# Peripheral Visions/Global Sounds

# Contemporary Hispanic and Lusophone Cultures

**Series Editors**
L. Elena Delgado, University of Illinois at Urbana-Champaign
Niamh Thornton, University of Liverpool

**Series Editorial Board**
Jo Labanyi, New York University
Chris Perriam, University of Manchester
Paul Julian Smith, CUNY Graduate Center

This series aims to provide a forum for new research on modern and contemporary hispanic and lusophone cultures and writing. The volumes published in Contemporary Hispanic and Lusophone Cultures reflect a wide variety of critical practices and theoretical approaches, in harmony with the intellectual, cultural and social developments that have taken place over the past few decades. All manifestations of contemporary hispanic and lusophone culture and expression are considered, including literature, cinema, popular culture, theory. The volumes in the series will participate in the wider debate on key aspects of contemporary culture.

# Peripheral Visions/Global Sounds

## From Galicia to the World

JOSÉ COLMEIRO

LIVERPOOL UNIVERSITY PRESS

First published 2017 by
Liverpool University Press
4 Cambridge Street
Liverpool
L69 7ZU

This paperback edition first published 2021

British Library Cataloguing-in-Publication data
A British Library CIP record is available

ISBN 978-1-78694-030-8 cased
ISBN 978-1-80085-575-5 paperback

Typeset in Borges by
Carnegie Book Production, Lancaster

# Contents

# List of Illustrations

# Introduction:
# Peripheries are not what they used to be

Periphery:
n. [countable], pl. -er·ies.
1. The outside boundary or perimeter of a surface or area. The outer
limits (of an aspect of social, cultural, or intellectual life).
*WordReference Random House Learner's Dictionary of American English*

Creo que la periferia ya no existe como la entendíamos,
porque tampoco hay un centro claro.
'I think the periphery is no longer as we once understood
it, because there is no clear center.'
Elena Oroz, "Las afinidades electivas"

If we look at the cartographic map of Western Europe, there are very few places that could be considered more geographically peripheral than Galicia. It has been historically considered the continental land's end, the *finis terrae*, a designation shared with Brittany—also on the outer limits of the continent and the Roman Empire—with which Galicia has many cultural and historical connections. Galicia's position in the geographical periphery has also often meant being away from the centers of political and economic power, and therefore situated in a marginal and inferior position. In some significant ways, its present political, economic, and cultural situation within the Spanish nation state is that of a double periphery, frequently invisible and inaudible from the center. But, over its history, the area that we now know as Galicia has gone through many changes in its geopolitical boundaries and cultural position in regard to the center, from the total autonomy of the Suevian kingdom to the medieval splendor to the progressive marginalization by the Castilian hegemony in the modern era with the formation of the Spanish nation state, and its massive expansion overseas through the Galician diaspora. Galicia's geographical peripherality did not preclude Santiago de

Compostela from becoming a center of Christendom for centuries, a crossroads of multiple routes leading to Santiago, which has re-emerged as a global cultural phenomenon in recent years and generated numerous audio/visual productions. Galicia's outward Atlantic position has historically enabled its people to travel far and wide, to build the largest fishing fleet in Europe, and to establish connections around the world, mixing with other cultures and creating a rich cultural tapestry beyond the confines of the Galician land. In our contemporary age, the decentralization and devolution of the Spanish nation state since 1978 has also meant a certain degree of political and cultural deperipheralization, and, with the entry into the global orbit, its long history of mobility and as a cultural crossroads has re-emerged with a new force. Today, Vigo is the largest fishing port in Europe, home of the most important fish company in the world (Pescanova) and the headquarters of the European Fisheries Control Agency. A Coruña (Arteixo) is the headquarters of the largest fashion multinational globally (Inditex). Santiago de Compostela is the destination of one of the most popular religious/cultural pilgrimages in the world and the source of numerous Galician and international films, books, and musical recordings. A new generation of Galician filmmakers working from the periphery under the umbrella term of *Novo Cinema Galego* ("new Galician cinema") has become the center of attention of film festivals around the world and celebrated as one of the most exciting and refreshing innovations in the area of non-fiction cinema. In many ways, the Galician periphery never felt more deperipheralized than in the global age.

Peripheries are not what they used to be. This is a theoretical proposition I have been arguing for several years in the context of Galician studies, which my own trajectory has only made clearer.[1] I am aware that I am positioned in a double periphery, since I research and write on Galician culture but live in and work from New Zealand, the exact antipodes of Galicia in the South Pacific, on the fringes of the anglo academy. But this remoteness has allowed paradoxically for a clearer focus, proving what they say about the proximity of the trees that does not allow seeing the forest as a whole. Sometimes you need a distant perspective, a peripheral vision, to get a fuller view of the field in front.[2] Geographical periphery is also perspectival. Almería may be

---

1 My first conceptualization of peripheral visions was formally presented in 2006 and later published as "Peripheral Visions, Global Positions". The concept has gained wide currency in recent years among Galician critics and creators, such as the collaborations in the *Atlas Ilustrado da Periferia* and the *(S8) Mostra de Cine Periférico* (see Chapter 7).

2 I develop this idea of the positive antipodean position in an interview with Nuria Godón ("Desde las antípodas"), where I vindicate the peripheral vision as the most complete and enriching.

seen as clearly peripheral from Brussels, but not so much from Morocco. Galicia appears as peripheral from Madrid, but maybe less so from Cape Verde or Montevideo. And distance can also be just a matter of perspective. Traveling, communication, and the flow of information and goods have never been easier or faster than today. The modern revolutionary advances in technology, transport, and communications have made a huge difference in shortening the time/space gaps and effectively making the world flatter. The greater global mobility of humans, as well as of production, capitals, and consumable goods, has erased or blurred many of the traditional obstacles and borders. Virtuality, digitalization, and the instantaneity of communication have changed the playing field, enabling new forms of connectedness between individuals and communities in remote locations, as creators, participants, and consumers. It is time to start looking at the periphery from a different peripheral perspective.

The periphery is traditionally defined in terms of its relation to the core, and therefore in a subordinate position to the center. The core/periphery conceptual model, with a strong structuralist component, became widely used in the 1960s and 1970s in the modern social sciences, whether economics, urban development, or ethnography. It establishes a power relations dichotomy that further privileges the center and marginalizes the periphery, seen as a minor satellite or a degraded version of the center. The center/periphery framework has experienced a new resurgence in the last few years, as a deconstructed theoretical model that can be adapted to the complexities of the new global age, since one of the effects of globalization is the potential fluctuation and redrawing of the traditional static and unidirectional geopolitical, economic, and cultural boundaries and binaries. In that sense, we could redraw this paradigm and take a different angle of vision, metaphorically exercising our peripheral vision, which can let us see things in a wider context, under a different light which may reveal a bigger and more complex picture. Paradoxically, a peripheral vision allows for a fuller perceptive experience and therefore one closer to reality, as the anthropologist James Fernandez has suggested. The center is near-sighted, while the peripheral is a far-sighted, curious eye, which sees the bigger picture. From that angle, the peripheral can also be a positive marker that is situated on the outer limits of the center, on the margins of the hegemonic mainstream, and beyond the limiting perspective of the center. This perspectival shift turns the periphery/center dichotomy upside down: the end of the known world, which we know as the land's end, can also be the beginning of another one. The periphery could be seen then as the frontier of new spaces to be explored, an area that allows freer experimentation on the fringes of the mainstream, therefore holding a cutting-edge position in the vanguard of cultural (ex-)changes. The periphery could also be understood as a border zone where boundaries are porous, cultures, languages and traditions cross, and tensions can generate creative and enriching possibilities—a space of gravitational tensions, towards and against the center, and of contacts with other centers and other peripheries.

Modern Galicia can offer some clear examples of the efforts of deperipheralization, from the *Rexurdimento* and the transatlantic mobility of yesterday to the emergence of the New Galician Cinema in the international arena and the global fashion phenomenon of our day. The long history of the Galician diaspora, through migration and exile, the creation of vibrant Galician communities overseas, and the tradition of Galician navigators, fishermen, sailors, and other seasonal migrant workers has created a deterritorialized Galician identity, a network of historical, cultural, familiar, and commercial connections and affinities with other peoples and lands which is unique in the Hispanic world. As a case in point, Galicia is the one nation outside Latin America where a central component of its cultural identity is closely tied to that region. It is for those reasons that Manuel Rivas has stated that Galicia has been a global village for a long time, even before the term was invented (Rivas 2001).

Galicia, with its strong diasporic transatlantic history and acute sense of cultural identity, is a particularly appropriate case study of the transformation of cultures, and culture industries, in the global age. Galician culture has experienced an unprecedented period of growth in all areas since the re-establishment of democracy and the development of its political autonomy. Audio/visual production (music and cinema in particular) has provided some of the privileged channels through which modern Galician cultural identities have been imagined, constructed, and consumed at home and abroad. Some of these Galician productions include innovative animation features in the leading edge of international production, avant-garde videos and non-fiction films winning accolades around the world, *Movida* groups emerging from the periphery, and ground-breaking folk artists merging into world music or the pan-Celtic music movement globally. This creative explosion has occurred in a productive dialogue with global currents at large and with considerable projection beyond the geopolitical boundaries of the nation and the state, but these seismic changes are only beginning to be the subject of attention of cultural and media studies.

This book aims to explore some of these dramatic changes in the Galician cultural landscape and argues for a perspectival shift towards a postnational and interdisciplinary cultural studies approach, based on a deterritorialization of the Galician cultural map. The traditional institutional channels of cultural identity—language, literature, territory, solidified in the discipline of philology—are thus set alongside new cultural formulations whose origins and channels are not only Galician but global. The focus of the book is to examine in particular the new developments in Galician audio/visual culture (broadly understood as including music and cinema in their many different manifestations) that have exploded and expanded beyond Galicia in the years since the democratic transition. New forms of cultural identity are being explored through images and sounds which cross traditional boundaries, blending the old with the new, the urban and the rural, the local with the global, the real with the imagined. These developments are profoundly transforming traditional definitions of Galician culture, but, with some exceptions, have so far been largely marginalized by academic scholarship, which has continued to focus mainly on the long-established and institutionalized philological model. Thus this book aims to explore the new areas established by new waves of audio/visual cultural production in the often overlapping areas of music and cinema which have emanated from Galicia in a dialogue with global currents. The study proposes an interpretation of Galician audio/visual creativity in which the peripheral is reimagined as central and the Galician as incontrovertibly global.

In a stateless nation such as Galicia it has been predominantly in the cultural arena, rather than in the political front, that Galician identity has found its main channels of expression. Precisely because of its traditional rural and diasporic history, Galicia has a strong sense of cultural identity but chronically weaker nationalist movements. The articulation of a strong nationalist political agenda has been historically obstructed by the realities of mass migration outside the land, the system of *minifundio* (crofting) and *caciquismo* (local bossism) prevailing in the rural areas, the uneven industrial development, and the co-option of *galeguismo* (Galician nationalism) by the political right during the Franco dictatorship, which has continued during the democracy.

Language and literature as identifying signs of cultural difference have been the fundamental modern tenets of the construction of a Galician national identity, with a series of official institutions dedicated to its administration, from the Real Academia Galega to the Día das Letras Galegas to the discipline of Galician philology and the process of linguistic "normalization." The traditional lack of interest by many Galician intellectuals in cinema or musical productions is the undesirable result of the great investment in the philological tradition, absorbed with the creation of a Galician literary canon as the essential and defining cultural formation of the nation. The result has often been a canonical, static, and exclusionary definition of Galician culture that has tended to reinforce its marginal and peripheral status, and its association with tradition, rurality, and isolation. This situation has somehow distorted the plurality, mobility, and hybridity inherent in Galician culture, which would be some of the main potential advantages of its peripherality.

Media studies are beginning to change this paradigm, realizing that the audio/visual fields have been key areas of formation of modern identities in the local/global contexts and are quite frequently intertwined. Hybridity and intermediality are recurrent features of audio/visual production. These media texts have the mobility and malleability for both internal collective identification and external projection, while also being cultural goods that have a potentially wide circulation at home and abroad. The voices and musical instruments are fundamental channels of cultural identity and, likewise, the moving images create collective forms of self-representation. In that sense we could say that musical productions function as an instrument for creating, communicating, and transmitting identity while audiovisual production acts as a medium for collective visual reflection and projection.

Since the nineteenth century traditional Galician music and folklore have been among the most prominent popular channels of Galician identity, in the rural areas as much as in the diaspora, while the visual arts have been a privileged channel of articulation of Galician identity for middle-class urban dwellers since the *Rexurdimento*. What has happened in recent decades is that new forms of music, such as *movida* rock, *bravú*, world music, and hybridized folk, have crossed urban and rural communities, as well as territorial boundaries of home and abroad, blurring distinctions of tradition and modernity, and have acquired in the process hybrid global inflections. Likewise, we have seen the development of a modern audiovisual culture in the form of cinema and television, video, animation, multimedia, and experimental non-fiction cinema that explores, reflects, constructs, and projects a modern Galician identity in relation to global trends. Both developments have effectively contributed to the progressive deperipheralization of Galician culture and the repositioning of Galicia on the global map.

My book aims for the deperipheralization and deterritorialization of Galician studies and Galician cultural production. In my analysis I cross the traditional boundaries delimiting the Galician cultural map to overcome long-established exclusions based on language, discipline, national origins, or territorial demarcation, while aiming to disjoint the center/periphery dichotomy that has relegated Galician culture to the margins. In essence, it is an attempt to address the perceived necessity of opening Galicia and Galician studies out of the periphery and into the world.

## From Galicia to the World

The subtitle of the book is a self-referential allusion to Galician media, as it echoes the title of a popular television program "Desde Galicia para el mundo" ("From Galicia to the world"), which is seen not only in Galicia and Spain but throughout the world via satellite broadcasts by TVE Internacional. The program started in 1993 and has continued uninterrupted over more than 1,000 chapters up to the present time. It has subsequently developed an interactive website and a mobile app, which provide around-the-world and around-the-clock access to the archive of all previous shows. Each program focuses on diverse aspects of Galician life and culture, including music and the visual arts, interviews, and various reports. As the title suggests, it is "made in Galicia," with the intention of projecting Galicia out of the periphery and into the world. It serves an important institutional function, as it aims to promote Galician culture, maintain and foster the connection with the diaspora, and attract tourism to Galicia, which are also major institutional goals of the government of the Xunta de Galicia (with the clear expectation of its translation into actual and symbolic capital). The program thus both constructs and represents the commodification of Galician culture in the global age.

In recent years variations of the phrase "Desde Galicia para el mundo," or, in Galician, "De Galicia para o mundo," have been widely adopted by Galician official institutions and mass media as a cultural brand. It aims to synthesize the concept of world-class Galician-made cultural goods, an image that underlines high-quality standards and modernity, created in dialogue with the world and suitable for export to the world. In the cultural arena, the World Music Expo (WOMEX), the largest world music festival in the world, took place in Santiago de Compostela in 2014 with a Focus Galicia section that was described in the website of the Consellería de Cultura of the Xunta de Galicia as "un espazo de proxección da música de Galicia para o mundo," ("a space of projection for the music from Galicia to the world") (cultura.gal).[3] Likewise, the Xunta has published the promotional volume *Libros & escritores de Galicia para o mundo*, ("Books and Writers from Galicia to the World"), with the intent of promoting Galician literature with publishers and at book fairs, and stimulating translation. Turgalicia, the official Galician tourist office, currently promotes the old monumental city of Santiago as "a grande creación de Galicia para o mundo e viceversa," ("the great creation from Galicia to the world, and vice versa") (turgalicia.es), underlining the

---

3 All the translations from Galician and Spanish to English in this book are my own, unless otherwise noted.

Figure 1    From Galicia to the World. Promo image from TVE program "Desde Galicia para el mundo", Pórtico de Comunicaciones S.L.

crossroads character of the city. And the controversial monumental project of the *Cidade da Cultura* in Santiago de Compostela has been referred to in the heavily subsidized Galician media as a space "De Galicia para el mundo" (Baltar). Likewise, the new visually stylish and critically acclaimed Galician TV series *Serramoura* (2014), now in its fourth season, set in an imaginary Galician rural area, has been described by its producers as "un thriller rural desde Galicia para el mundo," ("a rural thriller from Galicia to the world") ("Serramoura").[4] Even local visual artists who have successfully crossed the Galician borders are commonly referred to in the mass media as "De Galicia para el mundo," such as the sculptor Francisco Leiro ("Paco Leiro"), who has studios in New York and Madrid.[5] In the second issue of the *Revista bravú* and accompanying CD collection ("Hai alguén aí fora?," ("Is there anybody out there"), 1998), the countercultural *bravú* cultural movement (discussed in Chapter 9) was significantly presented as a message in a bottle sent from Galicia to the world, with its message formulated, in ironic Galician fashion, as a question. The wide use of this public discourse has almost turned the phrase into a commonplace that can be used on any occasion, but it suggests the prevailing conscious efforts to capitalize on the distinctive qualities of Galician culture while aiming towards its deperipheralization in our global

4  *Serramoura* currently has the biggest share of all Galician television series. It was nominated for 17 Mestre Mateo awards, the most important distinction in the audiovisual field in Galicia, and won the best television series category in 2014 and 2015. It has been commercialized internationally under the title of *Black Forest*, and was also nominated for best dramatic series in the Celtic Media Festival in Scotland.

5  The same phrase has been applied in reference to the international retail network of Galician children's fashion designer Pili Carrera, with franchises from Amsterdam to Venezuela (Mato, "Pili Carrera").

era. In sum, this language reflects the reality of a new global capitalist geography without borders, where Galicia comes out of the periphery using the channels of globalization.[6]

What all this points to is an overwhelming sense of the interpenetration of the traditional and the modern, the urban and the rural, the local and the global, in the contemporary definitions of audio/visual Galician culture, and its transformation into consumable cultural goods in the global market. In some ways we are living in the media utopia of the digital age that transcends time and space limitations. You can view, hear, and read almost anything, anytime, and anywhere. The digital era has brought a series of continuous and vertiginous changes in the audio/visual fields, with the convergence of different media (television, video, film, records), listening/ viewing platforms (television sets, radios, computers, MP3 players, tablets, phones), and hybrid creations that mix genres, forms of production, and circuits (fiction/non-fiction, commercial/non-commercial, local/global).

The acknowledgement of these technological advantages should not be interpreted as a blank endorsement of globalization, blind to the economic and political power asymmetries created, the risks of cultural hegemony, and the underlying neoliberal agenda promoted by the powerful international elites. We need to be always aware of the enticing trap of global neoliberalism, as consumers in a world supermarket of products, brands, ideas, and ideologies, and thus problematize the mixed reactions to globalization. While these global channels can provide easier access to cultural and material goods and improve transport and communication, globalization does not guarantee equal access for the global citizen and is often done at the expense of the weakest. I am fully aware of the privilege that is being a first-world citizen, with access to education, health, justice, democracy, a residence visa, and a secure job, but millions around the world today do not enjoy the same

---

6 The popular catchphrase has also been used as a logo and promotional name for a number of Galician enterprises with a global focus, such as the digital newspaper "Xornal de Galicia para el mundo," the gaming multinational EGASA, the videogame company Gato Salvaje Studio, and the export gastronomy company Galaicus Gourmet, just to name a few. The English language website of the public Zona Franca de Vigo (Vigo Free Zone Consortium) promotes 2300 high-quality Galician export products as "the best from Galicia to the world." Of course, the ultimate example of this new global model of "conquering the world" from the periphery is the Galician multinational Inditex, the number one fashion retailer in the world, with store brands such as Zara, Pull & Bear, and Massimo Dutti, among others. For Manuel Rivas, this glocal success story is the result in part of a long-established history in Galicia of family manufacturing, a tradition of commercial enterprises with the Americas, and the interpenetration of urban design and rural seamstresses (Colmeiro, *Galeg@s*).

privileges, merely surviving in terrible conditions. Globalization in many ways has created other asymmetries of power: those who have access to these channels and those who do not, those who benefit and those who perish. But my position is neither simply a unidimensional critique of globalization nor a nostalgic or inward-looking praise of the national. What is of interest are the tensions, fissures, and clashes between both poles, but also the opening of new spaces of exploration, negotiation, hybridity, and contestation from the periphery, aiming for its deperipheralization using the same channels and tools provided by the forces of globalization. The point is not simply to oppose globalization but to find alternative forms of globalization that do not conform blindly to the neoliberal logic, that allow for the deperipheralization of the periphery, with different forms of creating, distributing, and consuming (food, energy, material, and cultural goods). The channels of globalization can be used for the implementation of an imagined form of alterglobalization.

## Journeys

Every research project is a journey of multiple encounters, crossings, and discoveries, and this has been a long-distance project. Some 20 years ago I started a new journey in 1996 when I moved from the small and remote town of Hanover, New Hampshire, home of the Ivy League university Dartmouth College, to the American heartland to take a position at Michigan State University, one the country's Big Ten universities. There was a great opportunity to revamp and broaden the traditional program of Spanish (strictly composed of canonical literature in Castilian) in a new direction towards an interdisciplinary and multilingual cultural studies curriculum and a more inclusive concept of Iberian languages and cultures, particularly Galician and Catalan, which had traditionally been marginalized in Spanish and Portuguese departments across the US, but which could easily be approached for their proximity to Spanish and Portuguese. The situation of Catalan and Galician was very different, however. While Catalan was taught at some schools, and MSU offered it occasionally, and there were several Centers of Catalan studies in a number of American universities sponsored by the Catalan government, as well as a Catalan Studies Association and an academic journal, *Catalan Review*, Galician was almost completely absent from curricula in the United States, and there was no association, no journal, and no visibility.[7] Galician studies practically did not exist.

7 We should note, however, the pioneering work of Kathleen March, who founded the International Association of Galician Studies in the 1980s, with its first

Retrospectively, it seems as though it was the beginning of a momentous period for modern Galician culture, which was beginning to be recognized outside its borders. In 1996 Manuel Rivas was awarded Spain's *Premio Nacional de Narrativa* and the *Torrente Ballester* award for his short story collection *Que me queres, amor?*, which became an international bestseller translated into more than 15 languages after it was made into a film by José Luis Cuerda and Rafael Azcona. The movie, *La lengua de las mariposas* (1999), was an international art film favorite which visually projected Galician culture widely around the world. In the same year two folk albums were released onto the world music scene that again brought Galician culture to the forefront and gathered great critical and public success internationally: *Santiago* by The Chieftains and *A irmandade das estrelas* by Carlos Núñez. These led to my first two publications on Galician cultural studies.

Over the next few years I started to bring Galician culture into the academic curriculum by introducing Galician texts, mostly short stories and poems, but also other kinds of Galician texts in other media, such as songs and films. These audio/visual productions were particularly able to cross the inevitable language barrier. It was an opportunity to also develop a curriculum on cinema, and for several years I taught a series of courses on European and Latin American cinemas, which always started with *La lengua de las mariposas*, which was based on three short stories ("A lingoa das bolboretas," "Carmiña," and "Un saxo na neboa") from Manuel Rivas' *Que me queres, amor?* (1995). In parallel, I also started an acoustic music ensemble with my colleagues Miguel Cabañas and Kristy Byron, delivering workshops and recitals of traditional Hispanic music, which always incorporated some Galician songs and poems. These were the seeds for this present volume, stemming from the lack of availability of critical tools and channels to approach modern Galician culture, and more particularly its audio/visual cultural production.

*Peripheral Visions* has had a long gestation process. A small seed was initially planted with a presentation I gave on the musical and cinematic representation of the Camiño de Santiago, first as a seminar at Michigan State University in 1996 and then as a hybrid video/lecture at the Midwest MLA conference in 1997. My reading of these audio/visual journeys was subsequently published in the Galician journal *Grial*. The moment

two conferences taking place in Maine and Rhode Island, although they did not have much impact in the profession at large; and subsequently the work of Xoán González-Millán, with the creation of the first Center of Galician Studies at Hunter College (CUNY) in the 1990s, which further developed the philological approach to Galician culture, as will be discussed in Chapter 2.

was significant, as this presentation was prepared and delivered just after the almost simultaneous release of the now classic multi-awarded albums *Santiago* and *A irmandade das estrelas* and soon after Chano Piñeiro's commissioned film *O Camiño das Estrelas* (1993), which are the subject of Chapter 3. It also took place in the wake of the first stellar *Xacobeo* celebrations around the Camiño de Santiago in 1993 orchestrated by Manuel Fraga, the newly elected president of the Xunta de Galicia government. The *Xacobeo* represented Galicia's institutional entrance into the culture of global spectacle, which would only increase and accelerate in the following years, in a manner similar to the celebration of Barcelona's Olympics and Seville's Expo in 1992, and the opening of Bilbao's Guggenheim Museum in 1995. It seems, indeed, as if it was *escrito nas estrelas* (written in the stars), so to speak, with all the proverbial planets aligned, allowing Galicia to emerge from the shadows into full visibility. Something new involving the fusion of local cultural production and global projection in Galicia was developing, and the Camiño de Santiago seemed to be the tip of that iceberg.

This new development in Galician culture was particularly visible and audible in the music and film sectors, which desperately needed critical attention. It was something emerging from the periphery with the potential to affect the center, which had already started in the 1980s at the national level with the *Movida galega* and the beginning of Galician television and cinema production, the translation of Galician authors to other languages, and the explosion of Galician fashion globally, from Adolfo Domínguez to Zara. We could say that Galicia itself was becoming deperipheralized.

This book project started to germinate a little over ten years ago, with the invitation received from Kirsty Hooper to participate in the proposed volume on Galician cultural studies for the MLA with a piece on contemporary Galician cinema (another long-gestation project eventually published in 2011 as *Contemporary Galician Studies: Between the Local and the Global*). As I researched and drafted my piece, I became aware that we were collectively breaking new ground that required new methodologies and new critical tools. I could also sense that this volume clearly represented a turning point in the emerging field of Galician cultural studies in the English language academia. This served as enticement for developing my own book project. In addition, getting to know Hooper's evolving work on Galician literature and culture was exciting—it was so fresh and innovative in its approach and free from the old philological straitjacket—and I found her work extremely inspiring for my own project.

Conferences on Galician studies were excellent platforms for testing my working conceptual models and proved instrumental in developing my own critical tools and providing opportunities to engage in intellectual debate with other Galicianist colleagues. My participation at the conference of the Asociación Internacional de Estudos Galegos in Salvador, Brazil, in 2006 ("Galicia do outro lado do Atlántico—Voces reunidas na Bahía"), where I presented on the transatlantic Cuban/Galician connection, was an important and eye-opening experience to the reality of Galician diaspora and transculturation, and the far-reaching potentiality of Galician culture in a deterritorialized cultural map. The subsequent invitation to the ground-breaking conference "Coming out of the Nation: Beyond the National in Contemporary Galician Cultural Production" in 2008 at the Universities of Liverpool and Bangor (Wales) by Kirsty Hooper and Helena Miguélez-Carballeira was also another turning point for this project. It was there that I presented an early proposal of "Peripheral Visions" as a foundational new approach to Galician studies, which was a significant landmark in the development of this book.

The project was further advanced from that moment through continuous conversations with other Galicianist colleagues, who have provided a constant source of encouragement, such as Helena González, Eugenia Romero, and Silvia Bermúdez, and particularly my former colleague at Michigan State University, Joseba Gabilondo, who read some of the early drafts of the chapters and gave me generous and valuable feedback with always provocative food for thought. The project started to take shape and develop in an organic fashion; however, I eventually realized that the topic as originally planned was too broad to be able to be contained in a single book. For one thing, during the initial stages of research for this project I conducted a number of lengthy interviews with several Galician cultural figures in different areas (art, music, literature, performance, cinema, photography, graphic design). As a result of this extended process of conversations over the course of two years, in light of the vast volume of material gathered and the insightful quality of the views and ideas emerging from those conversations, I became aware that they needed to be published as a separate project. As a result, a volume of conversations and critical reflections with these Galician authors and artists was developed and a book contract signed with Edicións Xerais de Galicia. The manuscript was completed in 2009, but only finally published in 2013 due to the paralyzing effects of the economic crisis on the Galician publishing sector (*Galeg@s sen fronteiras: Conversas sobre a cultura galega no século XXI*). It should be seen as the first part of *Periperal Visions*. My deepest thanks to Uxía Senlle, Miguelanxo Prado, Bieito Romero, Manuel Rivas, Antón Reixa, Xavier Villaverde, Mercedes Peón, Xurxo Lobato, Teresa Moure, Antón Lopo, and Suso de Toro for their time, enthusiasm, thoughtful reflections, and inspiration.

Likewise, as I started to draft and revise different chapters of the book manuscript I became clearly aware that the critical issues of language, memory, migration, transculturation, and globalization I wanted to focus on, and the broad spectrum of contemporary Galician culture that I wanted to explore, from literature to cinema and television, music, performance, and visual culture, was just too much to be done justice in one volume, as it would require a multi-volume work of encyclopaedic proportions. For that reason, it seemed to me that it would be best to concentrate on the audio/visual areas that best exemplified the paradigmatic changes of Galician culture in the global age, and which have been less studied than have literature, language and history, which have received quite a bit of attention in recent years.

The final impetus for this project was the result of my move to New Zealand in 2010 to take a position at the University of Auckland. Paradoxically the change of hemisphere, the greater distance, and the isolation and remoteness of the South Pacific islands became positive stimulants to the development of my own conceptual framework on the merits of being in the periphery in a postperipheral, technology-driven global age, and the gain in acumen, perception, and perspective that peripheral visions can provide. Clearly, peripheries are not what they used to be.

In hindsight, the long gestation of the book has proven to be beneficial, since it has allowed for a wider temporal perspective that has obliged me to refocus some of my initial positions in view of the political changes experienced in recent years, the full impact of the 2007/2008 world crisis, and the coexistence of several generations of creators. As a result, the economic, political, and cultural tensions and the lights and shadows in the Galician audio/visual field have come into sharper focus.

I have presented different versions of parts of the book at conferences and lectures in A Coruña, Auckland, Barranquilla, Buenos Aires, Bangor, Chapel Hill, Chicago, East Lansing, Groningen, Liverpool, Minneapolis, Salvador de Bahia, San Francisco, Santiago de Compostela, Santa Barbara, Singapore, Sydney, Vigo, and Warwick. Each journey and each conference added another circle around the spiral of this project, while widening its angle and sharpening its focus. I am deeply indebted to the colleagues who extended invitations to speak at these public fora about parts of this project and to the editors and catalysts of related publications: Silvia Bermúdez, Kirsty Hooper, Helena Miguélez-Carballeira, Lou Charnon-Deutsch, Jo Labanyi, Tatjana Pavlović, Rosi Song, William Nichols, Helena González, Henrique Monteagudo, Samuel Amago, Cristina Carrasco, Manuel Puga, Gabriel Rei-Doval, Manuel Candelas, Susana Pérez Pico, Carmen Mejía, Kathryn Cramery, Olga Castro, Gabriel Pérez Durán, Benita Sampedro, José Antonio

Losada Montero, Olivia Rodríguez González, Mónica del Valle, and Pilar del Carmen Tirado. Likewise, my deep appreciation goes to Manuel Bragado from Ediciόns Xerais de Galicia, Damián Villalaín and Xosé Manuel Soutullo from Galaxia Editorial, and Isidoro Castellanos and José Luis Perales from the Instituto Cervantes, Sydney. I would also like to thank Nuria Godόn, Lourdes Varela, Silvia Pontevedra, Cristina Lombao, Rubén Fernández, Mayra Machado, and Belén Regueira for their thoughtful interviews which helped me to develop my own ideas and further disseminate my research work.

In the process of developing this project I have had the privilege of maintaining fruitful conversations and virtual exchanges with many artists, colleagues, and friends, such as Gabriel Rei-Doval, María do Cebreiro Rábade, Danny Barreto, Burghard Baltrusch, Carmen Becerra, Xabier Viana, Isabel Salgueiro, Tony Brazil, Nuria Godόn, Suso Hidalgo, Silvino Díaz, Silvia Bermúdez, Olivia Rodríguez González, Tamara Blanco, Marisol Manfurada, Susana Rey, Emilio Alonso, and Ekaterina Volkova, who assisted me with gathering documentation and giving me valuable insights. I would like to express my gratitude also to the artists and producers who facilitated illustrations for the book, including Xurxo Chirro, Eloy Domínguez Serén, Pancho Lapeña, Daniel Lages, Oliver Laxe, Lois Patiño, Felipe Laxe, Peque Varela, Guillermo Peláez González, José Paz Rodrigues, Julián Hernández, Cristina Pato, Fernando Cortizo, Sálvador Vázquez, and Diego Casal. Special thanks are due to the gifted artist who created the wonderful collage on the book cover, my dear friend Xulio Adán Eiroa. Lastly, I would like to thank the students at the University of Auckland and Michigan State University for their engagement and feedback, and their respective institutions for their generous support, particularly the Center for Global Studies and the Intramural Research Grant Program at MSU, and the Faculty Research Development Fund at UoA. I was fortunate to count also on the great competence of my research assistants Julia Niall and Gwyn Fox, who provided invaluable help with the development of the project and a final reading of the manuscript. *Graciñas!*

Auckland, April 2017

# Roots and Routes: Remapping Galician Culture in the Global Age

PART ONE

Roots and Routes:
Remapping Galician Culture
in the Global Age

# CHAPTER ONE

# Peripheral Visions, Global Positions

Ser periférico te sitúa en el centro del mundo
'Being peripheral places you in the center of the world'
Manuel Rivas

Today all cultures are border cultures
Néstor García Canclini

La visión periférica es lo más universal
'Peripheral vision is the most universal'
Antón Reixa

Borders, margins, and peripheries have been the subject of much scrutiny and revalorization across different disciplines in recent years. Postmodernist and poststructuralist theories (Jameson; Hutcheon) have helped deconstruct the notions of center and margin as natural and immutable relations of subordination, while postcolonial critics (Bhabha; Spivak) and global studies scholars (García Canclini; Castells) have accentuated the rich cultural hybridities that occur at borders and peripheries, which can actually impact, subvert, or transform the center. In the field of international relations, Noel Parker's *The Geopolitics of Europe's Identity* has proposed a "theory of positive marginality" (11) that highlights the potential for margins and peripheries to transcend their marginal status and use their position to their advantage. From an epistemological perspective, the wider range of peripheral visions can offer a more complete picture that goes beyond the narrow and confining viewpoint of the center.

Anthropologist James W. Fernandez has been a proponent of "peripheral vision" as a corrective, complementary, and fuller perspective to the central hegemonic vision: "In the most elementary and redundant sense, peripheral wisdom is awareness of the peripheries by active displacement to peripheral perspectives, enabling thereby the necessary and recurrent dialectic of identities with fully centred (not to say egocentric) wisdom" (140). His critical position is formulated on a series of basic assumptions:

> where there are boundaries there are centres and peripheries. [...] the experience of being in the peripheries shapes the sense of identity and the way of thinking, and [...] centres have need of peripheries, not only for their own identity but because there is always something to be learned from the peripheries. (117)

For Fernandez, the center/periphery dialectic is a constant in human relations and exchanges, although subject to reorganization, which may involve different articulations of power that are not necessarily geographically determined:

> It is also arguable that the globalizing process, with its intense inter-communication in virtually boundless cyberspace, will effectively abolish centres and peripheries, replacing that dynamic with the difference between being in the loop or out of it. But that of course is itself a centre/periphery phenomenon, although taking place in a less geographic medium. (118)

Fernandez turns around the traditional assumptions associated with center/ periphery relations, advocating for a perspectival shift to the periphery. He eloquently summed up the superior perspectival quality of peripheral vision, which, as in the case of peripheral wisdom, is "the most percipient and sensitive":

> Wisdom is customarily granted to the great centres of human affairs which are the generators of information and knowledge. It also might be argued in just the opposite vein that all wisdom, being perspectival, is peripheral. Objectivity, one might say, presumes peripherality. It might be argued even that the real wisdom, the most percipient and sensitive, like peripheral vision, is peripheral since, unlike central vision, it is necessarily comparative. It can hardly avoid comparing itself to the centre, whereas the centres can and often do ignore the peripheries. (118)

This perspective is particularly illuminating as it relates to the area of Galician studies. In this chapter I aim for a perspectival shift in the approach to remapping contemporary Galician culture and the challenges and opportunities it faces in a global environment. The transformation of the cultural landscape that has occurred in Galicia in the last few decades following the demise of Franco's dictatorship has been nothing but extraordinary, requiring a new epistemological and theoretical approach. Although unevenly evolved, contemporary Galician culture has been characterized by a remarkable cultural and political reawakening after a long history of neglect, the establishment of political self-governance under the statewide system of autonomy, rapid demographic urbanization and industrial reconversion, reversed migration patterns, and some significant advances towards gender parity and cultural and linguistic "normalization." It is certainly an ongoing development, rather than an already completed process, with visible lights and shadows, but its effects are quite noticeable. All these changes have taken place against the backdrop of the readjustment to new patterns of globalization and a rapidly evolving process of cultural hybridization.

The profound shifts that have occurred in Galicia and the world in the last decades dictate that we approach cultural production from new perspectives and conceptual models to produce an alternative cartography more inclusive of and better reflecting the new social realities. Beyond the established model of the disciplinary *criterio filolóxico* (philological criterion), to use the expression coined by Xoán González-Millán—a language-based national literature model which is still largely the norm in Galician studies, especially in its most institutionalized contexts—I propose to follow a postnational, non-canonical, and multi/interdisciplinary cultural studies approach in line with the recent innovative work of other Galician studies scholars, particularly in the Anglo academy (Bermúdez, Gabilondo, Hooper, Moreiras-Menor, Romero) on issues of transnational mobility, migration, and transatlantic studies, more in sync with the hybrid complexities of contemporary cultural production. My theoretical perspective is particularly sensitive to the multiple interactions between the local and the global, and the creation of "glocal" realities in complex relations of interdependence and interpenetration (García Canclini, *Hybrid Cultures*). This approach implies decentering language and Galician literary production as the privileged institutional channels of cultural identity, while still recognizing their crucial importance for Galician identity. This strategy aims to find a way around the overdetermined "fatal junction" of nation and culture which burdens minority cultures and stateless nations such as Galicia (Gilroy 4), as I will discuss later. In my analysis I propose the deterritorialization of the Galician cultural map to overcome long-established exclusions based on gender, national origin, language, or territorial demarcation, and the disjointing of the center/periphery dichotomy that has relegated Galician culture to the margins, which I call deperipheralization. In essence, it is an attempt to address the perceived necessity of opening Galicia and Galician studies to the world, and vice versa, while deconstructing their peripheral status.

## Remapping Galician Culture

The Galicia of the twenty-first century is rapidly coming out to the world. It could be argued that in these last few decades Galicia has been coming out of a lot of adverse historical constraints: coming out of the long night of the dictatorship, coming out of the legacies of patriarchal political *caciquismo* (local bossism) and cultural *minifundio* (fragmentation, atomization, and marginalization), and coming out of its own peripheral status. In one way or another, Galicians have been also coming out of the nation for a long time, as forced migrants and exiles to the Americas and Western Europe, or sailing around the world and the seven seas, reimagining the nation from afar, and in the process opening themselves up to new forms of cultural hybridity.

The tropes of travel and migration and the locus of the sea have been of paramount importance in regards to the development of modern Galician culture, characterized by its historical mobility, which has conditioned particular ways of being and seeing. A total of 1,500 kilometres of coast, more than any other region in Spain, and a geographical location in the Atlantic periphery of the nation state, with historically inadequate land communications, meagre resources, and neglect by the central power, has made modern Galicia a region of travelers, migrants, and marine explorers. Life in the coastal Galician towns is not only a history of massive migrations and relocations but also a history of seasonal migrancies, with a large floating Galician population of men who live at sea for months at a time— Galician sailors and fishermen who work in longliners, but also in merchant vessels, container carriers, oil platforms, ferries, navy ships, and expedition boats.[1] One could also argue that distant horizons have the potential to create a more perceptive and acute sight in those who have sharpened their vision in the wide immensity of the sea, such as sailors, fishermen, or those on the shores looking out. As Galician filmmaker and former sailor Xurxo Chirro has commented, his own experience as sailor and resident in a fishing port created a particular angle and way of seeing as a filmmaker.[2] It could

1 It can hardly be a coincidence that one of the most emblematic films of the New Galician Cinema boom of recent years (*Vikingland*, dir. Xurxo Chirro, 2012) is a found-footage documentary of life at sea on a ferry thousands of kilometers from Galicia, as will be studied in Chapter 7.

2 "En la ventana de mi casa, de mis padres, hay una línea de horizonte de mar y cielo de 180°. Es como estar viviendo cada día dentro de un cuadro de Rothko, donde la inmensidad te subyuga. [...] considero que el oficio del marinero es el oficio más parecido al filmmaker, porque construye una mirada perfecta. Me refiero a que cualquier atisbo en el horizonte, cualquier elemento ya te crea una atención

also be argued that this impetus towards the outside and contact with other cultures brings along with it a general broadening of the horizons that can potentially generate a wide-angle peripheral perspective, more open and less restrictive.

Mobility, migration, and displacement have a profound effect on the formation of one's cultural identity, individually and collectively. In response to the great modern diasporas associated with globalization, García Canclini has asked: "¿Cómo pensar una nación que en gran medida está en otra parte?" ("How should we think a nation that is in large part somewhere else?") (2005, 52). This question is particularly relevant in the case of Galicia, which necessitates an alternative conceptual model of the nation. It is symptomatic that the modern symbols of Galicia, the flag, the coat of arms, and the national anthem, all came from the other side of the Atlantic in Cuba, as did books, periodicals, cultural institutions, and new political ideas.[3] And from the margins of the British Isles and Brittany have come modern models of peripheral nationalism and cultural resistance, from the Romantic era exaltation of Celtic origins to the present pan-Celtic music revival, that have been instrumental for Galicia's reclaiming of its cultural identity.[4] Likewise, a myriad of migrant and exilic Galician

extraordinaria y comienzas a fabular de lo que puede ser. Eres capaz de distinguir azules, grises, tonalidades. Te ayuda a agudizar la mirada." (Bergner et al).

"... From the window of my house, my parents' house, you can see a 180° horizon line between the sea and the sky. It is like living every day inside a Rothko painting, where immensity overwhelms you. [...] I consider the job of a sailor to be the one most similar to the job of a filmmaker, because it constructs a perfect vision. What I mean is that a simple glimpse of a given element in the horizon generates in you an extraordinary level of attention, which leads you to start imagining what that could be. You are capable of distinguishing between different shades of blues and hues of grays. It helps you to sharpen your vision." (All translations from Galician are my own, unless noted otherwise).

3  The role of the transatlantic Galician migrant communities in the development of Galician modern cultural identity, particularly in Cuba, is well known. One of the crucial books of the nineteenth-century Galician *Rexurdimento* (Galician nationalist revival), Rosalía de Castro's *Follas Novas* (1880), was originally published in Cuba by the Galician émigré colony. The Real Academia Galega was also founded in Havana during Galician nationalist writer Manuel Curros Enríquez's exile, and the emancipation ideals of Cuban nationalists fighting Spanish colonial power also influenced early Galician nationalism. See Axeitos; Bermúdez.

4  The idealized association of Galician cultural identity with Celtic origins goes back to Eduardo Pondal and the *Rexurdimento* Romantic movement. Galicia's national anthem, based on Pondal's poem "Os Pinos" (The Pine Trees), claims to be the "nación de Breogán" (nation of Breoghan), the Celtic hero king of Galicia in Irish legends. For an overview of the modern "cultural reinvention" of Galician Celtic

communities have spread across Europe, north and south, across the Americas from Montevideo to Montreal, and across the Pacific from the Seychelles to Sydney. How, then, should we think Galicia if it is in large measure somewhere else?

Since the nineteenth century Galicia has greatly expanded her horizons and created new migrant communities beyond the confines of the geopolitical borders of the nation, on a par with other important migrant European groups, such as the Jewish and Irish communities. In a similar way to these groups, the Galician diaspora was the center of cultural and political activism. Havana was the cultural capital of Galicia at the end of the nineteenth century and the beginning of the twentieth in such key areas as journalism, book publishing, education, music, and theater spectacles (see Rivas, "A Galicia transn@cional"). In the twentieth century the greatest urban concentrations of Galicians were found not in Galicia or Spain but in the New World, in the metropolitan areas of Buenos Aires, Mexico City, and Havana. As one of the most common destinations of Galician migrants and exiles in the twentieth century, Buenos Aires has been commonly referred as Galicia's "fifth province," and it became *de facto* capital of the Galician cultural and political resistance during Franco's dictatorship. This reality is not simply confined to the past, since it still has its own very perceptible legacy in the present. In the census of registered voters for Spain's general elections of March 2008, there were 325,000 registered Galicians living abroad, a 5.5% increase since 2004.[5] And, in 2008, the percentage of absentee Galician voters from the total of voters residing in Galicia (a bit over two million) was 14%, more than the whole province of Lugo or Ourense. This situation is not merely a case of Galician magical realism, with the spectral reawaking of the dead to participate in the elections, but a present-day consequence of the great Galician diaspora of the past. A small percentage of this increase in numbers could be attributed to new migration patterns as a result of the 2007 crisis, but most of the new influx in migrant voters is composed of what could be called "post-migrants,"

music as an assertive act of reclaiming a distinctive identity, which will be discussed in Chapter 10, see Toro ("Bagpipes and Digital Music") and Romero ("Amusement Parks, Bagpipes and Cemeteries").

5 Between 2003 and 2007 there was only a 0.3% growth in local Galician voters, but a 12.3% growth in absentee voters (Sampedro). In 2016 there were 446,000 absentee Galician voters registered for the general elections. This increase, due to the new generations of "post-migrant" Galician descendants, is asymmetrical. The spectacular growth of registered Galicians in Latin America is a result of the economic and political crisis experienced in their countries of residence. The situation is not the same in Europe, where there has not been a similar increase.

second- and third-generation descendants of migrants and exiles who have reclaimed their ancestors' nationality for personal economic and political reasons, since their Spanish nationality is officially recognized and Galician governmental policies facilitate their integration through economic subsidies and cultural programs.[6] For this reason, Galicia is one of the few nations in the world where the main political parties regularly campaign outside of the nation, and candidates and representatives occupy billboards, tour the cities, have rallies, and meet voters.[7]

That diasporic dimension is integral to modern Galician cultural identity, and its dynamic condition could potentially be a major advantage in our global age.[8] Clearly, there are highly problematic issues related to the process of economic and cultural globalization, such as the real dangers of homogenization, deracination, and the reinstatement of world inequalities and asymmetries, which are real and troubling. For the purposes of this study I am focusing on the new forms of cultural hybridity and the strategic remapping that has become possible in the new global environment, as a result and in reaction to the forces of globalization. Interconnectedness and openness, cultural hybridity and creative fusion, social dynamism and global solidarity are some of the positive values that could be recognized and accentuated in this new horizon.[9] I propose that these visions from the periphery, coming out of the margins, can actually turn into valuable positions in the new global map. As we know, peripheral visions have a wider range of vision, and therefore are more open to what is beyond the limiting confines of the center. The locations of culture in the global age surpass the traditional geopolitical limits of modern nations. These peripheral visions are then turning into global positions, as we begin to visualize the

6 The fraudulent conditions of the Galician migrant vote have been repeatedly exposed in the media, with the appearance of dead voters in the registry, the non-secured conditions of the votes, and the true identity of the voters. See Baamonde. Since the introduction of the new restrictions for voting by mail in 2011, the number of migrant voters who cast ballots has decreased dramatically.

7 Some examples of the echo in the Galician press of the political campaign in Latinoamerica and Europe reveal the real scope of this important "post-migrant" connection ("Un total"). For another critical perspective on the Galician overseas vote see also Hooper (*Writing Galicia*), who also mentions the particular case of Haiti, where political campaigns are taken beyond the nation.

8 As Axeitos has noted, "en gran parte, nos conformamos como pobo desde a extranxería e non desde a familiaridade dos horizontes coñecidos" (18) ("in a large measure, we were constituted as a nation from afar and not from the familiar well-known horizons").

9 For a critical analysis of the negative aspects of globalization, see García Canclini.

establishment of a potential new paradigm that is both postnational and postperipheral, transcending the limitations of both concepts, one that we could label perhaps as "The Galician Atlantic," appropriating Paul Gilroy's concept of the transnational Black Atlantic diaspora, as Joseba Gabilondo has done for the "Hispanic Atlantic."

This remapping of Galician culture is, directly and indirectly, related to the political and cultural remapping of the nation state since the transition to democracy, with the official recognition in the 1978 Constitution of Spain's multicultural and multilingual diversity, which has enabled the recuperation and preservation of distinct subnational cultural identities. This realization is particularly significant in the contemporary context of the post-cold war remapping of Europe and the concerns about the erosion of local cultures challenged by political and economic globalization and furthered by the effects of the global economic crisis. My working hypothesis is that this double cultural and political delineation has created both a need and an opportunity to redefine Galicia's cultural identity in a wider cultural context exceeding traditional national and state parameters. The erosion of the traditional nation-state paradigm, by both centrifugal (nationalist movements) and external forces (supranational organizations and globalization), has provided a fertile ground and a creative impetus to redefine Galician culture and identity beyond the limiting confines of the nation or the nation state. This double bind has been redefined by some critics in Hispanic studies as the "postnational" paradigm (Bermúdez et al; Gabilondo, "Postnationalism"; Richardson; Hooper, "Novas cartografias nos estudos galegos"). And this is precisely, according to my thesis, the impetus behind the modern cultural reawakening of Galicia. These apparently opposing cultural forces create new hybrid realities and new forms of identity that bind the old with the new, the local with the global. A new Galician culture has emerged neither urban nor rural, but "rurban"; neither national nor colonial, but postnational; neither simply "authentic" or "foreign," but profoundly hybrid, as the interaction of the local and the global has produced new postperipheral "glocal" cultural forms that are transforming the inherited status quo.[10] The following sections will provide various examples of this hybrid redefinition in contemporary Galician culture.

---

10 García Canclini adopts the neologism "glocal," borrowed from the field of economics and social theory, to refer to those hybrid cultural realities resulting from the dynamic interplay of the local with the forces of global modernity (*La globalización imaginada*).

## Historically Speaking: A Postcolonial Coming-out

The study of contemporary Galicia can offer fascinating insights and potentially valuable lessons about the process of collective identity formation within a multicultural and multilingual context. Likewise, it can enlighten us about the creative interactions of local peripheral cultures with global forces in a postcolonial twenty-first century. Galicia presents an interesting case study of the demarginalization of subaltern identities and the fragmentation of absolutist power and monolithical thinking associated with postmodernity, and the parallel demise of the old colonial empires and emergence of postcolonial discourses. The critique of modernity by postcolonial thinkers and subaltern studies scholars such as Homi Bhabha, Paul Gilroy, and Gayatri Spivak has a peculiar inflection in the case of Galicia, where the nation has always been at the same time *more and less than a nation*. Galicia has been simultaneously a nation negated by the state and a nation overflowing the nation, marked by migration and deracination. This marginal and diasporic condition responds to the concept of *DissemiNation*, Homi Bhabha's metaphor of the modern postcolonial nation, which transfers (and transforms) the meaning of "home." This process follows in the footsteps of Eric Hobsbawm's history written from the margins, "the history of the modern Western nation from the perspective of the nation's margin and the migrants' exile" (Bhabha, *Location of Culture*, 200).

Galicia today is a stateless nation with its own particular cultural identity—one of only three officially recognized "historical nationalities" (with the Basque Country and Catalonia) in the 1978 Spanish Constitution; and one with its own language, Galician, which is one of the co-official languages recognized in the Spanish *carta magna*. Galicia is also one of a handful of relative "success stories" in the contemporary Western world where a minority culture, long repressed and marginalized, has resisted and grown despite all doom-laden predictions. It constitutes an exemplary case of the revitalization of a minority culture and language that have come dangerously close to disappearing through a long history of neglect and repression. This is an achievement brought about not by a simple return to a mythical past but by hybridizing and embracing the new (new technologies, media, urban idioms, and cultural channels) and engaging in a productive and creative dialogue between the local and the global.[11]

The multicultural and multilingual diversity of Spain has been

11 The language situation is quite diverse within the different autonomies. In spite of the institutionalization of Galician, the remarkable increase of cultural production in Galician, and the high number of "passive" Galician speakers, the

"discovered" and generally recognized only in recent years, after the long period of political and cultural repression exercised by Franco's dictatorship and the even longer five centuries of Castilian domination. But old legacies die hard, and Spanish nationalism is still strong and often dismissive of, when not aggressive with, its peripheral cultures. As some cultural theorists have remarked, empires begin at home. We should take into account MacKenzie's notion that "the building of empire is first an internal process with internalized others" (35). From this perspective, it could be argued that the formation of the Spanish empire actually began with the domination of conflicting internal others such as Galicia—what Alfonso Castelao named, following Zurita, the chronicler of the Catholic Monarchs, the "doma e castración de Galicia" ("the taming and castration of Galicia," 47). It is also true that the collapse of the imperial edifice often follows the inverse order of its construction, something that Ortega y Gasset already observed in *España Invertebrada*. This is clearly the case of the Spanish empire, with the progressive fragmentation of the old empire through the nineteenth century and then the vanishing of its latter-day vestiges in the twentieth, coinciding with the disappearance of the neoimperial Fascist ideology of Francoism. Thus 1975 marks the official end of Spanish neo-imperialism in Africa, with the transference of Western Sahara, as well as the end of Fascist rule at home.[12] As a result, the internalized "colonies" within the modern nation state (Galicia, Catalonia, and the Basque Country) were the last ones to obtain their autonomy from the central power during the democratic transition after the 1978 Constitution. From a postcolonial theoretical framework, we could argue, then, that Galicia was one of the first "colonies" of the Spanish empire, paving the way for the conquest of the new world overseas, and also one of its last, with the approval of the Statute of autonomy in 1981 and the establishment of self-governance.[13] The new

persistence of social diglossia is still a characteristic of Galician culture. See Niall for a comparative analysis.

12  Spanish rule over northern Morocco and Equatorial Guinea also collapsed during Franco's regime, in the 1950s and 1960s respectively, coinciding with the great global phase of decolonization after World War II. The enclave cities of Ceuta and Melilla and surrounding islands, regularly contested by Morocco, are the only exceptions to the end of Spanish rule in Africa.

13  I am aware of the theoretical stretch inherent in using the term "colony" to refer to the particularities of the historical nationalities within the Spanish nation-state. However, the historical situation of Galicia shares many of the attributes of colonial oppression and political and cultural dependence, something that has been argued by many leftist Galician nationalists (X.L. Beiras, X.L. Méndez Ferrín) since the 1960s and the emergence of anti-colonialist emancipation movements in the Third World. The postcolonial perspective appears as a valid way of conceptualizing historical

phase of multinational neoliberalism barely covers a new form of economic neocolonialism, where the global is the new stage.

The history of this Spanish "colonization" has had a huge impact on the development of Galician culture throughout the centuries, and has been marked by domination and subjugation. The old medieval kingdom of Galicia was incorporated into the Crowns of Leon and Castile in the early modern period, which led to a long period of political, economic, and cultural neglect. Galicia experienced an enduring decline since its cultural height in the Middle Ages, when Galician–Portuguese was the main poetic language of the Iberian peninsula and the pilgrim route to Santiago de Compostela traversed the European continent, thus forming the cultural nervous system of medieval Christendom—Goethe has been quoted as saying: "The idea of Europe was born along the road to Santiago" (Roseman 78).[14]

Galicia's long period of neglect and decline, with the tacit complicity of the Galician elites, lasted several centuries (commonly known as "os séculos oscuros," 'the dark centuries') until the intellectual regeneration that started with the nineteenth-century *Rexurdimento* regionalist revival and the subsequent Galician nationalist movement in line with the Iberian (Spanish, Basque, Catalan) and other European nationalist movements (the Irish among others), which continued through the 1930s, culminating with the approval of Galicia's Statute of Autonomy in 1936. This cultural and political revival was cut short by the Spanish Civil War (1936–39) and the four decades of repression and obscurity that followed, while a displaced Galician community flourished in exile and maintained a strong political and cultural identity away from the Galician mainland. Massive migration of the poor and subaltern classes to the Americas, and after World War II to Western Europe, and the exile of many nationalists and leftists have profoundly characterized the modern history of Galicia as a diasporic nation. With the transition to democracy in Spain in the 1970s and the establishment of self-government and the entry into the European Union in the 1980s, Galicia underwent a process of rapid transformation, reclaiming relative political autonomy, cultural and linguistic "normalization," and economic development, which, although uneven and still facing significant challenges,

internal others. It has been argued, for example, in the case of the British nation-state and its peripheral nations (Scottish and Irish in Reizbaum; Welsh in Aaron and Williams). I have articulated this position in my article on postcolonial detection in Spain ("The Spanish Detective as Cultural Other").

14  The pilgrim's route to Santiago was declared the first European Cultural Route by the Committee of Europe in 1987 and a World Heritage Site in 1993, symbolizing the construction of a new Europe. The significance of the Camiño in the global age is discussed in Chapter 3.

has no historical precedent in modern times.[15] The regained confidence in its own cultural identity and autonomy has offered some opportunities for coming out of the colonial mold of the centralist nation state.

But Galicia is also more than a nation, if a nation is traditionally defined in essentialist terms according to a monocultural mold and a clearly defined geopolitical space. As we noted earlier, Galicia has been a nation of migrants, dispersed around the globe, which has persistently expanded its horizons beyond the confines of the nationalistic definition of *A Nosa Terra* (literally Our Land, an essentialist geographic description of the motherland). In recent years Galicia has experienced a reverse phenomenon. While outgoing migration has not disappeared altogether, particularly since the onset of the global crisis, Galicia has become the destination of many migrants from abroad, much as in other parts of Spain after the country joined the European Union in the mid-1980s. In Galicia's case, this phenomenon has also had particular inflections, since a large number of the new migrants have come from areas with direct historic, cultural, and linguistic links, even with close family connections through the Galician Atlantic diaspora, such as Latin America and the Lusophone world.[16] This new situation, which alters the Galician migration paradigm but reinforces the centrifugal Atlantic orientation of Galicia, necessarily involves a more inclusive redefinition of the nation, presenting new challenges but also new opportunities for growth and cultural hybridity.

## Coming Out of the Periphery

Like other cultural identity markers (race, gender, class, language), those of Galician identity involve a particular way of perceiving reality and of interacting with the world, inflected by its history and geopolitical situation in the margins of the nation state. What I would like to argue, however, is that Galicia's historically peripheral condition has paradoxically facilitated its transition to the global condition. Galicians are geopolitically positioned away from the center of the nation state, in the margins of the center, but also

15 The dominant public discourse of the Transition has been widely criticized by cultural critics as triumphalist, highlighting some of the clear deficits of its inception and development, institutionally and culturally, which the current political and economic crisis has only exacerbated. For an overview of its causes and effects, see Martínez; Naharro Calderón; and Moreno Caballud.

16 Portugal is still the origin of the largest number of migrants coming to Galicia, followed by Latin America, particularly Argentina, Brazil, and Venezuela, traditional receptors of Galician migration (Izquierdo and Golías; Bouzada Fernández and Lage Picos).

beyond its confining boundaries, and perhaps are freer to develop their own alternatives and more open to movement and engagement with the outside world in Europe and the Americas, and beyond. This peripheral double position, both inside *and* outside, also suggests a wider angle of vision, a supplementary vision that augments and enriches the narrow angle from the center, as the following examples will illustrate.

As the traditional land's end of the European continent (*finis terrae*), Galicia is positioned in a double geopolitical periphery, at the farthermost point in the peninsula from the center of the nation state and from the center of political and economic power in Europe. Yet, on the other hand, Galicia's Atlantic position has also meant it is closer to other peripheral *Finisterres* in Europe, Africa, and the Americas, a transatlantic dimension of Galician culture that transcends geographical limitations and geopolitical national borders. This gravitational pull away from the center and reorientation towards other lands and nations has made possible the formation of other connections and alternative centers beyond the confines of its territory. Peripheral positions can thus lead to global visions.[17]

Galicia's geographical periphery has also frequently found a parallel in the political, socioeconomic, and cultural realms, as in modern history Galicia has been traditionally dominated by hegemonic groups subservient to the nation state (Beiras; Gemie). Galicia's peripheral condition (geopolitical and economic) was the key factor that opened the floodgates to massive migration, first to the new world in the nineteenth century and later to northern Europe in the mid-twentieth century. As a result, Galicians probably have had a more direct connection to the outside world historically than any other group in Spain, as even today there are still large numbers of Galicians living outside of Galicia and many more have personal, familiar, and commercial or professional links with overseas cultures.[18] This global

17 Galicia has a rich history of cultural and economic exchanges that are not subsidiary to the structures of the nation-state, from direct transatlantic relations with Latin America to the establishment of world fishing enterprises to the more recent Inditex global phenomenon. It would not be redundant here to reiterate the important migrant dimension of Galicia in this regard, as well as its direct cultural links with other European peripheries, such as through the Celtic music network of festivals and performances, or the rebranding of its peripheral status as the mythical "land's end" with the modern cultural redefinition of the road to Santiago (see Roseman), as will be analysed in subsequent chapters.

18 Officially there were around 500,000 Galician citizens living abroad in 2016, although 70% of those were born outside of Galicia and therefore should be considered "post-migrants." For more information see the website of the Instituto Galego de Análise e Documentación Internacional (http://www.igadi.org/index. html) and Campos.

connectedness has meant, for example, that Havana or Buenos Aires have a direct and familiar immediacy for most Galicians that is not commonly shared by the rest of Spaniards, or Europeans in general, and this is reflected politically, economically, demographically, and culturally. In that sense, peripheral positions have meant much wider global visions.[19]

Migration, uprootedness, transculturation, and the feelings of nostalgic *saudade* (melancholy) and *morriña* (homesickness) are Atlantic themes that permeate Galician culture, having an enormous influence on its literature, music, and visual arts, and are a large part of the Galician cultural hybridity. Attesting to this reality we encounter a solid literary history of novels, stories, poems, and memoirs, with contemporary examples such as *A man dos paíños* (The Migrant's Hand, 2000) by Manuel Rivas, *Tres Trebóns* (Three Thunders, 2005) by Xurxo Souto, or *Finisterre* by María Rosa Lojo (2005),[20] as well as a rich audio/visual culture that needs its own history, films such as *Mamasunción* (1984), *Gallego* (1987), *Sempre Xonxa* (1989), *Bs. As.* (2006), *Hotel Tívoli* (2007), and *Vikingland* (2011), or the Caribbean and Latin American rhythms of the Galician diaspora and its eternal return: the *habaneiras* and tangos from Marful; the *conga santiaguesa* from Carlos Núñez's "Para Vigo me voy" or his album *Alborada do Brasil*; the *corridos* and *cumbias* from the popular Galician *orquestas*; or the transatlantic album *Saudade* by Luar na Lubre with Pablo Milanés, Lila Downs, and Adriana Varela, as so many others.

Even today, when traditional migration patterns have reversed and Galicia is now the recipient of migrant workers from Eastern Europe, Africa, and Latin America (sometimes the grandsons and granddaughters of former Galician migrants), this Galician mobility has not stopped, and still today Galician workers travel around the globe alongside the new migrants in the new world economy, from the Seychelles Islands to South Africa. Manuel Rivas and Xurxo Souto have written extensively about the enormous challenges, life-changing experiences and intercultural exchanges of this working community, which signal a move from the Atlantic to the global. This redirection towards the global is manifest in the *Revista Bravú* (main press outlet of the 1990s rurban *movemento bravú*) which dedicated its third issue to this topic in 1998 ("7 portas, 7 mares").[21] As Xurxo Souto explains:

19 Sharif Gemie has commented that, as a result of the massive migration of Galicians to the new world, "Galicia was experiencing an early form of globalization: its people were learning to think in a bigger world. Stretching out beyond their region, which was shaped by international forces" (52).

20 For an in-depth analysis of a variety of cultural manifestations of the Galician diaspora, see Hooper (*Writing Galicia into the World*) and Romero (*Contemporary Galician Culture*).

21 A detailed analysis of the *bravú* movement appears in Chapter 8.

Galicia é unha rocha cativa chantada no Atlántico e tamén un inmenso país marino que abrangue todos os Océanos. [...] Outra xeografía. As distancias enrúganse e estrícanse no mar. [...] Reclamamos para o bravú o país invisible do mar.[...] Non hai límites nin fronteiras. Existimos entre a realidade e o misterio. O fuciño no Océano, a porta de todos os camiños. [...] Desde a hiper-periferia cara Capetón. ("Galicia-Capetón" 73)

Galicia is a small rock stuck in the Atlantic and also an immense marine country encompassing all the Oceans. [...] Another geography. Distances shorten and stretch in the sea. [...] We claim for the *bravú* people the invisible country of the sea. [...] There are no limits or frontiers. We exist between reality and mystery. Our snouts in the Ocean, the gate of all roads. [...] From the hyper-periphery towards Cape Town.

A clear example of this new paradigm are Galician traditional *cofradías* of fishermen and sailors, who form the second-largest fleet and fish industry in the world after Japan, now regularly employing large numbers of African and Latin American migrant workers relocated to Galicia. A case in point is the number of workers and sailors who relocated to Galicia in the 1970s from Cabo Verde, a Lusophone country off the northwest coast of Africa. A vivid testament of the resulting transnational hybridity is Batuko Tabanka, a women choir of *batucadeiras* (singers and players of *batukos*, traditional homemade percussion instruments) of Cabo Verde origin, who live in the small Galician fishing port of Burela (presently with a Cabo Verdean colony of some 500 people, many of them born in Galicia). Batuko Tabanka have become a definitive part of the Galician music scene, regularly appearing in the mass media and performing their songs across Galicia. The integration of Batuko Tabanka into the Galician musical landscape is particularly revealing of this cultural hybridization, blending well with the Galician tradition of female groups of *cantareiras* (singers) and *pandereteiras* (tambourine players) and the tertiary rhythm of Galician *jotas*, as well as the overriding feeling of *saudade* of the music. They have appeared in Os Diplomáticos de Monte-Alto's *bravú* rock band album *Kömunikandø* (2003) and the Televisión de Galicia program *Alalá*, which specialized in Galician traditional music, devoted one full program to them (see *Alalá*). Batuko Tabanka are produced by Galician musician and singer Uxía, a *raiana* product of the Galician–Portuguese border culture and an active advocate of the reunion of lusophone cultures and musics (from Galicia, Portugal, Azores, Cabo Verde, Mozambique, Angola, and Brazil) through her own work as singer and as producer of albums, concerts, and radio and television shows. Their first CD project, *Djunta mô* ("Lending a hand" in Cape Verdean Crioulo language, 2012), celebrates the co-operative solidarity of the women groups as well as the Galician/Cape Verde intercultural exchange.

Another example of this emerging cultural hybridity is the young Galician/ Palestinian singer Najla Shami. Born in Santiago de Compostela of Galician, Palestinian, and Argentinian origins, Shami pursued an international formal education as singer and music educator which has taken her to Norway, Kuwait, Jordan, India, Portugal, and the UK. Her work in music, like her own vital trajectory, is a compendium of many cultural threads, a result of the double impact of roots and routes. Thus it has a strong Galician base while exuding a variety of influences, such as Brazilian music, jazz, or world music. She is equally at ease singing an acoustic Galician folk *alalá* or a traditional Arabic song, or collaborating with Afro-Latin ensembles, funk, and rap bands. Her album *Na Lingua Que Eu Falo* "In the language that I speak" (2013), published as a CD-book by Xerais, was entirely devoted to new musicalized poems by Rosalía de Castro, the mother of modern Galician letters and one of the first writers to touch upon the topic of Galician migration. Mixing tradition and modernity, Najla Shami is showing the possibilities of working from the border zone of the local and global, while redefining the limits of modern Galician music.

Galicia's peripheral condition and its openness to the world have profoundly marked its cultural identity, to the extent that in many significant ways Galicia's collective imaginary has more in common with Latin America than with most of the rest of Spain, while retaining a particular cultural affinity with Brittany or Ireland, the other traditional *finis terrae* of Europe in the periphery of Europe and the British Isles. Galicia shares with Ireland a tradition of Celtic music, folklore, and mythology and similarities of landscape and climate, an isolated location, a minority autochthonous language, a colonial history of subjugation to the nation state, population dispersion, and massive diaspora. Not surprisingly, Galician musicians have in the last decades started exploring their common Celtic roots and experimenting with the fusion of other forms of world music (such as Latin and African music), thus profoundly renovating traditional Galician music by hybridization. As a result, a booming pan-Celtic neofolk music revival movement has taken place in Galicia, with the establishment of a circuit of international festivals, concerts, and music conservatoires. Today some of the best Celtic-inflected music produced in the world comes from Galicia, and some of its musicians, such as Milladoiro, Carlos Núñez, Susana Seivane, Mercedes Peón, Cristina Pato, and Luar na Lubre, are internationally known as composers, ethnomusicologists, experimental artists, and virtuoso performers.²² On the other side, alternative writer–musician and now film director and producer Antón Reixa has opted for the revolutionary hybrid mixing of dance grooves and hip hop beats with traditional Celtic bagpipes or Galician folk rhythms with electronic instrumentation over agitprop-like raps of urban disaffection and political activism, becoming in the process a national cult figure and mass media persona.²³

These peripheral visions, wide open to the world and fully aware of their gravitation in a global orbit, have enabled contemporary Galician artists to resist marginalization or assimilation and come out with strong original voices, relying on the large arsenal of a rich ancestral culture, but renovated and immersed in the new global currents, thus claiming a postperipheral, global position.

## Galicia in the Global World:
## Beyond/Coming Out of the Local

> Galicia está en el centro. En los siglos XIX y XX éramos periferia,
> pero en el mundo global ya no existen periferias.
> 'Galicia is in the center. In the nineteenth and twentieth
> centuries we were the periphery, but in the global
> world there are no peripheries anymore.'
> José Ramón García

Galician contemporary culture could be redefined primarily as a "post" culture: first, post-Franco; then, paradoxically, both postindustrial and postrural (or *rurban*) as well as postcolonial (profoundly marked by the experiences of colonialism and migration, but also struggling for its own identity and survival vis-à-vis the imperialistic legacy of the centralist Spanish nation state); and ultimately postnational and postperipheral (beyond the nation and immersed in the global economic and geopolitical order). The remapping of cultural boundaries in Galicia beyond the strict confines of the nation state corresponds to the postnational paradigm

---

22 This is the subject of analysis in Chapter 10.

23 Antón Reixa was the leader of the well-known 1980s/1990s Galician rock band Os Resentidos, the first modern group to use Galician exclusively in their lyrics. Their postmodern protest song 'Galicia caníbal' ('Fai un sol de carallo'), which mixed the rhythm of traditional *muiñeira* dances and the sound of *gaitas* with electronic dance beats, became one of the most celebrated songs from the *Movida galega* in Spain in the 1980s (with different mixes released in English and Basque, but not in Spanish). A detailed analysis of the *Movida galega* is contained in Chapter 8.

characterized by the erosion of the nation state and the emergence of new realities that signal the hybridization of traditional peripheral cultures with global forces.

The intimate relation between the local and the global is quite palpable in Galicia today, and is redefining its traditional peripheral status.[24] The worldwide phenomenon of the Galician fashion giant Inditex constitutes perhaps one of the more obvious industrial examples of this trend.[25] In 2008 Inditex became the leading fashion retailer in the world through its multiple brands (most recognizably Zara) with more than 7,000 stores in 90 countries, thanks to an innovative mix of speed, technology, creativity, and flexibility in adaptation to global demands. This interaction of the local and the global in Galicia is perhaps nowhere more conspicuous to the naked eye than in the postmodern transformation of Santiago de Compostela, the historic spiritual and cultural capital of Galicia and contemporary seat of Galicia's autonomous government, and perhaps the ultimate signifier of Galicianess. In recent years Santiago has become a veritable medieval "theme park" for the benefit of pilgrims, returning migrants, business visitors, and tourists alike, visited each year by several million people from all around

24 Significant in this regard is the statement by successful Galician entrepreneur José Ramón García, which synthesizes the potential of global technologies and transnational capitalism for remapping center/periphery dynamics: "Galicia está en el centro. En los siglos XIX y XX éramos periferia, pero en el mundo global ya no existen periferias. Internet es una gran autopista, además el mercado es global, no importa el punto del que partamos" (Blanco 2007). ("Galicia is in the center. In the nineteenth and twentieth centuries we were the periphery, but in the global world there are no peripheries anymore. Internet is a big highway; besides the market is global, it doesn't matter the point of departure"). García is cofounder of Blu:Sens, a booming Santiago-based manufacturer of international cutting-edge technologies (MP3, GPS, TV-LCD), with manufacturing plants outsourced in China.

25 The global emporium of Inditex is a case study in supply chain management textbooks. It is also one of the featured companies in Thomas L. Friedman's bestseller *The World is Flat* (2007). This global phenomenon has transformed the local reality of Arteixo, Inditex's main production center outside of A Coruña, into a multicultural enclave. As Alejandro Bolaños has stated, "la multiculturalidad es una rutina: en su sede central de Arteixo (A Coruña) hay empleados de más de 30 países" ("multiculturalism is the order of the day: in their headquarters of Arteixo (A Coruña) there are employees from more than 30 different countries"). On a less celebratory note, as a textbook example of neoliberal capitalism without borders, Inditex has been the subject of deserved criticism for its outsourcing practices offshore, and particularly for the use of under-age workers by local contractors overseas.

Figure 2   Performing Galicianess for global pilgrims and tourists in Santiago de Compostela (2016). Photograph by the author.

Figure 3   St. James ironically remade as a mass culture icon for global consumption, cannibalizing David Bowie's *Aladdin Sane* and the S.D. Compostela soccer team (2016). Designed by graphic artist collective Rei Zentolo, whose principles are Galicianess, creativity, and universality. Photograph by the author.

the world.[26] The cultural, and now also political and tourist, capital of this new Galicia has redefined its role as a hybrid of old and new, mixing the *enxebre* (traditionally Galician) and the global: folkloric *gaiteiros* (bagpipers) and *pandeireteiras* (tambourine players) and light-and-sound megaconcerts; a city of medieval *tunas* (traditional student music ensembles), *xacobeos* (pilgrimages), and world conferences; rural *zoquiños de madeira* (wooden crocks) can be found next to slick Zara stores, Galician artisan crafts next to souvenirs made in China; ancient medieval architecture and sculpture are juxtaposed with postmodern global *starquitects*, Mestre Mateo's Pórtico de la Gloria next to Alvaro Siza, Peter Eisenmann, and Norman Foster. All this consumable culture can be found within the small perimeter of the city, whose mystical ancient town is today surrounded by a colossal, overpowering ring of new highways. In all, it constitutes a perfect metaphor for the new "glocal" Galicia.

The Galician cultural industry has also profited from this "glocal" transformation, in the form of a blossoming tourist economy and the export of cultural products, such as the boom in Galician neotraditional popular music and its successful insertion into pan-Celtic world music, the production of cultural guides and books, the export of multimedia, audiovisual, and television productions with satellite transmission covering Europe and the Americas, and Internet broadcasting around the globe. Other indications of the potential projection of Galician cultural productions beyond the confines of the nation are the starring role of Galician culture at Havana's International Book Fair (2008), the first time a stateless nation has been invited as honorary guest;[27] the institutional and artistic representation of Galician music for the first time at the 2007 International Midem Festival (the most important international music trade show in the world); and the recent attention given to the New Galician Cinema, recipient of numerous awards at international film festivals.

Within this same "glocal" frame, one of the latest cultural developments in Santiago de Compostela, and the subject of continued public controversy, has been the project of the *Cidade da Cultura*, a monumental complex of several cultural buildings constructed on a mountain site overlooking Santiago. This indefinitely unfinished project underlines the tensions

26  For more on this cultural transformation see Gómez-Montero; Roseman.

27  This event was the object of much public controversy. The Galician representation in Cuba, understood as an endorsement of the regime by some and a costly self-publicity stint by others, was the subject of constant attack in the media, particularly by the PP opposition, coinciding with the general electoral campaign. For a report on the Fair and the response of Galician Conselleira de Cultura Anxela Bugallo, see Salgado ("La cultura").

between cultural and political institutions in contemporary Galicia, as well as the mutual implications of the local and the global. The *Cidade da Cultura*, originally planned by the *Partido Popular* conservative government during the years of the economic boom, could be interpreted as an attempt to create a Galician version, of gargantuan proportions, of the project commissioned from Frank Gehry by the Basque government, the Guggenheim Museum in Bilbao. The transnational dimension of that project, branded by an American cultural institution and signed by an American "starquitect," with funding from the official Basque government, highlights the trend of creating spectacular cultural projects for global consumption, whose origins may be found in the national but whose realization is indeed glocal. Two American cultural brands, Guggenheim and Gehry, carried out a postmodern intervention in the postindustrial urban wasteland of Bilbao, a controversial project that ultimately transformed the city and placed it on the postnational map for global consumption.[28] In both cases, in Bilbao and Santiago, we encounter postmodern spectacular buildings by leading world *starquitects*—Frank Gehry and Peter Eisenmann—publicly funded by historical autonomous communities to promote their global image. In both cases, the impact of the building as 'packaging' seems much more important than the actual contents of the package. The Guggenheim in Bilbao does not have an important permanent collection, and it is still unknown what the *Cidade da Cultura* will ultimately hold, thus perhaps creating their own metaphors of the void generated by the postmodern culture of simulacra. It is still unclear what the Basque or Galician component of these projects really is, other than their location.[29] In Eisenmann's defense, his project incorporates subtle references to Galician environment and history, such as the stone roof's curved shape, apparently inspired by the rolling hills of the Galician landscape, with its transversal cuts suggesting a Galician sea shell, which is also one of the symbols of the Camiño de Santiago, and the layout of the buildings suggesting the old street layout of Santiago. Likewise, the Hejduk Towers reflect in a postmodern fashion the familiar silhouette of the cathedral towers.

28 There has been a great deal of controversy on the subject of the Bilbao Guggenheim Museum. For an overview of the topic see Guasch and Zulaika.

29 As a result of the economic crisis, and the great popular opposition to the project, the Galician government stopped the construction of the *Cidade da Cultura* in 2012. With the rest of the original project pending its completion indefinitely, several buildings in the complex have been opened to the public – those housing the Library and Archive of Galicia, and the Gaias Museo of Galician history – while the building originally intended as international art center has been repurposed as offices for entrepreneur startup companies.

Figure 4  Partial view of the massive *Cidade da Cultura* designed by Peter Eisenman, with the John Hejduk Towers in the background, Santiago de Compostela (2015). Photograph by the author.

Nevertheless, the comparison between both projects ends there. Santiago was not a decaying postindustrial area, virtually unknown in the world. It already had a long and well-established presence in history, and had been for years a cultural and tourist destination of world importance in itself. The new project is on the periphery of the city, with no official efforts to bring it closer to the public, and is five times the size of the Guggenheim in a considerably smaller city with a much smaller budget.

Needless to say, there has been a great degree of opposition to the project of the *Cidade da Cultura*, in part for ideological reasons, since it was a legacy of the former Partido Popular government and a direct product of the megalomaniac vision of its autocratic leader, and former minister under Franco, Manuel Fraga, and a side-product of the construction bubble. The change of heart of the succeeding PSdG–BNG bipartite government (a coalition of the Galician socialist and nationalist parties, 2005–09), which finally endorsed the project and continued the construction after being vehemently against it while in opposition, and the return to power of the PP four years later, have only heated up the debate further. Beyond partisan political reasons, the widespread resistance to the project today is largely framed around conceptual as well as economic reasons. Critics have pointed out the gigantic scale of the project, which seems out of place for a small city such as Santiago de Compostela, the fact that it is removed from the city center—a periphery of the periphery—and the budgetary implications of building, maintaining, and operating such an enormous public project, which undoubtedly would diminish official subsidies for other cultural projects. While the long-term effects are unknown, the huge costs are certain and any cultural and economic benefit remains to be seen. Whether it will be another successful Guggenheim or not, its success will ultimately be determined by its ability both to connect in vital ways with the local population and to attract foreign visitors—that is, if it becomes a well-integrated *glocal* reality. For that to happen a new vision is needed to overcome the peripheral blindness that launched the project, which was autocratic and neoliberal in nature, seduced by its immediate political benefits and blind to its long-term effects. A new creative peripheral vision must be transformed into a sustainable and singular position on the global map.

An important interplay of the local and the global has manifested itself sometimes in the most dramatic and tragic ways. Such was the case in November 2002, when the *Prestige* oil tanker, a substandard ship from Liberia chartered by a European company, released 70,000 tons of fuel oil into the ocean and polluted hundreds of kilometers of Galician coastline and sea bed. This was one of the biggest environmental disasters in modern history (bigger than the Exxon Valdez). The spill affected all the main resources of the region, with devastating consequences for the ecology and the economy, particularly agriculture, tourism, and the crucial fishing industry. The spontaneous popular mobilization was also a "glocal" cultural phenomenon. The new grassroots organization *Nunca Máis* (Never Again), an umbrella of a myriad of collectives and groups, was formed and grew very rapidly. Thousands of individuals and members of non-governmental organizations from Galicia, Spain, and many other European countries volunteered in the massive clean-up effort and participated in rallies to mobilize complacent authorities, to gather international support, and to make international shipping regulations more ecology-friendly (i.e., by banning single-hulled tankers). Galician cultural figures responded just as vigorously and took charge of the popular movement, in light of the blindness of politicians and their inability to deal effectively with the emergency.

Significantly, the main "voice" of the popular movement was not a politician, a party leader, or a professional civic organizer, but a well-known female singer by the name of Uxía, the former lead singer of the folk band Na Lúa, who traveled around Galicia, Spain, and Europe to mobilize support for the cause.[30] Writers wrote in newspapers and spoke in the media; singers and musicians organized concerts and published CDs as fundraising activities; filmmakers and audiovisual producers made documentaries that traveled around the world. They organized a popular response denouncing the negligence of the authorities and demanding reparations and responsibilities. The collective effort showed a new form of solidarity and popular resistance

30 The *Nunca Máis* representation sent to Brussels included prominent diaspora Galician performers, such as the Galician/Belgian Verónica Codesal, the Galician/French/Basque Manu Chao, and the Barcelona-born female duo As Garotas da Ribeira, among others (see "Os europarlamentarios reciben a Nunca Máis").

that crossed national borders, and demonstrated the possibility of changing the status quo. In this sense, the massive mobilization in Galicia offered a good example not only of how the global directly impacts the local but, vice versa, of how the local can influence the global. We could say, then, in a double paradox, that a peripheral position demands a global vision, just as much as a peripheral vision implies its own positioning globally.

Several key cultural areas best represent this new creative hybridity in Galicia that goes beyond the confines of the national and is particularly visible in the literary, musical, and audiovisual fields. This is certainly the case of the "rurban" and "glocal" literature of Manuel Rivas and Suso de Toro, the most widely translated and successful of contemporary authors writing in Galician, whose novels have been taken to the big screen, but also applies to the transnational queer approach of Antón Lopo (*Ganga*, 2001), Teresa Moure (*Herba Moura*, 2005; *Benquerida catástrofe*, 2007), and María Reimóndez in their exploration of alternative sexualities and gender identities in a global context. Perhaps even more surprising is the emergence of new non-national authors such as Víctor Omgbá, the Cameroonian immigrant writer in Galicia who wrote a testimonial autobiography *Calella sen saída* (originally in French), or Erín Moure, the experimental Canadian laureate poet of third-generation Galician background who has written in a hybrid English/Galician–Portuguese transnational lyric language such works as *Little Theatres* (teatriños) or *O Cadoiro, poems*.

In the area of popular roots music and neofolk music, Galician musicians and singers have already established themselves firmly in the world arena. In fact, the two forms of roots music originating in Spain that have successfully been exported abroad to a significant degree are the ones that have been able creatively to hybridize their strong cultural heritage with new world music trends; one is flamenco, combined with African and Latin American rhythms, and the other is Galician folk, hybridizing with Celtic music and other forms of world music.[31] Likewise, the growing presence of immigration in Galicia has also translated to the local musical scene, where it is not uncommon to see performers of migrant origins (such as Batuko Tabanka) and multicultural hybrid performers (such as Najla Shami), as well as genre-crossing bands of rock, reggae, rap, and folk with members from

31 The list here is long – Milladoiro, Berrogüetto, Na Lúa, Uxía, Carlos Núñez, Luar na Lubre, Mercedes Peón, Cristina Pato, and Susana Seivane, among many others; but we could also include the Irish band The Chieftains, with their Grammy-winning and Galician-inspired album *Santiago*, or Belgian/Galician folk groups such as the female ensemble of *pandeireteiras* called Ialma (*Marmuladas*, *Nova era*) and the folk band Camaxe (*Imaxes*, *Airexa*), both led by singer and bagpiper Verónica Codesal, who have introduced Galician music into the repertoire of Belgian folk bands.

Galicia, Europe, and Latin America, as well as Senegal, Angola, or Tunisia (Pato).

A particular area of great interest in this regard are the visual arts and the so-called "boom" of the Galician audiovisual sector, with animation, multimedia, television, and state-national and transnational film coproductions made in or out of Galicia. Multi-artists such as Antón Reixa, the graphic artist, painter, and film director Miguelanxo Prado, the animators Peque Varela and Fernando Cortizo, and the documentarist Oliver Laxe, working in Morocco, are good examples of this new cultural hybridity.

These cultural agents and creators have been instrumental in the redefinition of Galician cultural identity, opening up to the world in the global age. They have been able to transcend both cultural essentialism and homogeneous uniformity by successfully incorporating the global in the local and by simultaneously exploring and inscribing their "Galicianess" in the global arena. The emergence of these creative artists and cultural performers with powerful, different voices is redefining what Galicia is, or could be, in this postmodern, postnational, and postperipheral environment. The new Galician cultural production (particularly the more traditionally consumable forms of culture, such as literature, music, and the visual arts) should then be understood in relation to its repositioning on the global map and to the process of construction of a new Galician cultural identity, post-Franco and postmodern, a/part of/from Spain, and fully immersed in the new global currents.

# CHAPTER TWO

# Deterritorialization
# and Deperipheralization:
# Galician Studies at the Global Crossroads

O único bo que teñen as fronteiras son os pasos clandestinos.
É tremendo o que pode facer unha liña imaxinaria trazada un día
no leito por un rei chocho ou debuxada na mesa por poderosos
como quen xoga un poker. [...] Pero, por sorte, esta fronteira
irá esvaéndose no seu propio absurdo. As fronteiras de verdade
son aquelas que manteñen aos pobres apartados do pastel.
'The only good thing about borders are the secret crossings. It's
incredible the effect an imaginary line can have. It gets traced one
day by some doddering king in his bed or drawn on the table by
powerful men as if they were playing poker. [...] Fortunately, however,
this border will soon be swallowed up in its own absurdity. True
borders are those who keep the poor away from the cake.'[1]
Manuel Rivas, *O lapis do carpinteiro*

Son galego da Arxentina, galego de Alemania,
galego de Cuba, da Suíza, da Holanda, do Canadá,
galego na Galiza imaxinaria.
'I am a Galician from Argentina, a Galician from Germany,
a Galician from Cuba, from Switzerland, from Holland, from Canada,
a Galician in an imaginary Galicia.'
Fran Pérez (Narf), "Galician lullaby"

Once we cross a border, we can't expect the border to
remain the same. It is marked by our passage.
Erín Moure, "The Public Relation"

1 *The Carpenter's Pencil*, translated by Jonathan Dunne.

## Shifting Grounds

Borders, frontiers, and maps are political and cultural constructs that reflect a particular ideological perspective of space in a given time. As such, they represent specific temporal/spatial crossroads and therefore are in a constant state of flux, subject to multiple changes and alterations. Cartographical representation is a reductive ideological instrument that suits particular needs and is subject to biases, exclusions, erasures, falsifications, and blind spots. However, in spite of the apparent fixity that a map imposes symbolically on territories, there is a continuing changing entity underneath that necessitates constant cartographical shifts and revisions to adapt to new realities and changing perspectives. This paradox is even more noticeable in our global age, with the transnational mobility of peoples, capital, and goods under the sign of neoliberalism, the development of intercultural practices and relations, and the virtual interconnections that have altered the traditional relations of time and space across the globe.

At this juncture I would like to focus on the relocation of Galicia between the local and the global and examine how Galicia's geopolitical and cultural borders are being redefined in the global age. My aim is to delineate a model for a new cultural cartography that redraws borders and alters the traditional center/periphery dynamics, allowing Galicia to be reimagined as a non-peripheral, open, inclusive space marked not by essential notions of origin but by mobility, cultural fluidity, and translateral relations. It will involve questioning the conventional relations between territory, culture, language, and nation, and challenging the disciplinary limitations that have traditionally defined the field of Galician studies.

In this shifting context it is important to examine the new crossroads for Galician studies in such a globalized world. This is a crucial issue that was discussed in one of the main roundtables at the recent conference of the International Association of Galician studies (AIEG) held in Buenos Aires.[2] In that presentation I tried to offer a general view of the new directions that Galician studies are taking on the international map, and the new crossroads facing us, particularly for those who work in Galician studies in English-language academic institutions around the world. The framework of the dialogue was particularly appropriate to reflect on the transformation and mobility of Galician culture and Galician studies in the age of globalization. On the world map Buenos Aires is a unique place of great significance for Galicians. It is a city almost more mythical than

2 "Os estudos galegos ante o cambio social e cultural: Identidades na fronteira, emigración e exilio," 6–9 April 2015.

real; a city full of memories and affects, migrants and exiles, and pendular movements across the Atlantic. A good part of the familiar and collective history of Galicians has been written in this city since the first waves of migration in the mid-1800s, creating sustained cultural links between both Atlantic shores. During the Franco dictatorship the cultural capital of Galicia moved to Buenos Aires, with a large proportion of the most relevant Galician intellectual and cultural figures in the arts, literature, and politics maintaining the vitality and vibrancy of Galician culture in exile. In fact it could be said that Buenos Aires constitutes a quintessential part of a deterritorialized Galicia, a fact that is reflected in the city being commonly referred as "the fifth Galician province." It would be impossible not to see the multiple layers of Galicia in the streets of Buenos Aires, in the museums, galleries, shops, murals, schools, civic associations, and dance and music groups. They give shape to a geography of mobility and transculturation. Teatro Castelao, Galerías Pacífico, Colegio Apóstol Santiago, Museo de la Emigración Gallega, and Galerías Santa Fe are just some of the numerous Galician historical *lieux de mémoire* present in the city, to borrow Pierre Nora's influential concept of the sites of memory that provide a historical continuity in collective cultural memory. In a further derritorializing manner, all people originally from Spain are to this day called *gallegos* in Argentina, as in other parts of the Southern Cone and the Caribbean where the Galician diaspora took root most firmly. The traditional demarcations of territory, nation, and culture do not fit the Galician experience. It seems to me a perfect illustration of the deterritorialized nature of Galicia, which has only increased in the global age, requiring a new critical approach and a new cultural cartography.

I would like to explore here the possibilities of such a new cultural cartography of Galicia in the era of globalization and examine the internationalization of Galician studies from the new critical horizons that have emerged in recent years, particularly attending to the realities and identities marked by movement and migration and the concepts of border crossing and hybridity. The starting point is a necessary cartographic reconsideration to reorder the traditional relations of territory, language, nation, and culture, which have produced, as Paul Gilroy indicates, the "fatal junction of the concept of nationality and the concept of culture" (2) in the case of transatlantic and African-American cultures. Similarly, Kirsty Hooper (*Writing Galicia into the World*) and other Galicianist scholars have recently referred to this junction in the case of Galicia, where the conventional notions of culture, language, territory, and nation must be re-examined from new perspectives that take into account mobility, biculturality, bilingualism, and transversality, and not as totalizing concepts that are absolute and

Figures 5–6 The enduring visual legacy of Galician muralists during their exile in Argentina. Mural allegories of Galicia in Buenos Aires by Manuel Colmeiro in Galerías Pacífico ("La pareja humana" "The Human Couple", 1946) and by Luis Seoane in Galerías Santa Fé ("Los músicos" "The Musicians", 1953). Photographs by the author.

invariable. This situation of "forced territoriality" is even more complex in Galicia, with the addition of rigid disciplinary limits imposed by official academic institutions, which creates a problematic system of inclusions and exclusions, as we will discuss later.

## Galicia on the Border of the Local and the Global

The transformation of Galicia that has taken place in recent years in the cultural field, as in the social, political, or economic realms, coincides with major changes which occurred in the era of globalization and the gradual erosion and disappearance of many traditional borders, both real and symbolic. The historical high mobility and transculturation of the Galician diaspora undergoes a new postnational transformation in this period. Since the 1980s, with the establishment of Galician autonomous government on the one hand and, on the other, its entry into the EEC (later European Union), a series of crucial political, economic, demographic, and cultural processes of a deterritorializing nature have developed, which have had a great impact on the redefinition of Galicia in the global era.

Since the political transition and the establishment of the Galician autonomy there has been a very visible boom in Galician cultural production both locally and transnationally, crossing the geopolitical borders of the nation and the state, which has been particularly noticeable in the arts, literature, fashion, music, and the audiovisual sector and is beginning to be recognized and appreciated beyond the geographical limits of Galicia. In parallel there has been a significant development in cultural infrastructure and industry, although still atomized in many ways and threatened by the effects of the global economic crisis and the pressures of transnational capitalism.

From an institutional point of view, these changes have included a continuous if uneven and rather unfocused policy of internal and external promotion and projection of the language, culture, and economy of Galicia, and of convergence in economic development within the new map of Euroregions. These institutional projects have not been without great controversy, often being seen as insufficient, inefficient, or politically partisan, particularly as advances in the "normalization" of Galician in schools have been at the mercy of the political parties in power, which has resulted in periods of Galicianization in schools during the PSG–BNG socialist/nationalist coalition (such as with the creation of *galegoescolas*) and periods of reflux and the introduction of trilingual curricula with the conservative Partido Popular (PP). Undoubtedly one of the most visibly successful of Galicia's revitalization projects internationally has been the rebranding of the Camiño de Santiago as a cultural heritage route for modern tourists and pilgrims alike, and the reinventing of the city of Santiago as a global theme park, which coincided with the presidency of Manuel Fraga in the Xunta de Galicia (1990–2005).[3] This should not be too surprising given Fraga's curriculum as Minister of Information and Tourism under Franco, his role as the creator of the "Spain is different" campaign, and his direct involvement in making tourism Spain's most important industry and Spain one of the preferred tourist destinations in the world.[4] Perhaps the most visible example of the top-down institutional approach to culture in Galicia has been the gigantic project of the *Cidade da Cultura* in Santiago, which stands as an unfinished monument to Manuel Fraga's institutional grandiloquence and autocratic governing style, as mentioned in the previous chapter.

Great advances in communications, transport, and urban renewal have taken place as a result of European Union convergence funding, which has in effect brought Galicia closer to the rest of the world and greatly contributed to its deperipheralization. In addition, the interactions between the local and the global are more visible than ever with the "discovery" of Galicia by visitors, tourists, and pilgrims. In 2007 Galicia received 5.7 million visitors, more than double its population, attracted by Galician cultural heritage (art and architecture, gastronomy, music, festivals, and so on) and the rediscovered Camiño de Santiago pilgrimage (declared a UNESCO World Heritage route), with several recently declared World Heritage Sites around Galicia (the historic city of Santiago and Lugo and A Coruña's Roman architecture) and the declaration of some Galician beaches among the world's best in international tourist publications. Galicia has undergone profound changes in its interactions with the world that are not simply limited to the experiences of migration and exile, and is more open and in sync with the world than ever before. But, in addition, the image of Galicia, for Galicians and for the world, has experienced a profound transformation in these years

3 The maps of the Camiño de Santiago would be good historic examples of a deperipheralized cartographic representation were Galicia constitutes not simply an annex to the nation estate, or an appendix to Europe, but a destination, a compass point of reference for millions, and a cultural center in its own right. The symbolic shell of the pilgrim has also become the modern emblem of a radial representation of the multiple roads crossing Europe and merging precisely in Santiago. For more on the resurgence of the Camiño in the global age, see Chapter 3.

4 During his years as Minister of Information and Tourism, Fraga started the process of reinventing the Camiño as a tourist destination. In 1964 the name Año Jacobeo was first introduced as a new "brand" by the Ministry to substitute the old Año Santo Compostelano.

as a rich, unique, and vibrant culture, a result of the historical confluence of different cultures—Latin, Hispanic, Lusophone, Celtic, Atlantic—giving shape to a moving cultural crossroads.

Paradigmatic demographic changes have also occurred in Galicia in recent years, such as the arrival and settlement of new immigrants, particularly from Latin America and Lusophone countries with traditional cultural and linguistic ties, which invert the traditional parameters of migration in Galicia and open her to new forms of cultural hybridity. Likewise, the general population exodus from rural to urban living and the parallel hybrid phenomenon of "rurbanization" in Galicia, where the rural peripheries acquire certain characteristics of the city and the urbanites in formerly semirural areas adopt traits of country life. The impact of borderless media, Internet, and virtual communication have further eroded these traditional distinctions. These transformations have proven the old categories of rural and urban to be simply inadequate and insufficient to describe Galician culture in the global age. They are intrinsically derritorializing movements which would effectively necessitate new mapping categories.

The economic engines of Galicia have also shifted gears drastically in these years. The primary sector, which was its traditional main economic foundation, is now heavily reduced. Because of production inefficiencies, European regulations, and global competition, agriculture and fishing currently accounts for less than 5% of the Galician economy. The majority of the Galician population today works in the tertiary sector. As a result, Galicia is a much less rural society than it ever was. It is also a lot less peripheral. The industrial reconversion after the crisis of the late 1970s and 1980s had a huge impact, with the closing of shipbuilding companies, metallurgic plants, and fish canneries, the traditional bastions of Galician industry, but other industries have boomed in recent years and expanded internationally. Evidently, the exigencies of global capitalism have left a profound mark in Galicia and created new economic inequalities, with some indeed profiting in vast ways. The Galician textile industry, which involves some 250 exporting companies, is one of the most visible. It is impossible not to see the giant shadow of Inditex in every major city around the globe, as it has become the leading clothes retailer worldwide with its different brands (Zara, Pull and Bear, Massimo Dutti, Zara Home, and others). Its main headquarters of Arteixo, a peripheral industrial park outside A Coruña, is now the center of the biggest textile empire in the world, and their products have become household names for millions of consumers. The world map of Inditex's complex system of supply-chain management and distribution redraws a very different cartography of center/periphery dynamics. Likewise, Estrella de Galicia has become a hugely successful brewing company with a comprehensive franchise and export plan around the world, from Miami to Singapore. The Galician service sector, and tourism in particular, is revitalizing the Galician economy, with established "brands" such as Camiño de Santiago, Albariño, and Islas Cíes regularly appearing in the travel sections of the world's major newspapers. In some senses Galicia has become its own brand, as in the institutional campaign "Galicia calidade," associating the name of Galicia with quality and excellence in the promotion of Galician products such as gastronomy, wines, jewellery, and tourist resorts.

As in other areas of Galician society, the glass of Galician culture may be half full or half empty, according to the angle of vision and ideological positioning of the observer. What seems evident is that Galicia finds itself at a cultural junction: facing a new crossroads between heritage traditions and innovations, flows of arrival and departure, the local and the global, homogeneity and difference, and cultural interests and supranational mercantile forces. At these crossroads the positive comes with the negative, showing the two sides of modernization and globalization. On the one hand, we encounter the more aggressive side of neoliberalism, with the imposition of asymmetrical structures of power and the strengthening of center/ periphery relations and a certain cultural homogeneity; and, on the other, we have the more positive aspects of access to new technologies and means of communication, new possibilities for integration and hybridization, and new capabilities for cultural expression as creators and participants in a global circuit, which also creates opportunities to alter center/periphery dynamics.

From these junctions it would be desirable to imagine a model of a deterritorialized dynamic Galicia, open to movement and hybridization, which finds its place in the world as a meeting point of a confluence of cultures. It would be necessary to create a new cartography where Galicia is not peripheral but at the forefront—an inclusive Galicia, open to the world and to herself, an idea of Galicia possible for the twenty-first century.[5] It would require designing a new cultural geography with new imaginary borders: Galicia as a meeting place between tradition and modernity, the rural and the urban, here and there, home and away, the real and the virtual, open to diversity, multiculturalism and *metissage*, as forms of creative

5 Carlos Mella has discussed his vision of a "possible Galicia," devoid of unattainable utopias, but of potential alternatives to present hegemonic conditions to overtake its economic peripheral status, based on a strong non-traditionalist national discourse. For Galicia's international cooperation and solidarity connections in the global scene, see Ríos and Teijo.

coexistence and cultural enrichment. It might seem somewhat optimistic or utopian, but, after all, if we are going to imagine a new cartography, it should be an improvement over existing ones.

The explosion of creative freedom that has characterized Galician culture in recent years seems to be going increasingly down that road: an expansive culture that is open to experimentation, change, and transformation, without fear of crossing boundaries, at the intersection of high culture and popular culture, at the confluence of assimilating the roots of the past, incorporating the contemporary aesthetic of the present, and in search of its own future; a culture open to cultural hybridity and mixing of forms and channels of expression in writing, communication, performance, music, visual arts, and animation as modern forms of expression and cultural intervention; a culture dialogically engaged with the world, made from the margins but against the margins, from a periphery that has become *deperipheralized*.

This undertaking would effectively mean the disrupting, expanding, and blurring of geopolitical, cultural, disciplinary, and imaginary boundaries. This new imagined Galician cultural paradigm could well be summarized in the song "Galician lullaby" from Narf, a multicultural postmodern nursery rhyme that tells us of the birth of this new deterritorialized Galician from a postperipheral "imaginary Galicia."

> Son galego da Arxentina, galego de Alemania,
> galego de Cuba, da Suíza, da Holanda, do Canadá,
> galego na Galiza imaxinaria.
> Son galego de Caracas, galego de Santiago,
> galego de Roma, de Lima, do Cairo, de Bogotá,
> galego na Galiza imaxinaria.

> I am a Galician from Argentina, a Galician from Germany,
> a Galician from Cuba, from Switzerland, from the Netherlands,
> from Canada,
> a Galician in an imaginary Galicia.
> I am a Galician from Caracas, a Galician from Santiago,
> a Galician from Rome, from Lima, from Cairo, from Bogota,
> a Galician in an imaginary Galicia.

Narf, the artistic name of Fran Pérez, a Galician born in Silleda (Pontevedra) and musically reborn in Mozambique, makes a strong statement of cultural hybridity in a multilingual electro-acoustic lullaby sung in Galician, Portuguese, and English, erasing geopolitical and cultural borders while reaffirming and resituating Galician local and national identities on a global map. His Atlantic@s tour around the Southern Cone in 2014 with fellow

Galician musicians and singers Uxía Senlle, Xosé Manuel Budiño, and Rosa Cedrón, developed in 2015 into a full-blown project of collaboration with Uxía entitled "Baladas da Galiza Imaxinaria" ("Ballads of an Imaginary Galicia"), which purposefully intended to deterritorialize Galician music beyond local/global, rock/folk, acoustic/electric, old/new, and here/there categories. For Uxía and Narf, the imaginary Galicia of their songs knows no boundaries; it is a deterritorialized network of travels, complicities, explored identities, and shared experiences.[6]

The phenomenon of deperipheralization is particularly noticeable in contemporary Galician cultural production, marked by its entry into the orbit of globalization and its gradual repositioning within the world map. In the cultural arena it is easy to see the mobility, real and imaginary, of Galician creators outside the region: the large number of transnational audiovisual co-productions and Galicia's participation in international cultural fairs, art exhibitions, literature conferences, music and film festivals, and so on. Galician music, one of the liveliest instruments of collective identity, travels well, as attested by the frequent appearance of Galician musicians and singers on the international circuit, in concerts, festivals, and recording collaborations. Luar na Lubre is Spain's most internationally recognized folk group. Carlos Núñez has become a superstar of Galician music around the world, and was named the "Jimi Hendrix of the bagpipe" by the magazine *Rock and Folk*. Mercedes Peón entered the circuits of world music. Uxía and Narf joined the Lusophone transatlantic orbit. Cristina Pato plays for millions of people on US

---

6 The mixing of Galician *alalás* and *pandeiretas* with electric guitars in this project echoes other territorial and cultural borders crossings that redefine the concepts of nation and culture, as Narf and Uxía explain in a segment of the TV program *Desde Galicia para el mundo* (#1131, 22 July 2015). "Entre conversas, encontros e concertos fomos debullando e compartindo a idea dun espazo emocional, que vai alén do puramente xeográfico, que latexa vivo e fértil, no interior de moitas almas espalladas por todo o mundo. Persoas que non beben necesariamente das mesmas fontes culturais, ou que nin sequera son galegas ou de ascendencia galega. Amantes do noso, sen máis. Habitantes da Galiza Imaxinaria. Pensala desde cualquera lugar ou sentimento, ou desde ópticas tan diversas como a curiosidade, a lembranza, a saudade, a esperanca, o descoñecemento, a crítica ou mesmo o desencanto é, dalgún xeito, facela real" ("Through conversations, encounters and concerts, we started to develop and share the idea of an emotional space, which goes beyond the purely geographical, beating live and fertile inside many souls scattered around the world. People who do not share the same cultural traditions, or who are not even Galician or from Galician descent. Simply lovers of our culture. Inhabitants of the Imaginary Galicia. Thinking Galicia, from any given place or sentiment, or from such diverse perspectives as curiosity, remembrance, *saudade*, hope, ignorance, criticism or even disillusionment, is already a form of making it real").

television, and thus to the world, with Yo-Yo Ma, and travels around the globe with her "Galician Connections," accompanied by the multicultural band The Silk Road. Likewise, Manu Chao comes to Galicia and associates with the *rock bravú* movement, while The Chieftains and Kepa Junkera have devoted whole albums to Galician music with Galician musicians. In the literary field, the number of translations of Galician authors into other languages and literary prizes awarded has grown dramatically in recent years and there has been an increase in non-Galician-speaking readers. Manuel Rivas, Suso de Toro, and Teresa Moure are some of the contemporary Galician authors most translated and recognized outside the region. Galicia is also becoming a powerhouse in the area of literature for young readers, with a catalogue of authors to export ("English Books for Children and Young Adults"), and authors such as Francisco Castro, Fina Casalderrey, Marcos Calveiro, and Agustín Fernández Paz translated into multiple languages. In the audiovisual sector, Galicia's animation industry is at the leading edge in Europe, with the first 3D productions having been made in Galicia and subsequently widely distributed internationally, winning consecutive Goya Awards for the best work of animation. Miguelanxo Prado is a well-established international graphic artist, writer, and animator, with a series of graphic novels published in 20 languages, who rubs shoulders with the best animators in Hollywood. Antón Reixa and Xavier Villaverde work from A Coruña and Madrid making international film co-productions that cross geopolitical and linguistic borders. A new generation of alternative filmmakers, such as Oliver Laxe, Peque Varela, and Lois Patiño, working from Morocco, London, and Portugal, are gathering accolades internationally. All these figures, and many others, are already effectively in some ways Galicians without borders.[7] But how do they all fit within the field of Galician studies as it has been traditionally conceptualized?

## New Directions:
## Galician Studies in Anglophone Contexts

I would like to turn my attention now to examine the new directions in Galician studies and their late emergence in English-language academia, which in practical terms is the equivalent of the global academe. From a historical perspective, we need to first point out the works of John Rutherford and Xoán González Millán, working from the UK and the US respectively, who pioneered Galician studies in Anglo-American academia

---

7 See an overview of this deperipheralization in my book of conversations with some of these figures, *Galeg@s sen fronteiras*.

Figure 7  Presentation of Galician digital fonts from the *artivist* collective Aduaneiros Sem Fronteiras (Custom Officers without Borders), featuring a photomontage of the traditional Carnival masked authority figures from Ourense known as *peliqueiros* or *cigarróns*, in a fictitious international border. Design by Pancho Lapeña (2007).

and were responsible for the establishment of the first centers of Galician studies in the early 1990s. John Rutherford has carried out important work as a critic and translator into English of modern Galician literature (of Méndez Ferrín, Castelao, and younger authors such as Xelís de Toro) and had an important role as mentor at Queen's College, Oxford of a new generation of Galicianists and Galician *lectores*, who have followed his path and are currently leaders in the field; later, he wrote Galician-language fiction, with *As frechas de ouro* (2004).[8] Xoán González Millán's theoretical essays have played an especially relevant role in the renewal of Galician studies; in addition, he was a founder of the Asociación Internacional de Estudos Galegos and its president between 1991 and 1994. He undertook solid intellectual work between the late 1980s and the early twenty-first century as a driver of modernization of Galician literary theory and criticism and a disseminator of Galician culture in the United States, and also as the mentor of a new generation of Galician studies scholars from the CUNY Graduate Center in New York. His proposals on literary nationalism and nationalist literature from a perspective of cultural resistance and subalternity were ground-breaking in the field, as was the introduction into Galician studies of both continental theorists such as Pierre Bourdieu

8  For an interesting personal perspective on the state of Galician studies in the UK, and the role of the Center of Galician studies in Oxford, see Rutherford.

and Jürgen Habermas and English-language cultural studies, which are still providing valuable outcomes. Despite his unquestionable significance for the development of modern Galician studies, González Millán does not totally escape the limitations of the literary studies model that he criticized. His introduction of polysystem theory by Itamar Even-Zohar to the study of Galician literature was very influential, and it represented an important revitalization in the stagnant area of Galician literary theory at the time, opening literary studies to the broader concepts of literary and cultural fields and examining the complex interactions of center and periphery, high and low cultures. However, it could be argued that it was a somewhat reductive and limiting perspective, still rather attached to cultural structuralist theories and semiotics. Similarly, his defense of the "philological criterion" as a conceptual basis for the definition of the object of study, already mentioned in the previous chapter, although it was important as a strategy of resistance and legitimacy, has been revised in recent years by other critics, who see it as an essentialist and excessively exclusionary conceptualization of the nation that maintains a problematic, naturalized identification of language, literature, and nation (Hooper 2007; Colmeiro, "Peripheral Visions, Global Positions").[9]

Even with these limitations, the theoretical renewal initiated by González Millán is still visible in the emergence of a new generation of critics who have continued to pursue the updating/reinventing of Galician studies. This critical wave of recent years presents a new challenge for Galician studies within a postnational and transnational dynamic that is multidisciplinary and interdisciplinary, open to the profound renovation in English-language cultural studies, and reacts to the new currents of globalization and its impact on cultural sites, while questioning the strict reliance on traditional philological disciplinary criteria. This revision aims for a better approach to the complexities of contemporary culture and, specifically, to the peculiar situation of Galician culture. It aims for the expansion and redefinition of the field of study, underscoring its transformation from the traditional and canonical focus on Galician literature and philology and undoing the crucial historic fusion/junction of nation and language.

Evidently, I am not proposing here the burial of philology—Galician, Spanish, or any other—as I actively participate in the field as a professor

---

9 González-Millán was also aware of the limitations of the concept in the contemporary Galician cultural context (see González-Millán). More recently, John Rutherford has also echoed the need to remedy the excessive philological focus of Galician studies as practiced in Galicia and exported overseas through the Centers of Galician studies (xx–xxiii).

and expert in literary analysis and criticism and am very conscious of its fundamental value and many positive aspects. Rather, I criticize the exclusivist and formalist philological criteria and the related nineteenth-century national model imposed by the interests of academic and administrative hierarchies that do not allow a broad vision of culture. The "big pink elephant in the middle of the room" that no one wants to see, and no one dares to speak about, is the slow death of the philological model, and of the invisibilities and exclusions that same model produces. The foundation of modern Galician national literature has a very clear canon that is called Rosalía de Castro. But the great taboo is that the canon is reduced to just two books of poetry, ground-breaking, magnificent and of the utmost importance, of course, but leaving out all her sustained narrative production in Spanish language and her last great book of poetry *En las orillas del Sar*, as Hooper and Gabilondo (in Hooper and Puga), among others, have indicated. Thus this unspoken exclusion reproduces the original marginalization of Rosalía, who was made to feel "a foreigner in her own country," forever exiled as a result of her crossing of the strictly enforced boundaries of Galician or Hispanic philology.[10] The cases of Pardo Bazán, Valle-Inclán, Fernández Flórez, and Torrente Ballester are even more shocking because they are not even considered an appropriate object of study as they do not fit the strict nationalist model, as much as they are some of the authors who have most contributed to the formation of the modern Galician imagination. And what to do with all the Galician authors with a bilingual literary production, such as Álvaro Cunqueiro, Juana Castro, and Marina Mayoral? And where to study the Latin American literature written about Galicia? Where do we place *Gallego* by Miguel Barnet, *La gallega* by Jesús Masdeu, or the border novel *Finisterre* by María Rosa Lojo, which could be models of transnational Galician transculturation? Which territorial map fits the literature of the Galician diaspora written in other tongues, such as the English-language poems of Erin Moure or the memoir *The Goobye Land* by Jose Yglesias? And what about all the other exclusions—of popular literature, women and sexual minorities, or anything that does not fit within the criteria selectively considered as a model? Not to mention other creative areas not necessarily unrelated to the literary field, but which exceed the strict philological parameters, such as a film text, a song, or a graphic novel. They all seem to fall into a disciplinary no-man's land.

Given the reality of the philological model in irreversible crisis, I propose an opening to cultural studies that expands the focus and disciplinary

10 For a discussion of the circumstances of Rosalía's status as "foreigner," see Davies; Rábade Villar ("Spectres"); and Moreiras-Menor ("El secreto revelado").

borders and is characterized by transversality, deterritorialization, and interculturality, and the use of new approaches informed by postcolonial critics, transatlanticism, diaspora studies, feminist theories, queer studies, and new areas of study open to the diversity and hybridity of cultural production, such as Galician cinema and audiovisual, music, performance, and other manifestations of popular culture.

Important contributions to Galician studies in English have been made in some of these fields in the past decade by critics such as Kirsty Hooper, Eugenia Romero, Helena Miguélez-Carballeira, John Thompson, María do Cebreiro Rábade Villar, Danny Barreto, Joseba Gabilondo, Cristina Moreiras-Menor, and Silvia Bermúdez, to name a distinguished few. The special interdisciplinary panel organized by Lou Charnon-Deutsch at the convention of the Modern Language Association of America in 2007 ("Galician Cultural Identity within and beyond Geographic and Linguistic Borders"), with interventions from several scholars mentioned above, was a conscious departure from traditional geographical and language-based disciplinary boundaries and showed the paths to deterritorializing approaches for Galician studies, while also provided significant visibility on the most important academic platform in the United States for the study of modern languages and cultures. Undoubtedly these paradigmatic changes represent a realistic note of hope for the future of Galician studies, and not only in the US academy. Likewise, the joint conference held at the University of Liverpool and the University of Bangor in 2008, "Saíndo da nación: máis alá do nacional na produción galega contemporánea," was another event of importance for Galician cultural studies internationally in its concerted effort to delineate a new postnational cartography. In parallel, various monographic issues have also reflected upon these same concerns: the special issues dedicated to Galician cultural studies in the *Journal of Iberian Cultural Studies* (2006) edited by Kirsty Hooper, in the *Bulletin of Hispanic Studies* (2009), coordinated by Kirsty Hooper and Helena Miguélez-Carballeira, and the *International Journal of Iberian Studies* (2008), edited by Sharon Roseman. The creation of the electronic journal *Galicia 21* has also provided an international platform for innovative and refreshing work in the field of Galician studies. Collectively these publication outlets indicate the momentum of Galician cultural studies in the English-language academy and justify the perception that the field is moving and expanding very quickly.

In terms of new academic initiatives, Gabriel Rei-Doval has been responsible for the foundation and development of the González-Millán Group for Galician Studies (GMGGS), the Anglo-section of the International Association of Galician Studies, and the recent entry of Galician studies into the Modern Language Association of America (MLA) with a discussion forum devoted to "Galician Language, Literature and Culture" (LLC)—undoubtedly historic achievements. The MLA is the most important organization in academic studies of modern language and literature worldwide and its congress brings around 10,000 participants, so it is easy to understand the importance of this symbolic and real achievement for Galician studies. This set of important events is not simply a happy coincidence, but proof of the fertility and increasing "deperipheralization" of Galician studies in the global era, and its slow but progressive incorporation into the field of cultural studies in Anglo-Saxon world. At the same time, we should note the progressive incorporation of cultural studies in the Galician scholarly context, as the work of "border" critics working on the Anglo/Galician line, such as Rábade Villar, Olga Castro, and Colmeiro, has been published inside and outside of Galicia.

Along the same line of deperipheralization of Galician studies in the Anglo-American academy, two important English-language monographs have been published recently that continue the same interdisciplinary direction of the special journal issues mentioned above: *Galicia Writing in/ to the World* (2011) by Kirsty Hooper and *Contemporary Galician Culture in a Global Context* (2012) by Eugenia Romero. These were published almost simultaneously by academic publishers in the UK (Liverpool UP) and the US (Lexington) and are closely related in their topics and critical approaches. They maintain a rich dialogue with current scholarship in contemporary Galician cultural studies produced on both sides of the Atlantic, in English, Galician, and Spanish, and both are positioned transversely between the local and the global.

As those authors acknowledge in their works, geographical and cultural mobility have been, and still are, crucial aspects of modern Galician identity, characterized by the collective experiences of massive migration and cultural hybridity. The authors examine the ways in which these experiences have defined and redefined Galician identity in relation to other cultures and languages, and how Galicia has been written beyond the confines of the nation. Both books aim, therefore, for a redefinition of the traditional principles of what constitutes Galician culture and literature, based on the junction of territory and language. They propose a new mapping and a new reading of Galician culture that exceeds the geographic and political configuration of the nation, focusing on the transnational and transcultural experience of migration.

In the case of Romero, this redefinition of the national culture of Galicia is in the light of global migration and mobility and the remapping of the parameters of center/periphery, rural/urban, and local/global. Among the most innovative aspects of her book are the careful examination of some texts and cultural phenomena that have not received adequate attention from critics and the variety of "texts" analysed (such as video, film, music, and novels, but also cultural myths, parks, museums, and Internet sites).

Hooper's book is mainly dedicated to the experience of migration in contemporary Galician poetic production. While the nineteenth- and early twentieth-century Galician diaspora to Latin America has been the subject of much attention from critics, the most recent European migration of the 1960s and 1970s, and the mobility provided by the subsequent entry into the European Union, have received minimal critical attention so far. Hooper's volume thus represents an important correction in this respect, focusing on cases of Galicians who write the experience of migration in the English-speaking world, particularly in the UK, and the new deterritorialized practices and poetics that have emerged as a result. *Writing Galicia in/to The World* is fresh and unique in its design, since no one has produced anything comparable to date. The author skilfully grounds the project on the theoretical formulations of Édouard Glissant's poetics of relation, Paul Gilroy's "Black Atlantic," Deleuze and Guattari's concept of deterritorialization, and current postnational critical discourses. The book strives for the remapping of both traditional time–space limitations of cartographies that have defined modern Galician culture and the conflation of the language-and-cultural identity triad of Galician nationalist discourses that has seemed to exclude those marginalized voices that do not quite fit the essentialist paradigm because of the language, the point of enunciation, or other markers of difference, such as gender, ethnicity, or sexuality.

Like Romero, Hooper does explore new territory, since the authors studied in her book—with the exception of Manuel Rivas, the most translated and studied among living Galician authors, and perhaps of Erin Moure, a leading contemporary Canadian poet—have not received much critical attention from academics till now. Both Hooper and Romero have thus expanded the territory for contemporary Galician cultural studies.

In a similar vein, I would like to mention here two reference books recently published in English of great importance to the field of Galician studies internationally, which also reflect the variety of approaches to and great momentum of Galician cultural studies: *Contemporary Galician Cultural Studies*, edited by Kirsty Hooper and Manuel Puga; and *A Companion to Galician Culture*, edited by Helena Miguélez-Carballeira. Both volumes are collective and multidisciplinary, and the contributions of their participants represent excellent examples of putting into practice the deterritorialization and deperipheralization of Galician studies from the different shores, literal and metaphorical, of Galicianist scholars in the twenty-first century.

The publication of the volume *Contemporary Galician Cultural Studies: Between the Local and the Global* (2011) by the Modern Language Association of America represented a major event in the field of Galician studies as it was the first reference book in the field available in English and, with the public recognition and wide distribution of the MLA, provided a timely and extremely useful research resource to encourage the study of Galician culture by way of interdisciplinary studies. The essays contained in the volume, which included major pieces from leading-edge Galicianist scholars in different disciplines, have a contemporary approach and offer a number of revisions of Galician cultural history and the formation of memories and individual and collective identities (around the concepts of language, migration, gender, and sexuality), and an analysis of cultural practices and politics in contemporary Galicia (in the literary, artistic, and audio-visual fields). As the subtitle of the volume indicates, the common thread of all the essays is the aim to deperipheralize and resituate Galicia and Galician studies away from the margins, between the local and the global.

The volume *A Companion to Galician Culture* (2014), edited by Helena Miguélez-Carballeira and published by the prestigious London publishing house Tamesis, is a noteworthy complement to the MLA publication. It was published in the *Companion* series dedicated to different Hispanic cultures (Iberian and Latin American) and internationally recognized figures such as Luis Buñuel, Pablo Neruda, Federico García Lorca, and Carmen Martín Gaite. The volume offers a broad historical view of Galicia and provides a balanced analysis of different moments and figures of Galician culture in prehistory, the medieval and Renaissance periods, and the modern age, with chapters devoted to music, architecture, cinema, new forms of rurality, and contemporary urbanism. The importance of the volume lies in both the new perspectives presented by its contributors and the symbolic solidification of the field, being part of a well-established academic series of more than 40 titles (anything from *Companion to Catalan Culture* or *Portuguese Culture* or *Companion to Mexican Studies* or *Latin American Cinema*), which is also in itself another form of deperipheralization of Galician culture.

The last book I will comment on, and the most recent among the new monographs of Galician cultural studies in English, is the volume by Helena Miguélez-Carballeira already alluded to earlier, *Galicia, a Sentimental Nation. Gender, Culture, and Politics* (2013). This book offers a unique and insightful critique of Galician cultural history from the nineteenth century to the present from the perspective of recent cultural studies on affect and emotions. Taking the concept of "cultural stereotype" as a political trope from the postcolonial critique offered by Edward Said and Homi Bhabha, Miguélez-Carballeira examines its use as a form of domination in the discursive construction of Galicia as a feminized and sentimental reality. Likewise, the author offers a critique of the process of institutional "normalization" or normativization from a feminist and postcolonial studies perspective, showing the marginalizing effects of this process caused by the hegemonic power. Her insightful analysis suggests what we would call another "fatal junction" in Galician studies, the overlay of two strong currents that have defined the field in recent decades in Galicia: the ideology and politics of linguistic and cultural "normalization" instituted with the establishment of Galician autonomy, and the polysystem theory conceptualized by Itamar Even-Zohar (discussed earlier), which was so well received in the Galician academy in the 1990s that it reached the level of academic institutionalization. These two ideological concepts are problematized as mutually supportive idealizing and compartmentalizing structures that ultimately sustain the status quo. I would also add a third element to this fatal intersection of language/culture normativization and the polysystem theory, the philological criterion approach: together, these constitute an overall normalizing and normativizing system. I think that this criticism of "normalization" could be considered part of a true normalizing process itself: to refocus the critical lens and "normalize" the use of available critical tools introduced by feminist and postcolonial theory in order to deconstruct and dismantle the hegemonic system, although I prefer to use the term "deperipheralization" because it represents a form of demarginalization on a wider scale and not a form of normativization, which has a certain canonical and exclusionary connotation. It is, after all, not a matter of homogenizing and normativizing, since rules and regulations always follow criteria for inclusion and exclusion that reflect the ideologies of power and hegemony.

In short, the new horizons of Galician studies in a globalized world have to be approached from different transnational and transversal multidisciplinary frameworks, deterritorialized and deperipheralized, as delineated by the recent work of the scholars discussed above. Galician culture is a movable border culture, European and Atlantic, Celtic and Latin, between Lusophone and Hispanic studies, local roots and global avant-garde, and that is precisely why our work should not be contained by borders, because Galician culture is not contained by them, and they are in a continuous process of redefinition. And that transcultural mobility is Galicia's true strength.

# The Critical Crossroads:
# Deterritorialization and Deperipheralization

The juncture of different space/time coordinates, of tradition and modernity, the local and the global, and the new cultural hybridity of mobility and border crossings, marked by "roots" as much as "routes" of travel and migration (Clifford), and the increasing erosion of categories between the canonical and the marginal, the high and low, demand a new approach and a new cartography for the disciplinary crossroads of our global age.

It would be instructive here to remember Deleuze and Guattari's reflection on the constructed nature of maps, their political, aesthetic, and cultural uses, and the latent possibilities they offered for their alteration, deconstruction, and reconstruction:

> The map is open and connectable in all of its dimensions; it is detachable, reversible, susceptible to constant modification. It can be torn, reversed, adapted to any kind of mounting, reworked by an individual, a group, or social formation. It can be drawn on a wall, conceived of as a work of art, constructed as a political action or as a meditation. (*Thousand Plateaus* 13–14)

In the area of Galician studies, Kirsty Hooper has led the way in the effort to redraw the existing cultural cartography, a crucially important task in the case of minoritized and peripheral areas such as Galicia. As Hooper acknowledges, "maps are especially meaningful in minority cultural positions, where questions of centre and periphery, the setting of borders and co-ordinates, the language of labels and legends, even the simple question of representation, carry a special urgency" (*Writing* 2). She echoes María López Sández's observation that this task is particularly urgent for stateless nations such as Galicia, which are contained in dominant cartographical representations:

> From a peripheral cultural position, like Galicia's, it is easier to be aware of the ideological implications of one's position on the map or of the simple question of whether a particular territory is the object of a map of its own or is systematically inserted into another map that covers a much wider territory. (quoted in *Writing* 3)

Following Antonis Balasopoupos's theorization of the interconnections of geography and history in postcolonial contexts and the need to challenge the received ideologically charged cartographic paradigms, Hooper aimed "to rethink the cognitive maps superimposed on 'minor' and 'peripheral' communities, so that the assumptions of metropolitan cartographical logic are revisited and even the categories of 'minor' and 'peripheral' called into question" (14).

Likewise, Rábade Villar has reflected on the need to rethink hegemonic center/periphery dynamics, which, as she states, "é un relato artellado polo centro" ("is a discourse articulated by the center"). From a Galician perspective, she instead advocates for redrawing the cartography and repositioning the peripheral in a center that is movable and can be located anywhere: "Non cómpre perseverar en sermos aceptados polo centro. Máis intelixente parece buscar o centro onda nós, sabendo que se move e pode estar en todas partes" ("There is no need to insist on being accepted by the center. It seems more intelligent to look for the center around us, knowing that the center is moveable and can be anywhere") ("Centro e periferia").

Galician history is an enlightening case in point in this respect, as the geopolitical borders imposed have tried to contain it within the limits of the nation state in a position of subordination, but at the same time Galicia's historic mobility has continually crossed and expanded those borders beyond the nation state. The traumatic experience of the Galician diaspora, marked by a collective history of political subordination, displacement, and loss, explains the deterritorialized sense of modern Galician identity, which, as Moreiras-Menor has discussed in reference to Manuel Rivas's novel *A man dos paíños*, is that of a "a nation which collectively forms itself from a permanently dislocated frontier" ("Galicia Beyond Galicia" 112).[11]

Living on a "dislocated frontier," a culture made out of and by crossing borders, is a transformative deterritorializing move that needs its own theorizing and its own cultural poetics. Erín Moure, the Canadian poet of Galician descent, has theorized about the personal experience of cultural border crossing and put into practice the deterritorialization of culture through language, by using English as a "minor" language, in Deleuze and Guattari's sense, transversed by other languages, including Galician. This bold border-crossing gesture effectively redefines the relations of space, culture, and identity, as she acknowledges: "Once we cross a border, we can't expect the border to remain the same. It is marked by our passage" (226). In her work, Moure problematizes traditional notions of territory, soil, and national origin as fixed entities intrinsically related to a patriarchal hegemonic perspective:

11 For a wider discussion of Spain's borders as spaces of negotiation and contestation, and a redefinition of the nation, see additional chapters in Sampedro and Doubleday's volume *Border Interrogations*.

What does *territory* mean—soil's sovereignty? Doesn't our capacity for 'de-localised' being—computer transfer and relations, internet, satellite positioning, laser-treated retinas, off-site manipulations, robotics prosthetics, networks—deafen static notions of *soil*, just as it deafens any reified notion of *body*? Doesn't 'national identity' risk returning us to notions of a closed familiar structure of origins, a basis for identity that mimics (in the end) the construct required to assure/secure stability for *paternity*? (226)

Moure thus questions the fixity and exclusions created by borders but does not simply call for their elimination, which in the case of stateless nations such as Galicia may be necessary for protection and to resist aggression and assimilation. In light of the realities of historical oppression and colonization, and the recourse to national discourse as a form of collective resistance, Moure opines that there ought to be a right to self-determination which includes the right to delimit one's own borders, but "there can only *be* a nation that has leaky borders not based on 'purities' or 'pure origins'" (228). Borders should be leaky, porous, and inclusive. Against the traditional concept of nation as "the collective *here*, in a *place*" (226), she proposed the alternative notion of "Cidadán," conceptualized as the "citizen as movement, and the troubled and transgressive relation of this citizen to borders" (227).

At the same time, Moure points out the paradoxical nature of nationalist discourses, which ultimately replicate the exclusionary practice of hegemonic systems, advocating instead for a transcultural form of citizenship:

The old nationalism of peoples maybe still associated with hope and "identity" but unless they are open, they risk too easily becoming monolithic echoes of the very supranational essences constructed by central states which they wish to contraindicate and defer. Better to have a nationalism which is locally based, and which bears upon languages, gestures and events, yet which admits the outsider to the soil and listen: one that says, with Castelao in Galicia, for example, "aquel negro era Galego." (229)

Likewise, the complex and paradoxical nature of the relationship of the local to the global, according to Moure, is that local cultures need borders to protect themselves, but these must be porous and open: "I believe that, in a movement that is paradoxical, the exceeding of frontiers without eclipsing them, frontiers of countries and of languages (and of mentalities), is urgent in order to defend local cultures. Yes it's paradoxical, but (I believe) we need paradoxes in our time" (230).

This paradoxical crossroads has been noted as well by other critics, such as Hooper and Rábade Villar, acknowledging the cultural and political tension between the need to maintain a certain concept of the nation, and therefore a nationalist ideology, as a defense mechanism in face of the challenges from the state and supranational global forces, and the need to be open, to recognize mobility and transculturation, to adapt and reconcile with the new global realities. As these critics maintain, the relative political and socioeconomic precariousness of Galicia still necessitates a national discourse to counteract and balance the undermining of its past and present, but this national discourse must be of a different kind that does not recreate essentialist notions of Galicianess. In this regard, Rábade Villar has discussed the exclusionary practices of Galician literary historiography, which condemns to the margins those who do not conform to a nationalist mould. Her suggestion to move from focusing on essences to refocusing on fissures is enticing ("Spectres").

We should consider borders as both political constructions and as bridge areas of intercultural exchange (Donnan and Wilson). Hooper has highlighted the relational nature of Galician cultural identity and practices (Glissant), entangled in a network of connections with the world. And both Baltrusch's concept of "portable identity" and Romero's notion of "movable identity" reflect on the historical mobility and translational aspect of Galician culture. For Romero migration and movement are key tropes in the imagining of modern Galician identity that erase the traditional coordinates of time/space and real/fantastic. It is Galicia's diasporic history that has created precisely a national identity located in the imaginary (*Movable Identities* 5).

Likewise, we should transcend essentialist nationalist constructions, but also the (not always so explicitly articulated) nationalist constructions of other hegemonic systems that cast a powerful shadow over Galicia and Galician studies, such as the Spanish, Hispanism, or even Eurocentric programs of comparative literature, for that matter. Redrawing the cultural cartography would thus be a way not only of demarginalizing Galician studies from the compartmentalization of hegemonic academia but of demarginalizing Galicia itself from its peripheral condition within the hierarchical structures of the nation state and the constrictions of the new global order.

Drawing on the concept of the nation as an "imagined political community," as famously theorized by Benedict Anderson, with the nation conceptualized as a limited and finite entity territorially defined, we could instead envision an imaginary cultural community, open, translateral, porous, and transgressive, which extends and exceeds imposed territorial demarcations. It would be instructive here to recall Edward Said's concept of "imagined geographies" (such as Orientalism) as perceptual reductive visions from the center (colonial power, Western thought) constructed through discourses, images, and stereotypes. Instead, what I'm proposing here would be an alternative reimagined geography from the periphery, which is perceptive of the network of lateral connections, cultural, historical, and affective.[12]

Enlightening examples of the possibilities of alternative "reimagined geographies" in the context of Galician cultural studies would be Antón Reixa's redrawing of cartographic imagery by subverting the geographic logic, a transgressive perspective informed by the map of postcolonialism, as in the album by Os Resentidos "Vigo, capital Lisboa" and songs such as "Galicia caníbal" (juxtaposing Galicia and Ethiopia), the invocation of Galician–Chinese, Vigo–Shanghai sisterhood ("Barrio chino"), or the rap litanies of the type "Melide, Sudán, Rianxo, Liberia, Soutomayor" of "Abdul" (analysed in Chapter 8); the "reimagined geography" of an alternative Galician Republic in their "Galicia, sitio distinto" album and subsequent TV program (a satiric angle on Manuel Fraga's "Spain is different" tourist slogan) or the postmodern, transnational mobility of Reixa's film *Hotel Tívoli*, an imaginary location continuously deterritorialized in a global setting; the border-crossing non-fiction films of Eloy Enciso, Xurxo Chirro, and Oliver Laxe, which defy territorial definitions of the nation; or Siniestro Total's take on "Sweet Home Alabama" for their Galician rock anthem "Miña Terra Galega" (as analysed by Hooper), or Miguelanxo Prado's graphic novel *Ardalén*, with an imaginary Galician reality created by the wind connecting both shores of the Atlantic. Other examples include the group Os Diplomáticos, with their album *Capetón*, and Xurxo Souto's essay "Galicia-Capetón," with its references to the popular renaming by Galician sailors of Cape Town as Capetón and Antwerp as Antuerpe, remapping Galicia according to "outra xeografia," ("another geography"), widening the territorial concept of Galicia in a deterritorialized nautical chart that is postperipheral and indeed global ("7 portas, 7 mares").

What I am proposing here is a rethink of the new horizons of Galician studies in terms of "deterritorialization" and "deperipheralization," two

12 It should be noted here that Álvaro Cunqueiro was an early proponent of imaginary geographies that blurred geopolitical boundaries, creating a new literary cartography of Galicia that was projected above all in Brittany, noting the parallel histories and cultural connections between these two land's ends of the continent. He even used the expression in an article ("Las geografías imaginarias"), where he creates a cultural remapping of Galicia by making connections with locations in other countries, particularly France, such as Terra Chá in Lugo with Orleans, and Os Bergantiños with Brittany.

concepts that bring us back to cartographic imagery by reversing and redrawing the ideological construct implicit in the categories of center/periphery and cultural territory.

The concept of "deterritorialization" is traditionally perceived as a loss of identity and a weakening of the relationship between the individual and the territory, as originally discussed by Deleuze and Guattari and more recently developed by other critics such as García Canclini in relation to the effects of globalization on modern cultures. Historically, the causes of this situation often go back to the phenomena of migration, exile, and political and socioeconomic colonization. This is clearly evident in the history and the reality of Galicia (with the great territorial fissures created by its subaltern peripheral condition, the experience of diaspora, and cultural and linguistic diglossia), which has gone through "dark centuries" and "long nights of stone" of political repression and subordination, and still has a visible legacy to this day. The sentimental attachment to the land and the feelings of *saudade* and *morriña* can be seen as direct consequences of that historic sense of loss, the most common channels through which to express that condition. The reawakening of Galician nationalist ideology since the nineteenth century would be another effect of that deterritorialization.

Deterritorialization is also related to Habermas's concept of the postnational, understood as reflecting a paradigmatic shift from the monolithic perspective of the nation state, which he theorized after the great diasporas following World War II and the effects of globalization. Due to the shifting nature in meaning of the postnational as employed by different critics, it sometimes overlaps with transnational, postmodern, and cosmopolitan identities inflected by global change. In general terms, the concept of deterritorialization tends to reflect the shifting of spatial relations with the globalization of the economy, politics, and culture, triggered by technological developments of digital information and virtuality and the new currents of global capitalism under the forms of neoliberalism and neocolonialism. In this sense, we could think of deterritorialization as the effects of the contemporary transformation of forms of living, working, and cultural practices, in terms of the blurring of traditional physical demarcations (here/there, local/global, real/virtual), which is also clearly felt in the case of Galicia.

But these are not the only effects of deterritorialization. We could also envision an additional layer of meaning to this term, which does not negate the troubling and often traumatic phenomena mentioned, but provides as a counterpart enriching possibilities opening towards lateral and transversal connections and hybridity. Deterritorialization would thus also entail the transculturation and formation of new shared identities, both individual and collective, as the work of Fernando Ortiz, Néstor García Canclini, and Homi Bhabha have demonstrated in the case of postcolonial cultural identities. Likewise, interdisciplinarity and multidisciplinarity would also be other forms of desirable and necessary disciplinary deterritorialization.

Conversely, the concept of "deperipheralization" would aim for a cartographic shift in perception, redrawing center/periphery relations in a new map where the local and the global undergo different forms of interaction. I understand deperipheralization here to be a dual process of *revision*: on the one hand, in the sense of refocusing, expanding the visual angle and incorporating the wider field of view provided by peripheral vision, an eccentric vision, toward the marginal, less visible and examined areas, which corrects the tunnel vision of the center; and, on the other hand, in regard to revising and rethinking cultural practices and identities from the margins and borders. Against the invisibility or partial blindness of the center, this peripheral revision seeks "deperipheralization" by decentering the focus and refusing to view the peripheral from the perspective of an immovable center, thus subverting the approach that makes the periphery peripheral.[13]

This new deterritorialized and deperipheralized perspective, characterized by movement, fluidity, and transversal connections, applies both to the processes of cultural formation and to the field of academic studies. And those are the critical lenses that we could use in order to examine the current situation of Galicia and Galician studies in the global era, at a critical rather than "fatal" crossroads which requires new methodological tools and new approaches to make it compatible with the realities of the globalized world.

The direction that I am proposing here is a continuation and expansion of some of my earlier proposals on the condition of Galician culture in the global era and my assessment of the situation of Galician studies, particularly in

13 Peripheral vision could be seen as a challenge to the unitary central vision of mainstream visual arts with the institutionalization of the rules of perspective since the Renaissance. Exceptional in this regard were the visual policentral representations of Brueghel and Bosch, which defied the single visual angle and the rules of perspective. In a sense, this poststructuralist perspectival shift has also some common elements with the "anamorphosis" or "curious perspective" of the Baroque period, which was a challenge to the classical perspective of the Renaissance, with the manipulation of linear perspective to create ingenious new optical effects when perceived from different angles, but which remain hidden to the viewer positioned in the center. Similarly, a peripheral vision shift would reveal a new different reality, hidden and invisible to the viewer positioned in the center.

the United States.[14] But now this remapping of the field is on a scale spatially broader and temporally more extended, with a global vision that includes the fertile activity produced internationally in the area of Galician studies in recent years. I will focus here on the areas that are closer to me through my work in the English-language academia (mainly North America and the British Isles, and now Oceania, which is another systemic semiperiphery) and certain academic frameworks that transcend traditional disciplinary divisions. Exploring the new research areas of cultural studies (on gender, sexuality, memory, language, and identity), border studies (studies of border "contact zones" and cultural crossings), and global studies, on the one hand, and the intersections with Latin American studies and the emerging field of transatlantic studies (focusing on exile, migration, memory, and identity), and postcolonial and postnational studies, on the other, allows for interventions in intellectual debates from transverse angles.[15]

These new crossroads logically require some new strategies and new critical tools. And so I propose a double deterritorialization and deperipher-alization of Galician studies, from the recognition that we live on the border, between the local and the global, the center and the periphery, here and there, in physical as well as virtual spaces. Overcoming rigid disciplinary standards and narrow philological criteria, this would encompass, first, a new and broader landscape that is open to the approaches of cultural studies, and the exploration of inter/multi-disciplinarity; and, second, the creation of intersections and convergences with other areas in search of new transversal, supranational, and transoceanic perspectives crossing borders and exploring inter/multi-cultural connections. One of the most exciting and illuminating ideas that surfaced in the last conference of the International Association of Galician studies in Buenos Aires from the discussions in the migrant centers and community groups related to the Galician diaspora was precisely the clear reconceptualization of a renovated field of Galician studies within a notion of a deterritorialized Galicia, redrawing the cartography of "a Galicia de aquí e a Galicia de alí" (the Galicia from this side here, and the Galicia from the other side there).

Given the reality of new forms of cultural contact, pendular movements, and hybrid identities, and the new network of virtual spaces and

14  See in particular my essay "Quen somos, de onde vimos, a onde imos: Reflexións sobre os estudos galegos desde Estados Unidos". For a complementary perspective, see Rei-Doval.

15  I will not get into the rather byzantine and sterile discussion of "Iberian studies" in the United States here, because I think it is like trying to reinvent the wheel or, speaking of maps, "rediscovering the Mediterranean," as the Spanish expression goes. For more on this aspect, see Godón.

connections, it is also necessary to strengthen the articulation of what is happening in these Galicias and beyond. It has to be also a pendular rather than a unidirectional movement. But the relative opacity between what is done within Galicia and without, particularly in the English-language academia, is a problem unique not just to Galician studies but to Iberian or Hispanic studies in general, subjected to the traditional disciplinary hegemony of philology and resistance to critical theory and cultural studies broadly speaking, practically ignored or at best perceived as fashionable trends of political correctness.[16] One obvious and necessary step to rectify this situation would be to disarticulate the rigid disciplinary walls and barriers and *de-philologize* Galician studies. That is, to discard what I call the national-philological corset, because, although the strict confines of disciplinary territories may allow in the short run the survival of the field, already increasingly weak and facing enormous challenges, it does not open it to the new directions and realities of our globalized world, and therefore it is likely to collapse in the long run. We should be moving in a new direction, because ultimately this philological criterion is a legacy of nineteenth-century nationalism, and I would say that responds to a form of covert colonialism that has resulted in the containment and peripheralization of Galician studies.

And since we are discussing the topic of containment and peripheralization, on the issue of cultural identity, gender and sexual difference are constituent elements of exclusion over which nationalist systems have been constructed, traditionally organized under a patriarchal and heteronormative order, as Hooper and Miguélez-Carballeira have noted, and the Galician case is certainly no exception. The definition of women as political subjects, their full incorporation into public life in general, and the role of women creators in particular are undoubtedly some of the most important cultural phenomena of recent decades both in Galicia and Spain. Likewise, integration and social acceptance of gays and lesbians, and their "normalized" legal status, are important achievements that resituate both at the forefront of human rights efforts worldwide. Nevertheless, remnants of a hierarchical patriarchal culture still survive, if sometimes less visibly. These are being confronted and contested by feminist theorists and activists, proponents of the assertion of the right to difference, and movements under the rainbow GLBT denomination. Thus, new alternative emancipatory

16  There are significant exceptions to this paradigm, as the work of scholars based in Galicia such as Rábade Villar, Reimóndez, Baltrusch or Bringas and Martín engage in productive dialogue with contemporary critical trends in cultural studies and postcolonial, feminist, and translation theories.

proposals have emerged recently that defend minoritized or undervalued cultural identities who refuse to be a mere "double minority" within the national culture, such as have been presented by Timothy McGovern (2011) and Bermúdez (2011) on queer authors Antón Lopo and Ana Romaní, and by Miguélez-Carballeira (*Galicia*) and Helena González ("Como prenden elas da nación?"). In that regard, the critical corrections proposed by women and sexual minorities in a society that is legally equal to all, but still fundamentally patriarchal and heteronormative in many respects, appear as necessary directions on the horizon, as María Reimóndez defends from a transverse postcolonial perspective.[17] These new deterritorialized critical horizons delineate new opportunities to generate resistance against the system, deconstructing from gender studies and feminist and queer critical perspectives the discourses that construct the traditional definitions of gender and sexuality, and to create a real alternative to patriarchy and heteronormativity. Is this perhaps the last frontier to conquer?

I end these introductory reflections with a last optimistic thought, recalling something I said in a previous article about the situation of Galician studies in North America. Working transversely from the periphery and against the grain has certain advantages, as a new generation of Galician audio/visual creators is showing to the world:

O lado positivo da atomización dos galicianistas [...] e da falta de estruturas tradicionais, de non ter cátedra de estudos galegos, de non ter facultade de Filoloxía galega, e polo tanto de non traballar dentro do estreito corsé disciplinario e dentro do canon, é a posibilidade de traballar e reivindicar as marxes, o rico campo das hibridacións, e de todas as manifestacións culturais que se escapan a mirada institucional. E aí si que eu vexo unha posibilidade renovadora de transcender a institucionalización da literatura e a cultura galega. ("Quen somos" 138)

17 Another step in the effort to deterritorialize and deperipheralize Galician studies from a feminist, postcolonial, transnational perspective of the peripheries, is the book by Manuela Palacios and Laura Lojo, *Writing Bonds: Irish and Galician Contemporary Women Poets* (2009) and some of the articles in the volume edited by María Jesús Lorenzo Modia and Roy C. Boland: *Australia and Galicia: Defeating the Tyranny of Distance* (2008), such as Olga Castro's. Likewise, translated anthologies of Galician literature such as Helena González Fernández's *A tribo das baleas* (2001), a trilingual anthology of new Galician poetic voices in Galician, Spanish, and English, Mary O'Donnell and Manuela Palacios's *To the Winds Our Sails. Irish Writers Translate Galician Poetry* (2010), and Jonathan Dunne's two volumes of *Anthology of Galician literature* (2010; 2012).

Figure 8   Demarginalizing the periphery. Emblematic image of the Galician *Movida* "reconversion" with a port crane turned into a radio mast, from the documentary *Periféricos* (2006). Productora Periféricos. The guiding principles of the producers are bold: "Somos periféricos porque … Venimos de la periferia. Creemos en la globalidad de las ideas locales" "We are peripheral because … We come from the periphery. We believe in the global reach of local ideas" (perifericos.org).

The upside of the atomization of Galicianist scholars [...] and the lack of traditional structures, such as not having chairs of Galician studies or Faculties of Galician Philology, and therefore not working within the narrow disciplinary corset and within the canon, is the possibility to work from and affirm the margins, the rich area of hybridizations and cultural expressions that fall beyond institutional control. And it is there that I see a possibility of renewal and of transcending the institutionalization of Galician literature and culture.

# CHAPTER THREE

# Sound and Vision:
# All Roads Lead to Santiago

Some sing with zithers, others with lyres, others with kettledrums, others
accompanied by flutes, others by flageolets, others by trumpets, harps,
violins, others by Gallic and British wheel fiddles, others by psalteries,
others by diverse musical instruments, they have a sleepless night. [...]
Here one hears different tongues, different voices in barbaric languages
–conversations and songs in German, English, Greek, and in other
languages of other tribes and diverse peoples from all over the world.
*Codex Calixtinus*, Book I, Chapter XVII

Cinema is the invention of a new reality; each film invents a life,
reinvents life. And Santiago is pure invented reality. Santiago was an
"inventio", which means "discovery" and also "creation". Santiago,
city that gave birth to so many other Santiagos throughout the world,
is a creation that is a religious myth, a legend, stories and History.
Suso de Toro, "Silencio se rueda"

## Beginning the Journey

I will start with some apparently paradoxical images. Anybody who visits
Santiago de Compostela these days can witness how the not-so-long-ago
remote provincial city has become a veritable theme park of Galician heritage,
medievalism, and the cult of St. James for global consumption. Traditions
are invented and reinvented. The old is now the new cool. What was once
the periphery is now a new center. It seems like a new cultural geography
has been written by the effects of globalization, which alters traditional
time/space coordinates and reshapes center/periphery dichotomies. After
centuries of neglect and peripheralization since its heyday in the Middle
Ages, the cultural and political capital of contemporary Galicia has become
one of the alternative hot spots of international travel in the global age.
Travelers from more than 100 nations now regularly come to Santiago each
year. Some are pilgrims, which could seem like an apparent anachronism

in a secularized western world, but for many that concept does not really reflect the variety of their goals or experiences as travelers in the twenty-first century.

The complex network of pilgrimage routes leading to Santiago de Compostela formed, historically and metaphorically, the backbone of a sort of European cultural nervous system during the Middle Ages. The pilgrimage to Santiago also constitutes one of the original founding myths and most influential chapters in the chronology of Galician history and cultural mythology, with an enormous transnational projection that has only increased in our age. The modern revival of the Camiño and the recurring *Xacobeo* celebrations have also been privileged institutional channels through which to promote Galician culture as a calculated series of measures orchestrated by the government of the Xunta de Galicia to resituate Galicia on the global map since the early 1990s. It is for that reason that the roads to Santiago are an appropriate focus for the first in-depth case study of this book, examining the remapping of Santiago and Galicia in the new global cartography. It is also fitting to initiate the journey here, since it was also the original first step in my own chronology as researcher of this book project, going back to the mid-1990s, as I explained in the introduction.

The historical pilgrimage route to Santiago is known by many different names: Camino de Santiago (or Camino Francés for its main itinerary) in Spanish; Camiño de Santiago in Galician; Chemins de Saint Jacques in French; it is also commonly known in English by the names of Way of St. James, St. James's Way, St. James's Path, St. James's Trail, the Route of Santiago de Compostela, and the Road to Santiago, among others. In modern-day global Spanglish it is sometimes known as "The Camino Trail" or simply "The Camino." The official denomination by the UNESCO is the "Route of Santiago de Compostela" (declared a World Heritage site in 1993), to which were added four additional routes in 2007, the primitive routes in northern Spain leading to Santiago. Throughout this book I will be using some of these denominations interchangeably, depending on the specific context—Galician, Spanish, European, or global. I will also use the expression Santiago/Camiño to refer to the combined cultural geography of the traveling routes and the city of Santiago de Compostela.

In this chapter I will emphasize a network of multiple roads: terrestrial and maritime, with all their multiple branches, national and transnational, historical and modern, geographical and metaphorical, and the roads to as well as emanating from Santiago. It is a journey where *roots* and *routes* cross and interact: the roots of cultural traditions, heritage, origins, and ancestral narratives and customs, and the routes of pilgrims and travelers crossing lands, nations, cultures, languages, and traditions on the roads to Santiago de Compostela. It is also a journey rich in old and invented traditions, such as carrying a shell and a gourd, making stone piles along the way, getting your *Compostela* certificate stamped, burning your boots, and leaving your clothes behind at the end of the journey. Through these rituals, the experience of Santiago/Camiño provides a sense of connection with the past and community, and an aura of authenticity in an age when collective memory is feeble and everything is plastically constructed. It is a comforting impression, which somehow forgets that everything is always already mediated through cultural media, a world data bank of sounds and images available at everyone's fingertips 24/7 from a computer terminal, laptops, tablets, or smartphones.

Thousands of websites, blogs, guided tours, and personalized travel plans can be found online, and a huge cultural industry has been built around Santiago/Camiño and the ways to get there. Santiago is nowadays a global tourist mecca, rather than merely a pilgrimage site, and the Camiño a must do for the contemporary international traveler, regularly being featured as one of the recommended places to visit in the travel section of newspapers and magazines around the world. To visit Santiago, and do the Camiño, is presented as one of the more memorable life-changing adventures a modern traveler can experience. Part of its appeal is its many different facets that combine elements from diverse traveling experiences, thereby attracting a wide variety of travelers: similar to a trip to the remote Antarctica; a photographic safari in Africa; an educational field trip in Latin America to learn about the culture and practice the language skills; a historical trail such as the Camiño Real of the missions in California; a religious experience such as visiting Jerusalem, Rome, or Tibet; a mystical experience such as going to Machu Pichu; a personal challenge in space such as climbing a high mountain or crossing a deep river; a trip back in time, such as going to Egypt, Turkey, or India; or a journey of discovery at the end of the earth, with the attraction of the limit, such as going to Patagonia or New Zealand.[1]

As a result, the city of Santiago resembles today a global theme park, offering a continuous sound and vision spectacle, with dazzling light and sound outdoor concerts, elaborate firework shows, Galician bagpipers and tambourine bands dressed in traditional costumes roaming the streets, ritual *botafumeiro* (censer) swinging performances, thousands of opportunities

---

1 The great success of the Camino as a global traveler destination can be further attested by the recent interest expressed by Japanese authorities to learn from, and collaborate with, the *Xacobeo* agency in order to promote their own Shikoku pilgrimage route, known as the Route of the 88 Temples (González, "Japón quiere copiar el Camino de Santiago").

for tourists' pictures, video projections on the cathedral's façade, flashy architecture by some of the world's *starchitects*, and an endless window display of t-shirts and Galician souvenirs made in China from gift shops selling Galician CDs of Celtic music.[2]

So how did we get here? The resurgence of Santiago/Camiño in recent decades has taken place as the result of a constellation of different local and global circumstances and a complex series of political, economic, social, and cultural changes. But let's start at the beginning.

## Reinventing Traditions

I would like to examine the cultural remapping of Santiago/Camiño, and Galicia, by focusing on the various contemporary forms of reinvention and resemanticization of the traditional pilgrim's road to Santiago, and the new secular patterns employed for the exploration of Galician cultural identity and its international projection beyond the geographic boundaries of the land's end of the Iberian Peninsula. Santiago/Camiño could be seen as a symbolic crossroads of tradition and modernity, the local and the global, roots and routes, reaffirming cultural identity while at the same time opening to the world as a statement of a common heritage of universality. The reinvention and remapping of Santiago/Camiño rewrites and translates the tradition in a contemporary language, or, rewriting Eric Hobsbawm's famous dictum, "reinvents the tradition," rebuilding a cultural identity rooted in the collective memory but also looking beyond and ahead to the future.

It is axiomatic that collective memory can explain the past only from the always-changing perspective of the present, as it illuminates that present and orients it towards the future. Its basic function is to create identity links between the past and the living present. Its meaning is constructed and continuously reconstructed, according to the different needs of an evolving present. The Camiño de Santiago has changed its meaning significantly over the centuries, but it still has an important place in contemporary

---

2 The same is true around the rest of Galicia, particularly in areas along the Camiño and in officially designated *Xacobeo* years. The Camiño is literally the stage for a number of audio/visual spectacles. The official institutions in charge of the promotion of Galician Culture and Tourism—the Axencia Galega das Industrias Culturais (Agadic) and Turismo de Galicia—co-organize the program Cultura no Camiño (Culture on the Road), which features a series of visual and musical performances in 93 towns along the Camiño. In 2015 this included 316 different Galician cultural activities (theatre, music, dance, new circus, among others), co-sponsored with the Galician food outlet Gadis (http://www.agadic.info/culturanocamino).

collective memory, as it gives meaning and cultural identity to different groups and communities. This is especially the case of those bound by the historical territorial geography composed of a rich architectural heritage of roads, bridges, and buildings along the Camiño, together with their customs, traditions, and narratives. These are effectively *lieux de mémoire*, as formulated by Pierre Nora, places of collective memory that signal continuity and permanence in time. But the Camiño also encompasses the community of travelers who year after year have traversed the roads, either physically or imaginatively. In our own era its renewed popularity as a polyvalent experience (spiritual, cultural, historical, leisure) and as a culturally mediated construction (with a myriad of books, travel publications, and media texts such as photobooks, films, documentaries, music projects, websites, and social media) also relies on a collective memory of narratives, sounds and images, rituals and reinvented traditions.

Collective memories are constructed on foundations that impose an interpretation on the past and build a link with the present. In actuality these collective memories can have weak or dubious grounds, or even lack a real authentic base. The legend of Santiago is part of the blurred history of national/religious founding myths that lie in the collective memory. Its earliest origins are extremely remote and practically inaccessible to modern historians. There are those who argue that the medieval Road to Santiago overlaps with another earlier pagan route of Celtic origin, the Milky Way or the Way of the Stars, of which only a legend remains. But, in actuality, it does not really matter how it started, whether or not the body of St. James arrived in the Galician coast, and whether or not his remains are buried in the cathedral of Santiago de Compostela. What is important is that collective memory has built that belief through the centuries. It is not so much the truth of the facts but the powerful weight that these images of the past have on the present. Authenticity may be important from a religious point of view, but is almost irrelevant from the point of view of its symbolic weight, accumulated in the collective memory as a cultural "heritage." Authenticity is only an effect of its aura. As the historian Américo Castro once stated, "la autenticidad del sepulcro de Santiago no es mayor ni menor que la de la estatua de la Libertad en el puerto de Nueva York" ("the authenticity of the tomb of St. James is no greater or lesser than the Statue of Liberty in New York harbor") (quoted in Sánchez Albornoz 30).

For Alfonso Castelao, Santiago was an invention that turned a periphery into a center: "a invención do corpo de Apóstolo [...] fixo sa nosa Terra un centro de universalidade" ("the invention of the body remains of the Apostle [...] turned our nation into a center of universality") (Castelao 47). Contemporary Galician writer Suso de Toro has also remarked, following

Castelao and historian Claudio Sánchez Albornoz, on the fundamentally invented nature of Santiago and the Camino as an *inventio* (a discovery and a creation), a product of the collective imagination, a narrative composed of "historias e Historia" ("stories and History"). For the exiled Spanish historian, the Camino de Santiago, built on the belief in the tomb of the apostle, should be treated as an *invention* in the double etymological sense of a *finding* and a *creation*:

> ¿Invención=hallazgo? El verbo latino *invenire* tiene el doble significado de hallar, encontrar y de inventar, imaginar. Y el mismo doble significado podemos atribuir al descubrimiento del sepulcro de Santiago que iba a galvanizar la resistencia de la cristiandad occidental española. (27)

> Invention =discovery? The Latin verb *invenire* has a double meaning –to find, to discover, and to invent, to imagine. And we can attribute the same double meaning to the discovery of the tomb of St. James that stimulated the resistance of Christian Western Spain.

The Camino, therefore, is understood by Sánchez Albornoz as an *invention*, both as a discovery and as an imaginary cultural construction, a complex net of invented traditions continually renewed and resemanticized.[3]

Eric Hobsbawm has studied the widespread phenomenon of "invented traditions" in the modern era, which seek to recover a lost link with the past while simultaneously hiding the marks of the suture that cover that break with the past: "The invented tradition is taken to mean a set of practices, normally governed by overtly or tacitly accepted rules and of a ritual or symbolic nature, which seek to inculcate certain values and norms of behaviour by repetition, which automatically implies continuity with the past" (1). Invented traditions attempt to reconstruct an imaginary notion of historical continuity. Thus, for Hobsbawm, the modern concept of nation, although it may be rooted in historical continuities, is always grounded in some invented or constructed components. Emblematic invented traditions such as the flag, the anthem, or even the national language are perceived as natural and always existing by the force of their repetition. The invention of traditions is "essentially a process of formalization and ritualization, characterized by reference to the past, if only by imposing repetition" (4).

According to Hobsbawm, invented traditions can be ascribed to three general types: 1) those that represent or symbolize social cohesion,

---

3 María Liñeira, following Bruno Latour's concept of "factish" (collapsing the distinction between real "fact" and fabricated "fetish"), has applied it to the "fabrication" of Santiago as a religious, cultural and political "factish."

reinforcing the sense of belonging to a group and community identification; 2) those that legitimize institutions and power relations; 3) and those that promote socialization, and the promulgation of values, beliefs, and conventions. The invented traditions of the Santiago/Camino fulfil all those functions. Founding myths such as Santiago are an essential part of a shared collective memory, which fill the need for the constitution, affirmation, and identification of the group. The original impetus for the invented tradition of the Camino de Santiago was the creation of a collective spiritual bond with the imagined territory of an earlier Christian Spain before the Muslim invasion and with the rest of Christian Europe. It symbolized that community cohesion and served as affirmation of the Christian beliefs and values supporting it, in opposition to those of the Muslims, who were seen as the Other. The roads to Santiago, which crossed the northern peninsular Christian territories, thus formed a vertebral spine serving as communal spiritual and cultural support and a form of resistance against the common enemy. The time of greatest weakness for Christianity in Iberian lands in the early Middle Ages saw the emergence of the myths of Pelayo in Covadonga, initiating the Christian Reconquest, and of Santiago/St. James, who would become Spain's unifying myth and future patron saint. The legend of Santiago was thus invented, invoking the name and the intercession of Santiago Matamoros (St. James the Moor-slayer) with the shout "Santiago y cierra España" during the centuries-long Christian Reconquest. This legend reached its zenith at the time of Santiago de Compostela's archbishop Xelmírez, who obtained the papal bull for Santiago from Pope Calixto II in 1122. As is well known, from the beginning the routes of Santiago have always had a versatile character. The project of national religious–military construction took place in a complex and evolving economic, legal, geographic, and cultural framework that went beyond the purely spiritual (thus serving as economic trade route, and power relations, establishment of borders, a form of redemption of convictions, for cultural and artistic exchange, and so on). The myth of Santiago gradually created a cultural bond giving cohesion to the peninsular Christian kingdoms, above the particular quarrels and struggles for hegemony, and later constituted the backbone of Christian Europe, which was heavily involved in crusades against the infidel.

The boom period of the Camino de Santiago, between the tenth and thirteenth centuries, coincided with an era of religious fervor and the need for the creation of a common Christian imaginary against the expansionism of the Muslim enemy. From that heyday the Camino started to show a slow but steady decline in the fifteenth and sixteenth centuries. The plague epidemics were certainly an important factor in the process of decline of the pilgrimage route, but there were multiple reasons. The progressive fragmentation of the unitary medieval universe owing to new Renaissance ideas, the end of the military and religious Reconquest in Iberia, scientific discoveries, exploration and conquest of new lands beyond Finisterre/Fisterra, and the Protestant Reformation and final separation from Rome would eventually peripheralize the Camino de Santiago, which would lose its protagonist role as Europe's backbone. Enlightenment ideas, the Napoleonic invasion, a string of Spanish civil wars, and anticlericalism would only sharpen its decline into oblivion until the latter part of the twentieth century.

In the late twentieth and early twenty-first centuries, when European unity is being rebuilt and renegotiated, it is appropriate to remember that the pilgrim's route to Santiago represents the first consciousness of a certain common European identity, serving for centuries as a major religious, cultural, and trade route, and as a driving force of European cohesion. For Goethe, as was mentioned in the first chapter, Europe was made precisely in the pilgrimage to Compostela, which generated a crossing of roads and peoples, giving a common cultural heritage and identity to the continent. The road in our own era has been officially declared by UNESCO a World Heritage site and the Council of Europe has named it the "first European cultural route." Similarly, the manuscript known as the *Codex Calixtinus* or *Liber Sancti Iacobi*—a compilation of manuscripts about the pilgrim's journey attributed to Aymeric Picard in the eleventh century—includes a pilgrim's companion book with practical information about the journey, which is regarded today as the first tourist guide known. Thus it is not surprising that the Camiño should be resignified in our global era as a cultural tourist route.

In our modern times the Camiño de Santiago is a newly reinvented tradition, necessarily resemanticized by the passage of time and the changes in political and cultural circumstances. Walter Starkie had already noted this shift when he referred to modern-day pilgrimages as "pilgrimages without tears" (33), acknowledging the impossibility of repeating the experiences of the arduous pilgrimages of former times and their transformation into often secular routes. The *Xacobean* tradition has come to be alive again, although most often resignified as a cultural journey, alternative tourism, personal challenge, field trip, study abroad, or any of the modern forms of leisure travel, as has been noted earlier. The founding myth of Santiago was not only an *inventio* but also a *translatio*, a transfer. *Translatio* also had a multiple meaning etymologically, as both a spatial transfer and a figurative transmission. In medieval religious iconography the representation of the ritual moving of a saint's body was known as the *translatio*—in the case of St. James the *translatio* from Jerusalem to the found place in Iria Flavia (today's Padrón) to the new site of Compostela. But there is a second sense. A *translatio* is also a metaphor, a transfer of meaning, from literal to metaphoric/figurative. The geographical change across space to another location also involves a symbolic transmission to a different context, a different culture, or different language. The invention of Santiago/Camiño has also been the result of a series of *translations*, across different time/space coordinates, cultures, and languages. In a contemporary sense, cultural critics of translation theory have emphasized precisely the hybridity and recontextualization process. Jo Labanyi understands cultural translation "en el sentido de la hibridación de culturas locales y globales en un momento presente compartido por ambas" ("in the sense of the hybridization of local and global cultures in a present moment shared by both") (Labanyi 48).

A constellation of important political, economic, and cultural factors explain the resurgence of the Camiño in recent decades, and its translation to a modern idiom. At the local and national level it is clear that it has coincided with the decentralization of the Spanish state and the establishment of Galician autonomy, with the recovery of local power and the transformation of Santiago de Compostela into Galicia's political and administrative capital, on top of its already established role as cultural and academic capital. It is therefore directly related to the political and cultural reawakening of Galicia after "the long night of stone" of the dictatorship and the new impetus for cultural projects reclaiming Galician identity, locally and globally. In the process of recovery of its own traditions, its unique history, its identity, and its collective memory, Galicia's political and cultural institutions have managed to strategically exploit the great symbolism of the Camiño de Santiago and its centrality in European history. The Camiño has been perceived as filling a void for founding myths in an important moment of symbolic reconstruction of collective identities in the postnational map of European integration. At the same time, through the Camiño de Santiago Galicia is "rediscovered" for the eyes and ears of the world, just as it was in centuries past. Again, following the already mentioned conceptualization by Sánchez Albornoz and Suso de Toro, it represents a (re)discovery and a self-(re)invention. In this regard, there has been a concerted institutional effort from the authorities of Xunta de Galicia and the city of Santiago towards the cultural rebranding of Santiago/Camiño, and the launching of Galicia itself as a tourist destination, reclaiming a central position in the global map of tourist/pilgrim/traveler routes.[4] Intense marketing campaigns

4 See Chapter 2 about the special role of Manuel Fraga in this reinvention, first as a Minister of Information and Tourism under Franco (in charge of censorship, propaganda, and tourist promotion), and then fully during his four terms as President of the Xunta de Galicia (1990–2005), when the new reinvented Camiño was launched, aquiring global proportions, starting with the 1993 *Xacobeo*.

were launched by the Galician governmental institutions after the forming of the *Xacobeo* consortium, starting with the big *Xacobeo* 93 celebrations of the Holy Year, which counted for their international projection on the sound and image of global icons such as Julio Iglesias, presented as "a son of Galicia."[5] A great number of sound and image spectacles were planned for that year. The focus was clearly to rebrand the Camiño as a ready-made multiuse destination, stressing a secularized cultural component, leisure cultural consumption, and the "cool factor" of a journey of discovery, personal growth, and self-improvement. The marketing campaign, which reflected the rise of neoliberal capitalism since the 1980s, proved to be quite successful globally, managing to multiply tenfold the number of travelers to Santiago in 1993 from previous years.

In the international context the Route of Santiago as a cultural/spiritual/tourist destination/adventure, and its spectacular festive celebrations, has experienced a pronounced boom with the globalization of culture. Some important factors are the transnational ease of mobility of the global era, the spectacularization of cultural consumption, and the new age mysticism and search for authenticity as a response to the hyper-stressed lives, disconnection, and materialism of late capitalism. There is an inherent paradox also in the fact that this supposed refuge from the constraints of modern life and market-driven consumption is itself an effect of the forces of neoliberal capitalism.[6] Santiago/Camiño is part of a thriving travel and culture industry involving marketing, hospitality, gastronomy, transport, and many other consumable goods, as well as the marketing of cultural products, particularly print and media texts.[7]

It would be appropriate to mention here the international boom in the number of narratives of the Camiño that have appeared in recent years, including memoirs, novels, films, documentaries, records, even cookbooks

5  The Galician public entity officially in charge of organizing the Santiago/Camiño re-engineering is known as *S. A. de Xestión do Plan Xacobeo*. Since its formation it has directed the restoration of parts of the Camiño, has been responsible for investment in infrastructure and the building of new facilities, and has led the collaboration with other national and international institutions related to the Camiño, among many other tasks. Attracting international celebrities to Galicia, from Umberto Eco to Bruce Springsteen, has been a regular element in successive *Xacobeo* marketing campaigns.

6  Among the critics who have commented on the commercialization of the Camiño, see Frey; Rasch.

7  A large number of museistic approaches to the Camiño in Galicia have been published, particularly photography and art exhibits. Thus, the Museo Centro Gaiás in the *Cidade da Cultura* featured in 2015 the special program "Camiño. A orixe," a comprehensive historical exhibition on the pilgrimage to Santiago.

and reality shows! The bibliography and discography generated by Santiago/Camiño is immense, as is the critical corpus. I will briefly mention some of those with the widest global impact, such as the international bestsellers by Paulo Coelho (*The Pilgrimage*, 1997) or Shirley MacLaine (*The Camino: A Pilgrimage of Courage*, 2001); successful international films such as *The Way* (Dir. Emilio Estevez, 2010), an English-language Spain/US co-production with Martin Sheen and Ángela Molina; and the international television miniseries *Camino de Santiago* (Dir. Robert Young, 1999), featuring a megastar cast including Charlton Heston, Anthony Quinn, Anne Archer, Lorenzo Quinn, Robert Wagner, and Joaquim de Almeida, and Spanish actors José Luis Gómez, Loles León, Imanol Arias, and Juan Echanove. There are also multiple print and media texts about the Camiño directly targeted to particular language/national groups, such as French, German, or Korean. The impact of each of these texts can be measured by the progressive increase in the number of travelers each year from different groups.[8]

The Camiño has also been the focus of a number of books by Galician authors, such as Suso de Toro (*La flecha amarilla*, 1998) and Marica Campo (*Confusión e morte de María Balteira*, 1996), and even by Galicianists such as the British professor John Rutherford, with his hybrid novel travelogue *As frechas de ouro* (2004). Particular mention should made of the numerous photo books devoted to Santiago and the Camiño by Xurxo Lobato, the best-known contemporary Galician photographer and the most prolific author of Camiño photography books in several languages, which he has coauthored in collaboration with Cesar Antonio Molina, Luis Carandell, Manuel Rivas, Víctor F. Freixanes, Xosé Ramón Barreiro, Francisco Fernández del Riego, and Ulrich Wegnera, among others (See *Galeg@s sen fronteiras*).

There has also been a boom in media texts made in Galicia related to Santiago/Camiño. Numerous shorts and documentaries on the Camiño, from

---

8 Some of the recent international film productions about the pilgrimage to Santiago include *Saint-Jacques … La Mecque* ("Santiago … Mecca") (Dir. Coline Serreau, 2005); *Brüder III—Auf dem Jakobsweg* ("Brothers III—On the Way of St. James") (Dir. Wolfgang Murnberger, 2005); *Ich trag dich bis ans Ende der Welt* ("I will take you to the end of the world") (Dir. Christine Kabisch, 2010); *Les doigts croches* ("Sticky Fingers") (Dir. Ken Scott, 2009); *If You Ever Get to Heaven* (Dir. Joe Atkins 2010). Spanish films include the action thriller *La rosa de piedra* ("The stone rose") (Dir. Manuel Palacios, 1999), based on a story by Manuel Rivas; the modern comedy set in the pilgrim's route *Al final del camino* ("At the end of the road") (Dir. Roberto Santiago, 2009); and the fantastic avant-garde *Finisterrae* (2010), directed by Sergio Caballero. An alternative pilgrimage, to San Andrés de Teixido, was the focus of *Pelerinages* ("Pilgrimages") (2016), by Galician–Italian director Simone Saibene, based on Ramón Otero Pedrayo's book of the same title. For a review of other films on the Camiño, see Herrera Torres; Sojo.

professional to amateur, can be found on YouTube, such as the collection of short films *Seis miradas de Compostela* (1999), made by well-known directors Antón Reixa, Isabel Coixet, Xavier Bermúdez, Manuel Palacios, Manuel Iglesias, and Ricardo Boo Valiño, commissioned when Santiago was named European City of Culture; the docufiction *Camiño de Santiago: A Orixe* (2004), directed by Jorge Álgora; or the multilingual *Tres en el camino* (Within the Way Without, 2004), directed by Larry Boulting in Japanese, Portuguese, and Dutch, blending the local and the global. In the field of animation, several media productions have also focused on the Camiño: *Os vixiantes do camiño* (1999), a fantastic adventure animation series inspired by O Camiño which was directed by Miguelanxo Prado for Televisión de Galicia, featuring characters from the celebrated *Xabarín Club* TV program (see Chapters 6 and 9); and *O Apóstolo* (Dir. Fernando Cortizo, 2012), a full feature horror animation film which was very well received at the animation film circuits worldwide and gathered six Mestre Mateo awards (out of ten nominations), not a small feat for the first crowdfunded Galician film. *O Apóstolo* is another example of a hybrid *glocal* production, with the collaboration of US composer Philip Glass, the Real Filharmonía de Galicia, and the traditional multi-instrumentalist Anxo Pintos from the Galician folk band Berrogüetto.[9]

Quite often the boom in media texts has been related to the sights and sounds of *Xacobeo* celebrations, and thus are frequently commissioned works by official institutions, which can be good or bad. An exemplary case would be the impressive orchestral composition *Iacobus Magnus* (1994) from Milladoiro, recorded with the English Chamber Orchestra for the *Xacobeo* 93, a continuation of the earlier Camiño de Santiago collection *Via láctea* (1993). There are also numerous record collections of traditional songs and newly "invented traditional" songs. A less positive example would be Alberto Comesaña's *Jacobsland* (1999) and the accompanying theatrical concert tour, both commissioned by the *Xacobeo* 99, which consist of a mixture of Galician folk-inspired music, mythical theatrics, and epic storytelling. This was an unusual, inauthentic, and ultimately not altogether successful career change for somebody like Comesaña, who was associated with the pop-rock Galician *Movida* scene in the 1980s (Comesaña, as former leader of well-known Vigo bands Semen Up and Amistades peligrosas, was the inventor of "porno pop"). It clearly reflects the institutional high stakes invested in the Camiño,

---

9 Other recent Galician animation features around the Camiño include *O Mago Dubidoso* ("The Little Wizard", 2013) (Dir. Roque Cameselle), set at the time of splendor when the Cathedral was being built, and the promotional videos *Santiago, a viaxe continua* (2009) and *Xis, ao encontro de Francisco* (2013). See Chapter 6 for more on Galician animation features.

in particular the sound and vision spectacles, and the new commercial boom of Galician Celtic folk, which will be analysed in Chapter 8.

As evidence of the phenomenon of the renewal and repositioning of Santiago and Galicia on the new national, European, and world map, among this considerable boom in Santiago/Camiño media texts I would like to examine two examples that aimed to rediscover and reinvent the Camiño in the field of audio/visual cultural production with a global projection: the hybrid travel documentary/fiction film *O Camiño das Estrelas* (The Way of the Stars, 1993) by Galician director Chano Piñeiro and the acclaimed album *Santiago* (1996) by the Irish Celtic music group The Chieftains. In these audio/visual productions the travel route is used as the central metaphor for the (re)discovery process of cultural roots and of the intercultural exchanges that reinvent one's identity in the present, as a modern project of an imagined Galicia oriented towards the future and the world. In the next two sections of this chapter I will focus on these two media texts, one made in Galicia for the world (*O Camiño das Estrelas*) and the other made around the world with Galicia as its core (*Santiago*). They both aimed for the discovery and remapping of Santiago and Galicia in the global age, and were the initial seeds that awakened my own interest as researcher in this project.

## Reimagining Galicia:
## the Visual Journey of *O Camiño das Estrelas*

> Non deixedes de inventar contos incribles, por favor. Seguide
> facendo películas. Quizais sexa o único xeito de sobrevivirdes.
> Porque, ¿que imos facer se non temos soños?.
> 'Please don't stop inventing incredible stories. Continue making
> movies. Perhaps it may be your only form of survival. Because,
> what are we going to do if we don't have dreams?'
> Chano Piñeiro

Chano Piñeiro (1954–1995) stands as the pioneering Galician film director, with a self-taught visionary trajectory that starts with the historic conversations in the Ourense film encounters of the 1970s and leads to the 1989 *Cinegalicia* film festival, which is generally considered the birth of the new Galician cinema (see Chapter 4). His short *Mamasunción* (1984) is a contemporary classic of the Galician cinema of the diaspora, and significantly was the first program shown when the public Televisión de Galicia was launched in 1985. He was also the director of what is considered by many to be the first Galician full-feature fiction film in commercial format (*Sempre Xonxa*, 1989), which was entirely shot in Galician. In 1992

Chano Piñeiro wrote and directed the promotional medium-length film *O Camiño das Estrelas* ('The Way to Stars' is the official subtitle), an atypical institutional commission that would be his last work. This project was commissioned by the Xunta de Galicia's *Xacobeo* consortium, presided over by the conservative PP *conselleiro* Víctor Manuel Vázquez Portomeñe, to celebrate the *Xacobeo 93* in a series of spectacular Holy Year celebrations of the Camiño—another invented tradition which takes place whenever Santiago's patron saint's day (25 July) falls on a Sunday. This event was conceived as the Galician answer to the various local/global cultural events of international projection held in Spain in 1992, such as the Olympics in Barcelona, the Wold Expo in Seville, and Madrid's European Capital of Culture celebrations, which intended to give a new image of a modern Spain, and Catalonia, to the world. The Galician institutional project was also envisaged as an opportunity to reimagine Galicia and project it to the eyes of the world, affirming a regained cultural identity rooted in popular tradition and the collective memory of Galicia, but also with a clear history in the European and western tradition, and with a recognisably modern and appealing wrapping for the global spectator.

*O Camiño das Estrelas* is of particular interest owing to its high visibility and intended wide audience (it was titled in four languages), the symbolic standing of the film director, and the distinguished cast and collaborators- including some key Galician figures of international renown, such as young artists Miguelanxo Prado and Carlos Núñez, and fashion designers Roberto Verino and Adolfo Domínguez. It also represents an important crossroads for Galician audiovisual culture with wider resonance in the field between mainstream and marginal production, commercial and *auteur* cinema, and local production and global audience. The film shows signs of the difficult balance between artistic vision and commissioned project, personal statement and institutional message, sometimes offering brilliant audiovisual perceptiveness and other times falling prey to aestheticizing impulses or cartoonish gimmicks. *O Camiño das Estrelas* is also at a crossroads from the point of view of artistic creation; a hybrid narrative fiction/documentary that seeks to provide a new dynamic image of Galicia, proposing a journey in which reality and fantasy, tradition and modernity, past, present, and future meet and merge at different cultural intersections. These bridges are constructed through a series of audio/visual crossfades and overlaps, subtly linking Galician heritage and landscape, industry and art (music, dance, sculpture, design, fashion), civil engineering and mythology, fishing and gastronomy. This is the case in one of the first scenes of the film, as the camera juxtaposes and sutures together the land roads and the sea passages of the Rías Baixas, one of the main international

Figure 9    All roads lead to Santiago. Galician *vieiras* (scallop shells) metamorphosing into billboard road sign for the Camiño. *O Camiño das Estrelas*, Bubela S.L.

tourist destinations in Galicia, regularly visited by cruise ships, gastronomy lovers, and beach vacationers. The film narrative forms a complex and heterogeneous cultural mosaic in constant motion, following the continuous rhythmic movement of a traveler through time and space. Thus, the camera starts by focusing on images of fresh Galician fish and shellfish—one of the traditional basic sources of Galician life, culture, and commerce. These images are literally transformed before our eyes in the next sequence, through filmic suture, into a visual metaphor of the road of Santiago (the Galician *vieira* shell as the recognizable emblem of the Camiño, commonly used as a road sign post), as a sign of its own identity and openness to the world. This symbolic visual metamorphosis "invents" the logo of the Camiño de Santiago, representing an iconic palimpsest in which the figures of the seashell and the star in the sky overlap. The Galician shell is a long-established emblematic sign of the Xacobean pilgrimage to Santiago, as is the figure of the star formed by various converging cartographic lines, suggesting "the Way of the Stars" that leads to Santiago/Fisterra, a central point that marks the metaphorical beginning and end of the journey, as if all the roads are leading to, and radiating from, Santiago. Piñeiro's film uses the narrative strategy of the pilgrim's wandering eyes that act as a guide along the paths of contemporary Galicia, across the old and new roads over land, sea, and air. The pilgrim's gaze links, like the still-standing medieval bridges crossed, the different Galicias, between past and present, the coast and the lands, interior and exterior, history and imagination.

As spectators of this new audio/visual journey, Piñeiro's camera symbolically removes our blindfold by taking off the blind hood of a peregrine falcon (*falco peregrinus*) and setting it free to fly, thus allowing us to see with new eyes a previously hidden world and open it to the imagination. It is an act of peripheral revisioning from a much wider and higher angle that invites us to participate in a journey rediscovering and reimagining Galicia. Piñeiro's roaming HD camera flies, with the ease, majesty, and powerful vision of the peregrine falcon, over the solid monumentality of Galicia's buildings, constructed of hard granite over the centuries and still standing in an apparent challenge to the passage of time. The high-flying camera also glides over the stunning natural monumentality of Galician landscapes—powerful, ancient, and magical—marked with a mix of prehistoric pagan elements and Christian landmarks. In the journey proposed by Piñeiro's images we follow a quest of cultural identity and witness as spectators the process of transformation of cultural identity into visual spectacle. Here the film spectacle functions as an instrument for constructing a collective identity: the social building of an imagined community that with each new generation takes on new life. Traditional identity and modernity, nature and culture, go hand in hand, as images of Galicia's ancient mountains and seas converge in this *finis terrae*, the old continental land's end, which is also the beginning of other modern routes across the ocean. It is a sound and vision spectacle in which tradition and modern technology overlap, like the ancestral Galician mussel-farm platforms in the *rías* under the sophisticated mechanical engineering of modern suspension bridges, displayed in a brilliant audio/visual metaphor with the musical punctuation of the traditional Galician harp. It is a Galicia open to the world beyond, just like its own estuaries, looking for new horizons yet to be discovered. A reimagined Galicia, collectively dreamed and rebuilt with new eyes; with ports and cities in a constant process of reinvention and reconversion; with resignified civil and religious monuments: manors, churches, medieval castles reimagined and transformed into hostels for the modern traveler and pilgrim; a traveling Galicia walking down ancient routes and new roads at once, with open ports of arrival and departure, and cities open to the world. Santiago, open city; with its Obradoiro Square, symbol of a diverse and concrete Galicia at once ancient and modern, ancient and cosmopolitan, open to locals as well as global pilgrims and travelers.

In this new Galicia reinvented traditions are reimagined, resignified, and translated to a contemporary language, such as the medieval carnival that has transformed its original religious meaning of pre-Lenten festivities to a secularized cultural performance that reinvents and collectively celebrates its own identity while adapting to the present (the carnivalesque celebration of the *cigarrones* from Laza, accompanied by futuristic machines designed by Miguelanxo Prado). Likewise, the traditional *muiñeira*—the Galician popular dance *par excellence*—is now translated and reimagined across time and space, in the contemporary urban setting of the sophisticated modern ballet, by Rey de Viana. Piñeiro's sound and vision are perfectly integrated in the scene, with the camera's movement harmoniously accompanying the dancers' jumps in the air to the sound of the dance, while invisibly suturing the spatio/temporal leap of the ancestral *muiñeira*. The camera thus visually leads us in a continuous *translatio* movement from the dance studio to the theater, from the rehearsal to the stage performance, and from the popular tradition to the public spectacle. Sequentially, the soundtrack also moves us, both musically and emotionally, from the conservatory piano to the traditional Galician bagpipe, and then to a full symphonic orchestra, which arranges all individual instruments in musical polyphony, thus blending popular traditional rhythms and philharmonic orchestration. The end result creates an audio/visual spectacle which is new and old at the same time, firmly rooted in a musical and visual tradition which reclaims the past while it opens itself to modernity (and thus years ahead of the Celtic revival dance shows of Michael Flatley and Riverdance, who would find global acclaim in the late 1990s).

Perhaps the biggest strength of *O Camiño das Estrelas* lies in the audio/visual impact of the representation and the high quality of its moving images and sounds—recorded with very fine resolution, high contrast, and color saturation, and an unbroken and lush symphonic soundtrack with an evolving tempo, which accompanies and enhances the film's visual impact. *O Camiño* enjoyed a generous budget, unlike all of his previous films, which were made in precarious conditions, and was shot with the most advanced digital HD video technology available at the time. The musical score was performed by the Orquesta Nacional de España, with additional string sections from the London Philharmonic Orchestra and the English Chamber Orchestra, and featured Carlos Núñez playing Galician traditional instruments. This unusual display of resources had the aim of projecting a captivating and high-quality sound and vision spectacle of Galicia for international audiences and, from a technical point of view, the film reaches its goal.

The varied images and geographical locations of the film revolve around a slight storyline, fragmented, disjointed, and thinly threaded, perhaps the weakest part of the narrative, which serves as a link between the various *fabliaux* represented, as in a modernized medieval painting. The narrative combines images of a documentary journey (or rather an invitation to travel) with imaginary scenes rooted in the Galician popular tradition of the fantastic. Piñeiro appeals to the roots of Galician magical realism through a romance fable story with clear symbolic elements of national foundation,

Figure 10    The lightning strike that leads to the liberation, from *O Camiño das Estrelas*. Symbolic stormy night of the past giving way to the new day of freedom, with highlighted symbolism by the dream-like dawn sequence and premodern horse-drawn caged cart pushed along the seashore.

to use Doris Sommer's notion. The story is a legendary love tale between a mermaid and a wolfman, two mythological creatures in the Galician imagination representing the two traditional bases of Galician culture, the sea and the land, and finding a creative fusion of both cultures.[10] The idyllic romance is recurrently threatened by a dark figure, a sinister paramilitary supervillain symbolizing the dark forces that have historically subjugated Galicia. The final release of mermaid and wolf from the cage and the destruction of the dark force thus symbolize Galicia's liberation and coming of age as a nation.

As has been noted before, the film is high in visual symbolism. The process of identity seeking and building is symbolized by Piñeiro in the socially framed process of artistic creation constructed from a natural and powerful material image: granite, base of Galicia's landscape as well as a recurring visual component in Galician art of all times, prehistoric, traditional, and contemporary. Piñeiro's camera again sutures the spatiotemporal dislocation and moves from the chisels of granite sculptors working in the stone carving school to the colossal cubist landscape built block by block in the gigantic granite quarries in the mountains of Porriño, extracted with the mighty force of hydraulic drills and dynamite. These quarries appear as a gigantic and slightly fantastic natural theater that suggests a vaguely surreal avantgarde spectacle, speaking without words of a strong telluric

10 This mythical nation-foundation romance of land and sea foreshadows Miguelanxo Prado's *De profundis* (see Chapters 4 and 6).

sense of identity and belonging, but also of the not so positive progressive transformation of the natural landscape by the forces of modernity. The camera's traveling gaze aims to capture the relationship of Galician men and women with their environment and their work material, elements that make up their ages-long history and culture and that Galicians simultaneously have shaped. On this visual traveling movement from the quarry to the workshop—and from the workshop to the quarry—a sense of continuity is replayed, stone by stone and block by block, between nature and culture, material and artistic expression. This constant *translatio* movement creates a bridge between archaic primitivism and creative modernity, popular tradition and high technology, the discovery of roots and a cosmopolitan opening to the outside world, which is visually alluded to in the images of the transatlantic commercial shipping of pink granite from Porriño to New York, traveling from Galicia to the world.

Movement, travel, and crossings, as we have seen, are key narrative symbolic elements of Piñeiro's film, cinematographically represented through numerous travelings, fades, and jump cuts. The narrative of *O Camiño das Estrelas* sutures together the activities of manual labor and industrial production (the granite quarries, shellfish harvesting, or designing) and cultural production of our time with a strong emphasis on the Galician audio/visual and performance arts (sculpture, architecture, music, dance) that travel more easily beyond its borders.[11] Centuries-long traditions— such as the carnival masks from Laza or the rituals of cutting the manes of wild horses (*a rapa das bestas*)—are juxtaposed to new traditions that reinvent tradition and give a new sense of collective identity—such as the contemporary ballet of Rey de Viana, or the Xoven Orquestra de Galicia (Young Orchestra of Galicia). Likewise, another peculiar feature of the film is that, apart from occasional voices in the background, it contains no dialogue or narratorial voices, relying solely on the raw power and beauty of the images and the non-stop accompanying soundtrack. This strategy enhances the successful communication with international audiences without the "noise" that would make difficult its passage across language boundaries.

As a journey across borders, times, and cultures, *O camiño das estrelas* effectively makes a contemporary sound and vision spectacle that merges

11   There are several interesting parallels between *O Camiño* and Lois Patiño's *Costa da morte*, a film analysed in Chapter 7. Piñeiro's film seems to foreshadow some of the techniques and themes in Patiño's work, including the wide panoramic frames and contrast with miniature human figures, the expressive use of sound, the fragmented flow and sparse use of voices, and the focus on certain Galician natural elements with high symbolism, such as the barnacle fishermen, the forest, the quarry, or the gathering of wild horses.

old and modern and transcends spatiotemporal barriers. It is an imaginative audio/visual journey, traveling from Galicia to the world, and vice versa, as all roads can lead to Santiago in the global age.

## Imagining Galicia: the Musical Journey to *Santiago*

Among the numerous musical recordings inspired by the roads to Santiago/Fisterra in the global age, there are two distinct but parallel projects which cross and overlap in significant ways: the albums *Santiago* and *A irmandade das estrelas*, by the Irish folk group The Chieftains and the Galician multi-instrumentalist musician Carlos Núñez respectively. These two albums have had a common trajectory and each represents a milestone in the rediscovery and reinvention of Galician folk music and its repositioning on the global map.

Of course, Galicia and Ireland have strong historical and cultural links, as has been mentioned in Chapters 1 and 2. The shared Celtic musical roots are one of the most evident connections, going back centuries, and have been greatly revitalized in our own era of exploration of fusion and "world music" hybridity. These two projects are a clear example of the richness of musical connections between Ireland and Galicia and the network of lateral connections with other musical traditions. Both recordings are widely considered as stellar achievements by the critics and were extremely successful nationally and internationally. *Santiago* was met with resounding success and received a Grammy Award for best "world music" recording in 1987, and *Irmandade* was widely acclaimed internationally, becoming a certified multiplatinum bestseller which launched the productive career of Carlos Núñez as a solo artist on the world stage.[12] The boldness of conception, the sense of discovery, the imaginativeness displayed, the richness of the multicultural musical tapestry, and the virtuosity of the musicians make both recordings epic achievements that represent a before and after of the remaking of Galician folk music and its repositioning on the global map.[13]

12 For a detailed analysis of Carlos Núñez's album, see Chapter 10.

13 The albums were twins in their gestation, development, and dissemination. The Chieftains' leader Paddy Moloney acted like a musical godfather, being responsible for Carlos Núñez signing a record contract with their own label BMG and producing his debut album. Interestingly, the astute marketing for both albums in the US followed parallel but different strategies. The multinational BMG used the New York-based marketing company Intercultural Niche Strategies (INS) to successfully market the records in the US addressing different ethnic groups. For *Santiago* the Galician, Spanish, and Portuguese language communities were addressed directly

The Chieftains are the best-known, and most appreciated, Irish band of Celtic music in the world, having being active since the early 1960s. They are directly responsible for the reawakening of traditional Celtic music and the relatively recent worldwide revival of Irish music, which, until they formed, had been largely neglected and forgotten by the advent of modernity. In their more than 50-year long recording career they have received five Grammy Awards and sold millions of records, an unheard-of achievement for a traditional folk group, and even more so for one from the Irish periphery. Part of their appeal has been their ability to combine and blend harmoniously *roots* and *routes*, their own musical traditions and the incorporation of others from around the world, particularly from other pan-Celtic musical traditions. Throughout their long career they have successfully crossed over into different genres, including orchestral compositions and other musical traditions of the world, such as the music of the Irish diaspora, as well as that of Brittany and Galicia, having helped to establish the validity of "world music." They have also collaborated with a myriad of different world artists and musicians, from classic flutist James Galway to new-wave artist Elvis Costello to the Rolling Stones, as well as many Galician singers and musicians.

Their relationship with Galicia and Galician music goes back to their concerts in international Celtic music festivals where Galician groups started participating in the later 1970s, such as the Interceltic Festival of Lorient in Brittany. This relationship solidified after The Chieftains's first outdoors concert in Vigo in 1984, when they fully partook of the richness of Galician folk music and its connections to the wider Celtic music.[14] From then on they started a long journey of collaboration with Galician groups and musicians, such as Milladoiro and Carlos Núñez, at the time a Galician 13-year-old *wunderkid* player of the Galician *gaita* who would soon be taken under their wing, starting to record with them and joining them in their world tours. That long and fruitful collaboration, which has continued until the present, was the breeding ground for their respective projects *Santiago* and *A irmandade das estrelas*. At the time of the release of these albums in 1996, Núñez and The Chieftains had been playing together for ten years, which gave Núñez the honorary badge of being considered "the seventh chieftain."

through mailing campaigns emphasizing the Latin aspects, or by giving away free CDs to the Galician restaurants in the Newark/New York area, while Carlos Núñez's album was sent to Irish radio stations across the country, employing a strategy of "reverse psychology" (Fitzpatrick 86). For more information, see Fitzpatrick; Halter.

14 For more on the reinvention of Galician folk and its connection with Celtic music see Chapter 10.

*Santiago* is an impressive musical accomplishment that took six years to complete, not only because of the heavy touring schedule of the band around the world and other time-consuming parallel projects, but also owing to the logistical complexity of a long list of guest appearances and recording locations in several continents.[15] The album includes the essential collaboration of Carlos Núñez, who serves as a sort of musical guide in this cultural pilgrimage and enjoys equal billing with The Chieftains. On this record Carlos Núñez played a multiple role, not only as a guest master multi-instrumentalist but also with a key role in conducting the musical research and the overall development of the album. In essence, it is a project with Galicia at its heart, but open to the world.[16]

*Santiago* is presented as a metaphorical musical journey. It follows the course of a modern-day multicultural pilgrimage, which explores the common Celtic *roots* of Galician traditional popular music (incorporating Galician voices, musicians, instruments, rhythms, melodies, and compositions) and the intercultural mixing of musical traditions along the multiple *routes* of Santiago, in Galicia and beyond, with the transculturation of its music through the historic Galician migration to the new world. It is a journey of cultural discovery of as yet mostly uncharted territory. As the founder and leader of the band Paddy Moloney indicates in the album's liner notes, Galicia could be described as "the world's most undiscovered Celtic country."[17]

This journey of discovery is characterized by a continuous experience of border crossing. The Chieftains chart in the record a new musical map of connections, crossing multiple geopolitical, cultural, musical, and language

15 The album includes studio sessions recorded around the world (in San Sebastian, Dublin, Los Angeles, Madrid, and Havana) and live recordings made in such diverse Galician locations as a stage theatre, a convent in Santiago de Compostela, and an Irish pub in Vigo. Some of the pieces were recorded in multiple tracks by different artists in distant places around the world, such as the famous "Rianxeira," which was recorded in three different cities, thus continuing its transatlantic history (the song was composed by Galician migrants in Buenos Aires).

16 With the participation of a wide variety of stellar guest singers and musicians from various lands, such as Ry Cooder and the legendary "Cachaíto" of Buena Vista Social Club fame, the Latino artists Linda Ronstadt and Los Lobos, and Iberian "world music" artists Kepa Junkera (the Basque player of the *trikitixa*) and Júlio Pereira (the Portuguese multi-instrumentalist recognized for the *cavaquinho* sound), this album offers both an example of ethnic music of great cultural specificity and "world music" with universal appeal.

17 In a similar vein to their previous achievements with traditional Breton music in *Celtic Wedding* (1987), where they collaborated with a number of Breton musicians and researchers, including Nolwenn Monjarret, Alain Guerton, Bernard Pichard, Michel Bertae, and Polig Monjarret.

boundaries and borders. Santiago here is not simply a destination but a multicultural crossroads. The roads of Santiago are metaphorical roads intersecting and merging at multiple points. The album is therefore more than a collection of traditional Galician music—which in part it is—but it is also an exploration of the different traditions that traverse Galicia, and are traversed by Galicians: played and sung with different voices, languages, instruments, and rhythms, along the many roads of the Camiño, from both sides of the Miño river and both shores of the Atlantic, mixing the old world and the new.

*Santiago* thus charts and records an alternative "imagined geography" not limited by traditional geopolitical, cultural, or language boundaries, but which encompasses the rich hybridity of border zones. This transcultural project invokes an alternative collective "imaginary" that goes beyond the time–space limits, crossing oceans, lands, and boundaries, literally and symbolically. It crosses distinct musical cultures, principally Galician, Irish, Basque, Asturian, Portuguese, Spanish, Mexican, and Cuban, with the unifying theme of a movable musical identity that intersects with other cultures at different musical crossroads.

The first part of the album includes a five-part set of traditional pieces entitled "Pilgrimage to Santiago." This journey begins in the Pyrenees foothills along the ancient pilgrimage route of Camiño de Santiago (the "French way"), and follows the northern peninsular corridor all the way to Galicia, starting in the Basque Country ("Txalaparta" and "Arku Dantza—Arin Arin"). The first piece, entitled "Txalaparta," is played with the ancient Basque instruments of the same name, wooden planks originally conceived to replicate the sound of horses' feet; their organic sound and repetitive tempo appropriately suggests the rhythm and feel of walking and the beginning of the ancestral journey. The journey resumes its course through neighboring Asturias, the other part of Iberia with which Galicia shares a common Celtic music heritage ("El besu"), and through the old greater Gallaecia south of the Miño river, which is today Portugal ("Não vas ao mar, Toino"), continuing all the way to Santiago. The musical pilgrimage discovers and imagines at the same time a sense of ancestral connection between the peripheries (Ireland, Basque Country, Asturias, Portugal, and Galicia). The Chieftains create a musical blend of the journey in this section by the continued accompaniment of the Portuguese *cavaquinho*, played by multi-instrumentalist virtuoso Júlio Pereira.[18]

---

18  The *cavaquinho*, a small stringed instrument and distant relative of the ukulele, is originally from the medieval Galician Miño river area. Its fast rhythmic strum conveys the tertiary rhythm of traditional Galician dances, such as the popular *muiñeiras*.

The different instruments played in this set, the Basque *txalaparta* and *trikitixa*, the Asturian *rabel*, and the *cavaquinho*, are instruments of cultural identity that reflect the merging of different traditions along the pilgrims' route.[19] The last stop of this journey takes us to Santiago de Compostela, ending appropriately with two pieces recorded in a convent in Santiago with the specialist Galician medieval choir Utreia, "Dum Paterfamilias" and "Ad honorem," which were originally contained in the *Codex Calixtinus*, thus completing the first part of the journey.[20]

The initial course following the tapestry of musics along the Roads to Santiago then leads to a much wider-ranging and ambitious itinerary, engaging with traditional Galician music and its multiple connections with other traditions from different shores. Thus the encounter of the Irish and Galician cultures is expressed in the form of a musical duel in "Dueling Chanters," a lively showpiece between the Irish Uileann pipes played by Paddy Moloney and the Galician *gaita* played by Carlos Núñez, blending two traditional tunes, the Irish jig "Sixpenny Money" and the Galician dance tune "Polka de Vilagarcía." The same fascinating blending of distant but closely related musical traditions is explored as another "imaginary geography" that connects Ireland and Galicia with the two-piece set of "Setting Sail" and "Muiñeira de Freixido."

"Galician Overture," Paddy Moloney's own orchestral composition dedicated to Galicia, is *Santiago*'s central piece, an 11-minute epic played with the Xoven Orchestra de Galicia (which was also featured in Piñeiro's film *O Camiño das Estrelas*). The overture musically represents the opening of a new journey of discoveries. The lush orchestration, melodic variations, and beat changes of the piece suggest the verdant Galician landscape with its sharp natural contrasts, as well as a great variety of dances and rhythms. The polyphonic ensemble of voices and instruments evokes a sense of collective project, mixing the Galician tambourine with other

19 The variety of instruments and languages reminds us of the commentary from the *Codex Calixtinus*, used as the epigraph of this chapter, about the assemblage of pilgrims in Santiago's cathedral with diverse musical instruments from different countries singing songs in many different languages of the world. This passage was taken by Galician folk group Milladoiro as a historical model of their embrace of different musical traditions, as we will see in Chapter 10.

20 The recording of this religious choral piece with its medieval aura echoes the global success of *Chant* (1994), a collection of old Gregorian chants from the Benedictine monks of Santo Domingo de Silos in Spain, which, surprisingly, made it to the top of the global music charts. That album was cleverly marketed as a new age response to the stressful conditions of modern life and sold some six million copies around the world.

non-traditional symphonic instruments, which reminds us of some of the Galician orchestral compositions inspired by traditional Galician music (such as those by Milladoiro).

The border crossing journey of *Santiago* then follows a second complementary itinerary with a more contemporary feel, as a modern supplement to the old medieval journey, following the trail of Galician migration. Here the musical waves echo those of the sea with their back and forth movement between the shores of the *rías*, rivers, and seas, as the lyrics of the ever popular "A Rianxeira" migrant song with their *ritornello* "ondiñas veñen e van" ("waves coming in and going out"). First we cross the Miño river border, which has historically united and separated Galicia and Portugal ("Minho Waltz"), and from there we embark on a new metaphorical journey to the other shores of the Atlantic, looking in the mirror of those other roads to Santiago across the sea. This is a transatlantic journey that takes us first to Mexico and the US with "Guadalupe," a culturally *translated* Mexicanized version, with *ranchera* cadence, of the "A Rianxeira," perhaps Galicia's most emblematic popular song identified with the diasporic experience. Finally the journey takes us to Cuba, where the Galician/Caribbean experience is celebrated as we reach the land's end of the island in another Santiago, which is also a pilgrimage site in honor of St. James ("Santiago de Cuba," "La galleguita").[21]

The musical odyssey of *Santiago* ends appropriately with a return to the point of departure, Galicia. Again a new "imaginary geography" is conceived with the closing set of "Dublin in Vigo," a six-piece medley of old Galician songs and dances recorded live at the Irish pub in Vigo called "Dublin." This performance includes a large ensemble of Galician dancers, musicians, and singers in the tradition, equally popular in Galicia and Ireland, of communal bar singing, which represents a sort of collective musical embrace and thus a fitting ending for this transcultural journey.

Inevitably, for such a transcultural hybrid project of transnational nature, there is bound to be controversy about the results of this endeavor. In spite of the many positive reviews received, the album is not without its critics. While many think that it is a heartfelt homage to Galicia, a celebration of its traditions, and a great projection of its rich culture *translated* internationally,

---

21 *Santiago* is not The Chieftains's last contact with Latin music. In 2010 they released the album *San Patricio*, which celebrates the Irish/Mexican connection, starting in the nineteenth century with the Irish "St. Patrick's battalion," commonly known as the "San Patricios," who sided with the Mexicans in the war against the United States. Carlos Núñez again participates in this album, along with other notable Mexican musicians such as Lila Downs, Chavela Vargas, and Los Tigres del Norte.

others see it as a "foreign" project, not authentically Galician, which distorts the cultural specifity of Galician culture by offering instead another version of "world music."[22] Some Galician musicians were thus critical of the overall project: for example, Bieito Romero, the bagpiper and leader of the well-known Galician folk band Luar na Lubre, although a fervent advocate of pan-Celtic musical connections, considers it basically an Irish/Latin fusion project with some Galician elements thrown in the mix (see Colmeiro, *Galeg@s sen fronteiras*).

But *Santiago* it is not about authenticity, it is about border crossing. It is an example of a contemporary approach to cultural issues not dominated by a narrow essentialist conception of national identity but coming from a peripheral and transversal perspective more open to hybridity, transculturation, heterogeneity, and diversity. It is not a purist project constructed on some essentialist notion of Galician identity, but an imagined geography of porous borders, hybridities, lateral relations, and collaborations, with the "foreign accents" of the diaspora across the ocean and the Latin American component of Galician cultural history.[23] And ultimately, that is why I see *Santiago* as a derritorializing effort to deperipherialize Galicia, made around the world with Galicia at its center.

22 Case in point is the song "Maneo," which is perhaps one of the most surprisingly "Spanish," questioned by purists for its obvious flirting with Spanish guitar music and flamenco clapping, but perhaps this is a reflection not of a cultural misunderstanding or a confusion of Galicia and Spain but of the Iberian/Southern undertones that Northern Celtic ears perceive in Galician traditional music. This is something that Carlos Núñez has often mentioned, and he himself has explored, as in his second album *Os amores libres* and his much acclaimed arrangement of Joaquín Rodrigo's "Concierto de Aranjuez" with which he starts his concerts. Likewise, Núñez has been criticized for his crossover tendencies and his commercial success internationally, and is perceived by some purists as not authentically Galician (see Chapter 10).

23 Even though *Santiago* is not a nationalist project by any stretch of the imagination, its imaginary geography is sympathetic to the larger Galician cause, as a strong affirmation of its cultural history. The Irish band, obviously conscious of their own historical battle for cultural and political recognition, reveals an awareness of the Iberian political context, as the liner notes indicate the Basque Country, Catalonia, and Galicia as the "three historical nationalities recognized within Spain."

# PART TWO

# Peripheral Visions

# CHAPTER FOUR

# Made in Galicia:
# Making the Invisible Visible

Hit and Myth in the Deep North. Forward-looking Rural
Area Transforming into TV and Film Heavyweight.
John Hopewell

## Fragmentation, Invisibility, and Political Devolution

In several vital respects, cinema has since its inception been marked by absence and loss and by a persistent tension between fragmentation and suture, visibility and invisibility, repression and representation. This tension is perhaps all the more acute in relatively peripheral and invisible cinemas, such as that of Spain, and even more so in the various cinemas that operate on the fringes of the nation state's official apparatus, such as that of Galicia.

On a general technical level, cinema provides a fragmented virtual take on reality, as a result of both the mechanical reproduction apparatus that magically tricks the human eye (the 24 frames per second produce a sutured ghostly illusion of an absent reality) and the particular narrative grammar of cinema based on continuity editing, which sutures a fragmented mosaic of images: the composition frame, the shot, the sequence. On a historical plane, cinema is also indelibly marked by fragmentation, because of the extreme fragility of the medium and the ephemeral nature of cinema, particularly in its first decades, complicated by belated or insufficient efforts at preservation. Any history of cinema will always be marked by a high degree of loss and fragmented remnants, a loss that means that cinema scholars and institutions aiming to reconstruct a meaningful whole must recognize such an aim as by definition an impossible enterprise. A history of cinema will always be an archaeological attempt at suturing the fissures and reconstructing the missing pieces of its own narrative. This situation becomes acute in cinemas that, in order to exist at all, have had to contend with major political, structural, and financial obstacles, as is the case in Galicia.

On a more culturally specific level, the historical mapping of cinema in Spain reveals a complex, fragmented picture composed of several singular cinemas, marked by particular political and economic developments as well as by cultural and linguistic diversity. As a mass cultural form cinema has been used as a major vehicle for Spanish nationalism at least since the Second Republic of 1931–36. It has also been crucial to the attempts at nation-building in the stateless nations within Spain, particularly since the transition to democracy and the process of administrative decentralization and political devolution initiated in the late 1970s. The historical narrative of Galician cinema is thus necessarily full of discontinuities, silences, and interruptions, marked as they have been by repression, migration, and/or exile during the years of the Franco dictatorship. The emergence of Galician cinema in recent decades has been closely related to the establishment, since the 1978 Constitution, of the regional autonomous government and new audiovisual media, particularly TVG, the public television channel, which has boosted the Galician audiovisual and film sectors. Another key factor is the new global dynamics that affect film production, which have encouraged local film producers to explore transnational projects; particularly after the 2007–08 global crisis, a new generation of creators is finding ways of operating on the global circuit from the fringes of the mainstream cinema apparatus.

The relation of local Galician cinema and globalization manifests in a variety of different ways, from joint co-production schemes, multinational patterns of film distribution, and marketing for targeted international audiences to working on the margins of the mainstream film industry in the new global digital network, sometimes working outside of Galicia or in "border zones." The large variety of situations, and the additional draw in recent years of film production to Galicia from other areas, raises the question of what is "Galician cinema" and whether we can really distinguish between "Galician cinema" and "cinema made in Galicia" (as will see in Chapter 5). We need to approach this complex map with a set of lenses that give us both depth of field and sharp focus, and that allow us to examine the interactions of the local and the global beyond the traditional confines of the national. Marsha Kinder's proposal that we think in terms of "microregional cinemas" and "macroregional cinemas" (1993) could be useful here, since it allows a double focus on the operation of local/regional cinemas both within the nation state and beyond its borders.

This map is not only fragmented and in flux but also complicated by a number of "invisibility factors." It can be argued that Spanish cinema is literally invisible in that, apart from a handful of exceptional films each year, it fails to reach a broad public. This reality points to the structural problem of Hollywood subsidiaries' monopoly control of distribution. It is a particularly acute problem for films made in, and associated with, "peripheral" autonomous communities. The openness to global currents has transformed the operations of film production but has not resolved its contradictions. The peripheral condition is not easily surmounted, and is not just a matter of semantics. While referring to the peripheral condition may appear to reinforce the centrality of the center and the marginality of the margins, we should remember, however, that all Western cinemas are regional and peripheral, as well as partly invisible, in relation to Hollywood—including Spanish cinema.

Another major problem is the general invisibility of films made in the autonomous communities in Spain's viewing circuits, reflecting Spanish nationalist culture's characteristic imperviousness to the multicultural, multilingual reality existing within the nation state. But this invisibility is evident even within the autonomous communities themselves. It may be easier to see a Galician film in Buenos Aires than Seville, and the showing of a Catalan or Basque film in Televisión de Galicia is practically unheard of. We must ask, then, to what extent there is a certain structural and institutional blindness that perpetuates the invisibility of these cinemas for general state-national audiences as well as for audiences in particular autonomous communities.

At the same time, the concept of the "national" seems too reductive or exclusionary. Many critics find the notion of national cinema increasingly problematic (Crofts; Higson). It has always been a convenient label that needs to be continually re-examined, and today it seems particularly insufficient to reflect the complexities of a globalized world. However, so long as the concept of Spanish cinema has some critical currency there are good pragmatic reasons for also talking of Galician cinema, out of parity.

The erosion of the "national cinema" conceptual model has run parallel to the crisis of the nation state and against the backdrop of re-emerging peripheral nationalisms and the new forces of globalization, all of which have created a new postnational paradigm, as has been previously discussed. At a time when the hegemony of the national model is being challenged by regional or national forces from inside the nation state and by supranational and global pressures from outside, it would be a mistake to assume any pre-constructed, essentialized notion of what the cinema of Galicia should be. The postnational focus of this study aims to rethink the conceptual models used to approach peripheral cinemas. Key questions that will be raised in this study include: the difficulty, theoretically and historically, of defining Galician cinema marked by fragmentation and invisibility; the role played in shaping it by political and cultural institutions (the autonomous government, television stations and other media, film schools, professional associations, and film commissions); the particular language map involved (monolingualism, bilingualism, diglossia, multilingualism, dialectalism); the intersections of nation, class, race, and gender; and cinema production and commercial branding efforts that exceed the limits of the nation.

With the process of political devolution that took place after the 1978 Constitution, the administrative control of local cinema and audiovisual production passed from the central state to the autonomous governments. The result has been the emergence of a significant corpus of cinematic production in autonomous communities with a strong sense of national identity, such as Galicia, with its vernacular language and history of non-state nationalism going back to the mid-nineteenth century. There had, of course, been some film production in Galicia before political devolution; what was new now was official recognition and sponsorship—that is, the emergence of the concepts of "Galician cinema," which originated in the 1970s but officially came into existence only in the late 1980s, expanding and diversifying from the late 1990s.

What appears clear is that the emergence of peripheral cinemas such as that of Galicia has the goal of winning visibility beyond the periphery and making a transnational impact. In this new cartography where the global joins hands with the local, bypassing the nation state, Spanish cinema may itself become decentered, if not peripheral. The arrival of the *Novo Cine Galego* or New Galician Cinema on the international stage of film festivals and digital platforms circumvents the limitations of the state.

## Screening the Spanish National Primal Scene

I will resort to a new conceptual model borrowed from psychoanalytical theory that can offer a fuller picture and a better understanding of the development of Galician cinema in the context of Spanish film history. Joseba Gabilondo has proposed the visual imagery of the primal scene as a powerful metaphor for a critical approach to peripheral national cinemas, in its tension between visibility and invisibility. The concept of a national primal scene is particularly relevant in the case of the "other cinemas" that have a conflictive relation with Spanish nationalism and authoritarianism and have struggled for visibility since their origins. If, as Joseba Gabilondo has argued ("The National Primal Scene"), the myth of *Carmen* can be read as the primal scene of nineteenth-century Spanish nationalism (constructed from outside and later internalized), I propose that the film *Raza* (José Luis Sáenz de Heredia, 1942) can be considered the primal scene of twentieth-century Spanish nationalism (constructed from within and imposed from above) as a form of co-option of other competing nationalisms from the periphery. A family-saga-cum-historical epic, *Raza* traces the national past from Spain's military defeat by the United States in 1898, leading to the definitive loss of its American and Asian possessions, to Franco's victory parade at end of the Spanish Civil War. The film thus rewrites the historical script into a triumphant nationalist epic according to Francoist mythology (as is well known, the film's original argument was written by Franco himself under a pseudonym). The Churruca family, which holds the narrative together, is a symbolic stand-in for the Spanish nation—a pedagogical instrument inviting identification with the film's lament for the end of the global empire where the sun never set, through a post-imperial narrative of loss and fragmentation that seeks historical transcendence. The film effectively announces a new spiritual and cultural empire in the form of "la Hispanidad," where the traditional values of the lost empire—patriarchalism, militarism, and Catholicism—are resuscitated and finally sutured in a montage of dissolved historical images. The anxiety of loss and fragmentation brought by modernity is neutralized through the imaginary apotheosis provided by the film's closure, restoring Spain to its central position in the occidentalist discourse of empire that has defined Europe since the sixteenth century.

The narrative begins in Galicia—specifically Ferrol, Franco's birthplace and one of Spain's oldest naval bases. The film's idealized Spanish patriotic family embodies the fragments of the nation that need to be reconstituted. The lesson taught by this cinematic primal family is the historical continuity and undivided territorial integrity of the motherland and the unity of the "Spanish race," overcoming loss and fragmentation. To that effect, the film conveniently erases recent history—in particular the birth of Catalan, Basque, and Galician nationalisms in the nineteenth century, their acquisition of political power and influence in elections and referendums during the Second Spanish Republic, and ultimately their defeat in the civil war and subsistence in exile.

The Churruca family can be seen as the expression of a national primal scene inasmuch as it rewrites national history so as to produce a mythical narrative of origins. Cultural and political difference is disavowed and integrated into the fabric of the nation. The mise-en-scène depicts the Churruca family's old *pazo* (country manor) as visibly Galician, accentuated by the use of traditional Galician imagery, landscapes, and musical soundtrack. Yet no reference is made to specific features of Galician history or language. Galicia is literally a backdrop for Spanish nationalist discourse, co-opting the audio/visual components of its cultural identity. The Churruca family may be Galician, but all that matters is that they are Spanish patriots willing to give their lives for the motherland. The navy officer patriarch instructs his children in the patriotic obligations deriving from their lineage. Interestingly, he reveals that one of their ancestors was Cosme Damián de Churruca, the Basque-born Admiral of the Spanish fleet who died heroically at the Battle of Trafalgar, fighting the British, in 1805. The third example of Spanish patriotism cited by him is that of the Almogavars, a medieval Catalan–Aragonese army that was instrumental in the Christian *Reconquista* and in the consolidation of Aragón's Mediterranean empire under the leadership of Roger de Flor, the hero who inspired the Catalan-language epic *Tirant le Blanc*. The patriarch's early patriotic lessons are later recited from memory by his grown-up daughter in the film's final montage sequence, subtly suturing the three discordant peripheral nationalisms (Basque, Catalan, and Galician) into the now triumphant narrative of Spanish fascist neoimperialism.

This rendering invisible of difference through a superficial act of suture, converting representation into a form of repression, is a historical determinant of Galician cinema production throughout its existence. This pattern is visible both in the *gallegada* films made under the dictatorship and in post-Franco cinema, such as the animation productions made by Bren/Filmax. The history of Galician cinema, like that of modern Galicia itself, is one of migration and dispersion, precariously balanced between the poles of subjugation and emancipation.

## The Cinema of Migration and the *Gallegada*

One of the earliest and most distinctive forms of Galician cinema, somewhat neglected by film critics and historians, was the creation of an autochthonous "cinema of migration." This cinema, sometimes called "epistolary cinema," had the novel format of a two-way exchange of documentary images between Galician migrant societies in Latin America, particularly in the Southern Cone and Cuba, and Galician communities in the homeland. These films were often commissioned by Galician migrant communities, and sometimes by groups of returning migrants, as a form of filmic cultural connection. This cinematic genre produced hundreds of films documenting communal celebrations, cultural activities, traditional Galician scenery, and the migration experience itself, on both sides of the Atlantic.

The "cinema of migration" lasted for several generations, from the early days of the silent era in the 1910s with pioneer filmmaker José Gil, and continued well into the 1960s with directors such as Manuel Arís Torres, Elixio González, and Amando Hermida Luaces, who were based in Argentina. These works included documentaries and docudramas, frequently shot in amateur or semi-professional formats, but shown in commercial film theatres. While many of these works remain anonymous and the large majority has not survived, a few have been recently recovered and restored by the CGAI (Centro Galego das Artes da Imaxe) (González, *Cine restaurado*).

This unique phenomenon has no known parallel among other European cultural diasporas in the Americas. What is most noteworthy is that the transatlantic constitution of this cinema of migration completely sidesteps the constrictions of Spanish cinema. All the basic elements of this cinema— means of production, technical and artistic crew, cultural themes explored, target audience, and circuit of distribution—were basically Galician. This cinema cannot be called peripheral to Spanish cinema since it was completely independent of Spanish cinema. It exceeded the parameters of Spanish national cinema, just as migration itself represented an excess that could not be successfully integrated into the Spanish nation state. The cinema of migration is thus the first film form that can unequivocally be called "Galician" in a broad sense that transcends national borders; it is also remarkable because of its longevity across several generations.[1]

The experience of Galician film directors already active during the Second Republic was also marked by dispersion. Of the three main established pre-war Galician directors—José Suárez, Carlos Velo, and Antonio Román— two chose exile, Suárez in Argentina and Velo in Mexico, from where they continued their association with Galicia; Román chose to continue filming in Franco's Spain. During the dictatorship, with Galician film professionals forced to relocate to Madrid or overseas, Galician cinema was subsumed within Spanish cinema.

This absorption of Galician film professionals into Spanish cinema during the dictatorship had its most emblematic figure in producer Cesáreo González. His company Suevia Films, named with a mythical reference to the ancient Galician kingdom of the Sueves, became the most important Spanish production company from the 1940s to the 1970s, notable for its well-established transatlantic production and distribution circuit and exclusive contracts with some of the mega-stars of export-oriented popular Spanish cinema of the period—Lola Flores, Sara Montiel, Carmen Sevilla, and the child prodigies Joselito and Marisol, not to mention the Mexican diva María Félix. A returnee Galician migrant who had amassed a fortune in Cuba, González was also responsible for inventing the "gallegada" (films of Galician topicality, customs, landscape, music, and stories of migration), popular in the 1940s and 1950s, including films directed by Ramón Torrado such as *El famoso Carballeira* (1940) and *Polizón a bordo* (1943), and rural

---

1 The Galician cinema of migration will have a new avatar in the global age, such as the "epistolary" non-fiction productions by Eloy Domínguez Serén, Xurxo Chirro, and Alberte Pagán (see Chapter 7).

caricatures featuring the comic Xan das Bolas, which film historian Castro de Paz has called "cine de gaita e pandeireta" 'bagpipe-and-tambourine cinema' (quoted in *O cine na Dictadura*). González was the first film producer to see the commercial potential of deploying the Galician landscape and rural types for a wide Spanish-language audience (Galán), which included the large migrant communities in Latin America—his popular remake of the Galician comedy classic *La casa de la Troya* (1948) was filmed in Churubusco Studios in Mexico. Thus was born the genre of Galician exploitation cinema, providing a stereotypical or nostalgic tourist postcard image of Galician life and customs, which proved economically successful in other films such as *Mar abierto* (1946), *Botón de ancla* (1948), *Sabela de Cambados* (1949), and *El pórtico de la gloria* (1953). Clearly, the prototype was the "andaluzada," which subsumed Andalusian topicality under the Spanish national banner, as González himself acknowledged: "Cada ano fago a miña película e os meus documentais de Galicia, pero Andalucía, para o cine español e para o espectáculo, é unica" ("Every year I make my film and my documentaries about Galicia but, for Spanish cinema and the entertainment world in general, there is nothing like Andalusia") (Galán 86).

## The Rebirth of a Nation in Cinema

In the 1970s important discussions about the conditions of possibility of Galician cinema started to take place, with a high degree of political awareness, in the context of the rebirth of Galician cultural nationalism. New conceptualizations of Galician cinema were discussed through a series of conversations, film festivals, and publication outlets. Particularly important were the early gatherings of the Semán do Cine en Ourense (Ourense Film Week), starting in 1973, which became the epicenter of critical debates about "national cinemas" in Spain throughout the mid-1970s. The conclusions of the first Ourense encounter were somewhat bleak in relation to the status of Galician cinema, but constituted a real starting point: They confirmed the non-existence of Galician cinema except as a utopian project yet to be developed, but at the same time they demonstrated the collective desire for a distinctive self-image and the need to create a sustainable local film industry capable of taking forward its own projects. In 1976 the Ourense Film Week was redefined to include "cine de las nacionalidades y regiones" ("cinema from the regions and historic nationalities"), bringing together filmmakers from Galicia, Catalonia, the Basque Country, Valencia, and the Canary Islands, who published a joint manifesto in the four languages of the nation state, "Declaración sobre los cines nacionales" ("Declaration on National Cinemas in Spain") (Williams 103).

Figure 11   The 1970s Ourense film encounters, the degree zero of Galician cinema. Poster of the *III Xornadas de Cine en Ourense* (1975). Courtesy of José Paz Rodrigues.

At the same time, different underground film collectives formed across Galicia, and groups of militant filmmakers with extremely low budgets started to produce shorts in amateur formats. Manuel Rivas ("Tres películas") has referred to this generation of Galician filmmaking pioneers as believers in the "utopía de un cine autóctono en el *far-west* galaico" ("the utopia of an autochthonous cinema in the Galician *far-west*"). These early initiatives laid the foundation for the birth of Galician cinema in the 1980s. Xavier Villaverde and Chano Piñeiro, who participated in those early discussions about Galician cinema, started their film careers as amateur cinematographers in the 1970s, and would be among the first filmmakers to make the leap into professional cinema in the following decade.

The post-1978 process of political devolution had a direct impact on this process, with the Xunta de Galicia constituted as an autonomous government in 1981 and the public TV channel Televisión de Galicia (TVG) established in 1985. Two top-down institutional projects emanating from the Galician government were particularly effective in this regard: a new policy of subsidies for Galician film production, and significant support and demand from TVG for autochthonous video and film productions, which generated a large number of audiovisual production companies. At this time, the exuberant cultural climate and the multifaceted activity of the Galician *Movida* (music, video, fashion, visual arts) were also decisive factors in the emergence of a new Galician cinema. Key figures here were Antón Reixa and Xavier Villaverde, who established themselves as successful music performance and avant-garde video artists (Reixa's *Salvamento e socorrismo* (1984), *After shave* (1986), and *Galicia Sitio Distinto* (1990); and Villaverde's *Veneno Puro* (1984), *Viuda Gómez* (1984), *Golpe de látigo* (1986), and *Galicia caníbal* (1987), the video clip made for Reixa and his group Os Resentidos's song of the same name, which is discussed in Chapter 8). Both Reixa and Villaverde later turned to professional filmmaking and film production in the late 1980s and 1990s, as we will see below.

The first major four films produced with institutional subsidies from the Xunta de Galicia were released in the late 1980s. The range of production schemes, genres, subject matter, and achievements of these four films is indicative of the trends as well as the limitations and possibilities of Galician cinema in those years. It is highly symbolic that the first of these productions was *Gallego* "Galician" (1988), a Galician–Cuban coproduction based on Miguel Barnet's testimonial novel of the same title (1981), which follows the life of two Galician migrants in Cuba. Directed by Cuban Manuel Octavio Gómez—author of the revolutionary classic *La primera carga al machete* "The First Machete Charge" (1969)—the film was shot on location in Galicia and Cuba, with an assortment of Galician (Sancho Gracia, Rosalía Dans), Spanish (Francisco Rabal, Jorge Sanz), and Cuban (Omar Valdés, Caridad Ravelo) actors. It is symptomatic that this first institutionally subsidized project should be a story of migration and a transnational initiative that exceeded the geopolitical parameters of both Galicia and Spain, with capital from Galician TVG, Sancho Gracia's production company, and Cuba's ICAIC. The production challenged a preconstructed notion of Galician cinema, necessarily predetermined in terms of use of language, nationality of directors or crew, or its certificate of origin, focusing instead on the particular issues of Galician cultural history, its deterritorialized experiences of migration and exile, and transnational collaboration and coproduction in the global age.

The other three films were premiered together in 1989 in Vigo at the special three-day gala event *Cinegalicia*, designed to inaugurate the new era of Galician cinema and technically the first ever Galician Film Festival. The event has traditionally been considered by film critics as a pivotal moment in Galician cinema, and its official 20-year commemoration received wide media coverage from Galician cultural critics, writers, and politicians. The three films launched were *Continental* by Xavier Villaverde, *Sempre Xonxa* "Always Xonxa" by Chano Piñeiro, and *Urxa* by Carlos López Piñeiro and Alfredo G. Pinal. *Sempre Xonxa* and *Xurxa* are stories of rural Galicia, shot on location in Galician, with Galician actors and crew and Galician-based funding. By contrast, *Continental* is a modern retro *film noir*, with a majority of Spanish actors, shot in Spanish and dubbed into Galician, and filmed in its entirety in a studio in Madrid, where Villaverde lives and co-directs his own multimedia production company, Continental.

While *Sempre Xonxa* and *Urxa* are recognizably Galician and possess a visual, linguistic, and cultural aura of "authenticity," mobilizing traditional tropes of Galicianess, *Continental* draws on an international film style, cosmopolitan mise-en-scène, and modern recycling of genres associated with Hollywood. The Galicianess of the first two films is also highlighted in their titles, which take a Galician female first name as an untranslatable emblem of the nation; by contrast, the cosmopolitanism of *Continental*, also figured in its title, does not need translating (at least, not for most European languages).

The first two films opt for a Galician poetic form of "magical realism" that has been common in Galician literature, in various forms, since the mid nineteenth-century *Rexurdimento* literary revival, including Álvaro Cunqueiro and Manuel Rivas. Both capitalize on the visual power and spectacularity of the Galician landscape, already present in *Gallego* and a hallmark of much subsequent Galician film production. As in much Galician literature, the land is present not so much as a backdrop but as a constituent element of Galician identity. Both films were also originally shot in the Galician language, an innovation that had no precedent in Galician professional cinema, adding a further aura of "authenticity." The rural Galician setting reinforced this linguistic authenticity, as Galician has traditionally been the primary language spoken in the rural areas, the urban areas being characterized by diglossia or Spanish monolingualism.

Both films, which are set in the postwar years, focus on traditional Galician rural life, giving a somewhat essentialist view of Galician identity at a time in the 1980s when Galicia was rapidly being transformed into an urban–suburban—even "rurban"—community, with traditional farming increasingly abandoned. These films nostalgically recapture the sense of collective loss as well as the experience of migration (*Sempre Xonxa*), but avoid addressing Galicia's modernization. While modern Galician literature was adjusting to social and cultural transformation (as seen in the works of Suso de Toro and Manuel Rivas), Galician cinema seemed to lag behind, fixated on filling the visual void of a past that had been for the most part cinematically invisible.

By contrast, *Continental* rejects traditional Galician themes associated with rural settings, natural scenery, and magical realist tropes. Instead, it opts for a neutral urban setting and cosmopolitan look. Indeed, the film is notable for its aesthetic experimentation and postmodern recycling and mixing of genres (film noir's sordidness, melodrama's theatricality, the western's archetypal characterization), and for being an ambitious commercial project, with a stellar Spanish and international cast including Fernando Guillén, Eusebio Poncela, Marisa Paredes, Jorge Sanz, Féodor Atkine, and Héctor Alterio.

While *Continental* is visually and musically exciting, it ends up falling victim to its overtly ambitious style, which at times disorients the spectator. The marks of its Galicianess are intentionally not obvious on the film's surface, or in its soundscape, which features mostly Latin dance music. Critics commented that the film "could well be set in Hamburg, Istanbul, or Brest" (Williams 105). Its Galicianess is more subdued, with many buried intertextual allusions to Galician literature (to Ramón Otero Pedrayo and Eduardo Pondal, for example) which would not register for most spectators, especially outside of Galicia.[2] Its director Xavier Villaverde has referred to the often misunderstood metaphorical Galician dimension of the film: "unha metáfora de Galicia como labirinto de rúas sempre molladas que se entrecruzan, onde ten lugar a traxedia duns personaxes sós, abandonados e de volta de case todo, perdidos na noite interminable de 'ese lugar húmido e pequeno' onde transcorre o filme" ("a metaphor of Galicia as a labyrinth of criss-crossing wet streets, where the tragic story unfolds of a lonely, abandoned, and disillusioned set of characters, lost in the endless night of that 'small, wet place' where the film's action takes place") (Villaverde).

Villaverde's film thus represents a key paradox of Galician cinema. In its effort to create and market a Galician film without obvious surface marks of Galicianess that can travel beyond Galicia, *Continental* could be said to symbolize the general invisibility of Galician cinema; but, at the same time, it also symbolizes a desire to expand the horizons of Galician cinema beyond Galicia itself, and beyond Spain, to the world at large. In this regard, the other two films discussed—*Sempre Xonxa* and *Urxa*—while unquestionably Galician, share with *Continental* the relative invisibility of Galician cinema, for they all failed to reach large audiences outside of Galicia.

---

2 For more of the intertextual allusions, see the interview with Villaverde in my *Galeg@s sen fronteiras.*

During the 1990s Galician cinema became partially consolidated in several key areas: the creation of a functional infrastructure; the establishment of professional film associations; the passing of legislation for the audiovisual sector, giving it official status as a strategic growth area in Galicia thanks to the regularization of film subsidies; the creation of the Galician Film Archives, with a mission to recover and disseminate Galician cinema; and the creation of public and private films schools. The proliferation of film shorts and short festivals can be attributed to a new generation of film school graduates as well as to the availability of new digital technologies. These various factors have contributed to increased levels of Galician film production since the 1990s. The steady growth of Galician cinema in the last 20 years has been accompanied by a growing diversification, with a large range of genres aimed at different audiences, from children's animation and youth comedies to documentaries, literary adaptations, popular genre films (urban thrillers, horror), and alternative films. Juan Pinzás's trilogy of films—*Era outra vez* "Once Upon Another Time" (2000), *Días de voda* "Wedding Days" (2002), and *El desenlace* "The Outcome" (2005), dealing with issues of cultural identity related to gender, sexuality, social class, and language use—stand out as the only films made in Spain that have been officially certified as Dogme 95, the avant-garde movement initiated by Lars Von Trier and characterized by an anti-studio and bare bones aesthetic. The rejection of artificiality and the aesthetic nakedness of the movement seem plausible choices for Pinzás's filmic exploration of the difficulties of coming out as both gay and a speaker of Galician in a homophobic and diglossic yuppy cultural context. However, as Ryan Prout has shown, in spite of its promising premises and potential international appeal, the trilogy has proven ultimately faulty, and only marginally successful, owing to excessive histrionics and a lack of linguistic and narrative verisimilitude. A picture much closer to reality, and also more traditional in narrative style, was presented in *Pradolongo* (Ignacio Vilar, 2008), which proved unusually successful with both urban and rural Galician youth audiences. *Pradolongo* explores the contemporary uses of land and language as two key forms of cultural identity, crucial parts of a sociocultural habitat that needs to be protected and invigorated. Picturing the rural lifestyle as both modern and appealing, if not devoid of problems, and a modern and realistic use of Galician language as spoken dialectally in the area of Valdeorras, the film has proven relevant and meaningful for a considerable segment of Galician youth. Given the fact that Galician language has been traditionally linked with rurality and the working classes, and for many young Galicians it is associated with an aging population and in general with the past, and is thus disconnected from an increasingly urbanized middle-class Galician youth, the fact that *Pradolongo* was able to connect with wide range of young audiences could be seen as showing promise for Galician cinema.[3]

## Global Visibility and Technical Innovation

In an article published in the widely read US film magazine *Variety* in 2004, film critic John Hopewell acknowledges a paradigmatic shift in the contemporary Galician audiovisual scene, which is encapsulated in the title: "Hit and Myth in the Deep North. Forward-looking Rural Area Transforming into TV and Film Heavyweight." Undoubtedly, in the last two decades there has been a quite significant development of the audiovisual sector in Galicia in such diverse areas as animation, multimedia, and television and film production. Whether this growth could be described as boom of "heavyweight" proportions, as John Hopewell's sensationalist headline indicates, it is perhaps more debatable.

In the last couple of decades mainstream Galician cinema production has become increasingly concerned with internationalization, in terms of both seeking outside funding and audiences for Galician film productions and attracting film production to Galicia from other parts of Spain and abroad. Official policies were put in place throughout the 1990s to encourage film production in Galicia by non-local film professionals, facilitating co-production schemes, thus prioritizing the idea of "cinema in Galicia." With that purpose in mind, the official Galician Audiovisual Report was published in English in 1999, and the Galicia Film Commission as well as the Santiago de Compostela Film Commission were set up in 2002. These initiatives have coincided with an increase in Galician films screened at international film festivals in our century, and a number of Mostras de Cine Galego (Galician Film Festivals) in various overseas locations, some repeated in successive years—for example, in Portugal (2000), Argentina (2003), Paris (2004), Berlin (2005), Cuba, Brazil and Chile (2007), and Brussels and New York (2008).[4]

The increase in film and television production in Galicia has been remarkable, especially taking into account its almost complete absence before the democratic period. Since 2003 Galicia has occupied third place in the statistics for cinema production in the various autonomous communities of

---

3  See Romero (*Contemporary Galician Culture*) for an analysis of *Pradolongo*.

4  In 2015 there was a concerted effort to export globally a Galician nation "brand" through the Galician Film Festival held in New York, in conjunction with an exhibit of Galician gastronomical products at the Instituto Cervantes. One of the reasons for this marketing strategy was allegedly the presence of 20,000 Galicians working in key places in New York ("Nueva York").

Spain, ranked only after Madrid and Barcelona, with some 20 films produced annually. Yet, while Galician films have been made with increasing regularity and the Galician audiovisual sector has become somewhat normalized, they still remain relatively invisible, as the large majority do not reach large audiences and only occasionally break even at the box office. And while a good number of the recent *Novo Cinema Galego* productions have received popular and critical recognition at international film festivals—such as Oliver Laxe's films, which have been awarded twice at Cannes, winning the FIPRESCI award for *Todos vós sodes capitáns* in 2010 and the Nespresso Grand Prize for *Mimosas* in 2016, or Álex Sampayo's *Schimbare*, which won the 2015 international award at the Independent Berlin Film Festival—they operate on the fringes of the mainstream and often work in precarious conditions. The most commercially successful Galician films of the last two decades have been co-productions made in Galicia, such as the acclaimed *La lengua de las mariposas* (José Luis Cuerda, 1999)—the first Galician-made international art film success which single-handedly "discovered" Galicia for the big screen, an adaptation of Manuel Rivas's equally successful collection of short stories *Que me queres, amor?*—*Los lunes al sol* (Fernando León de Aranoa, 2002), and Academy Award winner *Mar adentro* (Alejandro Amenábar, 2004).[5]

The one area of Galician-based and Galician-made cinema production that has been relatively successful at the box office outside of Galicia in recent years has been that of digital film animation, where Galicia holds a leading position in Europe as the top producer of 3D animation films (see Chapter 6). Some of the highest-grossing Galician films have been in the animation genre—for example, *El bosque animado* "The Living Forest" (Ángel de la Cruz and Manolo Gómez, 2001) and *Pérez, el ratoncito de tus sueños* "Pérez, the Mouse of your Dreams" (Juan Pablo Buscarini, 2006), both of which had sequels—aimed at the local, national, and international family market.

Indeed, some of the most interesting work in Galician cinema has been in the area of digital technology innovation. A case in point is Miguelanxo Prado's *De profundis* (2006), a fascinating example of how to bridge the two poles between which Galician cinema has swung since the 1980s: Galicianess and cosmopolitanism, the local and the global. Like the pioneering Galician films of the 1980s, *De profundis* shares the visual intensity of a utopian project that has overcome huge structural, technical, and financial obstacles. It almost inevitably invites a symbolic reading in its avoidance of the transparency of mimetic representation. The self-reflexive nature of this

5 To this list should be added those films made by Galicians or Galician companies outside of Galicia, such as *Celda 211* (Daniel Monzón, 2009). In contrast, the list of financial disasters and uncompleted projects in Galician cinema is large.

Figure 12   From the Land's End to the Far East. DVD cover in Chinese for *De profundis* (2007), Continental Producciones.

fantastic story of longing and loss between a male painter and a female musician suggests a further symbolic dimension, as a nation-building project. Prado, a Galician graphic novel artist and animator with a brilliant international résumé, responsible for the art design of the *Men in Black* TV series, embarked on the herculean task of creating a film single-handedly by digitizing and animating several thousand original oil, acrylic, and watercolor paintings made by him for this purpose, a project completed over an intense four-year period together with Galician musician Nani García. *De profundis* deals with a profoundly dramatic Galician topic with global repercussions—life and death at sea, inspired by the 2002 *Prestige* oil spill—

and its visual style, cultural referents, music soundtrack, and means of production are recognizably Galician. But the film also creates a new stylized language of images and sounds, without the use of words, which does not require translation, and the result is an exciting audio/visual product which communicates powerfully and effortlessly beyond the confines of Galicia. It does so by combining features traditionally associated with representations of Galician identity—natural settings, the sea-faring world, a poetic magical realist style—with universal motifs such as shipwreck, feelings of loss and isolation, the Atlantis myth, exploration of the unknown, imagination and fantasy, and rebirth in a New-Age style tapestry of color and sound.

Thoroughly Galician but open in its horizons, *De profundis* takes us to the deep waters of the ocean and the deep levels of the fantastic imagination, making the impossible seem possible and the invisible visible. More than an example of how Galician cinema can become an autonomous entity, *De profundis* constitutes a symbol of its possibilities. Its sunken ship does not invoke the heroic nationalist naval saga of *Raza*, with its eternal return of the imperial past and Fascist dream of a patriarchal united family that erases all differences. Prado's sunken ship, its fantastic transformation into a living sea creature, and its re-emergence on the face of the ocean—products of the fantastic imagination of a visual artist and a musician—stand as powerful metaphors of the death and rebirth of Galician culture, the revitalization of its artistic creativity, and its cinema's increased visibility.

# CHAPTER FIVE

# Reimagining Galician Cinema: Utopian Visions?

Este era un mundo de tebras e agora é un mundo de luz. Era
un mundo de ferro e é agora un mundo de ouro.
'This was a world of shadows and now it is a world of light.
It was a world of iron and now it is a world of gold.'
Xavier Villaverde, *Continental*

Primeiro foi a moda, agora é o audiovisual ...
'First it was fashion, now it's the audiovisual ...'
"O Audiovisual agora. Pintan Ouros," *Vieiros*

¿Cómo vai existir o cinema en galego cando case nin existe Galicia?
'How can a cinema in Galician exist when Galicia itself barely does?'
Marcelo Martínez, "¿Existe o cine galego?," *Vieiros*

T he question of the existence of Galician cinema has long been intensely
debated, defended, celebrated, and contested by critics and film
professionals alike. It is considered a glass half full or a glass half empty,
depending on the degree of optimism, ideological position, and relative
perspective of the onlooker. A large part of the debate has historically focused
on the definition of the ontological status of "Galician cinema": that is, what
exactly Galician cinema is or should be. It is a long debate deeply embedded
in a complex web of related social and political issues about Galicia's
struggle for national identity and cultural "normalization," reflecting a wide
spectrum of positions between culturally purist nationalist views, on the
one hand, and pragmatic possibilism, on the other. Global aspects of the
new economic, technological, and cultural realities have shifted the terms
of the debate since the 1990s towards wider notions such as "cinema made
in Galicia" or even "audiovisual productions made in Galicia," while, more
recently, others have coined the concept of "New Galician Cinema," which

is sometimes made away from Galicia or on non-Galician topics. Although frequently overlapping, it can be productive to maintain a methodological distinction between these concepts, from a merely analytical point of view.

In this chapter I will address the problematic situation of Galician film production in the larger contexts of the Galician audiovisual sector, the Spanish cinema industry, and the transnational currents of economic and cultural globalization affecting national and subnational cinemas. Galician film production is situated in quite peculiar, culturally specific circumstances, although it shares the general limitations of the Spanish film industry as a whole, struggling to compete in a global market dominated by US productions. It also faces the particular problematics arising from the marginal position of autonomous cinema produced in peripheral contexts, such as the Basque and Catalan cinemas, where questions of language, cultural identity, and nation-building overlap in intricate ways. The specific contexts of Galician film production reveal a complex interweaving of adverse historical, economic, political, and sociocultural conditions that historically have presented some challenges to its development. But the uniqueness of the Galician condition and its peripherality also provide a particular impetus, a different vision, and some unique opportunities in the global map.

The often expressed need for a "Galician cinema" and the enormous difficulties encountered in bringing it into existence must be analyzed against the complex backdrop of the Galician national struggle for cultural definition against Spanish state nationalism—before, during, and after Franco—and against a long history of cultural and political repression and uneven economic development. Furthermore, we must take into account the growing erosion of the "national cinema" paradigm as a conceptual tool in the context of economic, cultural, and political transnational globalization, which explains new conceptualizations such as "cinema made in Galicia" that have emerged in recent years.[1]

As we have seen earlier, to better address these complexities some Iberian cultural studies scholars have referred to a new "postnational" paradigm that could provide a more refined theoretical ground from which to analyze the decentering of Spanish cultural production, the emergence of peripheral cultures and identities, the hybridization of national cultures, and the interplay of the local and the global, advocating a remapping that would effectively deterritorialize the traditional boundaries of the national. This new conceptualization could be an effective tool to approach more productively the question of how to redefine what Galician cinema is, or could be. It could also have far-reaching implications for the redefinition of

---

1 For a review of these issues, see Crofts; Higson.

Galician studies as a field, traditionally centered around the *criterio filolóxico* borrowed from literary studies and the use of the Galician vernacular language, as was discussed in previous chapters. The study of Galician cinema and/or cinema made in/out of Galicia problematizes the definition of what constitutes Galician cultural studies and potentially offers a more encompassing alternative to traditional disciplinary philological approaches.

Intellectual debates since the 1970s have highlighted the need for a Galician cinema as a nation-building project, both to create *imaxe-país*, an image of/for the nation, and as a part of the process of cultural and linguistic "normalization." The need to reaffirm Galician cultural identity and project an image of Galicia in the global audiovisual market is seen by many film critics and professionals as a question of cultural survival nowadays (Acuña; Rozados). In the last two decades, Galician officials and institutions have also started to show clear signs of interest in the development of the audiovisual field, which encompasses video, television, film, animation, and multimedia productions. The audiovisual area has been officially declared by the Xunta a strategic and priority sector for the economic and cultural development of Galicia, although it is fair to say that Galician official institutions have frequently been erratic and dysfunctional in the implementation of their programs.[2] While there is a wide discrepancy of opinion about what Galician cinema is, or could be, there is nowadays a general consensus about the importance of the expanding Galician audiovisual industry and, more specifically, the steadily growing number of film productions "made in Galicia."

Since the early 1970s there has been a series of attempts to theorize the conditions of possibility of Galician cinema, asking: What makes a film Galician? How should this cinema be? And how should it come about?[3] The origins of the continuing debate about Galician cinema go back to the last years of the dictatorship and, in particular, the foundation of a *Novo Cinema Galego*, discussed at the Ourense film festival in 1973, in the aftermath of the new national film movements of the 1960s.[4] Without a unified conceptual framework, there were many different views on what would constitute Galician

2 Former President of the Xunta de Galicia under the bipartite coalition, Emilio Pérez Touriño, underlined the strategic importance of cinema made in Galicia for its economy and cultural promotion—using the expression "longametraxes con sabor galego" ("films with Galician flavour") ("Presentación"). For a summary of the legal measures for the establishment of the audiovisual sector in Galicia, see note 10.

3 For an overview of the bleak picture of Galician cinema in those days, see Rabón.

4 This should not be confused with the rebrand of the *Novo Cinema Galego* movement in our century, examined in Chapter 7.

cinema, such as the use of the Galician language, a Galician cast and technical crew, or a theme related to Galicia. Some had more abstract views, defining it as a way of "feeling" or "expressing" Galicia in images, while attempting to avoid traditional Galician "ruralism" or "folklorism" (Acuña 77–78). What all those views had in common is that they were expressing utopian visions of a still prospective Galician cinema—a cinema more imagined than real, a cinema that could *represent* the nation in all senses of the word. The catalog of the festival summed up the situation with sardonic Galician relativism, in a now well-known paradoxical statement pointing to this utopian *no-place*, which could be considered the degree zero of Galician cinema: "O cine galego é a conciencia da súa nada. Xa é algo" ("Galician cinema is the perception of its own nothingness. That is already a start") (Acuña 78).

Undoubtedly, many changes have taken place since then that have affected the development of Galician cinema. The end of Franco's dictatorship and the establishment of autonomy in Galicia propelled the reawakening of Galician culture with great force, and cinema has been no exception to this cultural revitalization. The intellectual debate between the creation of an alternative autonomous and self-marginalized but "authentic" Galician cinema, on the one hand, and, on the other, pragmatic possibilism, professionalization, and the creation of an industrial infrastructure, seemed to have leaned toward the latter in the global age (Hueso, "Anos," 188). That tension, however, has not disappeared altogether, although the debate has metamorphosed, particularly since the beginning of the global economic crisis, between a traditional concept of commercial cinema in a post-cinema age and the new, alternative, more purist approaches emerging from the margins of the industry, as we will see in the last section of the chapter.

Cinema production in Galicia is now part of a much larger and complex audiovisual field with blurred boundaries between different media formats, outlets, and technologies, such as film, TV, video, multimedia, and advertising (Nogueira, *O cine en Galicia*, 342, 361).[5] Digitalization and virtual networks have changed traditional patterns and allowed alternative modes of production and dissemination on the margins of the mainstream industry. In addition, the different regimes of coproduction, with national and international companies, directors, technicians, and cast members, and the international mobility of the creators and their works, have also blurred the strict defining parameters of a national cinema, in effect deterritorializing the concept and practice of Galician cinema.

5 The audiovisual *Mestre Mateo* awards organized by the Academia Galega do Audiovisual include different categories for cinema, television, web series, videoclip, multimedia, and advertising.

While Galician language remains a fundamental aspect of Galician cultural identity, even the language used in the films cannot be a meaningful distinctive marker. This is because a large part of the feature films shot in Galicia are filmed in Spanish and then dubbed into Galician in postproduction for their general release in Galicia, as the dubbing in Galician is required in order to obtain official production subsidies and be shown on Television de Galicia (TVG). The main reason for this practice is the widespread perception that films shot in Spanish are better suited for distribution and a commercially successful run, especially in Spanish-speaking areas outside of Galicia. This is particularly the case with mainstream long-feature films, which are dependent on established commercial channels for their distribution. Some exceptions to this rule are the original Galician-language films by pioneers Chano Piñeiro, Raúl Veiga, and Ignacio Vilar and, more recently, a new wave of films on the margins of the traditional commercial circuits, as we will see in the case of the *Novo Cine Galego* of recent years. Even such a well-known nationalist militant and supporter of Galician-language art and culture as Antón Reixa has shot his feature films in Spanish for pragmatic reasons: *El lápiz del carpintero* (2003) and *Hotel Tívoli* (2007) were coproduced with Spanish and other international companies. His adaptation of one of the most canonical novels of modern Galician literature, Manuel Rivas's *O lapis do carpinteiro*, received harsh criticism for this "fraud."[6] In this context, the surprising success in the theaters and video stores of Ignacio Vilar's ecological youth-theme *Pradolongo* (2008), originally shot in Galician, was understood by some as a first sign of the real "normalization" of Galician cinema ("'Pradolongo'"). This pattern has continued with his later films *Vilamor* (2012) and *A esmorga* (2014), which have met with both public and critical success.

*A esmorga* represents an important milestone, as it marks the maturity of Vilar's career and of a certain conception of Galician cinema. It has a highly symbolic value as perhaps one of the most emblematic mainstream Galician films of recent years, having received wide critical acclaim for its accomplished adaption of Eduardo Blanco Amor's contemporary classic Galician novel, and for exploring important cultural questions of identity, inflected by nation, class, language, gender, and sexual orientation. It would be tempting to perform an allegorical reading of the film, with its suggestive symbolic settings and elaborate visual metaphors (frames, labyrinths, walls, deforming mirrors, circular paths and camera movements), as representing the Galician subaltern condition marked by harsh social, economic, and

---

6 For an overview of the controversy between the collective Redes Escarlata and Antón Reixa's response, see "El lápiz del carpintero. Denuncia dunha mentira."

Figures 13–15   Decentering visions, mixing visual motifs from Galician prehistory, Baroque *pazo* architecture, and avant-garde aesthetics, in *A esmorga* (2014) by Ignacio Vilar, Vía Láctea Filmes. The *Pazo de Tor*'s stone labyrinths are suggestive of the spirals of ancient Galician petroglyphs and the distorting mirrors in the grotesque style of Ramón del Valle-Inclán's *esperpentos* reflect in expressionist style the characters' entrapment and the carnivalesque subversion of established order.

political constraints. Set in the dark years of the Franco dictatorship, the film offers a picaresque-like topsy-turvy perspective from the margins, focusing on the subaltern identities (poor outcasts, victims of patriarchal order, non-conforming masculinity), and offering a bleak non-romanticized outlook ultimately leading to abjection, self-destruction, and the eradication of difference.

Since the 1990s there has been a general understanding that a Galician production, incorporating in all or in large part a Galician artistic cast, technical crew, and means of production, would warrant the designation of Galician film. As Ángel Hueso has succinctly put it, "Cine galego sería aquel que utilizase uns recursos industriais, económicos, de producción e artísticos, propios de Galicia" ("A Galician cinema would be one that used industrial, economic, production and artistic resources from Galicia") (quoted in Galán, 14). For Xosé Nogueira, Galician cinema, *estrictu sensu*, would be "aquel pensado, producido e realizado en Galicia por empresas cinematográficas galegas" ("conceptualized, produced and made in Galicia by Galician film companies") (*O cine en Galicia*, 9). It is perhaps no coincidence that both statements were made in the conditional mood, subtly underlining their hypothetical status. The general consensus moved from the endlessly arguable and ultimately rather futile debate about the ontological status of Galician cinema, or the essentialist question of what makes a film "Galician." Rather than returning to the restrictive and often confusing notion of "Galician cinema," many critics and film professionals in Galicia prefer to use umbrella expressions such as "Cinema in Galicia" or "Cinema made in Galicia" (Hueso, "Anos," 190; Nogueira, *O cine en Galicia*, 358). These much broader categorizations encompass all the different facets of cinema production in Galicia, and are more attuned to the postnational political contexts and transnational economic and cultural conditions affecting Galician audiovisual production.[7] In my view, these are not mutually exclusive categories, but complementary and almost always overlapping. I use here the term "Galician cinema" restrictively to refer to those films

7  This trend can also be observed in the titles of recent books and articles on this subject (*Cen anos de cine en Galicia*, *O cine en Galicia*, *Historia do cine en Galicia*, *Diccionario do cine en Galicia*, *Libro branco de cinematografía e artes visuais en Galicia*), TVG programs such as Miguel Anxo Fernández's *Galicia no cine*, the website/publication *Rodado en Galicia*, and video collections such as the one launched by the journal *La voz de Galicia* as "Galicia de cine," which all avoid the ambivalent expression "Cine galego." Discussions on this topic (and the even older question of what constitutes Galician literature) have repeatedly taken place in the Galician Studies email discussion forum in the last few years. For access to the archive, see http://www.jiscmail.ac.uk/lists/GALICIAN-STUDIES.html.

that are rooted in Galicia and predominantly Galician in their process of production, independently of their language or other factors.[8] Cinema "made in Galicia," on the other hand, would be a much broader umbrella category that includes other films not necessarily involving a Galician production in plan or execution. In that sense, José Luis Cuerda's remarkable film *El bosque animado* (1987), although Galician in theme and location, is still technically a Spanish production "made in Galicia" (a traditional Elías Querejeta team production). Conversely, Ángel de la Cruz and Manolo Gómez's animated feature *El bosque animado* (2001), conceived and produced in its entirety in Galicia by Galician companies, is intrinsically a Galician film. There are important symbolic and pragmatic reasons to maintain this differentiation, even though both trends are part of the cinema produced in Galicia, and both should have a place within a broadly defined conception of Galician studies.[9]

The two quotes from the 2002 special *Vieiros* online dossier on Galician audiovisual production used as epigraph for this chapter highlight the intense debate generated at the turn of the millennium about the supposed boom of Galician cinema, ranging from enthusiastic celebration to Galician skepticism and resigned relativism. The beginning of the dossier synthesizes well the need to put things in perspective, without the exaggerated euphoria of the achievement or self-defeating fatalism ("neither 'boom' nor 'bluff'"), emphasizing the need to tell "our" stories and tell "ourselves" to the world:

> Primeiro foi a moda, agora é o audiovisual ... Falan de "boom" e amósannos un país maquillado nas estreas en pantalla grande. Ruborizámonos ao vérmonos alí, entre os focos, entre os protagonistas,

8 It has been noted by some that, while there has clearly been a considerable growth in the production of cinema in Galicia, there is not a unified set of characteristics that would establish Galician cinema as a unique national cinema different from other cinemas, as would be the case of, say, "Iranian cinema" or "Indian Cinema" ("Pintan Ouros"). The same, of course, could be said of other national cinemas, including the Spanish.

9 A strict categorization is of course arguable, since clear-cut distinctions cannot always be established, and intends only to clarify different patterns in the cinema made in Galicia. Jaime Pena offers an interesting angle on this issue, stating that both trends have almost converged in recent years, citing as an example the enormous parallels between two film adaptations of Manuel Rivas' works set in the civil war, *La lengua de las mariposas* and *El lápiz del carpintero* (the model of production, the look and film style, the literary referent). Beyond the intellectual debate, the argument has obvious political and economic ramifications: what films should receive the official subsidies provided by the Xunta de Galicia? Would a more restrictive subvention policy encourage more Galician productions, or discourage non-Galician companies from creating cinema in Galicia?

non estamos afeitos. Así que saímos do mundo da ficción e tentamos pensar con sentidiño: nin hai "boom" nin hai "bluff," non hai máis que unha incipiente e ilusionante industria que nos permite, por primeira vez, vernos reflectidos en caixas máxicas, xusto alí onde nunca chegaramos. O reto: contarnos historias a nós mesmos pero, sobre todo, contarnos ao resto do mundo. Velaí o inmenso potencial. ("O Audiovisual agora")

First it was fashion, now it's the audiovisual ... They talk about a "boom" and show us a tarted-up country on the big screen premieres. We blush to see ourselves there, among the spotlights, among the protagonists; we are not used to it. And so we leave the world of fiction and we try to think with some common sense: There is neither a "boom" nor a "bluff," there is only an incipient and exciting industry that allows us, for the first time, to see ourselves reflected in magical boxes, right there where we had never been. The challenge: to tell stories to ourselves, but above all to tell ourselves to the rest of the world. And that has immense potential.

The magical effect of the experience of Galicians seeing themselves reflected for the first time in the moving images of the theater marks indeed a historical turning point. It strongly resembles the primordial experience of the child who sees his image reflected in the mirror for the first time (the Lacanian mirror stage), and so we could say that it represents a sort of collective entry into the symbolic visual order. The passage quoted makes a passing reference to two different "mundos," the wondrous world of fiction where we see ourselves represented, and the world out there that works as a film screen on which to project our stories and dreams. This consideration points to a necessary double vision: the original conceptual visualization made in Galicia and the subsequent perceptual visualization of the viewer, for Galicia and the world to see.

In an even more enigmatic way, the earlier quote from Villaverde also has a high degree of symbolism: "Este era un mundo de tebras e agora é un mundo de luz. Era un mundo de ferro e é agora un mundo de ouro." These are the first words spoken in his urban thriller *Continental*, one of three films shown at the special premiere *Cinegalicia* in 1989, considered the official launch of contemporary Galician cinema, which could be seen as the staging of the collective moment of passage to the symbolic "mirror stage."[10]

10 The *Cinegalicia* festival was highly glossed by the media as the birth of modern Galician cinema. It was the official public premiere of the first results of the Xunta de Galicia's policy of subventions for the development of Galician films, initiated only

In a film with compelling imagery, ambiguous symbolism, and abundant self-referentiality, which is clearly a proposal for the aesthetic and thematic renovation of Galician cinema, the opposing worlds of a past iron age of shadows and a new golden age of light also have a strong metaphorical resonance. The shadows/light imagery evokes not only the historical *Séculos oscuros* and the reawakening with the new light of the day (*Rexurdimento*) but also the internal workings of the camera and the cinematic apparatus. Furthermore, these words are intertextually related to Eduardo Pondal, one of the great poets of the nineteenth-century Galician cultural *Rexurdimento* and writer of the lyrics of the Galician national anthem. Pondal's famous deathbed words referred to his founding role in constructing a modern literary Galician language: "Déchedesme unha lingua de ferro i eu douvos unha lingua de ouro" ("You gave me a language made of iron and I give you a language made of gold") (quoted in Iglesias). This literary connection reinforces the metaphorical reading of the film, underscoring its Galicianess and strongly suggesting a utopian vision for the future of Galician cinema.

Making Galician cinema in Galicia, with all its shadows and lights, in its journey from the iron age of the past to a golden age still to come, has always been a utopian enterprise. The idea of a Galician dream factory has itself been a dream, a utopian vision against all odds, marked by its peripherality, the lack of an industrial infrastructure, cultural and political marginality, and the domination of the Spanish and, especially, the hegemonic US film industry. The long and difficult journey of Galician cinema is perhaps best encapsulated in the well-known odyssey of the late director Chano Piñeiro, who defied all obstacles to turn his dream of making cinema in Galicia into a reality. Piñeiro became one of the first directors to make a feature-length Galician film in every sense of the term, as discussed in the previous chapter. His *Sempre Xonxa* (1989) is for many a highly symbolic example of the modern Galician cinema for its ability to transform a utopian vision into a reality, capturing the emotional involvement of great numbers of Galician spectators through its representation of Galicianess. This film could be considered a turning point, as it marks the transition from the earlier Galician cinema, comprised mostly of works of elitist auteur craftsmanship and underfunded amateur productions, and limited to traditional rural or

a couple of years earlier during the tripartite Galician socialist/nationalist coalition. The other two new films featured were *Sempre Xonxa* and *Urxa*, both originally shot in Galician with Galician actors and settings, as discussed in the previous chapter. Manuel Rivas described in *El País* the audience's enthusiastic acclamation of *Sempre Xonxa* as a communal "auto de fe" ("act of faith") (Acuña 125).

folkloric themes, to a new era of progressive professionalization, economic and cultural expansion, and access to wider audiences.[11]

Rather than a black-and-white picture, contemporary Galician cinema is a complex puzzle, with many shades of light and shadows, greatly shaped by various important social, political, and cultural developments. Galician cinema of the last two decades must be seen against the substantial accomplishments in the recuperation of Galician language, culture, and historical identity in the years since the restoration of democracy. A result of this collective cultural reawakening has been the considerable success and recognition beyond Galicia of young Galicians working in the arts, design, fashion, literature, and popular music, which started to gain great visibility with the "Movida galega" of the 1980s (see Chapter 8 on the "peripheral movidas"). The considerable development in the audiovisual sector in Galicia since the mid-1990s and the conceptual and artistic renovation of recent years with the *Novo Cinema Galego* are some of the examples of this continuing cultural revitalization.

## The Golden Age of Light?
## The *Boom* of the Galician Audiovisual Sector

The development of cinema production in Galicia is directly related to and inseparable from advances in the audiovisual sector as a whole (encompassing television, multimedia, video, cinema, animation, advertising, and so on). Significant administrative and legal measures were taken to regulate and promote film production in Galicia soon after the establishment of the Xunta de Galicia, thus filling a public policy audiovisual vacuum and increasing the vitality of this sector.[12] Two important official measures enacted by the Xunta

11  Also see Chapter 3 for a discussion of Piñeiro's last opus *O Camiño das Estrelas*. For an extended analysis of his film career and its pioneering role in the vitalization of Galician cinema, see Acuña. For the production of *Sempre Xonxa*, see the section "A odisea dunha longa e compleza rodaxe." As a vivid illustration of the degree zero of Galician cinema at the time and the lack of local infrastructure Piñeiro had to deal with, he used to tell how there were no audiovisual support companies in Galicia at the time that could provide a Galician oak tree for a prop, a crucial symbolic element in the film to represent the passage of time and the changing of the seasons. After many frustrating and costly delays, a fiberglass tree had to be ordered for that purpose from a company in Madrid, but unfortunately the resulting product didn't remotely resemble a Galician oak tree.

12  The official *Lei do audiovisual* in Galicia, approved unanimously in 1999, is one of the most comprehensive in Spain and clearly spells out the special status of the sector in Galicia: "Os poderes públicos de Galicia recoñecen a importancia cultural, económica e social das actividades cinematográficas e do audiovisual, do papel

to promote Galician cinema were the creation of institutional subsidies for Galician film production—with ever-changing rules, regulations, and budgets, but firmly established since the mid-1980s—and the creation of the public and autonomous Televisión de Galicia (TVG) in 1985. The combined effect of these official programs has had a direct and continued influence on Galician cinema and the audiovisual sector as a whole. Subsidies for the Galician audiovisual sector became the basic *sine qua non* for the initial development of a double minority cinema that can hardly compete in equal terms against other national and international film products, especially given the hegemony of the US film industry in Spain and Galicia.

The launch of TVG, with its strong support of, and indeed great demand for, Galician audiovisual productions, such as video works, TV series and movies, shorts, and feature films, proved to be equally instrumental for the gradual establishment of an industrial audiovisual infrastructure in Galicia. This infrastructure resulted in the creation of a plethora of small audiovisual companies, dubbing studios, production companies, and animation studios. The influence of TVG undoubtedly accelerated the process of linguistic and cultural "normalization" in the sector, although its institutionalized approach has been problematic in several key areas, as we will see later.[13] The emergence of the audiovisual sector has also meant the slow but progressive development of the cinema industry in Galicia and the gradual professionalization of the industry as a whole. The formation of film production companies such as Continental, Filmanova, and Filminvest with the direct participation of major Galician financial institutions was perceived as the definitive pillar for the strengthening of the film industry. For instance, the main investor in the last two companies was the savings bank Caixanova, and one of the private investors in Continental was Rosalía Mera, the cofounder of the Inditex textile empire.[14] However, the economic

---

que poden desempeñar como creación artística, información, coñecemento e imaxe de Galicia, a prol da consecución da normalización cultural de Galicia, polo que a consideran sector estratéxico e prioritario" ("Galicia's public authorities recognize the cultural, economic, and social importance of cinema and audiovisual activities, of the role they can play in terms of artistic creation, information, knowledge, and image of Galicia, in favor of the attainment of Galicia's cultural normalization, and therefore consider them a strategic and high-priority sector") (Sempere 267).

13 The popular acceptance of Galician TV fictional series and sitcoms has had the surprising result of TVG becoming one of the leading producers of fictional television series in Europe (Sempere 260). In the last few years there have been more than 25 fictional TV series made in Galicia—many of them lasting multiple seasons and successfully exported outside of Galicia—and more than 30 TV films.

14 Between 1994 and 1999 there was a 296% increase in the number of audiovisual production companies, a 125% increase of employment in the sector, and a 113%

crisis of recent years and the subsequent collapse of the Galician savings banks Caixanova and Caixa Galicia (artificially merged as NovacaixaGalicia and then refloated as Abanca) has meant that many Galician film production companies also collapsed, and filmmakers have had to search for alternative forms of financing and low-cost production schemes.

Official governmental support from the Xunta has also been a key factor in the development of the audiovisual sector in terms of providing financial subsidies, funding technical education, promoting audiovisual productions, and fostering professional associations. In that regard the foundation of new institutions that promote and support the Galician audiovisual sector has been significant. The creation of schools of cinema and audiovisual arts and film archive centers in Galicia have also proved instrumental in the training of a new generation of audiovisual professionals and technical, artistic, and creative crews, as well as in the preservation and dissemination of knowledge about Galician audiovisual culture. The official Escola de Imaxe e Son (EIS), the first professional film school in Galicia, and the Centro Galego de Artes da Imaxe (CGAI), formed from the ashes of the defunct Arquivo da Imaxe, were both established in A Coruña in 1991.[15] While both centers opened their doors after Manuel Fraga took the presidency of the Xunta de Galicia in 1990, they were in actuality projects already planned and approved by the former tripartite socialist–nationalist coalition government in power in the late 1980s.

Public organizations and private associations related to film production in Galicia have also formed, representing the interests of the community working in the audiovisual sector. These include APAG ("Asociación de Profesionais do Audiovisual Galego," 1983) and AGAPI ("Asociación Galega de Produtoras Independentes," 1994).[16] In 2003 AGAPI formed the "Clúster

increase in volume. For a summary of the expansion of the audiovisual sector see the chapter "Audiovisual galego, as cifras," in the online dossier "O Audiovisual agora. Pintan Ouros" from the Galician web portal Vieiros. The most recent official update from 2011 is available from the Xunta de Galicia website "As cifras da industria cultural galega."

15 Other audiovisual schools, private and public, have appeared in more recent years throughout Galicia. Aside from the EIS, new audiovisual training schools include O Raio Verde (Santiago) and the Escola de Imaxe e Son, in Vigo and Ourense, as well as the private Escola Superior de Cinematografía (Vigo). The three public universities in Galicia have also started offering the *diplomatura* in Audiovisual Communication, with a specialization in Film Direction and Screenwriting (Santiago), Film Production (Vigo), and 3D and Multimedia (A Coruña).

16 A new alternative association was created, seceding from AGAPI, the AEGA ("Asociación de Empresas Galegas do Audiovisual," 2001), encompassing the major media and communication groups of Galicia. Artists and creators have also formed

do Audiovisual Galego," an organization that encompasses a group of Galician companies from different sectors—film production, consulting, finance, mass media, and communications—to support the audiovisual field. This initiative was a conscious effort to counteract the tradition of *minifundio* individualism—in this as in other sectors of Galician society— and to become a more competitive industry in a globalized world. Also recently created are the "Galicia Film Commission," which promotes and facilitates film production in Galicia at the national and international level, and the Academia Galega do Audiovisual, established in 2002, which, among other activities, awards the annual Mestre Mateo prizes in the audiovisual sector. All these initiatives further attest to the growing recognition of the potential of the audiovisual sector in Galicia.

In the last couple of decades a great variety of audiovisual productions has been made in Galicia by Galician companies, with Galician men and women, in the form of feature films, documentaries, shorts, video art, video-clips, TV movies and series, multimedia, and animation, among others. By the first decade of the twenty-first century a certain degree of "normalization" was achieved in the sector, which appeared more in sync with other more established cinemas. As far as feature films are concerned, a remarkable diversity of genres and approaches was apparent, going beyond the traditional rural Galician setting—exploring new areas such as the urban thriller, fantasy, comedy, adventure, animation, documentary, and other hybrid forms.[17] This heterogeneity was also manifested in the diverse quality and style of the films produced, as well as their critical and public reception.[18] Current social issues and controversial topics—

professional associations, such as the "Asociación de Actores, Directores, e Técnicos de Escena de Galicia" (AADTEG, in 1985), the "Asociación Galega de Guionistas" (AGG, in 1997), and the "Asociación Galega de Directores e Realizadores" (CREA, in 2001).

17  *Rodado en Galicia* had a list of 176 films made in Galicia between 1916 and 2009. In the last 20 years examined some 50 films were made in Galicia, of which half could be considered Galician productions in a strict sense. For a list of films with the number of spectators and box office results between 1986 and 2003 see *Libro branco* (155). The most successful of the films made in Galicia during that period was *Los Lunes al sol* (2002), which made 7.5 million euros at the box office in Spain alone; and, among the Galician productions, *El bosque animado* (2001), which made almost two million euros, and much more internationally. *Mar adentro* (2004) is the highest-grossing film ever made in Galicia, making 38 million dollars at the box office worldwide (boxofficemojo.com).

18  In a poll taken in 2001 among critics and historians of Galician cinema by the CGAI, the best Galician films of the previous decade were judged to be *Sé quien eres, Fisterra, Arde Amor, Martes de Carnaval, El baile de las ánimas*, and *La lengua*

such as illegal migrant workers (*Ilegal*, 2003), drug trafficking (*Entre bateas*, 2002), unemployment (*Los lunes al sol*, 2002), contemporary youth culture (*O ano da carracha*, 2004), political violence and historical memory (*Sé quién eres*, 2000; *El lápiz del carpintero*, 2002), migration (*Un franco, 14 pesetas*, 2006), ecology and sustainability (*Pradolongo*, 2008), and, more recently, the effects of the economic crisis and the real estate bubble burst (*Somos xente honrada*, 2013; *Os fenónemos*, 2014) and the continuing recovery of repressed historical memories (*Lobos sucios*, 2016)—were commonly explored in mainstream films. This diversification can also be attested in the continued diversification of genres and film styles: urban thrillers (*Lena*, 2001; *O descoñecido*, 2015), horror/gothic films (*13 badaladas*, 2002; *La promesa*, 2004; *O Apóstolo*, 2012), Dogme 95-style films (*Era outra vez*, 2000); *Dias de voda*, 2002; *El desenlace*, 2005), documentaries (*Un bosque de música*, 2003; *Santa Liberdade*, 2004), surrealist comedies (*Crebinsky*, 2011), and award-winning animated features such as *El bosque animado* (2001), *De profundis* (2006), and *Arrugas* (2011).

Other encouraging developments were the "discovery" and recognition represented by Galician cinema's participating in film festivals and receiving awards. This has been particularly the case in the area of animation, such as Ángel de la Cruz and Manolo Gómez's *El bosque animado*, winner of two Goya Awards in 2001 and released in some 50 countries, or *Pérez, el ratoncito de tus sueños* ("The Hairy Tooth Fairy"), the biggest domestic box-office success in Spain in 2007 (for more on Galician animation see Chapter 6). Also noteworthy are the established careers of a generation of Galician audiovisual creators who started their careers in the 1980s and 1990s, such as Antón Reixa, Xavier Villaverde, Patricia Ferreira, Xavier Bermúdez,

---

*de las mariposas* (*Libro branco* 156), all vastly different in terms of genre, location, historical setting, look, and inspiration, and all of them except *Arde amor* directed by Madrid-based directors. The only one that was a box-office success was *La lengua de las mariposas*, which also did very well on the international art film circuit. How much has changed since then in the consolidation of Galician cinema, and how rapidly, can be measured by the different titles that would make the list only a decade later. An informal online poll conducted in 2012 ranked the best Galician films in the following order (first ten): *Arrugas, Celda 212, O bosque animado, Pradolongo, Mar adentro, O lapis do carpinteiro, Vilamor, 18 comidas, Sempre Xonxa*, and *O ano da carracha* ("A mellor película galega!"). The new ranking does not include any of the titles or directors in the first list, and almost all of them could be categorized as "Galician films" with the exception of *Celda 212* and *Mar adentro*. As a reflection of the popular vote, the titles are more or less in line with their success at the box office and general circulation. *Sempre Xonxa* is the only one that could not be considered a box-office hit by normal standards, but it is regularly shown on TVG and therefore well known to Galician spectators. See also Chapter 7, note 7.

Jorge Coira, and Héctor Carré. Juan Pinzás is the only director in Spain with three films carrying the official Dogme 95 seal of approval from Lars von Trier, although their uneven aesthetic quality has been questioned by some (Prout). We should note the acclaimed trajectory of Galician actors such as Uxía Blanco, Manuel Manquiña, Nancho Novo, Chete Lera, Tristán Ulloa, and Martiño Rivas—who have all worked in Galician and Spanish film productions—and the special case of Luis Tosar, winner of three Goyas and six Mestre Mateo awards, who has made frequent appearances in international films such as Michael Mann's *Miami Vice* and Jim Jarmusch's *The Limits of Control*. Likewise, Galician animators have been hired to work in US studios, such as graphic artist Miguelanxo Prado, who was appointed as art director for the animated television series *Men in Black* by Steven Spielberg. Also encouraging for Galician cinema was the arrival in the 2000s of filmmakers such as Jorge Coira and Ignacio Vilar, who have produced commercially successful films that have been able to connect with young Galicians (*O ano da carracha*, *Pradolongo*) and older audiences (*18 comidas*, *A esmorga*), thus underlining the potential of cinema in Galicia. These developments seem to have paved the way for the exciting emergence of a new generation of filmmakers in the last decade, which will be discussed in Chapter 7.

The combination of financial incentives provided by the Xunta de Galicia in the form of subsidies and the gradual formation of an industrial infrastructure with capable technical crews and support companies, and at lower costs, made Galicia's natural scenery an attractive location for many Spanish and even international films, with Galician financial, technical, and artistic participation. Some of the better-known film productions made in Galicia by well-known Spanish directors include José Luis Cuerda's *La lengua de la mariposas*, *Los girasoles ciegos* and *Todo es silencio*, Fernando León de Aranoa's *Los lunes al sol*, Alejandro Amenábar's *Mar adentro*, Gracia Querejeta's *Cuando vuelvas a mi lado*, Isabel Coixet's *Los que aman*; films by foreign directors include Emilio Estevez's *The Way*, Adolfo Aristarain's *La ley de la frontera*, Bent Hamer's *Water Easy Reach*, Stuart Gordon's *Dagon*, and Roman Polanski's *Death and the Maiden*.[19]

All these developments have had the surprising result that in 2002 Galicia, of all the autonomous communities in Spain, showed the third greatest expansion and volume of its audiovisual sector (*Libro branco* 163).

---

19 Aside from the attraction of the Galician settings, the promotion done by Galician film commissions and the positive quality–price ratio offered by Galician audiovisual companies are also major reasons why so many Spanish films have been shot in Galicia in recent years.

These all seem like positive signs of progress, but some relativism is required. In essence, Galician cinema has some advantages going for it: a developing infrastructure in its diverse components—institutional, industrial, economic, educational—although uneven and still inadequate in some areas; a slow but regular and varied stream of films, especially since the mid-1990s, with increasing budgets and cinematographic values; the growing public acceptance of Galician audiovisual products, especially through TVG; the emergence of a new generation of alternative cineastes; and the recent "discovery" of Galicia by film audiences and film companies beyond Galicia's borders. This is a new paradigm beginning to be explored in the twenty-first century, which indicates the progressive deperipheralization of Galician cinema.[20]

## Utopian Visions:
## Not All that Glitters is Gold

On the other side of the coin, there are certainly significant shortcomings in the field of Galician audiovisual and cinema arts that cannot be overlooked, and are cause for some concern. These constrictions are the result of particular political, economic, and sociocultural realities that affect in a similar manner other areas of Galician cultural production, which have been exacerbated by the onset of the global economic crisis. Many of these deficiencies are structural problems that are difficult to circumvent. The official report *Audiovisual Galego 2003* stated that the audiovisual sector in Galicia was characterized "por ter unha estrutura fragmentada e atomizada" ("by a fragmented and atomized structure") (*Libro branco* 18). This is a challenge that corresponds with what I call the Galician *minifundio cinema* infrastructure, a chronic atomization of the audiovisual industry sector that is parallel to the economic, geographic, and cultural *minifundismo* running deep through many areas of Galician society. The

---

20 In addition, the increased interest in Galician cinema on the part of academic researchers and specialists should be noted here. A growing bibliography of critical and historical works has made possible the recovery and conservation of Galician film history. A good number of online publications are now devoted to film studies in Galicia, such as the web platform *A cuarta parede*. In addition to the established film festivals of Ourense and Carballiño, a myriad of new film festivals have emerged in recent years, such as the Doc-Play International Documentary Festival in Tui, already in its 16th edition, the "Mostra de Cine Periférico" in A Coruña, the "Cineuropa" in Santiago, and the more radically *enxebre* ("culturally autochthonous") indie "Festival de Cans" in Porriño—the Galician *agroglamor* response to Cannes—and the "Festival Internacional de Cinema Rural Carlos Velo."

audiovisual industry in Galicia is composed mainly of a large number of small independent companies, often with insufficient financial resources and equipment to operate adequately in a stable and continued manner.[21] This situation has often resulted in a necessary reliance on other audiovisual institutions and complex co-production schemes, and alternative circuits. In 2003 226 companies were registered in the audiovisual sector in Galicia, of which 150 were dedicated to audiovisual production (*Libro branco* 15). In 2008, just before the world financial crisis, the number of audiovisual companies had reached 495, with some 300 devoted to production ("As cifras"). These may seem like very high numbers, but it must be noted that a considerable percentage of these companies were single-digit person operations established around a particular project. Furthermore, the total amount of business sales generated by production companies in the sector for the year 2001 was 51 million euros, which was equivalent to the average budget of one regular Hollywood studio movie (*Libro branco* 162).[22]

In the first years of the century before the world financial crisis there was a noticeable trend towards greater specialization and capital expansion by many of the audiovisual companies operating in Galicia. That situation, however, has not shown many signs of improvement as a result of the economic downturn. Although audiovisual company associations and clusters are steps in the right direction, the atomization of the sector and the relative lack of strong and stable companies, and difficulties in access to equipment and financial resources, make the task of creating audiovisual works professionally in Galicia still a rather challenging proposition. Successful projects are often carried out through the tenacity of creators, with minimal budgets and relying on self-production and other financial alternatives, such as crowdfunding.[23]

21 Significantly, two of the biggest production companies involved in Galician cinema in the last decades were Barcelona-based Filmax and Madrid-based Continental, both run by relocated Galician migrants, which points out the historical reality of the economic Galician diaspora. In addition, both of them have been on the verge of collapse as an after-effect of the economic downturn (see Chapter 6).

22 The average audiovisual production company in Galicia was composed of three members, with one owning almost 60% of the company, which made it a de facto one-person business. 79% of all audiovisual companies in Galicia were small businesses (less than 600.000 euros generated in business), 17.7% were medium-sized companies (between 600.000 and 3 million euros), and only 2.7% were large corporations (*Libro branco* 18, 47). According to more recent statistics, production sales generated 89 million euros in 2006 ("Cadro de mando do sector audiovisual galego"), and 98 million in 2008 ("As cifras").

23 Non-mainstream approaches to film production and alternative distribution practices have developed in Galicia in recent years as a result of the crisis, including

Another major challenge for film and audiovisual production in Galicia has been the excessive dependence on official subsidies, typically to producers rather than creators, and on commissioned works, which relates to other chronic patterns of Galician society, political *caciquismo* and economic paternalism, almost to the point of servitude. Galician film production is often put at the mercy of the arbitrariness of the selection committees, the changing official policies, and political parties in power. Galician filmmakers have resorted to a number of sources of finance for their productions, such as local governments and public and private television companies from Europe and Latin America. They have also turned to Spain's Ministry of Culture, the ICAA, or the European Union, or to the strictly one-off subsidies from the *Quinto Centenario* or the *Xacobeo* celebration agencies. In reality, however, the bulk of the subsidies come from two main sources: official subventions from the Xunta de Galicia's Consellería de Cultura and advance payments from TVG for television showing rights.[24] Excessive dependence on public funding from these two main sources only aggravates the *caciquismo* syndrome in Galician film production; another and no less undesirable result is that it has tended to promote conformity and conservative choices, both aesthetic and ideological, and has rarely fostered formal experimentation or dissidence on the part of the film directors.[25] Hence the conspicuous absence of overtly political themes in Galician feature films, which constitute almost a taboo subject.[26] In a similar vein, the scarcity of films out of the mainstream

crowdfunding (*O Apóstolo*) and crowdticketing (*Encallados*), and the creation of other circuits, such as schools, town halls, and town main squares (*Pradolongo*). These non-mainstream practices are particularly common in the *Novo Cinema Galego*, which is discussed in Chapter 7.

24  As much as 50% of the income generated by audiovisual production companies in Galicia usually comes from TVG, in several cases reaching practically 100% (*Libro branco* 18–19).

25  A welcome departure from this trend would be the alternative productions of the New Galician Cinema, as discussed in Chapter 7.

26  Low budget shorts and documentaries have been the principal means for politically challenging audiovisual productions, with many focused on ecological concerns, such as Marcos Nine's *Carcamáns* (2003), Ángel Peláez's *Las voces del Prestige* (2005), and Alfonso Zarauza's *Encallados* (2013), on the aftermath of the *Prestige* oil spill; Xabier Blanco and Luís Montenegro's *Cason 1987* (2008), on the toxic spill from the *Cason* on Costa da Morte, Xosé Bocixa's *As encrobas a ceo aberto* (2007) on Franco-era expropriation of Galician farmlands for coal extraction; and Susana Rey's experimental mock-documentary *Cousas do Kulechov* (2007), an original meta-exploration about the montage of wars in the media, based on everyday images of Galician life.

defying gender or sexual normativity is notable.[27] For example, the early treatment of homosexual characters in Juan Pinzás's trilogy (*Era outra vez*, *Días de voda* and *El desenlace*) is stereotypical and sensationalist, and the discourse on sexual orientation in *O ano da carracha* is conventional and seems ultimately reactionary.[28] In this light, the result of the old debate between a purist cinema and a cinema of possibility reveals the negative consequences of excessive accommodation to the socioeconomic realities of the status quo and the cultural mainstream.[29]

The paternalism of official institutions can also manifest its influence in perverted ways. Thus, in spite of the often-stated preference in official subsidy guidelines for films to be shot in Galician, this has often not been implemented by the institutions or exercised by the filmmakers. For the purpose of obtaining official subventions and selling broadcasting rights to TVG or making co-productions with TVG, it was enough for films to have a dual-language track, in Galician and Spanish, which allows its commercialization in both languages, and its broadcasting on TVG in Galician. In reality, until a few years ago only a limited number of long feature fiction films were originally shot in Galician (*Sempre Xonxa*, *Urxa*, *A metade da vida*, *Pradolongo*, and Pinzás's first two Dogme 95 films come to mind). The majority, however, relied on the conventional practice of dubbing into Galician in postproduction (endorsed by TVG) for the sake of expedience and economic viability beyond Galicia. Casts were often headed by recognizable non-Galician Spanish actors (Carmen Maura, Fernando Guillén, Ángela Molina, Jorge Sanz, and so on), who are dubbed by Galician actors—Javier Bardem is unusual, having learned Galician for parts of his role in *Mar*

27  Two provocative exceptions deal with the taboo topic of incest: Xavier Bermúdez's *León y Olvido* (2004), whose protagonists are a young woman who defies and contests traditional gender roles and her mentally disabled brother; and the Galician–Catalan co-produced TV film *Más que hermanos* (Dir. Ramón Costafreda, 2005), about the alternative family born out of the incestuous relationship of a brother with his sister, and their common daughter, based on real facts. It is not clear, however, to what extent these films reinforce the perception of deep Galicia's backwardness.

28  One of the segments of Jorge Coira's film *18 comidas* (2010) contains a dramatic coming-out scene, albeit with the histrionics of TV drama. *El sexo de los ángeles* (2012), by Xavier Villaverde, offers an interesting exploration of pan-sexuality through the love triangle formed between two men and a woman, while Ignacio Vilar's *A esmorga* examines repressed homoeroticism in the post-war context. On the fringes of the industry, working from London, Peque Varela directed the acclaimed *1997* (2007), a short animation feature about gender non-conformity based on her own life, which is analysed in Chapter 7.

29  For an extended analysis of the complex entangle of protectionist measures and the politics of official subsidies for audiovisual production in Galicia, see Sempere.

*adentro*.[30] As a result, many of the films dubbed in Galician typically sound affected, artificial, unrealistic, and aesthetically deficient. A number of problems surface: the noticeable traces of translation, the overpowering of the vocal track over the background sound, the recourse to the same limited group of actors' voices, and the prosody and vocal patterning inherited from Spanish.[31] While it could be argued that at least this dubbing practice effectively assists in the linguistic normalization of Galician, in fact it promotes an excessive conformity to a Galician standard that is the product of TVG's linguistic department, rather than Galician social reality and customs (with a varied linguistic map, subregional and social class varieties, linguistic code-switching, and chronic diglossia).[32] While the dubbing of foreign language films is an accepted practice in the Spanish film market, rather than the use of subtitles, as in other countries, it is a highly questionable practice on aesthetic and intellectual grounds, and indeed is another legacy of Francoism's cultural and ideological manipulation.[33] In that sense, it is distressing to see that Galician audiovisual practices, and TVG in particular, have tended to follow the hegemonic Spanish model. And we could even ask ourselves: If the practice of dubbing remains the dominant one in Spain and Galicia, why are Galician films not shot in Galician and then dubbed into Spanish or other languages in postproduction?[34]

30 Similarly, the Basque actor Karra Elejalde also learnt Galician for his role in *A esmorga*, but it was a different situation, as it was not a "film made in Galicia," but made from Galicia and shot entirely in Galician.

31 This situation is common to much of TVG programming. A remarkable breakthrough was the hugely popular series *Mareas vivas* (1998–2002), directed by Antón Reixa, which actually highlighted popular Galician dialectal varieties such as *seseo* and *gheada*. As a result of this, new Galician TV series have been more attuned to the social realities of Galician language.

32 Galician director Raúl Veiga (*A metade da vida*, 1994; *Arde amor*, 1999) has insisted on the need for Galician films to address these issues more critically, by incorporating the linguistic conflicts into the film narrative. For an overview of the linguistic issues of Galician audiovisual production, see his essay "A lingua do noso audiovisual."

33 The obligatory dubbing into Castilian of all films in other languages under Franco's dictatorship—intended as a form of ideological control and censorship of foreign films under the guise of the defense of the Spanish language—forced the accommodation of Spanish audiences to the practice of dubbing rather than subtitles.

34 The dubbing situation also points to the lack of a coherent vision from the Xunta de Galicia, or of consistent official policies regarding the audiovisual arts, which are highly conditioned by political changes. This is perhaps most notable in the great ideological divorce between TVG's original impulse at its foundation and the official leaders who were appointed by the conservative Partido Popular,

A final but no less serious challenge to Galician cinema is the lack of a supportive system of distribution and exhibition, which remains largely in the hands of subsidiaries of transnational US companies. This is a chronic problem that Galician cinema shares with Spanish cinema, where many national films never make it to the theater screen, and in general terms with all cinemas, whose distribution system is controlled by the de facto Hollywood monopoly. The situation is, however, particularly acute in a minority (or double minority) cinema such as Galician, in the periphery of the periphery. As a result, relatively few Galician films make it to the commercial circuits at large, aside from their showings on TVG or alternative circuits.

The market limitations of a minority cinema within a minority national film industry create a *Catch-22* situation that has no easy single-approach solution. With some significant exceptions, Spanish distributors, critics, and the officials in control of film subsidies simply have not shown a great deal of interest in Galician films, which makes their access to wide audiences complicated. Perhaps this is a trend that can be reversed, and the emergence of the New Galician Cinema on the global arena is encouraging. But for all the talk about a "boom," the audiovisual sector in Galicia is still developing, and the situation of Galician cinema is still far from "normalized." Perhaps, on the day that one can go to a video store or film library—brick and mortar or more likely virtual—and browse the Galician cinema section, next to other national, or perhaps postnational, cinemas, it will feel finally "normalized." Until then, the vision of Galician cinema will likely remain partially utopian.

in power with Manuel Fraga between 1990 and 2005 (and again with Alberto Núñez Feijóo since 2009), which has been sharply criticized by EIS director Manuel González (Acuña 98). As a result, TVG has largely developed as a populist entity with an institutionalized folkloric view of Galician culture, which has earned it the ironic popular name of "Telegaita" ("Bagpipe TV").

# CHAPTER SIX

# The Galician Magic Kingdom: Nation and Animation from the Glocal Forest

## The Enchanted Forest

Let us imagine an enchanted forest of fables, where plants, trees, and animals can speak, feel, and sing; a remote and lush magical forest where imagination can roam free. Galician literature since Romanticism has imagined and re-imagined this fantastic magical forest: from Rosalía de Castro and Eduardo Pondal in the nineteenth-century *Rexurdimento* Galician revival to Álvaro Cunqueiro and Wenceslao Fernández Flórez in the post-Civil War period to Manuel Rivas and Miguelanxo Prado in our day: all have inhabited this forest of the poetic imagination, redoubt of pan-Celtic romanticism or peripheral magical realism, that identifies this natural enchanted forest precisely with Galicia.

In this magical and timeless fable, one good day the peace and quiet of the forest is altered with the appearance of a new kind of tree, a dry tall tree with long thin branches and no leaves, which is soon followed by many others of the same kind. These new trees could transmit voices very far from the woods and communicate with other faraway lands. This audio/visual image representing the arrival of the first telephone post to the forest symbolizes the late arrival of modernity to Galicia, with new technologies and means of communication, a complex reality reflecting its inescapable transformation by the forces of modernity and the possibilities of progress and improved living conditions. But this image also symbolizes the anxieties produced about the destruction of its natural habitat and its cultural traditions, including the most basic form of communication, language, and the uncertainties about the future of the forest that is Galicia in this new historical era.

This narrative is the main story line of the Galician animation feature *El bosque animado* (The Living Forest, 2001), widely considered as the beginning of the animation cinema boom in Galicia. As a self-reflexive metaphor, it seems to me a suggestive starting point from where to speak about the animated digital forest that has been growing in Galicia in the last decades. Immersed in an environment of global economic and cultural trends and new technological developments, this remote forest away from the center aims to embrace modernity while keeping its roots firmly planted on Galician soil. It is not mere coincidence that *El bosque animado*, a free adaptation of the novel of the same name by Wenceslao Fernández Flórez, was precisely the first digital animation feature film made in Galicia; it was followed later by its sequel, *El espíritu del bosque* (Spirit of the Forest, 2008), and both had notable success internationally, putting Galicia on the global map of audiovisual animation production.

## From the Periphery to the Leading Edge

One of the areas in which the emerging audiovisual sector in Galicia has been prominent in recent years has been in digital animation and multimedia creation. The two main animation studios specializing in feature films in Spain—Dygra and Bren Entertainment, responsible for some of the most awarded and biggest box-office animation films made in Spain—were originally established in Galicia in the late 1990s. They managed to make a dent in the global audiovisual market, being in the lead of 3D animation and CGI graphics generated with digital processes in Europe.

In the article published in *Variety* in 2004, John Hopewell described for an international audience the transformation taking place in the contemporary audiovisual field in Galicia, which was starting to make waves internationally. The title of the article nearly said it all: "Hit and Myth in the Deep North. Forward-looking Rural Area Transforming into TV and Film Heavyweight." In an ironic reversal of conventional wisdom, the title suggests the wave of change and innovation that Galicia has experienced in recent years, and its impact in the audiovisual sector: thus the proverbial "hit and miss" is replaced by "hit and myth," signaling the entrance into the global arena of a culture rich in popular mythologies, and that rural peripheral areas away from the center are not necessarily backward-looking anymore. The question remains, however, whether the transformation into a "heavyweight" referenced in the article is an accomplishment already achieved or still a work in progress, given the economic downturn of the last few years and its local effects in the financial difficulties of Galician production companies.

But how can we explain this apparent explosion of high technology and specialized creators and technicians in a peripheral zone such as Galicia, with strong rural roots, traditionally behind in technology (with some exceptions), and until now not very competitive in the export of its cultural products? The situation of Galicia could be compared to some extent with the remarkable technological take-off in another of the Galician sister cultures of the European periphery, the "Celtic tiger" of Ireland, which for Galicia has often functioned as a cultural and political mirror, with similar historical and socio-cultural conditions. The parallels would point to an economic and industrial reconversion based principally on the utilization of new technologies and the adaptation of its traditional models to the transnational trends of globalization and economic neoliberalism. As in other sectors of the economy, however, in both the Irish and Galician cases the boom has been followed by a crisis, which still lingers and makes the future at least uncertain.

In the last couple of decades an official discourse about the audiovisual sector has emerged in Galicia, which has been favored by the Galician industry, the local media, and political institutions. It is a discourse firmly based on the foundational role of audiovisual technology and development and their possibilities for generating a sustainable cultural industry while projecting a modernized image of Galicia to the outside world. This discourse emphasizes the invigoration of the sector, shaped by the favorable legislation of the Xunta de Galicia, the strategic utilization of new digital technologies involved in the processes of information and communication, the training of creative and technical talent in the use of innovative technologies, and the creation of new products of high added value that can compete successfully in the global market. In practical terms, this would translate as the encouragement of certain practices of *glocalization*, adapting local subjects, methods, and strategies to new stages, models, and languages marked by global trends in an effort to create culturally hybrid and compatible products from a post-peripheral perspective, which can function across national/cultural borders. However, the recent economic crisis has revealed the limits of this model, as the cash-strapped Xunta has itself not kept its financial commitments to local production companies, credit has not been forthcoming from banking institutions, competition for distribution has become even more fierce, and the bigger companies with the largest overheads have struggled to survive, as is the case with Dygra and Bren.

From a historical point of view, the surge in audiovisual animation in Galicia could be explained by a series of confluences that are, directly and indirectly, related to the two key events that have come to reconfigure the traditional concepts of nation and culture in the last 30 years in Galicia: one at the level of the Spanish nation state (the autonomous decentralization process started with the Transition) and another at the transnational level (the effects of globalization in the local environments), which are reconfigured as a new cultural map that we could call postnational.

On the one hand, we encounter the development in Galicia of an emerging audiovisual industry since the 1980s and 1990s, albeit with all the limitations of a deeply atomized cultural economy with a chronically weak infrastructure. This surge, as we have seen, was directly related to the official establishment of the Xunta de Galicia autonomous government and the creation of the official TVG channel, which generated a great need for all types of Galician audiovisual products. In order to fill this void, new public and private audiovisual schools were established in Galicia, which trained a new generation of young professionals. In addition, this fertile ground was strengthened with the creation of a network of Galician professional groups related to the audiovisual sector, and new local production companies and an institutional support program with important subsidies to the Galician audiovisual industry (see Chapters 4 and 5). To this we can add the entrepreneurial spirit of some local small and medium-size companies that decided to invest in the sector with a vision of the possibilities opening up for commercialization in transnational markets.

All of this, however, would have been insufficient without the remarkable technological take-off and acceleration of global trends that introduced substantial changes in the modes of production and enabled the development of the sector. The engines of economic globalization that have impelled the transnational mobility of human and capital flows, also facilitated the co-optation of highly specialized international professionals, as well as the participation and experience of local specialists in foreign projects (although with a considerable brain drain effect as well). The reality of the globalized market opened the doors to audiovisual co-productions and the development in parallel of joint projects, often working virtually across the planet, physically separated by long distances and different time zones. And, indeed, the technological revolution of digital information and communication was able to increase productivity and allowed the undertaking of labor-intensive projects that before were simply not feasible economically. In the field of animation in particular, the development of new digital tools was especially important, for they helped to simplify processes and routines significantly, and to unify finished styles, reducing costs and shortening production times. The introduction of these new digital technologies also enabled the displacement of the modes of production, favoring access to new resources that were previously inaccessible for small independent producers. This has substantially decreased production costs and has allowed for more fluid, creative collaborations between technicians and creators from different, and at times very distant, workplaces.

Moreover, the field of animation has certain unique characteristics that would seem to make its development particularly attractive for peripherally located audiovisual companies, since it levels off two of the biggest stumbling blocks for the distribution of their products internationally. On one hand, it facilitates its commercialization overseas, since animation films are nearly always necessarily dubbed by real actors, which avoids the negative commercial stigma of foreign language cinema with subtitles of conventional feature films; and, on the other hand, it fills the absence of a *film star* recognized internationally, a necessary condition for mainstream commercial releases which is normally out of reach for Galician productions. The conjunction of all these factors helps to explain the reasons for the development of the animation audiovisual sector in Galicia and its international impact.

In spite of all these developments, the real advancements in the field need to be closely examined and put into context, with all their lights and shadows. The area of animation began to develop in Galicia in the 1990s, particularly in relation to television programming for children and teenagers by TVG (such as the hugely successful program *Xabarín Club* or Miguelanxo Prado's animation series *Os vixiantes do camiño*, the first Galician animated TV series), as well as video clips of musical groups for a young audience ("Carmiña Vacaloura" from Maestro Reverendo) and some film shorts for the general public. It is precisely in the late 1990s that the adventure of animated feature films begins properly with Dygra, a small independent multimedia company established in A Coruña. Its example is soon followed by Bren Entertainment, a company based in Santiago de Compostela and backed by the conglomerate of Filmax Entertainment companies (video, TV, film production, distribution, and exhibition), headed by the Galician businessman Julio Fernández. At the same time, other animation studios on a lesser scale begin to appear with alternative animation projects.

As we will see below through an analysis of the trajectory of both studios and of the feature films produced for young audiences, the technological reconversion of the cultural industry in areas of great creativity but limited resources, as seen in Galicia, have allowed the creation of productions of relatively high quality and low cost that could be competitive internationally, or at least find adequate niches in the global market. The shortcomings, as in other areas of the audiovisual sector in Galicia, are the lack of capitalization and a solid industrial infrastructure, a dependence on contracts and subsidies from official institutions (mainly TVG and the Xunta de Galicia), and, as is the case with other peripheral cinemas, limited access to the wide distribution circuits controlled by the major Hollywood studios. These limitations also affect the reliance on traditional cultural representations of Galicianess that tend to tend to focus on a rural, mystic, and timeless Galicia, quite often at the expense of the modern and urban side of Galicia, or the co-option of Galicianess into Spanishness.

## Dygra:
## Deep-rooted in the Land, a Digital Forest for the World

Dygra Films, which officially closed its operations in 2012 after a period of financial struggle following the global economic crisis of 2008, was an independent animation studio which specialized in 3D films with Galician roots and landscapes, rewriting the local for the global. From its beginnings in 1987, Dygra established itself as a high-tech company dedicated to audiovisual communication and multimedia. In 1997 it entered the field of 3D animation, spending the following four years engaged in the production of its first feature animation film, *El bosque animado* (dir. Ángel de la Cruz and Manolo Gómez), a new free adaptation of Fernández Flórez's novel of the same title, originally published in 1943, which had been previously taken to the big screen on three occasions.[1] A relatively low-budget production of only 750 million pesetas (4.5 million euros), the film was screened in 2001 with considerable public and critical success, and is considered a milestone for animation in Galicia and Spain, being the first European film completely made in the new 3D system and created integrally in digital form in CGI, the same technology employed in the animated films *Toy Story* or *Bugs*, produced by the major US animation studios.

*El bosque* represents an ambitious challenge, a Galician-focused local production combining a pioneering artisan spirit and the use of innovative technology, with aspirations of quality and distinctiveness so as to compete within the international markets practically monopolized by the US animation industry (Disney, Pixar, and DreamWorks). The film is in this sense a *glocal* production, rooted in a specific local context but in a permanent process of hybridization with globalized forms, technologies, and markets. The production process of *El bosque* was highly singular and innovative in multiple aspects. The directors worked with a modest budget, much lower than the average costs of the super productions made by US studios, for which reason they had to devise appropriate strategies vis-à-vis the local reality. Part of the success of their work model consisted in the innovative

---

1 *Afan-Evu/El bosque maldito* (Dir. José Neches, 1945); *Fendestestas* (Dir. Antonio F. Simón, 1975); *El bosque animado* (Dir. José Luis Cuerda, 1987).

use of technology.[2] The technical characteristics of the 3D animation processes used in *El bosque* were impressive, particularly for an independent low-budget production, where the extensive use of leading-edge technology is essential.[3] Dygra's association with the new Master's program in Communication and Digital Creation of the Universidade da Coruña was also innovative and advantageous, with the incorporation of student interns and postgraduates in the production of the film. In fact, nearly all the creators and technicians involved in the film, a team of several hundred people including sketchers, animators, computer graphic artists, and programmers, had been trained in Galicia.

A significant distinguishing trait of Dygra is that all the basic elements of the production have their roots in Galicia. In this case, all the work was carried out in their own studios in A Coruña, from the initial designs to the animation and postproduction processes, in contrast to other production companies such as Bren/Filmax, which specialize in certain creative aspects and outsource other areas of production to distant companies. Likewise, the large majority of creators, from the documentation team to the artistic direction and production teams, were Galician. This characteristic explains the special attention that the production company gives to local Galician details. For example, the pre-production of *El bosque* entailed a long and exhaustive process of visual documentation of the 1920s and 1930s in Galicia, based on magazines, photographs, and postcards of the era, which was employed in the creation of hundreds of period objects and decorative elements which appear in the film. In addition, an extensive process of documentation to record Galician nature was based on botany books, documentaries, and other visual sources; and for the exterior localizations repeated trips were made to the Galician local forests, such as the *Fraga de Eume*, to capture the natural settings and the different lights during the day

2 Several sets of powerful personal computers were configured, working from six different places and interconnected by an intranet system designed specifically for them by Sun; and the studio technicians developed many of their own tools including up to 50 different applications, such as management tools, protocols of information exchange for the intranet and Internet, and special programs to modulate the subtle changes of light and color in the Galician forest. Similarly, the animation of the river was created with the Spanish program Real Flow and the open code software program Maya, in which many modifications were introduced to make them suitable for the specific needs of the production (Pérez de Eulate).

3 As an example, 80 different types of Galician plants and trees appear in the film, with 15,000 leaves for each tree and six layers of texturing, and more than half a million pixels used for a regular forest scene. Some of the main characters have up to 12 layers of texturing and each head of hair comprises between half a million and two and a half million individual hairs.

and through the seasons of the year. But, at the same time, an important part of the visual inspiration was based on the nineteenth-century classic fairytale iconography created by Arthur Rackham, Gustave Doré, and Gustaff Tenggrem, to recreate the ambience of the Nordic and Celtic mythical tales and of the central European Atlantic forests, which points to the hybrid and local character of the production.[4] The evocation of the natural and fantastic world of Galician myths and legends, with evident parallels in the Nordic and Celtic European mythology, as in the case of the pan-Celtic enchanted forest, serves as a unifying element appropriate for an animation product with international ambitions.

Unlike the well-known previous adaptation of the novel directed by José Luis Cuerda, which centered mainly on the gallery of human characters and their relations, Cruz and Gómez opt for focusing on the fantastic and magical aspects of the novel, intending to animate "*la otra historia que quedó sin contar,*" ("the other story that remained untold") (Cruz, 23). The film by Cruz and Gómez thus rescues the most fantastic part of Fernández Flórez's book, the wondrous magical forest, animated by plants and trees with human characteristics, which had been considered as an ideal text for animation since its publication in 1943.[5]

The film by Cruz and Gómez, which is directed mainly to a family audience, capable of attracting parents and captivating children and youth, is an ecological fable. The central points of the film are the animals and the plants of the Galician forest and their survival, not the human characters, who represent a constant threat to their habitat and are on a secondary plane. The plot centers on the hunting of moles by humans for experimentation and for the value of their coats, which encounters resistance from an army of insects self-called "el pueblo pardo" ("the brown people"), and the vociferous protests by the resonant trees of the *fraga* (ancient Galician forest of native flora and fauna), which act as the totemic symbolic witnesses of the nation. The values of solidarity, community building, collective struggle, and ecology are prevalent in the film. It is important to recall here that the words of the Galician national anthem were taken from Eduardo Pondal's poetry book "Queixume dos pinos" (the lament of the pine trees), allegorizing the rebirth/reawakening of the nation with the regeneration of the forest, since the idea of the Galician nation was symbolized in the natural land. The forest acts, then, as an affirmation of cultural identity

---

4 Nogueira (2001) also highlights the visual references in this film to many cinema classics, from *Citizen Kane* to *A Phantom Menace*.

5 In fact, Walt Disney was interested in producing the adaptation of the novel as an animation feature, but an agreement was never reached before Fernández Flórez's and Disney's deaths.

(together with the landscape, the architecture, the music, and other local cultural references). The ecological message of the film is simple, direct, and appropriate: the future of the forest needs to be saved from human depredation. This message entails evident indirect references to the actual Galician social reality and the deterioration of its landscapes—in recent years plagued by bushfires, deforestation, reforestation with non-indigenous trees, neglect, land speculation, and the negative consequences of territorial reorganization plans and ordinances.

As is normally the case in films of this type directed at a general family audience, with the aim of reaching an audience predominantly composed of children, but which could potentially appeal to youth and adult audiences as well, there are different levels on which the film can be appreciated. The pretty and innocent moles appear as adorable little white furry animals, which are meant to seduce a younger audience; the flies Hu Hu and Ho Ho, who speak in current street slang, represent the rebellious hip side, which might be attractive to a general teenager audience; meanwhile, cultural references, ecological consciousness, and the symbolic capital of the literary adaptation would attract the adult audience. For example, one of the details that surely did not escape the adult audience was the similarity of the facial features of the telegraph post—with hieratic gestures and arrogant, pompous, and authoritarian in nature—which symbolizes utilitarian economics and the material deforestation of the forests, to the then President of the Xunta de Galicia, Manuel Fraga, from the conservative PP (although ironically the directors had made him out to resemble Galician writer and Nobel prize winner Camilo José Cela, who had somewhat similar personal attributes and political inclinations).[6] On another level, the transatlantic cultural subtext of the Galician migration to American lands, with the actual return to Galicia of the descendants of the migrants, also appears to be reflected in the story of the mouse *Piorno*, a happy and funny migrant who speaks Galician with a Cuban accent, opening in the film an Atlantic perspective on Galician modern history and culture that is unfortunately lost in translation.

6 For more on the intertextual allusions in the movie, see Nogueira (2001). The film makes many explicit intertextual references, through both visual and audio cues, to well-known international films, such as *Citizen Cane*, *Superman*, *Apocalypse Now*, and Sergio Leone's spaghetti westerns. More subtly, there are local references to the old *gallegada* films, such as *Sabela de Cambados*, and it is tempting to see a veiled reference to *Raza* in the setting of the traditional Galician *pazo* (country manor) and the caricatured representation of the authoritarian family of the violent hunter and the fashion-obsessed tyrannical wife as satirical allusions to Francisco Franco and Carmen Polo.

Figure 16   Promotional image from *El bosque animado* (2001), Dygra. Telephone pole bearing a striking resemblance to both Camilo José Cela and Manuel Fraga, with a Galician country *pazo* in the background.

The film presents a straightforward defense of the values of ecology and solidarity against the violence caused by humans and the blindness of materialist interests. This is a theme with wide resonance in the destructured contemporary Galicia, characterized by chaotic development, rural abandonment, and neglect that sees, as its forests are burnt, oil tankers sunk, and waters polluted, the irreparable cannibalization of the land by its inhabitants and the incapacity of its government to defend the ecosystem. "Qué el hombre te ignore," ("May the men ignore you"), the repeated greeting of solidarity between the animals and trees in the film, basically turns itself into a form of cultural resistance. *El bosque animado* is thus a film with solid roots in the land and nature, Galician in its origin and content, but with clear international ambitions that could appeal to the interest and sensitivity of wider audiences. As director Manolo Gómez stated:

> queremos vender Galicia y España a través de nuestra belleza natural, cultura y forma de ser y sentir. Pretendemos aportar nuestro granito

de arena y sensibilizar al público en la conservación de la naturaleza. El esfuerzo se hace extensivo a la vida salvaje autóctona más cercana a nuestro hábitat, asociando este aprecio hacia cualquier forma de vida. (Cebrián)

we want to sell Galicia and Spain by means of our natural beauty, our culture and our way of being and feeling. We aim to contribute a grain of sand to increase the audience's concern for the preservation of nature. This effort is extended to the native wild life closest to our habitat, associating this appreciation to any form of life.

Another aspect of *El bosque animado* that reinforces the connection with the local, while opening it to the global, is the use of music in the soundtrack. From the beginning, the orchestral score by Arturo Kless is clearly inscribed in the musical tradition of Galician pan-Celtic folk, which is superimposed on the lush Galician landscapes, creating a strong audio/visual marker of cultural/natural pan-Celticism. The collaboration of Galician singer Luz Casal, who composed and sang the two main songs of the film (for which she won the Goya Award in 2011), is also very significant. Luz is a very well-known singer from A Coruña with a long career behind her, who has achieved great international recognition, especially by European and Latin American audiences, after her vibrant and dramatic bolero covers in Pedro Almodóvar's film *Tacones lejanos* (1992)—"Piensa en mí," "Un año de amor"— and her participation in the widely successful album *A irmandade das estrelas* (1996) by Galician bagpiper Carlos Núñez (triple gold album in Spain, and a bestseller on the Celtic world music circuit, as analyzed in Chapter 10). Her shivering version of the well-known anthem "Negra sombra," written by Rosalía de Castro, caused a sensation and would afterwards be reused to even wider acclaim by Alejandro Amenábar in his Academy Award-winning film *Mar adentro* (2004).

Furthermore, the promotion of the film was conducted along the lines set by the Hollywood industry. The marketing campaign was carried out in the manner used by the big studios, with a series of high-profile media events orchestrated to generate anticipation in the audience months before its screening. The film was accompanied by a line of merchandise, in the style of Disney, with costumes, school material, and soft toys related to the film. Another promotional innovation was the itinerant interactive exhibit about the processes of animation "*Paso a Paso*," which traveled around seven Spanish cities, as well as Paris, Lisbon, and Espinho, and was visited by more than 250,000 people. In addition, as an important component of the film's global promotion, an interactive webpage was created, which received on average 200,000 hits per month, with visitors coming from 46 different countries. All these ingredients help to explain the movie's successful run at the box office, both nationally and internationally. With nearly two million Euros earned in Spain alone, it became one of the top ten grossing films of the year in Spain, was the recipient of two Goya awards (best animated feature film and best song), was dubbed into more than 20 languages, and was exhibited in some 50 countries. The film reached a million spectators in Europe and received 20 international awards. Besides this important career in the theaters, *El bosque animado* became the second bestselling film on DVD of all Spanish cinema, fundamentally thanks to the child/family audience. In all, it was a most promising opening act, but almost too hard to follow.

The second animated feature film produced by Dygra, *El sueño de una noche de San Juan* (2005), also had a four-year gestation and was also directed by Ángel de la Cruz and Manolo Gómez. The film was co-produced with the Portuguese company Appia Films and represents an even more ambitious project than *El bosque animado*. An important quantitative and qualitative jump is evident between the two films, with the availability of more resources and increased use of innovative technology.[7] This second production had a workforce of 400 people and a substantially higher budget of 8 million euros, which almost doubled the budget for *El bosque* (Estrada). For the voices of the characters, recognized popular actors from Spanish cinema and television, such as Gemma Cuervo, Emma Penella, and Diego Gabino, were sought, adding another element of attraction to bring the family audience to the theaters. For the marketing of the film in the English-speaking market the voices of popular British actors Miranda Richardson, Rhys Ifans, Brian Blessed, Bernard Hill, and Fiona Shaw were employed. There were also significant improvements in regard to marketing techniques. Thus, before its commercial release the film had already been sold for distribution to 65 countries (Estrada). Its official release in Spain was a big media event that took place simultaneously in 180 theaters and generated numerous licensing and merchandizing products (from the powerful mass media group PRISA, among others), which fundamentally targeted the schoolchild audience. Likewise, an interactive Internet portal was created for the film, and an exhibition ("*Oniria: Atrévete a soñar*") was organized to show the insides of the work of animation, which visited a number of cities in Spain and abroad.

7 Dygra Films is one of the "cases" that the US technology company Sun Microsystems have used in their promotional campaigns, qualifying them as a "strategic partner" in the implementation of the operative system Solaris 10. Dygra Films doubled the work capacity of animation with the technological development of Sun, reducing the production time of *Sueño de una noche de San Juan* compared with *El bosque animado* and at the same time making them more competitive commercially. See "Dygra Films Selects."

Despite these successful figures, as well as receiving the Goya award for the best animated feature film in 2005, the results from a creative point of view were somewhat mixed and some weaknesses were evident in the script. Once again, like *El bosque*, the film was a free adaptation of a classic text of fantastic literature, in this case inspired by Shakespeare's *A Midsummer Night's Dream*, adapted through a peculiar local view and targeted at a family public, while trying to capture the imagination of the younger audience. In the film, Shakespeare's fantastical reverie is mixed with fairy tales and Galician folk traditions. As director Gómez pointed out, this film alludes both to the classic dramatic text as well as to a widespread European popular tradition with ancient roots: "trataba un hecho con una larga tradición en Europa y Galicia como es la Noche de San Juan" ("it dealt with an event which has a long tradition in Europe and Galicia, Saint John's Eve (the Midsummer night)") (Estrada). Indeed, the film explores another enchanted forest of sorts, some 400 years later than the English original text, exposing the disappearance of the spirit of magic and illusion in the modern world, while revindicating the capacity and need to dream in a materialistic and consumerist world. The theme of the film is the resistance of the world of dreams and imagination against the pressures of a market-driven reality, or the power of personal conviction against the loss of a magical world of illusions. This is also quite an appropriate metaphor for Dygra's pioneering efforts and their quixotic determination to make Galician fantastic animation a reality against all odds and the constrictions of global hypercapitalism. But, as we will see, the reality of the market has its own laws too, which may prove invincible.

The magical natural setting portrayed in *El bosque animado* is also depicted in *El sueño*, an unreal world of fairies, witches, and goblins inhabiting a timeless fantasy, but the results are not totally convincing. As an adaptation, it bears very little resemblance to the original, while, as a story, the narrative is minimally developed, with an excessively schematic script.[8] And, as animation, its magical world generally fails to cause a demanding spectator to marvel, with some exceptions, such as the fantastic scenes of the palace and the ornate architectural constructions. The first part of the film functions well, portraying the dreaming architect and his Sancho Panza-like sidekick with some brushstrokes of humor and a certain degree of quixotic madness. The characters, however, are little more than flat types: the duke Theseo, lover of the arts and misunderstood inventor; his

---

8 In addition, the inclusion in the film of autochthonous "hip hop" musical numbers appears somewhat out of place, and may be intended a concession to the teenage audience and to modernize the story with newer musical trends.

princess-like angelic daughter; the disloyal aristocratic pursuer; and the inept helper of the inventor who finally conquers the heart of the female protagonist. Although the quality of the animated work is in general quite acceptable, the film suffers from a somewhat rudimentary script that follows a fantastic path similar to that of *The Wizard of Oz*, with a traditional happy ending where conventional values are celebrated: the poor helper marries the rich girl, the duke's authority is finally restored as he is recognized as a genius by his town, and the bad guy (a greedy banker) is punished.[9]

On the aesthetic plane, there are some successful achievements in the artistic references to the modern visual Hispanic tradition that highlight the imaginative and the fantastic. Certain interesting elements of the absurd and surreal are used, such as the band of animated instruments that reappear every time the word "time" is mentioned (perhaps a nod to Salvador Dalí and his surrealist "soft watches"). Certainly there are abundant references in the film to modern Iberian art, with other allusions to paintings by Picasso and Dalí, including grotesque elements reminiscent of Buñuel (such as the monstrous characters and the witches). Likewise, the fabulous architectural constructions and the organic domestic ornamentation are clearly inspired by *art nouveau* and the exuberant and imaginative style of both Galician and Catalan modernism.[10]

Manuel Cristóbal, executive producer of Dygra, also highlighted the characteristic hybridity of the film, rooted in one's own culture but managing to connect with the tastes of international audiences, thus bridging the gap between the local and the global:

> ... lo que nos gusta es contar historias universales con raíces propias y que fundamentalmente tengan contenido. Tenemos una raíz gallega evidente, al igual que tenemos una española, pero creemos que si la historia es universal, la película funciona en todos los lados, aunque hay que darle un sello para que se haga personal. (Michelín 31)

> ... what we like is to tell universal stories with native roots and substantial content matter. We have some evident Galician roots, and Spanish roots as well, however we think that if the story is universal,

---

9 It is tempting to see in this finale a symbolic prophecy in reverse, anticipating Dygra's future collapse because of its financial problems with banks.

10 A variety of different visual styles are cited in the film, as director Ángel de la Cruz acknowledged: "La estética del filme es modernista y supone un homenaje, no sólo a Gaudí, también a Klent [Gustav Klimt], a Dalí, al modernismo gallego y catalán" ("The film's aesthetic is modernist and represents a homage not only to Gaudí, but also to Klent [Gustav Klimt], Dalí, and to Galician and Catalan modernism") (Lobo 38).

the film will work everywhere, but you have to give it your imprint to make it personal.

For their third animated feature film, Dygra returned to well-known territory. Following the successful path opened with *El bosque animado*, they produced the obligatory sequel, *El espíritu del bosque* (Spirit of the Forest), directed by David Rubin and Juan Carlos Pena, which was released at the end of 2008, three years after *El sueño*. *El espíritu* insists again on the ecological message, with the defense of the environment and a critique of the mistreatment of the natural habitat as its main themes. Following the commercial techniques established by Hollywood, the film took advantage of a ready-made audience by creating a sequel to a popular film, capitalizing on a recognized and successful "brand" ("el bosque"), which guarantees a certain level of return. In addition, from a practical and economic perspective, reusing the characters and pre-existing settings reduced the costs and accelerated the production process. In this sense the film represents a lesson in creative economics by taking advantage of the resources available. For that reason, the film was produced in less than three years and paved the way for faster productions schedules. As pointed out by Pamela Rolfe in *The Hollywood Reporter*, Dygra was aiming to quicken production processes and add incrementally to its work plans, thus positioning itself in the European leading edge:

> Dygra typifies the exponential growth some Spanish toon companies are experiencing. The Coruna-based studio has picked up the pace from releasing a film every four years to one every 18 months. "Not only have we had a radical change in our pace and presence in the market," Dygra president Manolo Gomez says, "but no one that I know of creates the totality of their 3-D films like we do. We are in the leading edge in Europe."

*El espíritu del bosque* represents another important quantitative leap: its total budget was some 20 million dollars, almost three times more than that of *El sueño* and nearly five times more than *El bosque*'s. Important international distribution operations took place, resulting in the film's dubbing in English with the voices of recognized actors Anjelica Huston and Ron Perlman, as well as those of Sean Astin (from the *Lord of the Rings* trilogy) and Giovanni Ribisi (*Avatar*). Clearly, the big challenge for Dygra was to introduce itself into the difficult US market, which had proven impenetrable until then. Manolo Gómez acknowledged the enormous difficulties and resistances of the North American film market to foreign products, even in the age of globalization, showing clear asymmetries of power:

Es curioso que nos hablen de términos como la globalización. Claro que la hay, pero vete tú a globalizarles a ellos, a venderles tu película. Resulta poco menos que imposible ... Ya sabemos que ellos son, a la vez, muy competitivos y grandes productores, pero es que también mantienen demasiadas medidas protectoras. [...] resulta difícil plantarle cara a los americanos cuando ellos se gastan en publicidad la misma cantidad de dinero que tú has necesitado para crear tu película. (Estrada)

It is interesting that they use terms such as globalization. Of course it exists, but just try to globalize them, try to sell them your film. It is almost impossible ... We already know that they are both very competitive and great producers, but they also uphold too many protective measures. [...] it is difficult to compete with the Americans when they spend in marketing alone the same sum of money you required to create your film.

Another important aspect that shows both Dygra's commitment to the growth of the Galician audiovisual sector and the innovation introduced in the world of animation is the didactic and research activities undertaken by the company. In this sense it is important to highlight Dygra's pioneering collaboration with the *Centro de Supercomputación de Galicia* and with the three Galician universities, especially with the *Master de Comunicación e Creación Dixital* of Universidade da Coruña. In addition, as part of their didactic and training initiatives, Dygra developed the interactive program "Anímate," targeted at a young school-age audience to encourage them to discover the inside workings of 3D animation. Likewise, their organization of animation conferences in A Coruña for Spanish professionals, the *Xornadas sobre Cinema e Imaxe de Síntese "Mundos Dixitais"* and the "Cartoon Master Future" for European creators, have helped to situate Galicia on the map of the European animation circuits.[11]

---

11 Besides the three above-mentioned feature films, Dygra also produced several educational and experimental animation shorts that continue the didactic and consciousness-raising profile of the company's films and their interest in a young school-age audience. *Taxia* (2002), by David Robles, is an animation short created integrally by a computer that presents a gory view of the *rurban* and *glocal* cannibalesque Galician reality, a result of the tragic-comic clash between tradition and modernity. The three animation shorts of *O Señor dos Mosquis* (*Mosquis, Os dous tarros,* and *O Regreso da Lei,* 2003–2005), by David Rubin, made for the Spanish NGO *Manos Unidas,* were described on Dygra's own website (now disappeared) as *"una trilogía sobre la globalización"* ("a trilogy about globalization"). The main themes are, once again, solidarity, ecology, and the critique of economic exploitation, with the reappearance of the flies Hu Hu and Ho Ho from *El bosque* y *El espíritu,* now turned

For all these reasons, it is particularly discouraging to see the end of Dygra, which officially closed its operations in 2012, leaving behind a complete animated feature film, the intercultural family Christmas comedy *Noche ¿de paz?* (Holy Night!) that has not been able to be distributed commercially, among other other unfinished projects. The film was co-written by Billy Frolick (*Madagascar*), David Muñoz, and Antonio Trashorras, who co-wrote Guillermo Del Toro's *El espinazo del diablo* (The Devil's Backbone), and cost 12 million euros. Because of the closing of the company and the lack of funding for distribution, the film remains in limbo. As the film's director Juan Galiñanes stated in his blog, its production was plagued by all kinds of problems, including legal suits, dismissals, and employees leaving the company, against the backdrop of the global financial meltdown: "Todo un culebrón. O making of da peli daría para unha ficción que pecaría de pouco crible" ("It was a real soap opera. The film's *making-of* would be a story that nobody would believe"). As he explains, this sad outcome was the by-product of the financial crisis and the forced merging of the two biggest Galician savings banks, which were originally behind the project, with colossal corruption and huge operating losses passed on to the taxpayers:

> ...a *Holy Night!* le tocó vivir todo el proceso de fusión de Caixanova con Caixa Galicia, sin saber siquiera si quienes poseían los derechos de explotación de la película seguirían ahí para preocuparse de sacar algún rendimiento de su estreno en cines.

> *Holy Night!* lived through the merging process of Caixanova with Caixagalicia, without even knowing if those who had the rights to the commercial use of the film would still be around and could care to make some profit from its exhibition in film theatres.

This limbo condition of *Holy Night!* may be sadly an appropriate metaphor for the current uncertain state of the animation industry in Galicia.[12]

---

into humorous and socially aware didactic flies for the young audience. Last is *El bufón y la infanta* (2007), directed by Juan Galiñanes and inspired by Oscar Wilde's story "The Birthday of the Infanta," a film that insists on the pictorial subject as a source of fantasy, this time animating the painting of *Las Meninas* by Velázquez.

12 Similarly, the disappearance of Dygra's former website, which contained very valuable documentation and bibliographical sources about its films, has left behind a fantasmatic absence/presence.

## Bren Entertainment:
## Globalized Visions and Eclipse of the Local

At the other end of animation production in Galicia we find Bren Entertainment, a company founded in 2000 that has become the largest animation studio in Spain. Bren is located in Santiago de Compostela and is an affiliated company of the gigantic media conglomerate Filmax Entertainment, a private enterprise based in Barcelona and dedicated to the production, distribution, and exhibition of audiovisual cultural products (film, video, music, and television). Filmax's president is Julio Fernández, a Galician migrant who relocated to Barcelona in the 1960s, who has arguably become the most important producer in Spanish cinema, noted above all for Filmax's internationally successful popular genre films (particularly in the fantastic thriller and horror genres) such as the *REC* series and the international box office hit *The Way*.[13] Because of his personal connection with Galicia (he was the founding president of the Clúster Audiovisual Gallego), Fernández concentrated the animation branch of his companies in Galicia, situating in Santiago its production units for cinema and television, the animation studio Bren Entertainment and the production company Filmax Animation.

Bren's first project was the animated children's television series *Goomer*, comprising 26 half-hour episodes made over the course of two years. Since then the focus has been on the production of animated feature films mainly targeting children and teenage audiences. In comparison with the small-scale independent model of Dygra, Bren represents a very different scale and mode of production. The company works on a diversified horizontal plan of large international co-productions and production segmentation (concentrating almost exclusively on the 3D animation component), and is organized vertically in its association with Filmax in relation to funding, production, and distribution. This peculiar organization resulted in Filmax Animation receiving the Cartoon Movie award in Potsdam, the most important festival of animated feature films in Europe, for the best production and distribution strategy.

13 Filmax is the most diversified company of the audiovisual sector in Spain and the biggest in business volume. In 2007 it was the producer with the highest box-office returns in Spain thanks to hit films such as *REC* and *Pérez, el ratoncito de tus sueños* (a Bren production). Their international campaign (particularly in the US market) has proven quite successful. The US remake of *REC*, *Quarantine*, whose executive producer was Julio Fernández himself, was the second film with the highest box-office returns on the first week of its release in October 2008 ($15 million), and made a total of $30 million in the US market.

Owing to its diversification and segmentation strategy, the number of animated projects in different forms of co-production is relatively high, and there is a determined plan to increase its presence in the international markets. According to Bren's director José Manuel Barreira,

> Dende o punto de vista de volume de investimento e de risco que se toma, o volume de producción de Bren Entertainment, de seis películas en seis anos, maioritarias ou en coprodución con outros países, é dunha dimensión que nos sitúa como unha das empresas referentes, non só en España, senón a nivel europeo. (Correa)

> From the point of view of the level of investment and risk taken, the volume of production of Bren Entertainment, with six films in six years, as the main producer or in coproduction schemes with other countries, is of such a scale that it situates us as one of the leading companies, not only in Spain, but in Europe as a whole.

Bren's intense production program, benefiting from the numerous technological tools developed in its own studio and the outsourcing of processing work around the clock and around the world, has allowed the studio to release approximately one animated feature film per year (even releasing two of their own feature films in 2008). Among the most important productions made by Bren are some hybrid films, mixing animation with real scenes and actors (the big box-office hits *Pérez el ratoncito de tus sueños* and its sequel *Pérez 2*); films combining traditional 2D and 3D (*El Cid, la leyenda, Gisaku, Nocturna, una aventura mágica*); and feature films made totally in 3D (*P3K Pinocho 3000, Donkey Xote*). The percentage of Bren's participation in these productions varied greatly, from a mere 10% in *El Cid*, corresponding to the animated scenes in 3D, to nearly the totality of *Donkey Xote*.[14] The budgets for their films have increased exponentially, from three million euros for *Pérez* to ten million for *Nocturna* and 15 million for *Donkey Xote*, its most ambitious project to date. Its animated productions have received important awards, such as the Goya for the best animated feature film on four occasions in a five-year period, for *El Cid* (2003), *P3K Pinocho 3000* (2004), *Pérez* (2006), and *Nocturna* (2007), during a decade which could be considered the "golden age" of Galician animation.

As in the case of Dygra, Bren's productions have recurred repeatedly to the practice of literary adaptations, appealing to notions of cultural prestige,

---

14  As part of its global strategy, Bren also carried out diverse animation projects for the Expo 2005 of Aichi (Japan) and for European producers and television stations.

resonance with the public, and ready-made marketing campaigns, a singular example of the commercial use of the national cultural heritage for both interior and exterior projection. For this purpose, they resorted to two of the greatest universal myths of Spanish literature, *El Cid* and *Don Quijote* (in *El Cid, la legenda* and *Donkey Xote* respectively), completely reworked and treated as mere source of inspiration, and recontextualized as politically correct contemporary visions of intercultural sensitivity and gender awareness. Thus, the films show tolerance and respect to Islamic culture, in the first case, and a nod to feminism, with a modern Dulcinea representing a new model of a determined and enterprising woman, in the second. In addition, they have repeatedly made use of children's stories, legends, and traditional popular stories with international resonance, as in the case of *Pérez* (the tooth fairy) and *P3K Pinocho 3000* (Pinocchio), which is a fairly common practice in US animation features since the early days of Disney. The only feature films that do not follow this path are *Gisaku* and *Nocturna*, whose inspiration comes from the international language of the cartoon and Japanese *anime*. *Gisaku* was the first anime feature film produced in Europe and *Nocturna* was inspired in part by the influential work of Japanese animator, director, and producer Hayao Miyazaki, considered the Walt Disney of *anime*.

In Bren productions, therefore, the global frequently eclipses the local, and Spanish as an international "brand" imposes itself as a totality, with only a small connection to Galician local reality reflected in their productions. For that reason, the Galician references in these films are in general minimal and casual. For example, the collection of fists used in the tournament scene in *Donkey Xote* is a clear visual reference to the fetishes and amulets of the well-known ceramics of Sargadelos, considered a modern sign of Galicianess, which are inspired by the ancient popular traditions of the *meigas* (witches).[15] This reference, however, would go practically unnoticed by a non-Galician spectator. The globalized vision of

---

15 One of its recent animation feature films, *Copito de nieve* (Snowflake, the White Gorilla, 2011), again shows no obvious connection with Galicia. This disconnect with Galician reality in its commercial animation projects contrasts with parallel projects of the company, where Galicia takes center stage as commissioned work from Galician institutions. That is the case of a number of animation promotional shorts related to the Camiño de Santiago, such as *Santiago, a viaxe continua* (2009), and *Xis, ao encontro de Francisco* (2013). Although not animation, *Eloxio da distancia* (2009) is also a promotional documentary of Galician rural tourism in the Fonsagrada area (the old entryway of the Camiño de Santiago in Galicia) prepared for the Xunta de Galicia, clearly marked within a *glocal* orbit, and narrated through the perspective of a Belgian tourist with roots in a rural hippie commune in Galicia.

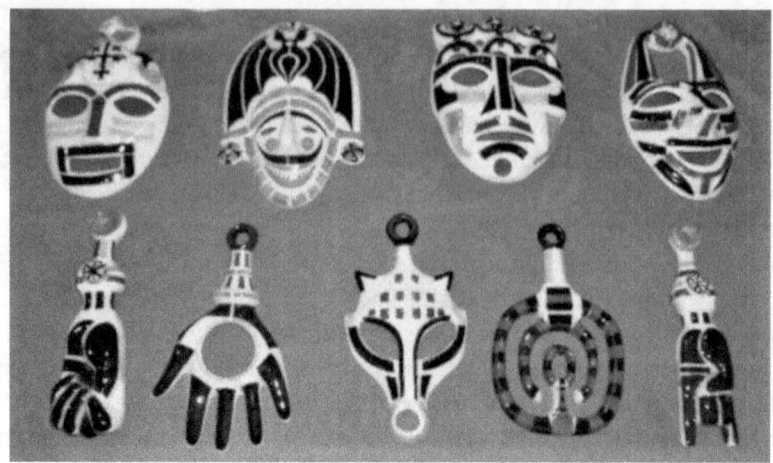

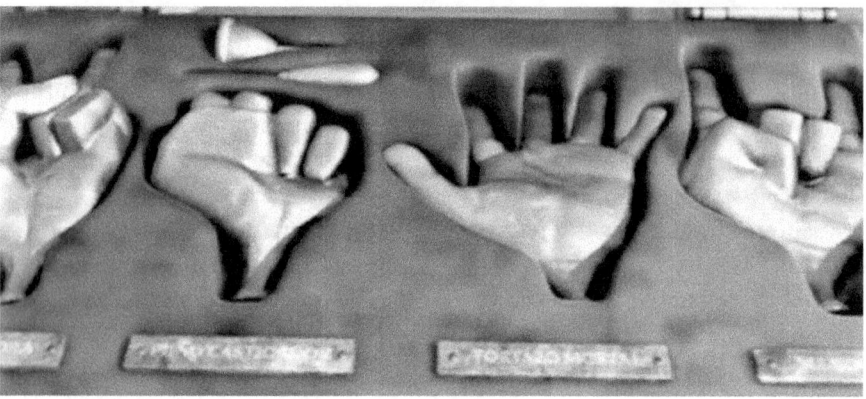

Figures 17–18   Masks and lucky charms inspired by Galician traditions. Iconic modern porcelain from Sargadelos, including a *peliqueiro*, and jousting lance fists from *Donkey Xote* (2007), Bren/Filmax.

Bren applies to the content of the films just as much as to their production and distribution.[16]

16 In its animated productions Bren have collaborated closely with other companies from around the world—France, Germany, Italy, Canada, Argentina, Israel, and several Asian countries—and they have also been sold and distributed internationally. But, as in the case of Dygra, English-language markets, particularly the US, have proven most resistant until now. One strategy to ease their entrance into these markets, as employed also by Dygra, has been to hire recognized English-language actors for the dubbing of the dialogues. Thus, for *Pinocho 3000*, for example, Whoopi Goldberg was hired to dub Cyberina and Malcolm McDowell Scamboli.

Like Dygra, Bren has encountered serious financial troubles as a result of the recent economic meltdown. Even what might be considered relatively low-budget productions by international/Hollywood standards represent a serious investment requiring external financial backing and, in a time of economic crisis, lack of financial credit, loss of clients and subsidies, and general uncertainty, the situation has become unsustainable for many production companies. Thus Bren filed for bankruptcy in 2012, with six animation features in production, and is currently in the process of restructuring its debt.

The technological take-off of animation in Galicia is evident in view of the cases discussed above, but the creation of a sustainable industry capable of competing in the rest of the world has proven much more difficult. The feature films realized in the last years have achieved success and international recognition. Their results are generally quite professional, on occasion even brilliant, and perfectly comparable to what is done internationally, sometimes surpassing it. One of the challenges still remaining for the animation studios in Galicia is at the level of content, particularly when there is a lack of connection with Galician reality, as is the case with Bren's productions, or a reliance on stereotypical representations of Galician culture as magical and exotic. The great achievements with leading-edge technology do not hide, but on the contrary perhaps underline, the facts that more consideration is needed to the storylines and the development of the characters, that the scripts of their own creation should go beyond adaptations of literary works or popular legends already known, and that a reliance on conventional narrative clichés should be avoided in order to be more in tune with Galician social and cultural realities. In that sense, the content often lags behind the technological advances. The narratives are frequently excessively classic and stereotyped in their patterns, modeled after the filmic conventions imported from Hollywood. This is not a characteristic exclusive to Galician animation, but something that affects the field of animation globally in general, which tends to place much more emphasis on the technological development than on the content (Martín Núñez 9). A notable exception to this pattern would be *Nocturna*, which, although not directly related to a Galician reality, is an imaginative film in narrative terms, surprising and unconventional in its inventiveness, and visually against the current trend of 3D hyperrealism, as the 2D animation employed offers in this instance an appropriate and unique nostalgic effect.

## Alternative Visions

The economic crisis initiated in 2007–08 deeply impacted the film industry in Galicia, as in Spain as a whole, an industry that already showed signs of weakness due to a number of structural problems, such as the low number of spectators in relation to US productions, the decline of movie theaters in rural areas—and lately urban areas as well—the recent increase of streaming platforms, and the lack of legislation on piracy and intellectual property, among others (see Alonso García). Nevertheless, the reality of the crisis has also encouraged alternative initiatives, often on the edges of the mainstream (Romero Suárez, "Low cost"). As we have seen, the recent economic crisis has particularly affected the established studios of Dygra and Bren/Filmax, and it is now the smaller production companies, sometimes one- or two-person studios, that have been able to carry out their animation projects. In that regard, it is important to point out other types of animated project made in Galicia in recent years on the fringes of the industry—those that are more personal and artisan-like, which at times the great trees of the forest do not let us see. The experimentation is abundant above all in the area of animation shorts and in a variety of diverse mediums from traditional 2D to claymation, stopmotion, or flash animation, at times realized from a personal computer, such as the children's animation short *Meigallos* (2001), directed by Tomás Conde and Virginia Curiá, or the multi-awarded *1977* (2007), directed by Peque Varela as her film school graduation project (see Chapter 7). Another very successful project made from the fringes was the short *Birdboy* (2012), directed by Alberto Vázquez, an illustrator and author of comics. *Birdboy*, based on his own comic *Psiconautas*, has gathered more than 40 international awards, including the Goya Award for the Best Animated Short.

An interesting example of alternative innovation in Galician animation, in terms of both artistic creation and production scheme, was Fernando Cortizo's *O Apóstolo* (The Apostle, 2012), winner of six Mestre Mateo awards and widely praised at several international film festivals. *O Apóstolo* was the first stereoscopic stop-motion animation film made in Europe, with an estimated budget of 5 million euros largely raised through crowdfunding. This film is innovative in its use of technology and its thematic and stylistic approach, as well as its mode of financing, with the budget partly covered by selling shares in the film online. While 100% Galician in its theme and production, involving a hybrid fantastic/horror/humorous story set along the Camiño de Santiago, with supernatural undertones of magical realism, the film is clearly transnational in terms of its target audience and the film professionals involved: its music soundtrack was composed by Philip Glass

Figure 19   Troubles along the Camiño. English language poster for *O Apóstolo* (2012), a glocal production with music composed by Philip Glass and a complex financing scheme involving crowdfunding and private investors, including Rosalía Mera (cofounder of Inditex). The ill-starred trajectory of *O Apóstolo*, which was marginalized by the mainstream distribution circuits, highlights the challenges of competing in the global market. Courtesy of Artefacto Producciones.

and it had an international technical team whose members had worked on *The Lord of the Rings*, *Coraline*, and *Matrix*, to cite just some examples. However, the odds seemed to be against it. Although critically praised, the film failed at the box office, as the distribution circuit controlled by the majors did not make room for this type of independent production.

Perro Verde Films is another independent Galician audiovisual company that has produced several animation features to have garnered wide recognition, including *Gritos en el pasillo* (Going Nuts, Dir. Juanjo Ramírez, 2007), which has bragging rights as the first animation film in the world made with nutshells. They also produced the award-winning feature films

*El lince perdido* (The Missing Lynx, Dir. Manuel Sicilia and Raúl García 2008), a co-production with Antonio Banderas's company Kandor Moon, which won the Goya for best animated feature; and *Arrugas* (Wrinkles, Dir. Fernando Ferreras, 2012), also winner of two Goya awards (best animation film and best adaptation, done by Ángel de la Cruz), which was based on the internationally awarded comic book by Paco Roca of the same title and successfully commercialized as a hybrid DVD/graphic novel.[17]

But probably the most personal, innovative, and ambitious experiment in this field was the work of Miguelanxo Prado, commented on earlier. His first feature film, *De profundis* (2006), was a particularly remarkable project made between creator/animator (Prado) and musician (Nani García), carefully crafted from Prado's own home studio over several years. Prado's situation is quite unique, as he is very well known internationally as a graphic designer and graphic novel artist. He has to his name more than 20 graphic novels published in various languages. He was also the illustrator of the international bestselling novel by Laura Esquivel, *La ley del amor*, the first major "multimedia novel" published (integrating literature/graphic/music). His leap to animation began in the 1990s as art director and animator for TVG's *Xabarín Club*, which over the years would become a landmark of children's programming in Galician television. He then spent four seasons as artistic director for the US television series *Men in Black*, produced by Steven Spielberg. Perhaps as an antidote to the impersonal conditions of serialization and the industrial production of animation which he experienced at first hand in Hollywood, Prado afterwards embarked on a very personal and artisan project of animation, which received the financial backing of Continental Producciones.[18] His quixotic undertaking consisted of creating, digitalizing, and animating 40,000 oil, acrylic, and watercolor paintings: a colossal enterprise and an intricate work of passionate dedication.

*De profundis*, directed towards a general adult audience rather than to small children, is a fantastic story on the powerful influence of the sea

17  2012 was a good year for critical recognition of Galician animation, with three different Galician productions candidates at the Goyas: the feature films *Arrugas* and *O Mago Dubidoso* (The Little Wizard, Dir. Roque Cameselle) and the short *Birdboy* (Dir. Alberto Vázquez).

18  The film's production also showed another side of the difficulties of obtaining financial funding in a weak Galician cultural infrastructure, and the need to recur to alternative private sponsorship. Thus, among the main investors in this film was the Galician brewing company Estrella de Galicia, which has sponsored a number of important cultural activities in Galicia, such as the musical *Galicia Caníbal*. As another sad corroboration of the recent financial struggle of the audiovisual sector, Continental filed for bankruptcy in 2013.

on the life and imagination of humans, and has Galicia as its very center. Prado creates a magical marine fable of submerged cities, mermaids, and mythological beings, sunken ships that return as whales, and drowned men who fly like seagulls, in a sort of Galician magical realist story in the tradition of Fernández Flórez, Álvaro Cunqueiro, or Manuel Rivas.[19] Prado portrays with meticulous detail this other enchanted forest that is the sea for Galicia: a dark and mysterious mirror in which Galicia sees its reflection— the sea as a source of life and death, which takes away and brings back emigrants, sailors, fishermen, that communicates Galician across the waters, and that at times brings with it enormous catastrophes. Its submersion in the great depths of the sea, to the less transparent regions where death and oblivion dwell, is an ode to marine life, to this other enchanted and submerged forest, to the oneiric world of dreams and fantasies, anxieties, magic, and wonder, but it is also something of a symbolic response to the series of tragic ecological disasters that have taken place in Galicia, such as the infamous *Prestige* oil spill of 2002 and many others before, which have spoiled the Galician coasts and, in particular, the Costa da Morte, with its wretched history of shipwrecks. Animation in the hands of Prado appears as another alternative form, profound and poignant, to imagine the nation.[20]

It is clear that animation in Galicia has been able to surface from invisibility and come out of the dark corner of the periphery; however, there are still some serious challenges ahead. In order to really convert itself into a leading-edge sector, supportive financial backing and infrastructure needs to be created, and it still has to make the qualitative leap so that its content and imaginative capacity to create a world of its own is commensurate with its admirable technological innovation. The innovative work of creators such as Prado, Varela, and Cortizo indicates a new direction that perhaps could serve as a reference and a guide for a renovation of content truly rooted in the Galician reality and imagination, capable of reimagining the nation and projecting it to the world, with its own stories that respond to the cultural questions emerging from the present. As we have seen, the cultural representations of Galician animation still play a key role in the promotion of a magical, timeless, and exotic Galician "imaginary." In that sense, the animation/film sector could use the opportunities not only to redefine but also to debunk romanticized national stereotypes and examine alternative cultural definitions of the nation.

19 Prado's submerged story has certain similarities with Fernández Flórez's "subterráneo maravilloso" ("marvellous underground"), from his novel *El bosque animado*.

20 For additional comentary on *De profundis* see Chapter 4.

# CHAPTER SEVEN

# A Peripheral Focus:
# The Rebirth of the *Novo Cinema Galego*

Nuestro cine es bastardo, exiliado, emigrado, fronterizo.
Ser artista ya implica ser extranjero, inadaptado.
'Our cinema is a bastard, exiled, migrant, border cinema. To
be an artist already implies being a foreigner, a misfit.'
Oliver Laxe, "Cine gallego: viento del norte, a favor" (quoted in Calzada)

La memoria, aquello que somos, se construye con una mezcla
de la realidad y la construcción mítica de esa realidad. [...]
La realidad se construye, ante todo, imaginándola.
'Memory, what we are, is constructed with a mixture of reality
and the mythical construction of that reality. [...]
Reality is constructed, above all, by imagining it.'
Eloy Enciso, "Efectos Especiales" (quoted in Koza)

En la periferia nacen las olas
'Waves are born on the periphery'
José Luis Castro de Paz, *En la periferia nacen las olas.*
*Nouvelle Vague y documental*

## Rethinking Peripheral Cinemas from the Margins

In recent years there has been an emergence of the notion of the periphery/
peripheral as a conceptual framework for the study of contemporary
cinema. In the Iberian context, Josetxo Cerdán was one of the first critics to
approach the production of experimental documentary non-fiction cinema
in Spain though the conceptual lens of the peripheral, which he defines as
avant-garde cinema on the margins of the mainstream audiovisual industry.
His attention, however, has been mostly on Catalan experimental filmmakers
and his essay, published in 2005, does not include any references to Galician
documentary films. In the global sphere, Iordanova, Martin-Jones, and Vidal
have edited the volume *Cinema at the Periphery* (2010), which offers a more
theoretically informed peripheral view of world cinemas from a postcolonial

perspective, focusing on cinemas "located in positions marginal to the economic, institutional, and ideological centers of image making" (5).[1] Recognizing also the geopolitical location, the volume aims to "explore the connotations of the peripheral as a mode of practice, as a textual strategy, as a production infrastructure, and as a narrative encoded on the margins of the dominant modes of production, distribution, and consumption" (9). They thus propose a new model of polycentric vision, "*by making the periphery the center of our study*" (6, original emphasis). This also includes the conditions of production of minor cinemas within nation states: "These peripheral cultures may or may not feel that the nation or state speaks with the same voice as they do, and, accordingly, their cinematic output often represents a different view from yet another peripheral position" (7). Although none of the essays refers to the particular case of the Galician audiovisual sector, this view suggests the condition of pluriperipherality, a particularly important one for Galician cinema, which is subject to different forms of peripherality vis-à-vis the state and other supranational organizations, as in other areas of Galician cultural production.

Also in 2010 the peripheral became a central point of attention in the Galician audiovisual sector with the launch in A Coruña of the film festival *(S8) Mostra de Cine Periférico*. Already in its seventh edition, the *(S8) Mostra* was originally conceived as a forum for "experimentation, dialogue and reflection" about experimental cinema made from the fringes. Its focus has been on new trends in avant-garde cinemas not only from Galicia but also from Spain and overseas.[2] Paradoxically, this forum on the fringes of the mainstream has served as a center for the articulation of new theoretical discourses emanating from Galicia about peripheral cinemas, which in the process has been able to deperipheralize the Galician audiovisual sector and bring it out of invisibility.

Thus a number of critics, filmmakers, and audiovisual culture agents, from within and without Galicia, but all involved as collaborators in the launch of this project, have discussed their particular views on the different positive aspects of peripheral cinemas. Their intersecting positions have been posted on the *(S8) Mostra*'s internet platform "Atlas Ilustrado da Periferia"

---

1  Earlier, in *Los cines periféricos* (1999), Alberto Elena studied non-Western cinemas (African, Middle Eastern, and Indian) from the perspective of their peripherality to hegemonic Western cinemas. Another volume published in 2010 (Conn Holohan, *Cinema on the Periphery*) deals on the peripherality of contemporary Irish and Spanish cinema from a comparatist approach. The book focuses on the changing representations of both national cultures, which have evolved from traditionalist cultural perspectives and merged with European modernity and globalizing trends.

2  The website platform is www.s8cinema.com.

(Illustrated Atlas of the Periphery) in Galician, Spanish, and English.[3] The word "atlas" is significant, as the platform intends a cartographic remapping of the field of audiovisual production from its margins, as its presentation clearly indicates:

> The periphery of cinema is a territory seldom explored, traversed only by a handful of fearless individuals who attempt to forge new and daring paths to the heart. The Peripheral Film Festival, in its first edition, started an indispensable cartography work [...] Putting the edges on the map, making them sharp and visible. That is a purpose of this Illustrated Atlas of Periphery. [*sic*]

For such a new cartography, this group of critics and filmmakers proposes a new peripheral positioning which questions the hegemonic values emanating from the center while aiming to bring visibility to the fringes. They all coincide on seeing the peripheral as more than merely a geolocation, but rather a conceptual, ideological, and aesthetic positioning. Thus Galician film director and critic Alberte Pagán has advocated for a "peripheric cinema, excentric, alternative," opting for the symbolic position of the mole, undermining the norms and values of mainstream cinema: "I prefer underground, clandestine art that destroys the shapes and formalities that we accept just without thinking" ("A toupeira"). For Barcelona-based Venezuelan filmmaker Andrés Duque the periphery is a voluntary process of distancing from the center, which represents a visual and ideological shift in perspective: "La periferia deviene de un proceso mental y de distanciamiento. La periferia es un espacio de posicionamiento frente al orden establecido" ("The periphery is the result of a mental process and distancing. [...] The periphery is a location positioning against the established order").

Galician film critic, screenwriter, and producer José Manuel Sande also defines peripheral cinema as an ideological and artistic position rather than a mere territorial location. For him, peripheral cinema is characterized by an attitude of contestation against the mainstream commercial industry and a perspectival shift that stretches the limits of the visual field towards a wider symbolic territory and a fuller image of reality:

> Lugar marxinal e *maudit* da cidade, universo ninguneado polo corporativismo vinculado á arte [...], a periferia é unha actitude sumada a unha perspectiva aberta desde a que otear os riscos da

---

3 Some of the English translations provided on the website have substantial differences and errors. Wherever I quote the original source in Galician or Spanish, the English translation has been edited by me.

fanfarria e os extremos da experiencia artística. Rebelde, punk, bardo, farsante, filibusteiro ou insensato, se a vida contribúe a estreitar marcos, a periferia se extende e crece. A unidade desaparece, o universo exemplarizante se pecha e a ilusión dos límites infinitos prolonga o espazo ata que quizais non quede máis territorio.

A fringe and forgotten area of the city, a universe neglected by the corporate interests in the arts [...], the periphery is an attitude and an open perspective from where to observe the risks of the great fanfare and the limits of artistic experience. Unruly, punk, bard, fake, filibusterer or reckless; while life keeps trying to narrow the boundaries, the periphery spreads and grows. Uniformity disappears, the exemplary universe vanishes and the illusion of endless limits extends the space beyond the existing territory.

Furthermore, audiovisual promoter Elena Oroz highlights the multiple conditions of invisibility and intersectionality of peripheral cultural production:

To explain what periphery means (or even what it may mean) involves, first of all, to assume there is some kind of centre that, in metaphoric terms, it almost always, worked as a centrifugal point which not only pushes out what doesn't fit in the center but always makes it invisible.

Oroz emphasizes the need to visualize a new map with a plurality of centers and peripheries:

... a la hora de abordar el audiovisual contemporáneo no podemos hablar de un único centro, sino de diferentes puntos de fuerza, cada uno de los cuales genera su propia periferia y sus propias relaciones de desigualdad e indiferencia con lo que le es ajeno: ya sea el formato, el género cinematográfico, el país de producción o el sexo del director o directora.

... in regard to the contemporary audiovisual we cannot just talk about a single center but about different strength points, and each one of them creates its own periphery and its own relations of inequality and indifference to what is different: not only with respect to format but also cinematographic genre, country of production or the gender of the director.

As an alternative to the traditional marginality and invisibility of the periphery, she proposes new spaces of rhizomatic connections and a multilateral network of affinities that alters the center/periphery divide through alternative forms of production, sharing, and collaboration between the peripheries:

> Creo que la periferia ya no existe como la entendíamos, porque tampoco hay un centro claro. Y que es este sistema de redes y de afinidades el que, los que alguna vez nos hemos sentido periféricos, debemos potenciar y reforzar. No se trata sólo de constituir un espacio de resistencia, sino de construir uno que sea habitable.

> I think the periphery is no longer as we once understood it, because there is no clear center. And it is this system of networks and affinities which must be enhanced and strengthened by those of us who have ever felt peripheral. It is not just a matter of establishing a space of resistance, but of building one that is livable.

Miguel Fernández Labayen and María Mallol González, curators of the first *(S8) Mostra*, insist on the valuable plurality and hybridity of the periphery as positive values that need to be fostered. They also advocate for the eccentric nature of peripheral cinema, both in the alternative conditions of film production, creation, and distribution and in the counterhegemonic practices and non-mainstream forms of cinematic representation:

> … nos interesa revindicar el carácter híbrido, variable, complejo y plural de 'la periferia'. Periferias que en el terreno audiovisual van unidas a unos contextos de producción anómalos (generalmente unipersonales y autofinanciados), a unos modos de representación marginales en su sentido contrahegemónico. Pero también, y no menos importante, a unos circuitos de exhibición paralelos, capaces de generar un tejido comunitario ex-céntrico en su sentido radical y primigenio.

> … we want to assert the hybrid, changeable, complex and plural character of 'the periphery'. In the audiovisual arts, the peripheral goes hand in hand with anomalous contexts of production (typically self-produced and self-funded), and marginal counterhegemonic forms of representation. And also, which is equally important, it is linked with parallel exhibition circuits, capable of generating an ex-centric network community, in the radical and original sense of the term.

Galician filmmaker Ángel Santos discusses the multiple positionalities of the center/periphery dichotomy and the changing nature of their relationship, advocating for a widely disseminated audiovisual culture that defies borders and does not necessarily depend on a center (industrial or economic) for its existence, opting instead for a more artisan-like creative experience:

> ... periferias hay tantas como puntos para situar el eje de una imaginaria circunferencia (bien sea en relación a criterios industriales, de creatividad, independencia, etc.). Hoy en día los círculos parecen haberse expandido y multiplicado exponencialmente, tanto que hasta ahora no habíamos asistido a una oferta tan amplia e inabarcable de obras y de cineastas/creadores, ya no como puntos a situar dentro o fuera del circulo [*sic*] formado por la(s) industria(s) sino, lo que es mucho más interesante, puntos diseminados aquí y allá sin vinculación alguna con cualquier tipo de industria y sí con el arte/artesanía de las imágenes y sonidos en movimiento.

> ... there are as many peripheries as points where to situate the axis of an imaginary circumference (according to industrial criteria or measurements of creativity and independence). Today the circles seem to have expanded and multiplied exponentially, in a way that we had not witnessed before such a wide and vast display of works and cineastes/creators, and not as points to situate inside or outside of the circle formed by the industry(ies) but, more interestingly, as points disseminated here and there not linked with any type of industry but with the art/artisanship of moving images and sounds.

Xurxo González (AKA Xurxo Chirro), a film critic and academic as well as a filmmaker associated with the new wave of Galician cinema of recent years, defends a peripheral positioning as an ideological and aesthetic standpoint of resistance against the market-driven conditions of film production:

> ... a periferia é un posicionamento que incide sobre todo no individuo que involucrado no seu presente creativo actúa nunha contraposición consciente ou afastando os criterios establecidos polo mercado da disciplina na que se atope. O sistema capitalista amosa a súa tendencia máis avasalladora e cruel dotando de invisibilidade a todo elemento discordante coas súas regras do xogo. Ante isto, é o creador quen adopta un posicionamento periférico para salvaguardar a súa singularidade e independencia da súa obra. ("Posicionamento periférico")

> ... the periphery is a positioning that impacts, over all, on the individuals who, immersed in their creative present, consciously act against, or even refuse, the criteria imposed by the market in their respective areas of work. The capitalist system shows its most dominating and cruelest trend, making invisible any discordant element which

goes against the rules of the game. In view of this, creators adopt a peripheral positioning aiming to protect their own singularity and the independence of their work.

Xurxo González's outlook summarizes well the general conceptualization of peripheral cinema as it applies to Galicia. His work as film critic and audiovisual culture agent with José Manuel Sande and Martin Pawley, organizing the first *Novo Cinema Galego* (NCG) exhibit at the Centro Galego de Arte Contemporáneo (Santiago) and creating the web platform *Acto de Primavera* for the Galician audiovisual sector, has been influential in the conceptualization of the *Novo Cinema Galego* among critics, filmmakers, and the audiovisual sector as a whole.[4] The work of these critics is partially responsible for the new visibility of peripheral Galician cinema, in Galicia and abroad, at a time when, paradoxically, the general economic and political conditions might appear as less than ideal.

## After the Bubble

Some of the most dramatic and iconic images of the recent economic crisis in Spain are the thousands of unfinished and vacant buildings dotting the landscape, seemingly in a state of permanent paralysis, while many homeowners who have lost their jobs and their unemployment benefits are forced to leave their homes. These eerie constructions effectively constitute ghost towns that remind us of the unbridled wave of neoliberalism that dominated Spain in the late twentieth century and the early years of the twenty-first. Galicia was no exception in this regard. Incomplete institutional projects abound, most noticeably the controversial *Cidade da Cultura* in Santiago, a monumental visual metaphor for unfinished business, and perhaps for a misguided institutional path in pursuit of grand dreams which should have been more modest, better aimed, and in alignment with Galician social realities (see Chapter 1).

After the bonanza years of the 1993–2008 real estate bubble, a new lean period started that has already surpassed the proverbial seven-year period of *vacas flacas* (economic hardship). The situation of the culture industry, and the audiovisual sector in particular, has followed exacerbated patterns of recession. Perhaps the most disastrous cases in the Galician audiovisual sector have been in the field of animation, one of its most visible

---

4 A compendium of Xurxo González's influential critical reflections on the NCG is available as "Caldeirada de Novo Cinema Galego" on the website http://novocinemagalego.info. This website also includes a historical timeline of the development of the NCG, starting in 2005.

flagships, particularly in the case of commercial feature films involving bigger budgets, complex production schemes, and large teams, which were engulfed by the financial tsunami. Several animation feature films were literally paralyzed in midstream, or were completed but remain in financial limbo awaiting legal adjudication, while the two major animation studios in Galicia have collapsed (see Chapter 6). These animation film projects are the audiovisual equivalent of the empty buildings of the burst real estate bubble.

The field of audiovisual production in Galicia was profoundly shaken as a result of a sort of political and economic "fatal junction" of global and local events: on the one hand, as we have noted, the negative effects of the global economic crisis, which is still having a ripple effect on Galician society at large; and, on the other, the political landslides in the governments of the Xunta de Galicia—first, the ascent to power of the socialist–nationalist coalition in 2005–09 and the removal of the PP after 15 consecutive years in power with Manuel Fraga, largely a result of popular mobilization against the management of the *Prestige* oil spill disaster; and, second, the return to power of the PP in 2009, largely as a consequence of the coalition's internal divisions and the onset of the economic crisis.

At the local level, in the allocation of political competencies in 2005, the Consellaría de Cultura was assigned to the Galician nationalist party (BNG) and Ánxela Bugallo was appointed as director. As a result, a new set of official criteria was instituted in relation to the promotion of the Galician cultural industry. In 2006 Manolo González, a documentary maker and academic founder of the EIS, was named director of the newly created Axencia Audiovisual Galega (AAG), designed as a meeting platform between Galician audiovisual creators and the administration. One of the results of these political changes was the establishment of new programs of official subsidies for film creation. The AAG and later the AGADIC (Axencia Galega de Industrias Culturais) instituted the new "axudas ao talento" (subsidies for talent), which at the time were resisted by the audiovisual industry sector and harshly criticized by the PP in opposition. These subsidies were aimed at directly supporting projects undertaken by creators (writers, directors, editors), including shorts and experimental films, rather than at production companies and full feature commercial films, as had been the norm in the past. This institutional shift would be a game changer in its ability to promote different kinds of projects that were more personal and more inventive, with fewer commercial considerations and more grounded in Galicia. Another important initiative was the creation of web-based platforms for the diffusion and exchange of Galician audiovisual creations, such as Teutubo and Flocos. This new cultural direction would eventually prove to be the breeding ground for the emergence of a new generation of Galician audiovisual artists.

At the global level, the financial collapse that originated with the subprime mortgage crisis in the United States did not take long to make itself felt in the rest of the world. Spain was hit particularly hard, as it had been riding high on the real estate bubble during the years that the PP were in power. The PSOE, unable to stop the effects of the collapse, the financial strangling of the markets, and the increasing sovereign debt, gave power back to the PP in 2011. The newly elected government, under great pressure from the EU, started a harsh austerity plan which heavily curtailed social services, including investment in education and culture, while raising IVA taxes to unheard-of levels for cultural goods, such as DVDs, CDs, and cinema tickets. Thus one of the indirect effects of the crisis in Spain was the dismantling of the cultural infrastructure. In Galicia, where the PP had been voted back to power in 2009, at the beginning of the crisis, the dismantling of the previous government's programs was already a reality. The newly appointed directors of TVG were not interested in funding new projects, particularly alternative non-mainstream projects. The AAG was disbanded and official subsidies and public investment in the cultural arena suffered huge cuts or were simply abolished.[5]

The crisis also accelerated the general transition to a post-cinema era, marked by the obsolescence of the traditional forms of production and distribution and exhibition channels. The post-cinema age has been characterized by great changes in consumption patterns, already begun with the advent of new digital formats and the ease of copying and sharing, followed by the general desertion of film theaters and video stores, a reality exacerbated by each new technological development: digital cameras, smart TVs and phones, video streaming, new forms of video sharing such as Vimeo, Youtube, and Dailymotion, and social media platforms such as Facebook.[6]

5 The "axudas ao talento audiovisual galego" program has been maintained, with some interruptions and reductions in the allocations, as the result of a grassroots campaign by audiovisual culture agents, critics, and filmmakers (González, "Novo Cinema Galego"). The actual description of the criteria for the category of "experimental shorts" in 2010 clearly matched the new directions of the Novo Cinema Galego ("RESOLUCIÓN").

6 The same is true of the music industry as a whole, with the decay of traditional record companies and sales of physical records, as well as new channels opened with the availability of digital tools and internet connections. As a result, the chain of creation, recording, production, sharing, and distribution for new artists does not necessarily depend on the record companies hiring them, or the department stores

The combination of these sweeping political, economic, technological, and cultural changes, related to the patterns of globalization and neoliberalism, had unforeseen consequences for the audiovisual sector in Galicia. While the industry experienced a serious contraction, like the cultural industry in Galicia as a whole, and many companies collapsed, a new generation of independent filmmakers started to come to the surface as a reaction, with alternative approaches, methods, and aims. Manolo González, the former director of the AAG, expressed this surprising development through a strong visual analogy with the end of the Mesozoic era, when "dinosaurs died but small mammals survived" (Azalbert). These interrelated events have given us a new audiovisual lexicon, a new look, a new outlook, and even new brands, such as low-cost films, crowdfunding, peripheral cinemas, and *Novo Cinema Galego.*

## The Rebirth of the *Novo Cinema Galego*

The lack of available resources for cultural projects has often been a motivation to look for alternatives on the fringes. In this case, what started as a major financial constriction and developed as a regression in cultural politics has generated an alternative response characterized by different visual aesthetics and cultural ethics. A new paradigm started to emerge in which innovative filmmakers could entirely sidestep the mainstream system and experiment with new forms: a new way of looking with a more direct and more personal perception of reality, crossing established borders and defying received notions with a broader peripheral vision, as it escaped the conditions of mainstream cinema; a new way of creating, experimenting with new digital tools, smaller teams, and greater mobility. In this new *guerrilla* cinema scenario, the reality of the cultural and economic atomization of Galician *minifundio cinema* could be turned into an advantage. The combination of the earlier audiovisual policies and direct incentives to creators from the AAG, with the availability of new technological applications and forms of electronic distribution, enabled possibilities for creating a more personal artistic work without the encumbrance of commercial trappings, and at the same time deperipheralizing the Galician audiovisual sector. These were fundamentally the conditions for the emergence of the *Novo Cinema Galego.*

The development of the NCG was thus an indirect result of positive encouragement by the Xunta's audiovisual subsidy policies and a reaction

selling their records, or radio and television stations playing their music being more interested in easily digestible mainstream music formats.

against the progressive collapse of the traditional film production companies during the economic meltdown. Young filmmakers who had started to produce personal and experimental shorts, animation films, and audiovisual school projects on the fringes of the industry soon began to get recognition outside Galicia and moved to longer projects. The visible starting point of the movement is considered to be the first feature film by Oliver Laxe, *Todos vós sodes capitáns* (You Are All Captains, 2010), which was financed with a subsidy of 30,000 euros from the AAG and went on to win the FIPRESCI award at Cannes. The film displayed a unique and bold personal vision in the form of a self-reflexive documentary that crossed the conceptual, territorial, and aesthetic boundaries of mainstream cinema while exploring and questioning the politics of filmmaking, identity, and representation. It was received with wide international acclaim, setting the tone and giving visibility to a new unconventional way of making cinema from the fringes.

*Todos* was only the first visible tip of the iceberg that had been slowly forming in previous years. Its success turned it into a new paradigm for Galician independent cinema. A new generation of innovative filmmakers started to emerge from invisibility with Oliver Laxe, Peque Varela, Xurxo Chirro, Eloy Enciso, Lois Patiño, Ángel Santos, Lara Bacelo, Sonia and Miriam Albert Sobrino, Susana Rey, Xacio Baño, Sandra Sánchez, Xacio Baño, Alberte Pagán, and Sonia Méndez, among others. They form a very diverse group of young men and women, working within and outside Galicia and within and outside the film schools. Significantly, a good number of them are women, reflecting the new roles of women in Galician society and the progress towards a certain deperipheralization of gender-based forms of marginalization in the audiovisual sector. Although they do not constitute a strictly unified movement, they have followed similar paths of experimentation on the margins of the commercial industry, consciously aware of their peripheral position and determined to have their visions projected on the global screen. As Villarmea Álvarez has observed:

> This group of filmmakers addresses identity issues from a peripheral position, which is transnational in itself: they consciously avoid the centre to settle down in the margins, borrowing ideas from global non-fiction genres such as the travelogue, the found-footage documentary or the correspondence film in order to enrich their film tradition without giving up its particular idiosyncrasy. ("Transnational Identities," 242)

Their single trajectories have crossed and influenced each other, and their multiple roles as filmmakers, writers, producers, actors, educators, critics, and cultural agents means that they have often been mutual supporters and collaborators. A series of common elements among these creators was succinctly identified by Xurxo Chirro in what appears to be almost a cultural manifesto: "The New Galician Cinema filmmakers share: cinephilia, small crews, the democratization of technology, self-management, risk, experimentation, improvisation, process, meta-language, referentiality, landscape, pantheism, irony, humour" (Naughten). Some of the most emblematic films of the NCG include: *Todos vós sodes capitáns, Vikingland* (Dir. Xurxo Chirro, 2011), *Arraianos* (Dir. Eloy Enciso, 2012), and *Costa da Morte* (Dir. Lois Patiño 2013), and film shorts such as *1977* (Dir. Peque Varela, 2007), *Paris#1* (Dir. Oliver Laxe, 2008), *12 noites con Piedad* (Dir. Otto Roca, 2009), *Eclipse* (Dir. Alberte Pagán, 2010), and *Anacos* (Dir. Xacio Baño 2012).[7] These experimental films, made on the periphery, on the margins of the commercial industry, and away from the centers, have crossed literal and symbolic borders and received accolades in festivals around the world, including Locarno, Marseille, Cannes, Mar del Plata, Sundance, and Clermont-Ferrand.[8] Significantly, there have been several film festivals outside Galicia with a focus on the NCG, such as the "Nuevas Estrategias" at the Buenos Aires BACIFI (2011), the "Jornadas del Novo

7 A recent 2013 poll about the best Galician films conducted among 11 influential Galician film critics and filmmakers revealed a very different perspective and result from earlier polls (see Chapter 5, note 16). In general, they tend to favor foundational films, ethnographic and documentary cinema, and contemporary experimental cinema, particularly short films. Thus they give nods to Galician historic film documentaries (known to academics, but hardly seen by most viewers), including film shorts and animation. They show obvious bias towards the recent wave of NCG, not altogether surprisingly, as some of the critics are also filmmakers and producers associated with the movement. The ranking order was as follows: *Vikingland, Galicia* (Carlos Velo, 1936; re-edited in 2011), *Mamasunción, Arraianos, O carro e o home* (Antonio Román, 1940), *Paris #1* (Óliver Laxe, 2008), *Montaña en sombra* (Lois Patiño, 2012), *1977* (Peque Varela, 2007), *Eclipse* (Alberte Pagán, 2010), and *Todos vós sodes capitáns* ("Votación películas gallegas"). None of them could be considered commercial successes by mainstream standards, but most have had widespread circulation in the alternative art film circuits, nationally and internationally. Again, another poll taken in 2014 of the best Galician films since Cinegalicia (1989) among critics, academics, and filmmakers tended to reflect the overwhelming bias towards NCG, with only two "commercial" films in the top ten: *Vikingland, Todos vós sodes capitáns, Arraianos, Costa da Morte, Bs. As.* (Alberte Pagán, 2006), *León y Olvido, 1977, 18 comidas, VidaExtra* (Ramiro Ledo, 2013), and *Belas dormentes* (Eloy Lozano, 2001).

8 While the full features have received prestigious awards at major festivals, such as *Todos*, which has gathered more than ten awards internationally, it is perhaps the shorts that have been most successful at film festivals, with both *1977* and *Anacos* receiving more than 15 international film awards.

Cinema Galego" in Bilbao Arte (2014), or the "New Galician Cinema" section at the Edinburgh and Glasgow *Iberodocs* film festivals (2015), evidencing the growing international currency of the NCG.

The appellation *Novo Cinema Galego* was the creation of several film critics and audiovisual culture promoters, among them Xurxo González, José Manuel Sande, and Martin Pawley. They refloated the old NCG denomination, which had been in use since the 1970s, giving it a new context and a new perspective, as well as an international projection.[9] As Xurxo González explains, the coining of the term NCG in 2010 was originally intended to call the attention of the new Xunta government to the need to maintain investment in an area of growth; it was also a strategy to give it some visibility ("Novo cinema Galego"). But the Galician cultural sector as a whole more or less ignored these developments on the fringes of the industry. The official Xunta agencies, the TVG, the mainstream media, the producers, and the universities hardly acknowledged them. Instead, it was mostly the impetus of creators and the exterior projection of their works, mobilized in festivals, websites, and publications outside Galicia, that energized the movement.[10] The name rapidly took root, being adopted by critics and viewers. Blogs, personal websites, and online film sites have been the common breeding ground for the conceptualization of the movement. One of the earliest academic attempts at a preliminary categorization of the NCG is the article by Isabel Martínez and María Gallego, "El Novo Cinema Galego" (2012), which provided a general overview of the movement, although

9 Particularly important in this regard was the work of Xurxo González, who was very involved in the early development of the NCG through his work at the AAG and AGADIC, and as coordinator of the audiovisual web platforms Teutubo e Flocos during the bipartite, among other activities. Equally important for its visibility was the launching of the NCG exhibit at the CGAC and the yearly "Panorama Audiovisual Galego" section of the Cineuropa in Santiago.

10 This situation is beginning to change. The NCG is already the subject of a course at the University of Oviedo (Asturias) in 2015–2016, and the course description explicitly recognizes its leading-edge position internationally: "Acercamiento teórico al Novo Cinema Galego, uno de los movimientos cinematográficos, al margen o en la periferia de la industria, más interesantes desarrollados en los últimos años en el estado español, que logró situar a Galicia y a los cineastas gallegos en el mapa mundial del cine de calidad, consiguiendo una repercusión y un reconocimiento internacional sin precedentes en la historia reciente del cine español." ("Theoretical approach to the Novo Cinema Galego, one of the most interesting film movements developed in recent years in the Spanish state, from the margins or on the periphery of the industry, which managed to place Galicia and Galician filmmakers in the world map of high quality cinema, achieving unprecedented international recognition and impact in the recent history of Spanish cinema.") ("Aula de cine.")

without extensive critical analysis.[11] The movement gained wide recognition in international festivals and influential film journals and newspapers, such as the prestigious *Cahiers du cinema*, which dedicated an article in 2013 to examining the emergence of the *Nouveau Cinéma galicien* (Azalbert). The exposure of these new filmmakers on the international film festival circuit was far-reaching, and has since grown exponentially: *Vikingland* has been seen in more than 40 festivals around the world, *Todos vós sodes capitáns* in more than 60, and *Costa da Morte* in almost 100.

The NCG nomenclature made a subtle reference to the national cinemas of the 1960s and 1970s (including the prospective Galician cinema of the era, with Chano Piñeiro at the forefront). It followed the experimental tradition of *free cinema*, the various new waves of film of the period (British New Wave, French *Nouvelle vague*), and avant-garde video creation of the 1980s. In some ways, it is also related to the Dogme 95 cinema initiated by Lars von Trier in terms of its alternative ideological bent and purist aesthetic positioning, although they don't adhere to any kind of decalogue.

The filmmakers associated with the NCG exercise a plurality of aesthetic approaches, often not from within the straitjacket of traditional film schools, but they are related by the common goal of experimentation with new techniques and new forms of story-telling from the margins. Thus avant-garde strategies of fragmentation, estrangement, ambiguity, use of long takes, black-and-white, and footage manipulation are frequently employed. Their films tend to represent a purist vision of cinema, a poetic cinema free of the corporate trappings of the cinematic apparatus. They are characterized by an anti-establishment aesthetic standpoint, an unconventional and innovative style, and their peripheral position on the fringes of the film industry. These filmmakers boast an independent and iconoclastic spirit, engaging with current social issues, both local and global. Generally they do not aim for a space in commercial film theaters, but instead their films are shown in museums, film archives, festivals, schools, and other public spaces, and of course through the Internet. Rather than following the paths of commercial cinema already known, and repeating with fewer resources at a local level what has been done before, they aim for innovative new approaches. One of the paradoxes of the NCG is that by escaping from conventional commercial patterns and refusing to replicate the hegemonic imported models, instead exploring their Galician identity

11 For other general overviews of the NCG from Galician studies see Redondo; Gómez Viñas; Pablo Suárez; and Villarmea. Film scholars in Iberian studies have also started paying attention to the NCG. Thus Amago examines Laxe's self-reflexive questioning of the rethorics of authenticity in *Todos*.

and affirming their difference, these filmmakers have been able to create a niche for themselves in the international arena of avant-garde cinema, something that as a whole Galician cinema had never done before.[12] It is thus a new cinema born on the periphery of the periphery, not behind the times, but on the leading edge of innovation and avant-garde experimentalism.[13]

The NCG could be considered as a border cinema defined by its liminality and hybridity, regularly exploring and stretching the boundaries of cinematic representation. These films move easily across genres, languages, and geopolitical borders. Indeed, mobility and migration are recurrent themes, sometimes reflecting the directors' own trajectories, which have often involved living and working overseas, in London, Paris, Portugal, Morocco, and Sweden, or at high sea. They typically cross the established border zones between fiction and non-fiction, documentary and essay, reflection and imagination, the autobiographical and the collective, narrative and non-narrative, memory and identity, the real and the fantastic. They experiment freely with diverse forms bordering on the documentary, but diverging from traditional styles, exploring instead the multiple faces of non-fiction, such as the fake documentary or mockumentary, the found footage, the docufiction, or the film essay, among others. Some directors prefer to refer to their work as documentary fiction, creative documentary, or non-fiction cinema.

In some ways, the NCG represents a return of the *auteur* model, a concept somewhat abandoned since its heyday in the 1960s and 1970s. In the Galician context, the NCG is connected with the foundational cinema of Chano Piñeiro and his early experimentation with the ethnographic look in *Mamasunción* and *Sempre Xonxa*, as well as the exploration of the landscape and the mixing of fiction and non-fiction in *O Camiño das Estrelas*. Likewise, their avant-garde aesthetic is also related to the original countercultural creative impetus of the Galician *Movida*, as in the video works by Xavier

---

12  Reflecting on the possible constitution of a canon for Galician cinema, Iván Villarmea Álvarez argues that, with the NCG, "por primera vez el cine gallego está a la altura de las obras internacionales que los cinéfilos autóctonos más aprecian" ("for the first time Galician cinema is at the same level of the international works that native cinephiles appreciate the most") ("Un canon"). Likewise, Gómez Viñas states: "It is remarkable that a cinema defined in production terms by low costs, light formats and the absence of an industrial infrastructure should again be garnering prestige and visibility in both Spain and the international arena" (154).

13  Spanish and Galician mainstream media have recently started to echo the forefront position of the NCG internationally. Thus *El País* notes that Galician cinema is positioned as "la vanguardia del cine mundial con películas que transmiten identidad," ("the avant-garde of world cinema with films that transmit identity") (Calzada), and *Faro de Vigo* states "la vanguardia del cine se filma en Galicia" ("the avant-garde of cinema is filmed in Galicia") (Mato).

Villaverde (*Veneno Puro*, 1984; *Viúda Gómez*, 1985) and Antón Reixa (*After shave*, 1986; *Ringo Rango* 1990).

Self-production and self-management schemes are commonly employed by NCG filmmakers, resembling in that sense the resourceful and personal investment strategies of amateur production models. The new means opened up by the availability of low-cost digital technologies meant that anybody could potentially create, share, and distribute their audiovisual productions from a computer terminal, tablet, or smartphone with internet access, thus bypassing the constraints of traditional industrial circuits and the lack of infrastructure and financial resources. As Villarmea Álvarez has commented, these filmmakers "no longer work in a standardized film industry located in a particular territory, but within a decentralized digital network" ("Transnational Identities" 233). Experimental films, shorts, and web series don't even have a space in traditional commercial circuits, but they can blossom in the new virtual spaces.

## Crossing Borders:
## Tensions and Frictions through the Galician Peripheral Lens

I intend to explore in the next section the tensions, frictions, and resistances that appear in the NCG, as the traditional fiction/non-fiction categories and space/time boundaries are crossed: rural and urban, home and abroad, tradition and modernity, local and global. I will be examining some of the most emblematic and widely recognized works associated with the NCG, starting with Oliver Laxe, the first internationally appreciated author of this group. *Paris#1* (2007) is Laxe's first film work, a 16mm black-and-white medium short of 30 minutes, shot on location in Galicia in the remote mountains of Os Ancares and the coastal village of Muxía. It is the first part of a trilogy which the credits describe as "ensayo cinematográfico en 3 actos chamado 'Paseos e polifonías para unha Galicia contemporánea'" ("cinematographic essay in 3 acts called 'Wanderings and polyphonies for a contemporary Galicia'"). The title of the trilogy already alludes to its hybrid nature, mixing qualities of the film documentary and narrative ethnographic essay, and the collective mobility, plurivocality, and multiperspectivism that encompasses the vision and soundscape of modern Galicia.

A number of tensions and frictions are revealed at the core of *Paris#1* between documentary/fiction, modernity/tradition, urban/rural, and nature/culture. The film presents a selective view of Galicia, focusing the gaze exclusively on the rural areas, although of course the categories of urban and rural are constantly crossed behind the cameras, just like fiction and non-fiction. In that sense, it appears to continue a certain ethnographic film tradition of looking at the rural as the roots and essence of Galicia, from Antón Román to Chano Piñeiro, but from a self-reflexive and self-questioning perspective, something that we will see in other works associated with the NCG.[14]

Geographical dislocation also starts with the title of the film. The pre-credits alert us that Paris is one of the locations to which people from the Os Ancares area have migrated, in a sort of collective autobiographical gesture (Laxe himself was born in Paris, of Galician migrant parents). Thus from the beginning there is a personal investment and perspective in the story told, which somehow clashes with the traditional "objective" ethnographical documentary. There are other significant disjunctures in the film, since as viewers we keep expecting to see the images of Paris, or of the migration, but that expectation is endlessly deferred through the duration of the film, and is ultimately frustrated. The migration alluded to in the credits is never seen on the screen, thus producing a double sense of dislocation. It acts as a ghosted presence—we know that it is there, but we cannot see it, replicating in reverse the ghosted effect and dislocation that migration, and the modernity represented by the experience of the metropolis, has created in the contemporary fabric of Galician society.

Fiction and non-fiction categories are also constantly crossed. A number of techniques associated with experimental cinema are employed in *Paris#1*, which intend to create a friction with reality rather than recreating reality though fiction. Thus numerous marks of self-referentiality are inserted in the film, which continually alert the viewers to the filming process, making them aware of the camera's intervention in reality and of the constructed nature of representation. The first scene starts as a picnic in the mountains with a group of young friends setting up their film cameras and recording equipment. The rural idyllic setting is immediately interrupted by the deafening sound of the helicopter coming for water next to them. What follows after that is the result of their engagement with the surrounding Galician reality as seen through the camera lens, witnessing and interrogating the relationship of people to their natural habitats and the formation of a cultural identity. Likewise, the film uses a number of techniques that call attention to its own construction, such as long takes, repeated fades to black, and continuous changes of perspective,

14 The film is also in the tradition of experimental films and *auteur* cinema, with echoes of Fellini, Buñuel, and Saura. The initial image of the helicopter approaching to gather water to control forest fires is reminiscent of Fellini's *La dolce vita* (later used by Icíar Bollaín in *También la lluvia*), whereas the stark treatment of the hunting scene reminds us of Saura's *La caza*, and the sometimes surreal ethnographic look suggests Buñuel's *Las Hurdes, tierra si pan*.

alternating distance and proximity, close shots and full shots without following the traditional suture practices of mainstream cinema. The film employs techniques that emphasize the Brechtian sense of estrangement, aiming to break the false (sense of) transparency of the images represented. Thus continuous jump cuts create a disjointed narrative, while multiple angles and takes of the same subject create a distorted multiperspectivism, thus simulating the working of a wide-angle peripheral vision versus a narrow central vision.

In addition, *Paris#1* repeatedly creates dislocations of image and sound through different technical processes, such as lack of continuity, mismatch, or turning the sound on and off intermittently. One means of highlighting the blurring of borders between reality and fiction in the film is the addition of "noise." This can be visual, in the form of dust speckles and blank frames of white light, or aural, such as the camera's own sound, creating a non-edited amateur/family video style, the feeling of "found footage," and a fake patina of historical elapsed time. The blurry, grainy quality of the black-and-white images suggests the ethnographic approach to a remote location in both time and space, but from a poststructuralist perspective that questions those conceptual boundaries. Thus these technical strategies foreground the frictions of tradition and modernity, urban and rural, challenging the transparency of the camera and disturbing the viewer's cinematographic logic. But spectators can also be disturbed by the tensions produced by the way the content is presented. Some of the film images are thus "difficult" to watch, in particular the inhumane treatment of animals in the hunt sequence, or their auction afterwards, which again has Buñuelian undertones. A form of Brechtian estrangement is employed effectively in one of the scenes, as the group of hunters are merrily gathered and eating bacon and sausage after the hunt, with no other sound than the persistent tolling of the cowbells in the background, thus foregrounding the tensions between nature and culture. The wanderings and polyphonies captured by Laxe's camera oblige the viewer to confront the clash of tradition and modernity, the relationship of people and their habitat in the formation of their cultural identity, and the multiple temporalities of Galician rural life in the modern age, produced by movement, migration, and hybridity. At the same time, they make the viewer confront the limits of representation, revealing in a postmodernist fashion the self-effaced false objective gaze of the camera.

Oliver Laxe's feature film *Todos vós sodes capitáns* is paradoxically exceptional and paradigmatic of the NCG at the same time. This film defines the kind of "border cinema" associated with the NCG, unapologetically experimental avant-garde fiction from the fringes, with a strong peripheral perspective. As the first long feature film that received a great deal of international recognition after its Fipresci award in Cannes, it has been seen as the visiting card of the NCG. At the same time, Galicia is conspicuously absent from the film, almost in an exact reversal of the invisibility of Paris in *Paris#1*. Indeed, *Todos* is a film that crosses traditional geopolitical and conceptual boundaries, as a hybrid production mixing documentary and (meta)fiction, ethnographic and verité styles, and territorial, cultural, and language borders (with its dialogues in Arabic, French, and Spanish, and the director's DVD commentary in Galician). The film's small technical crew was mixed, featuring a French-born Galician director, a German cinematographer, a Galician sound engineer, and two Moroccans as film editor and sound assistant. It was conceived and shot in Tangiers with Moroccan children as protagonists, and produced by a Galicia-based company. In that sense, it is a deterritorialized film that defies the traditional definitions of a national cinema and therefore does not quite fit the traditional paradigm of Galician cinema.[15]

*Todos* was the first production of Zeitun Films, an independent A Coruña-based company created by director Oliver Laxe, producer Felipe Lage, and film critic Martin Pawley. Zeitun has also had a key role in the development of the NCG, as it subsequently produced some of its most emblematic films, such as *Costa da Morte, Arraianos, O quinto evanxeo de Gaspar Hauser* (Alberto Gracia, 2013), and Laxe's *Mimosas* (2016). Interestingly, the expressed goals of the company as stated on their website are explicitly transnational, reflecting its peripheral vision and possibly a call for the attention of co-production partners: "Our objective is to promote co-productions between Europe and North Africa, which are committed to producing films that represent the core elements of cinema, and created by emerging auteurs from both sides of the Mediterranean." The two films produced to date that indeed engage in a dialogue with North Africa are Laxe's own *Todos* and his second feature film *Mimosas*, both of them shot in Morocco.[16]

We could ask ourselves: What is the interest of a Galician director in Tangiers? In principle it could be seen as no different from any other first-world director who has ever shot an ethnographic film in northern Africa, attracted by its difference, or its primitive exoticism, with the underlying weight of a history of an orientalist colonial gaze, including the new postcolonial perspective of progressive cineastes (starting with decolonization, such as Gillo Pontecorvo's classic *The Battle of Algiers* or Fernando Arrabal's *Viva*

---

15 The film has been criticized for its non-Galicianess at least by one Galician film critic, who called it a "Moroccan film" (Romero Suárez, "Idioma").

16 Zeitun ("olive tree" in Arabic) reflects Laxe's connection with the Maghreb and the symbolic centrality of the olive tree in *Todos*, as well as ironically nodding to his own first name.

Figures 20–21  You have to understand that this image is not going to be this image. Self-reflexive cinematic lesson in *Todos vós sodes capitáns* (2010), Zeitun Films.

*la muerte* and *J'irai comme un cheval fou*).[17] The difference, of course, is that because of its historical peripheral position and the limitations of its film industry, Galicia has never participated in that sort of filmic exploration of the other, on the other side of the Mediterranean. Laxe's border cinema thus

17  Morocco was the subject of a good number of Spanish neocolonialist films, such as *La canción de Aixá*, *¡A mí la legión!*, *¡Harka!*, or *La llamada de África*. In the years since decolonization, several films have also focused on the region, including *Morirás en Chafarinas*, *El deseo de ser piel roja*, as well as the popular TV series *Tiempo entre costuras*.

offers a new vision of the periphery from the periphery, as it interrogates precisely the boundaries of filmic representation, the ideological boundaries in the construction of the filmic gaze, and the self/other, center/periphery dichotomies.

Oliver Laxe's personal trajectory is familiar with border crossings, as he was born in Paris from a Galician migrant family, lived in Galicia, studied filmmaking in Barcelona, worked in London, and, since 2007, has been living in Morocco. In Tangiers he worked in a shelter for marginalized children, where he developed the idea for the movie, and eventually shot *Todos*. The location is of paramount importance. Tangiers is a historical border city, international and multilingual, a traditional crossroads between north/south and west/east, and at the same time it encapsulates a radical form of otherness, the traditional religious, racial, ethnic, linguistic, and cultural other to European identity. But its history of European (French and Spanish) colonization and peripherality could be seen through the same lens as that of Galicia, only magnified in the distance. It is thus an appropriate border zone to explore questions of exclusion/inclusion, home/abroad, native/foreigner, which are central to Laxe's own cultural identity and conceptualization of border cinema: "Nuestro cine es bastardo, exiliado, emigrado, fronterizo. Ser artista ya implica ser extranjero, inadaptado" ("Our cinema is a bastard, exiled, migrant, border cinema. To be an artist already implies being a foreigner, a misfit") (Calzada).

*Todos* was based on Laxe's own experience teaching at the Dao Byed cinema workshop for socially excluded youngsters in Tangiers. It is a metafilm, in the form of a fictionalized documentary about the making of a documentary. The film employs different techniques to highlight the process of construction of the cinematographic gaze, such as the duplication of scenes and the use of multiple perspectives which alter the meaning of the images and break the narrative linearity of traditional filmic representation. The film features Laxe in the first part of the movie acting as the director of the workshop, in a constant struggle with his surroundings. As a self-reflexive documentary, the film reveals the underlying tensions and fissures in its own construction, the children's different ideas about the project, the local teachers' opposition to and criticism of the director's self-centered interests, the problems with the crew, the difficulties of shooting in the city, and the director's own ambivalence and eventual "surrender" of the project in midstream. The last half of the film changes the tone, location, perspective, and narrative rhythm, allowing for a different set of visions, which theoretically corresponds to the expressed interests of the children behind the camera (but are also aligned with the director's escape from the conventions of mainstream cinematic representation): non-narrative shots of fields, olive trees, animals, or a group jump in the river, which represent an act of collective creative freedom.

The film adopts a postcolonial and postmodern perspective that resets the lens to decenter the focus and let us see the world from the margins, and not simply by providing the children with a mediated "voice" or giving them the tools to tell their own stories in front of the camera, but by inscribing the tensions and frictions of such a proposal in the film's texture. Thus, *Todos* does not merely document the "good deed" of giving cameras to a group of disadvantaged African children who had never had contact with such technology, which would allow the morally virtuous feeling of empowering marginalized children by allowing them to tell their own stories. That might be the subject of a "feel good" television documentary program. The film instead questions the motivations and the implication of such a move. Rather than legitimizing the paternalistic and superior perspective of the first world, the film explores the effects of the crossing of boundaries, problematizing the relations of power, raising questions of cultural appropriation, the ethical implications of filming the other, and the underlying positions of center and periphery, without giving any final answers.

Another border crossing film that also highlights cultural dislocation, migration, hybridity, and personal storytelling is the eight-minute animation short *1977* (Dir. Peque Varela, 2007), which has also received great international recognition. In this film issues of cultural identity, marginalization, tradition, and modernity are also examined, but from a peripheral queer perspective which questions the social assumptions of heteronormativity and gender conformity. Varela is also a Galician border-crossing director in between languages, cultures, and geopolitical territories. Originally from the peripheral neighborhood of Caranza in Ferrol (A Coruña), she has developed her career as a London-based filmmaker, although with one foot set in Galicia. She obtained a Masters in Animation Direction from the National Film and Television School in the UK and *1977* was her graduation project. The title of the film makes a personal and collective reference to particular time and space coordinates, as 1977 is the year she was born as well as the year that democracy was reinstated in Spain. The film has had enormous circulation, has been shown at many film festivals, including the prestigious Sundance and Clermont-Ferrand festivals, and is widely available on many platforms on the Internet. It has had great critical acclaim, having received more than 20 international awards. It is clever and poignant, conceptually and stylistically well designed, innovative, and thought provoking.

Varela's film, as her own trajectory, shows the blurring of periphery/center dichotomies and binary thinking, as seen in her own geographical mobility from the periphery to the center, and her ability to transcend borders with her work and demolish hegemonic constructions from the margins. Technically, visually, and conceptually, *1977* is also a border-crossing film. It was partly made in Galicia and partly in the UK, with a Galician/ UK team and the support of UK film institutions. Although it does not contain dialogue or voice narration, it mixes Galician, English, and Spanish through words and phrases seen on signs or blackboards, in books, and heard in songs.[18] Musically, it incorporates Galician popular traditions (bagpipers and *pandereteiras*) with modern English indie rock. Visually it effectively mixes color and black-and-white, hand-drawn sketches, computer animation graphics, and real images with stop-play animation. Conceptually it questions the culturally constructed divide of male/female identities and heterosexuality/homosexuality, affirming gender non-conformity and defying sexual heteronormativity.

One of the most visually appealing aspects of the film is the creative use of graphic symbolism taken from the children's domain, which creates its own imaginative narrative logic. Thus, doodles are a constant visual reference throughout the film, marking the drifting into the imaginary, like the drawings in the margins of school notebooks or the internal untangled knot that represents the unresolved confusion in the protagonist's core. Similarly, the use of doll cut-outs (as a color-coded cultural imposition), paper boxes coming unglued, foosballs, boardgames, school blackboards, and calligraphy notebooks alert us to the enforced narrative of cultural conformity. In the same fashion, the film makes constant symbolic references to children's toys, sports, and games, all riddled with cultural rules. This is clearly the case when the protagonist imagines herself as part of a Playmobil figure set; playing games of football, basketball, and foosball; or living her life as a boardgame, such as Guess Who or Game of Life, which act as metaphors for society's cultural identity constructions and normative patterns. Thus the city of Ferrol is represented as the backdrop for the board of Game of Life, with María and her father in a car following a curving road around major locations—the neighborhood, the school, the church, and so on—while receiving rewards (in the form of accumulated money) for achieving societal expectations and good behavior. The Game of Life thus functions as an appropriate visual metaphor for the capitalist system of ideological subjectivation.

The storyline of *1977* is based on the autobiographical experience of the director growing up in Galicia. The film's protagonist is a young schoolgirl

18  This mixing of languages sometimes happens surprisingly in the same context, as in the math book page about subtraction, with the chapter title in English and the problems explanation in Spanish: perhaps a commentary on the politics of bilingual education.

from Ferrol named María, who we see struggling to reconcile herself with familiar and societal expectations as we follow her outward trajectory from her home, neighborhood, school, playground, and city, until her eventual coming out and final liberation. One significant sequence in the film takes place in María's classroom. The school, as Althusser has conceptualized, is a major part of the ideological state apparatus, which reinforces the dominant hegemonic ideology, and one of the central loci of interpellation for the constitution of subjectivity. The lesson of the day written on the blackboard is "resta o substración" (subtraction), described as "diferencia entre duas cantidades" ("difference between two quantities"). The writing on the school blackboard, also repeated in the young María's book, states that difference is the result of the operation of subtraction. It also suggests that cultural "difference" (gender/sexual) itself is subtracted in the school uniformity, an impression corroborated by María's somber face. In the next sequence, she "escapes" from the classroom by imagining the math problem (represented in the book as a set of balls inside a circle) turning into actual soccer balls that come out of the pages of the book and take us outside into the playing field. There María runs happy and free with other boys in pursuit of the ball. The free movement in the field ends, however, when she is trapped in what is now a foosball game, where the protagonist does not fit within the group of players uniformly aligned and attached to the bars. Laughter and insults about gender and sexual orientation non-conformity start to come out as written words from a group of girls watching the game (*machito*, *marimacho*, *tortillera*) while dehumanizing sounds are heard coming from their mouths (the sound of hens clucking). These offensive words become part of María's internal knot, as does the word *maricon*, pronounced by the boys when she rides her pink bicycle in a later sequence, and end up taking over the whole screen, which fades to black. The active knot, seen growing graphically throughout the film, visually represents the internalization of social normativity, the rules of the game, and the pressure to conform.

Similarly, the social construction of gender is allegorized by the Playmobil human figures, with the head of the protagonist trying different body parts that do not fit. This stop-play animation segment finally gives way to an outline drawing by numbers of her body that configures her own transformation from child to adolescent, with her first menstruation and consciousness of her own physicality and sexuality. In a similar way, as her struggle with gender identity was exemplified by toys and games, the discovery of her sexual orientation is shown through a color-coded card-matching game, which also ends with indecipherable words covering the whole screen to black. Finally, after a long internal struggle, she is able to untangle her knot and come out of the black social yarn that contains

Figure 22   Alternative visions from the mainstream margins, deconstructing heteronormativity and gender conformity. Image from the short film *1977* (2007), National Film and Television School, UK.

her, and turns the knot into a writing trace of seagulls that fly away free, and, with that, the last vestige of insulting words collapses in the end. The internal knot, graphic metaphor of the internalized anxiety, confusion, and self-doubt induced by the external pressures of a patriarchal and heteronormative social environment, finally comes out of her body and becomes a tool of empowerment, of creativity, and of constructing her own identity in a way not according to society's expectations.

Other provocative experimental Galician films that deconstruct received notions of gender roles are the creations of Lara Bacelo. Her film short *Varona* (2010) refocuses the old cultural binary divide that makes men the center and women the periphery, starting with the rewriting in its very title that appropriates and feminizes male centrality, deperipheralizing female subjectivity. The film reappropriates the patriarchal gaze and deconstructs sexist discourses of women through sound and vision disjunction. Thus it juxtaposes voice-over narration taken from biblical passages advocating the subjugation of women with modern images of women in pop art style and visual representations taken from media footage. The result is a subversive exploration of women's bodies and sexuality from a non-patriarchal position, appropriating the male gaze and symbolically the central phallus position.

Lara Bacelo's later short *Así falou Penélope* (Thus Spoke Penelope, 2013) also effectively opposes visual and written/aural discourses, in this case poetic and academic texts, echoing the growth of Galician women's writing and feminist discourses since the 1990s. The film revisits the myth of Penelope in the modern Galician imagination, which has had a long history, particularly in the poetic tradition, from Rosalía de Castro to contemporary female writers Ana Romaní, Chus Pato, or María do Cebreiro Rábade Villar. The title of the film makes an explicit reference to Xohana Torres' feminist poem "Penélope," which rewrites the classical myth from a feminist perspective and ends with the lines "Así falou Penélope." The director appropriately calls her film a "videopoema" ("videopoem"), articulated with deconstructed poetic lines from Xohana Torres, Álvaro Cunqueiro, Rosalía de Castro, and X. Díaz Castro, all of whom have produced influential texts rewriting the Penelope myth.[19] The film creates an intertextual palimpsest of representations of self-fulfilling women, from Rosalía's poem about the woman of an emigrant who has departed ("Tecín soia a miña tea" ["I wove my own fabric alone"]) to Torres's feminist rewriting ("Eu tamén navegar" ["I can also sail"]), which effectively deconstructs the image of the subservient and homebound female model in the mythical representation of Penelope, opposing the model of passivity and resigned waiting with the image of a woman who is also a traveler.

The film creates a suggestive visual and audio collage, mixing religious imagery of virgins and female saints with new and recycled found images of everyday women, from old movies to underwear advertising, who are seen sawing, knitting, ironing, and typing, or to inscriptions advocating silence. They are images of women waiting and creating, highlighted by the continuous sound of a clock ticking.[20] The overlay on the aural track of the voice-over from critic Manuel Forcadela, who is later seen in a video conference analyzing the different representations of Penelope in Galician literature, also creates a destabilizing effect. Through able editing, the voice-over narration of the lecturer appears to be the voice the women are listening to while they complete their domestic tasks, as if it was a traditionally "sedative" mainstream radio or television program, thus creating a powerful jarring effect in the narrative of female submission.[21]

---

19  For a critical reading of the myth of Penelope in Galician literature see Helena González Fernández, "La ausencia".

20  The clock ticking reminds us of the central place it occupies in *Mamasunción*, which also mobilizes the Penelope myth as a visual and acoustic metaphor for a lifetime of waiting for the return of the migrant son.

21  Some new documentaries that offer a female-centered perspective on Galician migration include the films *A cicatriz branca* (Dir. Margarita Ledo, 2012), about women migrating to Latin America; *12 horas con Piedad*, focusing on the plight of Piedad, an elderly woman who relocates from the countryside to the city; and *Bs. As.*, about the Galician diaspora in Argentina. Mobility and migration are also featured themes in *Tralas Luces* (Dir. Sandra Sánchez, 2011), which follows a family traveling around from fair to fair with their dodgems.

The manipulation of found images is an often employed technique for questioning the limits of filmic representation, as in the much acclaimed *Vikingland*, a neocompilation film made by manipulating found video footage shot by a Galician ferry worker in the North Sea 20 years earlier. Similar is the lesser known *Cousas do Kulechov* (Dir. Susana Rey, 2006), a mockumentary short with apocalyptic overtones about the popular resistance to an army invasion in Galicia made by recontextualizing through editing everyday images of Galician life and additional found footage: festivals, celebrations, political demonstrations, forest fires, ecological disasters, rural exodus: all become part of a war narrative. The film gives an implicit nod to Orson Welles and his experiments in blurring the limits of fiction and documentary and an explicit one to classic soviet cinema (Lev Kulechov's theoretical writings about narrative order and montage), demonstrating how our perspective of things can change through film editing. Everyday Galician realities are altered to create the effect of war newsreel footage through skillful audio and visual editing: from image selection, fragmentation, and decolorization to changes and additions in the music soundtrack and the overlay of voice-over narration. Thus *bateas* (mussel farm platforms) are magically transformed into naval flotillas, fire-fighting hydroplanes become bombers, and collective *festas gastronómicas* (gastronomy feasts) turn into war rationing lines. Cleverly, Rey's manipulated images suggest Galicia's internal cultural and political contradictions as well as the tensions between the local and the global, the nation and the state. Speaking from the double plane of the mock/documentary, over the realities of Galician culture—its festivities and celebrations, as well as its tragedies, ecological disasters, and political mobilizations—another level of the war narrative is superimposed. This duality creates a constant ironic tension between reality and fiction, the real and the symbolic, which offers a provocative and critical view of both the editing/montage of everyday reality and the media manipulation in the justification of war (which the final credits describe as "the most unjustified and cruel type of montage"). Through the cannibalization of everyday images of Galicia, the film thus offers a picture of Galicia's own cannibalization: ecological disasters, abandonment of the rural, deforestation, exodus, the depoliticization and passivity of the population, all wrapped in festivities and official celebrations, and its continuing peripheral/subservient status within the nation state.

One of the recurring elements of the NCG is the new ethnographic fiction focus on rural Galicia, but it is not a return to a folkloric or an essentialist vision of Galicia. The rural focus might seem perhaps somewhat paradoxical, taking into account Galicia's demographic transformation in the recent decades of fast urbanization and rurbanization, with increased migration from the rural and general abandonment of farming and agricultural activities. Another aspect of this perplexing impression is that avant-garde experimental art is associated with modern city life, while tradition is associated with country life.[22] Likewise, it may be even more puzzling given the fact that most of these young filmmakers are fundamentally urbanites.[23]

It appears symptomatic of the times that for the most part this avant-garde cinema has its focus not on the modernity of urban life, technology, and its comforts but on the miraculous survival of ancestral traditions, the discontinuities of rural life, and its slow disappearance. Often the depictions of rural life transmit a strong sense of place, as if witnessing the last vestiges of a fast-disappearing reality or lamenting something that is already lost. Perhaps this attention to the rural reflects a new vision, with the will to cross the urban/rural borders defining tradition and modernity, old and new, local and global. There may be an even more profound vision, with a determination to scratch through the surface of modernity and see the inherent hybridity and porosity of contemporary Galician culture and the realization that there is a lot of the rural in the urban (and vice versa). An innovative aspect of these films that has attracted the attention of viewers internationally is precisely the new focus that they bring by using experimental film techniques which highlight the tensions underneath the surface of the urban/rural divide and offer a new and more profound vision of the periphery from the periphery. These underlying frictions are highlighted by the use of non-naturalist film approaches that produce breaches of continuity, sound and vision clashes, fades, unstable images, and fictional stagings, which reiterate the marks of their own construction as films. In every case, the new focus on the rural in these films functions as a metaphor for the reimagination of Galicia in the global age, with all its tensions and frictions.[24]

Thus, common tropes in many of these films are isolation, uprootedness, and deracination, as seen in *Paris#1, Arraianos, 12 noites,* and *Rural Pretérito*

22 We should remember, however, that the historical avant-garde used the rural space as a way of shocking the consciousness of bourgeois audiences. That is the case, in the Spanish context, of Luis Buñuel in *Las Hurdes, tierra sin pan,* which audiences and authorities found to be as provocative and subversive, and therefore subject to censorship, as the earlier surrealist experiments done in Paris.

23 Although some were born in the metropolitan diaspora, such as Oliver Laxe in Paris, and Marcos Nine in Hannover (Germany), or have developed their careers overseas, such as Peque Varela in London, their particular strain of cosmopolitism might be inflected by their family background and their contact with the rural.

24 Mónica Delgado has reflected on this aspect of the NCG: "el espacio rural como cobijo natural, el único espacio de preservación de la tradición, y por ende de un estado del alma" ("the rural space as natural shelter, the only space where tradition is preserved, and by extension, a certain state of the soul").

(Dir. Sonia and Miriam Albert Sobrino, 2010). As indicated in its evocative title, the documentary fiction short *Rural Pretérito* focuses on a double temporal and spatial dislocation, a chronotope apparently removed from contemporary reality. It refers to a remote rural enclave that no longer exists, but the memory of the place is still strong in the people who left for the city, which creates tension and gives a spectral presence to the images. The voice-over commentary from two former inhabitants, reminiscing about what was lost and what was gained in the exchange, reveals contradictory feelings. The evocations of the peacefulness and tranquility of the remote village, without any of the comforts of modern life, clashes with memories of the repression of the *maquis* by Franco's forces, who killed the father of one of the informants. While they admit that they are better off now, with access to modern utilities and health care that they did not have in the past, for example, a certain uneasy emptiness invades the film frames, symbolized in the recurring images of dead trees and stumps. The tension between past and present, urban and rural, presence and absence, identity and loss, is reflected in the jagged instability and uncomfortable mobility of the camera, as the lenses try to apprehend the images of the abandoned forest, creating a somewhat phantasmagorical effect of that in-between time/space.

Similarly, *12 noites con Piedad* also focuses on rural/urban tension and temporal/spatial dislocation as it examines two overlapping forms of alienation merging in the figure of Piedad, the last inhabitant of the village, who is diagnosed with Alzheimers and must leave for A Coruña to live with her son. The film thus focuses on the disorienting experiences of forced migration (relocating in old age from the village to the city) and of illness, which creates an alienation from her own memory of her past. Both are dramatic forms of deterritorialization and uprootedness. The clash of tradition and modernity and the end of rural life are literally embodied in Piedad, who at the end is reunited with her young son in the city, but has lost crucial parts of her cultural identity.[25]

These tensions are also palpable in *Arraianos*, an ambitious full-length documentary fiction film focusing on the cultural time/space capsule of A Raia, a rural border zone in Galicia between Spain and Portugal that has maintained its unique cultural hybridity and autarkic nature for centuries. Its strong sense of place and its border location on the periphery of the periphery

25  The focus of these films on the cultural problematics of old age is a repeated trope in other films, such as *Arraianos* and *Arrugas*, and earlier in *Mamasunción*, in part a reflection of Galicia's aging population, the traditional diaspora of young people from the rural to urban centers and beyond Galicia, and the situation of the Galician language, such a determinant of Galician cultural identity, which is commonly associated with both rural areas and old age.

strongly suggests a metaphorical reading of Galicia. Historically known as Couto Mixto, this remote and isolated area did not have any formal political or administrative alignment to either the Spanish or Portuguese states until the late nineteenth century. Couto Mixto was in practice comparable to a free trade zone or an independent state. The reality of this Galician microstate and its uniqueness is a powerful historical example that has captured the imagination of many Galician writers, such as Luís Manuel García Mañá, Jenaro Marinhas del Valle, and X.L. Méndez Ferrín. García Mañá has referred to the Couto Mixto as "unha república esquecida" ("a forgotten republic"), reminding us that Thomas More conceptualized his utopia as an imaginary republic. This forgotten island between Spain and Portugal, historical and legendary, resonates powerfully as a metaphor for the cultural uniqueness of Galicia and the power to imagine other alternative cartographic geographies.

The location in A Raia is of course not casual, as this is a film that is fundamentally defined by its constant crossing of borders. *Border cinema* and *frontier cinema* are terms often employed by many of the filmmakers and critics associated with the NCG to refer to their films, reflecting the crossing of traditional conceptual boundaries, the self-conscious awareness of their peripheral vision positioning, and their production on the fringes of the mainstream. *Arraianos* is a perfect example of the concept of border cinema that explores cultural tensions at the junctions. The film alters the perception of traditional time/space demarcations as fixed, immutable, and impermeable territorial and temporal boundaries. Instead it crosses the geopolitical boundaries of Spain, Galicia, and Portugal, the cultural borders marked by Spanish, Galician, and Portuguese languages, including non-normative and integrationist forms of Galician, and the temporal borders between past and present.

Likewise, the boundaries of the real and the imaginary, fiction and non-fiction, are constantly crossed. The film aims to reflect the duality of a community that exists in a border zone between a prominent enclosed physical world, deeply entrenched with the land, the forest, and the animals, and the no less powerful world of imagination, legends, and myths. In this regard, the director has stated his objective of making his film grounded "on two feet": one in the plane of the real and the other in the plane of the oneiric.[26]

26 Director Eloy Enciso has expressed his goal of accentuating these tensions, rather than settling for harmonic synthesis, conscious that our cultural memory is already a mix of reality and the mythic construction of that reality: "Instead of working in the boundary of genres with a single hybrid language, I decided to explore two apparently antagonistic languages that have no other alternative but to coexist and to create a dialogue between them, as man and animals or reality and

As in the case of other filmmakers of the NCG, the references to the "non-reconciled cinema" postulates of Jean-Marie Straub and Daniele Huillet are recognizable in the use of anti-naturalist strategies that reveal the internal contradictions and frictions, such as non-professional actors, immobile takes, and the insert of literary fictions in the documentary film. Enciso frequently quotes one of their prescriptions as a guiding principle in his films: "Filmar las palabras para que sean como piedras y las piedras como palabras" ("to film words so that they appear as stones and stones as words") ("La celebración del viajero"), crossing the demarcations of sound and vision, orality and visuality.[27]

The tension of reality and fiction in the film is mostly expressed through the clash of realist and anti-naturalist strategies, such as the friction between the naturalist documentary style and the visibly staged acting of non-professional actors who recite literary passages. Their lines are taken from the play *O Bosque* (The Forest), which depicted life in A Raia. It was written in the 1960s by Jenaro Marinhas del Valle, an anti-Franco avant-garde Galician playwright influenced by existentialism, symbolism, and the theatre of the absurd. This strategy creates a double temporal and visual dissonance that reveals glimpses of reality that would not be visible merely through traditional realist representation.[28]

The exploration of these latent tensions through the use of disconcerting strategies is one of the characteristics that makes the NCG visually exciting and conceptually thought-provoking. This is the case of the frequent disjunction between natural settings and the sophisticated technical manipulation employed, as seen in *Arraianos*, *Costa da Morte*, *Montaña en sombra*, and *Eclipse*. One of the new Galician filmmakers who has experimented more

dream do. In this sense, *Arraianos* uses a geographical border just as a cover story to make a frontier film in the sense of the duality of reality and imagination: what is printed in our memory is the mixture of reality and a mythical construction of this reality. [...] My wish is to create a dialogue with memory, which is full of conflicts, contradictions and meanings that change over time. Overall, I tried not to embalm the images, but to make them porous enough so they keep alive after the film is finished" ("Director's Statement").

27  The Brechtian estrangement effect is consciously invoked by Straub and Huillet in their *Non Reconciled* film, which starts with a quote from Brecht: "Instead of wanting to create the impression that he is improvising, the actor should rather show what the truth is: he is quoting."

28  This idea of crossing borders is also reflected in the careful construction of the soundscape in the film, with the repeated use of sound crossfades and overlays, which transmit the idea of connection between apparently disconnected different scenes, planes, words and actions, the forest and inhabited spaces, and humans and nature.

Figure 23  Waves are born in the periphery. The lighthouse in Cabo Vilán, from *Costa da Morte*. Border zones of land/sea, day/night, light/darkness, visible/invisible, here/there, and reality/imagination, lighthouses appear as recurring motifs in Galician maritime culture that redraws these binaries and alters center/periphery demarcations, from Manuel Rivas or Luar na Lubre to Miguelanxo Prado and Xavier Villaverde.

profoundly with this type of sound and image disjunction in his films is Lois Patiño. By mixing naturalist and anti-naturalist techniques, his documentary fiction films aim to give a fuller picture of the relationship between the Galician natural world and its inhabitants. Patiño employs an unorthodox cinematographic approach in examining the interactions of nature and culture, the landscape and its people, and their mutual influence and effects. Through the use of anti-naturalist techniques he makes nature come alive in full force with an almost magical quality, focusing on the otherwise imperceptible movements and sounds in the landscape and the magnificent force of nature on the lives of the people.

In his acclaimed film *Costa da morte*, sound and vision clash in a large canvas of carefully composed natural scenery and sophisticated sound design, aiming to capture both the depth and the detail of the landscape and its inhabitants.[29] His visual approach to nature is therefore not simply

29 Costa da Morte (Coast of Death) is the popular name of the coast in the traditional land's end of Galicia and the continent (Fisterra), where the sun sets, between the land and the sea, the end and beginning of the old known world. This legendary space between reality and fiction, life and death, with its rugged coast, heavy winds and mist, and long history of shipwrecks, has given it a magical, mysterious, and ghostly character in the Galician imagination, while its location in the hyper-periphery makes it an almost symbolic representation of Galicia.

naturalistic, but more as seen through the lens of a painter.[30] Thus his films create extraordinary estrangement effects through the repeated use of long and static shots of the Galician coastal scenery, the exaggerated dwarfing of human figures against stunning panoramic images, and the frequency of extreme high-angle shots from humanly impossible observation points. These techniques avoid the flat unidimensional central view of mainstream cinema, opting instead for a fuller and wider peripheral vision which offers a more complex approximation to reality.[31]

As an audiovisual experimental artist, his approach to sound is equally non-naturalistic. Patiño has explained his development of the technique of visual–sound dissonance as a "double distance" between the image and the sound. The filmic representation is visually distant, as seen through the panoramic camera lenses, but acoustically close, as heard through the amplified remote microphones:

> I sought to relate the vastness of the natural space to the intimate experience of people through a double perceptual distance to the human figure (far in the image close in the sound). Eventually through the deep contemplation of the image we will dissolve in the whole and disappear into the landscape of Costa da Morte.

This "double distance" technique is employed to maximum effect in *Costa da Morte*, where distant opening shots of the immensity of the sea or the magnificence of a mountain are typically juxtaposed with the close-up of the voices, body noises, and tools of the humans in the far distance, which create visual–sound clashes aiming to capture "the voice of the landscape." A good example of the effective use of this technique is the panoramic image of the Galician forest wrapped in mist, which forcefully communicates the

---

30  In that regard, and for all its breathtaking natural images, the film is not simply a "postcard," as it has sometimes been described (Pagán, "Algumhas consideraçons sobre a língua de Costa da Morte"; Romero Suárez, "Idioma e identidad en el Novo Cinema Galego"). The director has admitted that his painter's perspective is a result of his own family background and education, as both his parents, the influential founders of the 1980s *Atlántica* movement Antón Patiño and Menchu Lamas, are painters. Likewise, in some of his shorts Patiño even experimented with distortion through the use of filters and petroleum jelly on the lenses to create non-realistic visual effects closer to abstract painting.

31  The peripheral vision shift could be seen as a recurring feature in the non-reconciled NCG, but it is a key visual component of *Costa da Morte*. The experimentation with non-central visions and the display of panoramic landscapes with decentralized human figures thus defy traditional visual notions of perspective and central vision established since the Renaissance, as was mentioned in Chapter 2 in reference to Brueghel and Bosch.

Figure 24  Wide-angle peripheral vision focusing on the margins of the frame, from *Costa da Morte* (2012), Zeitun Films. The foggy vision and magnified sound of the falling trees allow viewers to fully perceive the effect of the disappearing forest.

deforestation of the Galician habitat by unnaturally amplifying the sound of the logger's breathing and the menacing sound of the power saws barely seen in the distance.[32]

This technique also adds multiple layers to the "texture" of the film. Different temporal layers are superimposed through the distant/close dialogues of the people commenting on events in the collective memory of the place, such as tragedies which occurred during the Spanish civil war or famous shipwrecks in the nineteenth century. As Patiño explains, "their voices breach through new strata of the landscape to shape the collective imaginary of that place and leave us in a timeless space." The ultimate goal of this multi-layered visual–sound representation is to build the collective imaginary and identity of this landscape.[33]

Conceptual and technical disjunctions, cultural fissures, and temporal/spatial disruptions are also at the heart of *Vikingland*, one of the most

32  This image of the pine trees is the long opening shot of the film, which acquires special significance given the metaphoric importance of the pine trees as symbols of the nation, as has been previously discussed, and its correlation with the title of the film, Coast of Death.

33  The film has been criticized for the use of language, which reflects the actual speech of many working-class Galicians (using "castrapo," a Galicianized version of Spanish, with Galician vocabulary, syntax, and entonation). See Pagán ("Algumhas consideraçons sobre a língua de Costa da Morte"); Romero Suárez ("Idioma e identidad en el Novo Cinema Galego").

Figure 25   Found footage manipulation and the symbolic "rebirth" of Galician cinema. Blurred positioning between two lands in *Vikingland* (2011), Filmika Galaika.

widely acclaimed documentary border films of the NCG. Here the territorial polarities of sea and land, home and abroad, function as reflectors of other tensions: between tradition and modernity, culture and nature, documentary reality and fiction, home video and professional production, as well as the local and the global. All these tensions converge in the film as it explores cultural mobility, migration, isolation, and deracination, which are central issues of Galician identity, as well as self-reflective issues of film language and visual representation. For these reasons *Vikingland* has acquired a certain emblematic character in the NCG, and it could be seen to represent a filmic metaphor of Galicia in the global age.

The main locus of the film is a ferry boat in the North Sea, where some Galician sailors work as seasonal migrants.[34] The film employs real found footage, made by one of these workers with his newly bought camera to document the trip for his friends and family. This unique location/dislocation and the relationship of man and camera encapsulate the essence

---

34 Another director who has focused on Galician migration in Northern Europe is Eloy Domínguez Serén, in *Pettring* (2012) and *Ingen ko på isen/No Cow on the Ice* (2015), where he explores his own experience as migrant and his relationship with Galicia.

of the film. All the cultural tensions seem to be metaphorized in the video images of the ferry boat, a chronotope of an interstitial space, in-between coasts, permanently dislocated. The idea of passage, the journey back and forth across the shores, also dramatizes a struggle for survival, cultural identity, and sense of (collective) self. This appears as a perfect metaphor for Galician diasporic mobility and hybrid cultural identity, also reflected in the mixing of Galician, Spanish, German, and Dutch in the film.[35] At the same time, the interrelationship of land, sea, boat, and man through the mediation of the camera represents the irruption of modern technologies and, metaphorically, Galicia's "discovery" of the cinematographic gaze.

*Vikingland* is a story of journeys and discoveries, essentially made by the careful manipulation of found footage. The director, Xurxo Chirro, discovered several old VHS tapes that contained original camera footage recorded by Luis Comba, a Galician sailor who had been working in the North Sea 20 years before. Vikingland was the name written on the transferred tapes, and the name of the ferry boat where Luis, the cameraman and main "actor" of the movies, worked, servicing the journey between the port of Rømø in Denmark and the German island of Sylt. There were more than 12 hours of unedited footage, which documented the daily lives of Luis and his working mates away from Galicia, his interactions with the surroundings, and his own experimentation with the camera. Chirro was fascinated with the intense raw power of the found images and the possibilities offered for further manipulation, and decided to use them to make his full length film. However, rather than using the found footage to recontextualize it and give it a new meaning, as is usually the case in other experimental films, he preferred to maintain it intact and expand the communicative power of the images. In spite of all the technical limitations, artistic deficiencies, and deterioration of old home video, Chirro's guiding idea was to respect the original significance of the found images. There was a personal proximity and an emotional charge to these tapes, as his background was similar to Luis Comba's. They were from the same coastal village of A Garda, both had been sailors—Chirro was on board a high-seas fishing vessel in the South Atlantic at the time when Luis was shooting his movie—and Chirro's father had been embarked on the same ferry as Luis, being one of the original intended recipients of the tapes. This gave him a close understanding of

35 This dislocation and in-between status is highlighted visually and musically in the powerful sequence in which the protagonist strikes different poses in front of the camera while listening to the edgy rock song "Entre dos tierras" ('Between two lands') by the Spanish band Héroes del silencio: "entre dos tierras estás, y no dejas aire que respirar" ("you are between two lands, and you leave no air to breathe").

the images and an appreciation of the uniqueness of the vision. He was also conscious of the rarity of a true worker's point of view in the history of cinema, without preconceived notions or intermediaries. And in this found footage he had the direct vision of a Galician working man behind the lens, who becomes the subject and protagonist of his story and not just the object of the camera. Thus Chirro initiated a process of filmic reconstruction, which was at the same time personal, familiar, and collective.

Chirro's purpose was not to rewrite Luis' story but to retell it with better means while amplifying its message. He defined his role as, rather than director, "manipulator" of Luis's original images, who receives credit as cinematographer in the movie. He worked on the montage continuously for four years, creating 12 different full edits. A fictional narrative structure was superimposed onto the original footage, inspired by the great novels of maritime travel in the tradition of Conrad and Melville, and in particular following the structure of *Moby Dick*, with the narrating role of the sea-wandering Luis/Ishmael, the different challenges experienced, the symbolic use of white and the fades to white. As a result of his manipulation, Luis's images are transferred from analog to digital format and passed from the small story to the big story, from the register of the personal to the collective, and from the realm of the domestic to the epic.

The technique of "found footage" manipulation offers many possibilities for experimental cinema. It is a low-cost material for production purposes and is conceptually exciting in its easy malleability for visual experimentation.[36] As in the case of the "finding" in other founding myths (such as Santiago, as we saw in Chapter 3), we could see this found footage also as an *inventio*, in the sense of being both a finding and a creation. The process is initiated with a discovery which generates a process of self-discovery: something that was invisible and was made visible. The found footage in *Vikingland* generates a journey of identity discovery away from home as well as a journey of visual discoveries.

This finding, which Chirro has called a "magical" apparition, powerfully suggests the discovery of the magic of the reels and the preservation of the collective memory of a community.[37] The discovery of the visual

---

36  Found footage has been employed often in a number of NCG non-fiction films, such as Xurxo Chirro's earlier *Cellular Movie*, Marcos Nine's *Manuscritos* and *Aarón*, Magín Blanco and Otto Roca's *Memoria*, Susana Rey's *Cousas do Kulechov*, and Alberte Pagán's *Bs. As.*

37  As Chirro stated to the UK press, symbolically emphasizing the "magical" and "miraculous" nature of the finding: "that's why I say that Vikingland is made from a miracle, that the images were on the point of being lost, the facts that they document forgotten, and something erased definitively from history" (Naughten).

reflection signifies the mirror-stage entrance into the symbolic order with the communal act of (self)-reflection on the big screen.[38] Luis's process of discovery is thus shared in Chirro's movie with the experience of the spectator, who follows the different stages of the metaphorical journey: the exploration and interaction with the camera, the possibilities of the new technology, and the experimentation with filmic language.

The found footage has also the quality of the primitive, raw, untouched, resembling in that sense the origins of visual representation. Although devoid of artistic ambitions, it has the innocence of the virginal gaze, as if contemplating reality for the first time, and the virginal materiality of the analog blank tape which captures the images in its magnetic reels. It has also been argued that *Vikingland* becomes a metacinematic reflection that narrates in parallel a dialogue with the history of cinema: starting at its very beginning, from the images of the workmen's exit at the Lumière factory and Méliès, primitive films, amateur movies, and proletarian cinema, to the spectacular scenery of John Ford and the avant-garde manipulation of experimental cinema, while summing up several decades of technological innovation (from analogue Hi8 and VHS tapes to digitalization in miniCV and DAT).[39] As the director has commented: "This technological evolution works as a metaphor for history where what happened to these men does not count for the 'History' written in capital letters" (Naughten).

We could say that *Vikingland* also encapsulates a history of Galician cinema: from its humble amateur beginnings, the cinema of the diaspora and of its later development, with all its discontinuities and holes, to its resurgence and growth and its latest transformation with the avant-garde documentary fictions of experimental cinema. Perhaps most significantly, the film reconstructs an important lost page of the history of Galician cinema: its unique origins as amateur epistolary cinema of migration

---

38 Delgado has also noted this important symbolic dimension of the film-within-the-film, which includes: "Tomas de lo cotidiano, del día laboral, del ingreso y salida de pasajeros y mercancías, y de ocio son capturados desde lo que se podría llamar un acto primigenio, y que encuentra una analogía perfecta en el juego del niño que por primera vez descubre su reflejo en el espejo, un símil del hallazgo del artefacto tecnológico con el estadio lacaniano, una celebración del encuentro del yo a través de la imagen." ("Shots of the everyday, the workday, the entry and exit of passengers and goods, and times of leisure are captured from the perspective of what could be called a primal act, with the perfect analogy of the child who for the first once discovers his reflection in the mirror, making a simile of the finding of a technological gadget with the Lacanian mirror stage, a celebration of the encounter of the self through image").

39 See Pagán, "Vikingland, película perfecta," for a detailed analysis of *Vikingland*'s creative dialogue with film history.

(discussed in Chapter 4).[40] Like the epistolary cinema of earlier decades, Luis Comba shot his film with the intention of sending it to the people "at home" so they could see what his life was like in the distant land where he worked and maintain alive the communicative emotional bond during the long absences. In that sense, *Vikingland* represents a return to the beginning, a return home, and a full closing of the circle.[41]

In essence, *Vikingland* narrates an experience which is at the core of Galician identity, marked by travel, migration, dislocation, and cultural hybridity. In that sense, Chirro's reassemblage and reconstruction of the loose tapes acquires a metaphorical quality, as a way of regenerating the fragmented identities and discontinuities of Galician culture and history. It is the great allegorical Galician movie of cultural mobility and emotional separation, of *morriña* and *saudade*, which portrays the anonymous life of Galician sailors, the experience of migration, and working at sea far away from home.[42] *Vikingland* is a film in which we can say that the sea becomes a protagonist, as in other recent emblematic Galician films such as *Costa da Morte*, *Crebinsky*, and *De profundis*.[43] The sea is a recurring central element, uniting and separating, giving and taking lives. It has a historical and mythical significance for Galicia, a border zone between reality and imagination, with the powerful imagery of sunken and resurfacing treasures.

Perhaps it is true that waves are born on the periphery. The reappearance of the forgotten video tapes from the ferry in *Vikingland*, like the re-emergence of the sunken ship in *De Profundis*, then acquires a magical aura, which powerfully suggests the resurgence of the Galician visual imagination, coming out of the darkness into visibility. With the cannibalization of the old images and the long metaphorical voyage towards the home port, *Vikingland* could thus also be seen above all as an allegory of the rebirth of Galician cinema, rising from its ashes.

---

40 Also within the Galician epistolary cinema of migration are Pagán's *Bs. As.*, Domínguez Serén's *Pettring*, and his collaboration with Marcos Nine's *Carta 1* and *Carta 2* (2012), relying on the family/friend correspondence exchange as the main narrative structure.

41 Chirro accentuates the collective nature of the addressees by leaving out of focus the main intended recipient of the original video images, which Luis shot to send to his Mexican girlfriend Lupita, so that she could understand the nature of his work, the life at sea, and why he needed to be away from home for six months at a time. Chirro later recovered the discarded images for his short *Lupita* (2012).

42 See Cascudo for an analysis of *Vikingland* and the Galician migration cinema.

43 The sea has been a central motive in many films set in Galicia, from the old *gallegadas*, such as *Botón de ancla*, *Sabela de Cambados*, *Polizón a bordo*, and *Mar abierto*, to the new commercial cinema made in Galicia in recent years, such as *Los lunes al sol*, *Mar adentro*, *Ilegal*, *A praia dos afogados*, and *Entre bateas*.

# PART THREE

# Global Sounds

# CHAPTER EIGHT

# Peripheral *Movidas*:
# Cannibalizing Galicia

Galicia pasó de exportar "latas de sardina" a emerger como competencia
que había que tener en cuenta en el ámbito de la creatividad.
'Galicia went from exporting "sardine cans" to emerging as a competent
player that had to be taken into account in the area of creativity.'
Fernando Franco, *Periféricos*

Una ciudad que intenta superar el franquismo sumida en una cruda reconversión
industrial, con enormes desigualdades sociales a la orden del día y aires de
libertad brotando a borbotones por todas las esquinas. Un contexto propicio
para el desafío, la transgresión, la imaginación, el surrealismo o la ironía
[...] Una ciudad epicentro de la movida gallega, ese babel de estilos que
marcó para siempre una de las épocas más creativas de nuestra historia ...
'A city trying to overcome Francoism in the midst of a severe industrial
reconversion, with great social inequalities everywhere and airs of freedom
bubbling over with force on every street corner. A propitious context for
confrontation, transgression, imagination, surrealism, or irony [...] A
city that was the epicenter of the movida gallega, a babel of styles that
defined forever one of the most creative periods of our history ...'
*Periféricos*.

Con reconversión ou sen reconversión, Vigo é unha nación.
'With the reconversion or without the reconversion, Vigo is a nation.'
Os Resentidos

The modern transformation of Galician culture, from exporting "cans of
sardines" to exporting images, music sounds, and fashionable concepts
in the 1980s, could be seen as indicative of a significant paradigmatic
shift from the industrial era to a postindustrial phase of postmodernity.
The commercial image of the "can of sardines" has often been recycled in
Galician contemporary visual arts and graphic design, conveying ironically

Figure 26   *Letras Galegas en Escabeche* (Pickled Galician Letters), ironic cultural reconversion of Galician identity from the *artivist* collective Aduaneiros Sem Fronteiras. Design by Pancho Lapeña (2007).

both the specter of industrial decay and the construction from its ashes of modern new forms of Galician identity.[1] It is in itself a sign of cultural reconversion. The meanings conveyed in this symbolic image, with its implicit Galicianization of Andy Warhol's iconic Campbell's soup can, suggest the cultural transformation of a Galicia associated with the old and decaying industrial past into a new form of Galicianess redefined creatively within the scope of pop culture. This image is indicative of the profound industrial and cultural reconversion of Galicia during the years of the *Movida galega*, symbolically converted in a new Warholian "factory" of products for cultural consumption through the internal self-cannibalization of its past and traditions.

In parallel, a second form of cultural cannibalization has also occurred from outside. Much has been written in recent years about the cultural

---

1  A recent example of this type of image reconversion was fashioned by Pancho Lapeña, from the collective *Aduaneiros Sem Fronteiras*, who created a new Galician typography commemorating the Día das Letras Galegas "Day of Galician Letters" in 2007, converting old Galician fonts into TTF digital fonts for the twenty-first century.

production of *la Movida* years in Spain, with almost exclusive attention paid to the phenomenon centered around Madrid, to the detriment of other manifestations across the Spanish nation state. Such has been the case of the cultural productions of one of the most active peripheral *Movida* "centers" during the 1980s, that of the *Movida galega*, and specifically its cultural "epicenter," the *Movida de Vigo* or *Movida viguesa*. In spite of the great explosion of creativity in music, fashion, graphic design, and the visual arts during the 1980s in Galicia, which aimed to define a modern urban Galician culture, the phenomenon has received only minimal academic attention to date.[2] For all the interest generated, these have been, and still are, "peripheral *movidas*," largely co-opted and appropriated by the cultural industry and media apparatus of *la Movida madrileña* as a form of cannibalization of the exotic.

There are, then, several distinct meanings to the concept of cannibalization in relation to the *Movida galega*: internal self-cannibalization (recycling and reconversion) and external cannibalization (appropriation and co-option). This chapter aims to offer a critical overview of the *Movida galega*, examining the peripheral/center and Spanish/Galician dynamics of the phenomenon, as well as its internal process of formation and cannibalization. I will focus on several key figures where the musical, the visual, and language cut across different definitions of Galician culture, cannibalizing tradition and modernity, as well as local, national, and international symbols, images, and idioms, to create a new Galician urban culture. I will examine in particular the creative output of the seminal bands of the *Movida viguesa*, such as Siniestro Total and Os Resentidos, and the video creation of Xavier Villaverde and Antón Reixa, authors of the anthem of the *Movida galega* "Galicia caníbal," which offers a template of the cultural tensions and anxieties of the movement resolved with postmodern irony and serves as a main point of reflection for the chapter, extending the concept to examine the process of appropriation and co-option by *la Movida madrileña*.[3]

Some exceptions to the general critical neglect of the *Movida viguesa* are the local documentary *Periféricos* (2006), underlining its peripherality as the one single identifying characteristic, and Emilio Alonso's recent monograph

---

2 The area of fashion related to the *Movida galega* has received some academic attention in recent years, particularly Natalia Quintas Froufe's study and the retrospective exhibit "Los 80 Moda en Galicia. Singularidades," curated by Silvia García González and Cristina Varela, from the Escuela de Bellas Artes in Pontevedra (Issuu.com, *Os 80*). See also Lara Varela.

3 *Galicia caníbal* was also the title of Antón Reixa's film documentary about the music of the *Movida galega*, released in 2011. As noted below, *Galicia Caníbal: El Musical* was staged in 2012–13.

*Vigo a 80 revolucións*, both of them local productions with limited reach.[4]
The title of my chapter thus reflects the problematic peripherality of this
phenomenon in a double sense. On the one hand, the *Movida galega* has
often been relegated to little more than a historical footnote in the existing
critical accounts of *la Movida* in Spain (such as José Luis Gallero's pioneering
*Sólo se vive una vez: Esplendor y ruina de la movida madrileña*). On another
level, the *Movida galega* was an ambiguously decentered phenomenon from
its inception, subject to negotiations with the center while fully aware of
its marginal positionality. In this regard, and unlike the minority *Rock
Radikal Vasco*, which generally did not intend to reach audiences beyond
the limits of the Basque country, the rock groups of the *Movida galega* had
an active relationship with *la Movida madrileña* and the rest of the nation
state. In that sense, there was a fundamental tension between a centripetal
movement towards national exposure, commercial success, and acceptance,
and a centrifugal resistance to being a mere appendix of the geopolitical
and cultural center, consciously positioned in the margins as a critical and
self-questioning gesture of cultural identity. In a certain way, the struggle to
resist assimilation was closely related to its ultimate collapse, as we will see.

## *Vigo Capital Lisboa*

In order to understand the origins of this cultural development it is
necessary to gather some historical background and consider the crucial
political, economic, and social processes taking place in Spain, and those
particularly relevant in the Galician context. The late 1970s and early
1980s in Spain coincided with the period of the political Transition, which
was characterized by a sudden acceleration of systemic changes on a scale
perhaps previously unknown in modern Spanish history. This was even
more noticeable in the case of Galicia. Because of its peripherality, modernity
had never been fully and evenly implemented, but suddenly it was caught in
the eye of the storm of modernity with full force. The general transformation
of Spanish political structures by the democratic process of the Transition
years was accompanied by the ensuing process of political devolution
and administrative decentralization and the formation of the Galician
autonomous government between 1979 and 1981, when the Xunta de Galicia
was officially constituted. There was also a parallel process of cultural
liberalization and revitalization, reinforced by the new political climate,
which had peculiar inflections in the case of Galicia. After the centuries-long

---

4 Emilio Alonso's book offers a detailed chronicle of the *Movida viguesa*, with an
excellent resource of visual materials, but it has not reached beyond Galicia.

history of Galicia's political and economic domination by the Spanish nation state and the repression of its cultural identity, greatly reinforced by Franco's military dictatorship, Galicia was again starting to stand on its own. This was noticeable in the affirmation of long-repressed Galician identity, the rediscovery of its roots, and the revitalization of the local autonomous culture. At the same time, this process of cultural reinvention was also marked by a widespread interest in experimentation and creativity, a general embrace of innovation and modernity, and a distinct cultural openness to the outside world in sync with contemporary cultural international trends, perhaps as a reaction to the long-term peripheral subordination within the nation state.

The years of the Transition were also marked by major economic and social shifts at the national level as a result of a sustained and profound economic crisis. Paramount in this context during the first stage of neoliberalism was the process of "reconversion," or restructuring of the obsolete industrial sectors that had developed in the protectionist Franco era, in terms of outdated equipment and processes, inefficient policies, unprofitable businesses artificially maintained, excessive labor costs, and an unbalanced workforce. In Galicia this general situation had particular inflections, with a dramatic crisis in the key shipbuilding, steel, and textile industries of the urban coastal areas, particularly around Vigo and Ferrol. These sectors were particular targets of government adjustment measures in the context of Spain's accession to the EEC, such as the 1981 Industrial Reconversion Act and the 1984 Law of Reconversion and Reindustrialization, which included severe and wide-ranging forced reductions in the workforce in those particular sectors (López-Claros 18).

At the same time, a rapid demographic urbanization was taking place in Galicia, with large population shifts from the rural areas to the urban centers, which caused a general abandonment of an agriculture-based economy in favor of a consumer services economy. These changes created significant pockets of unemployment and underemployment and a parallel underground black economy, in which drug trafficking and consumption suddenly became widespread activities.[5] As a result of these developments, the transition years in Galicia were characterized by social unrest and major mobilizations of urban workers and unions protesting against plant

5 Significantly in this respect, the cultural and industrial reconversion in Galicia paralleled the reconversion of the long-established small-scale contraband channels of consumer goods (such as tobacco) into full-blown drug-trafficking cartels operating globally, as a result of which Galicia became one of the main points of introduction of cocaine into Europe.

closures and layoffs and demanding better economic conditions. Amid all these demographic, economic, and industry-driven changes, Vigo saw the emergence of a new urban youth culture. If it is true that moments of crisis can also represent moments of opportunity for reinvention, perhaps the moment was particularly ripe in Galicia, and even more in Vigo, the industrial and economic capital of which was most heavily affected by the governmental reconversion policies. As the rest of the chapter will argue, these social phenomena had a real impact on the development of the *Movida viguesa*.

The terms *Movida galega* and *Movida viguesa* were, and still are, used practically interchangeably, as the urban area of Vigo was the recognized epicenter of the cultural effervescence of the 1980s in Galicia, with an unprecedented upsurge in the areas of music, design, fashion, and the visual arts (Xelís de Toro). One has to wonder why this was the case in a city that had always defined itself as fundamentally industrial and away from the centers of administrative and political power. I would like to highlight several aspects of Vigo's unique history and modern development as the largest Galician urban area, and of its reconversion crisis, that are important determinants for the emergence of the phenomenon known as *Movida galega*.

Comparatively speaking, Vigo is a very recent urban phenomenon. It had one of the fastest growth rates in Spain of the twentieth century, seeing its population increase from a mere 15,000 inhabitants at the end of the nineteenth century to 300,000, with a metropolitan area of around 500,000, at the beginning of the twenty-first century. It has become the largest fishing port in Europe, with a fishing fleet working around the world, and is at the time of writing the headquarters of the European Union Fisheries Agency. Its fast and unplanned growth, and the legacy of the excesses of *desarrollismo*, make it a chaotic modern city to live in from an urban planning perspective, where rurality and urbanism collide in strange surreal ways. Thus bizarre images such as a university built on top of the highest mountain, a major multinational automotive plant surrounded by small cabbage patches, the tallest skyscraper erected on a tiny Celtic settlement island, or a massive car-parking dock sprawling in the middle of its bay evoke a savage process of urban self-cannibalism.

Politically, Vigo has faced some paradoxical circumstances. It is the most important urban center in Galicia and the main engine of its industrial growth, but has been historically relegated to the margins of political power. It is also the largest city in Spain that is not a provincial capital (since the national territorial reorganization of 1833). Vigo was again marginalized when Galicia's Statute of Autonomy was enacted in 1981, and Santiago de Compostela was selected as the political and administrative capital of the Autonomous Government (A Coruña also felt initially marginalized, but to a much lesser extent, owing to its proximity to Santiago and its position as the capital of the same province). This situation has resulted in a perennial detrimental position away from the official centers of power. *Vigo Capital Lisboa*, the ironic and polysemic title of Os Resentidos' debut album from 1984, should be understood in this cultural context. On one level, it deterritorializes the geopolitical space and imagines an alternative cartography in which Vigo is symbolically repositioned and realigned on a postnational map. And, on another level, Vigo may not be a political capital, but its cultural capital is emphasized and the city resituated as the epicenter of a possible new Atlantic alliance (with a nod to the Vigo-based *Atlántica* movement in the visual arts). A similar irony was also central in Siniestro Total's 1984 album, titled *Menos mal que nos queda Portugal*.[6]

We should remember also that Vigo was one of the cities most adversely affected by the crisis of the shipbuilding, steel, and textile industries, which represented (with the automotive sector) the largest industrial employers in the region. The process of industrial reconversion caused the restructuring and final closure of many plants, big and small, which had been family-run for generations and were the backbone of the modern city's identity. This process was punctuated by massive layoffs and strikes. Vigo, which has a long tradition as a center of political agitation, experienced renewed social unrest as a result of these events. Many of these themes will make ghostly appearances in emblematic songs of the *Movida de Vigo* groups ("Sector Naval" and "Economía sumerxida" by Os Resentidos, "Superavit, superavit," "¿Qué tal homosexual?" and "Fuimos un grupo vigués" by Siniestro Total).[7]

As a result of this complex situation, marked by economic unrest, unmet demands for greater political autonomy, and a symbolic recognition of its role as a catalyst of modernity in Galicia, it might be expected that a certain amount of collective pent-up frustration, politically and culturally, would grow in Vigo in the years of the Transition. Unemployment and the lack of either traditional job opportunities or the possibility of continuing the family business meant that many young people had to choose different solutions and imaginative alternatives. Many recent university graduates, unemployed or underemployed, opened bars and cafes or started producing fanzines, playing live concerts, and putting on cultural performances and

6  There is also a local in-joke involved in the title ("Thank goodness we still have Portugal"), as, in the soccer fandom subculture, Deportivo da Coruña fans derisively refer to Celta de Vigo fans, and people from Vigo in general, as "Portuguese."

7  Vigo's tradition of political agitation and violence is ironically invoked in "Fuimos un grupo vigués," ("We were a band from Vigo"), which overlaps the biography of a musical group with the terrorist group GRAPO, founded in Vigo.

art exhibits, and the borders between all these activities were extremely porous.

The recently launched TVG also offered new opportunities, and a major media platform, in the audiovisual arena. The new and active night scene, with the proliferation of bars, clubs, and cultural events, represented an opportunity for creativity, while its neon brilliance also offered for many a form of escape from the gloomy economic realities. The industrial reconversion was thus accompanied by a parallel cultural reconversion, with a peculiar mixture of a rebellious spirit, restlessness, creativity, fluidity, and hedonistic practices. Paradoxically, euphoria and *desencanto* were two complementary sides of the *Movida* phenomenon. A general sense of disillusionment with the political establishment was often accompanied by the embrace of cultural and sexual liberties and hedonistic excesses allowed by the new, liberal political and cultural climate.

A related issue involves the difficult efforts to reconcile the spontaneous outbursts of individual creativity with the establishment of a proper cultural industry. It is not completely surprising that the *Movida viguesa* was characterized by this bicephalous nature, whereby creativity was channeled through both the countercultural alternative youth movement expressed most audibly in the musical arena and an entrepreneurial side most visibly expressed in fashion and design. Yet, the visual arts, fashion, photography, design, video, and music were not separate, but were contiguous areas with a great deal of porosity in between. In fact, this multidisciplinary aspect may be one of its defining characteristics. There was a confluence of musicians, artists, designers, writers, and journalists in the time-space that is known as *Movida viguesa* as an expression of a modern Galician cultural identity. The embracing and enjoyment of the new vibrant local scene of bars, music concerts, happenings, cultural magazines, fashion shows, and art galleries was representative of this cultural affirmation as a young and free urban culture, and of its openness and its desire to project itself towards the outside world. There may have been "Malos tiempos para la lírica" (bad times for poetry), as the Golpes Bajos song famously stated after Brecht, but there were very good times for creativity in a range of disciplines.

The political context was also an important factor for the emergence of the *Movidas*. With democracy newly regained, Spain experienced in the late 1970s and early 1980s a collective outburst of freedom and liberation of forces. The failed coup in 1981 was a reminder of a recent past that nobody wanted to remember. In Galicia, the first autonomous government of the Xunta was just being established and the first democratic municipal elections held after Franco in 1979 brought to power a new socialist mayor in Vigo, Manuel Soto, who was to oversee the municipality in the crucial years

1979–91. Soto soon became a keen promoter of the new modern image of the city, and would become the orchestrator of the Vigo–Madrid official *Movida* connection, as will be seen later. What is clear from the above analysis is that there is not one single explanation for the emergence of the *Movida viguesa*. It happened because a given number of political, social, and economic circumstances aligned, gathering together a group of creative individuals with common collective desires at the right time and at the right place. Likewise, the *Movida viguesa* did not form a unified movement, as it was ideologically extremely varied, but its diverse participants shared common cultural contexts and a large degree of interactivity in a reduced space.[8]

## Bad Times for Poetry? Rock and Nationalism

In fundamental cultural, economic, and political aspects, Spain's democratic Transition and its cultural *Movidas* implied a profound reconversion and creative recycling of the past into something new. There was a definite epochal "newness" in the air, in terms of aesthetic trends, urban language, forms of self-expression, moral attitudes towards sexuality and gender identity, urban spaces, and interclass mobility and confluence, particularly in the social spaces created around the rock music and drug subcultures. In the area of popular music, the emerging youth music movement was referred as "nueva ola," in a direct allusion to the British post-punk "new wave" that was its closest reference, but soon it would be rebaptized as part of the general urban youth *"movida"* of sex, drugs, and rock'n'roll by the Spanish media, and the new term was then applied to the new underground cultural scene as a whole, as a general rubric to include the emerging performance and visual arts as well as the parallel areas of design and fashion.

In the late 1970s in Galicia there was, musically, an interregnum. The old generation of Galician *cantautores* associated with the anti-Franco resistance of the late 1960s and 1970s had quietly began to disappear from the music scene or had followed a voluntary "reconversion" to modern forms of urban music (jazz, rock). This was the paradigmatic case of Bibiano, a former member of the pioneering Galician *cantautor* collective Voces Ceibes and the Movemento Popular da Canción Galega (MPCG). Interestingly, Bibiano is also a crucial point of departure to understand the development

8 To briefly delineate the ideological positions of the main figures discussed in the essay: they varied from the remains of the anti-Franco political resistance and Galician left-wing nationalism (Reixa; Bibiano) to the punk anarchism of Julián Hernández, the non-nationalist socialist agenda of the Vigo city council, and the non-denominational or apolitical *desencanto* characteristic of many urban youth during the Transition.

of the *Movida viguesa*, as he became one of its major catalysts. In that regard, his own trajectory is highly emblematic. By the early 1980s Bibiano had experienced a radical musical "reconversion," assembling an electric rock backing band, Trenvigo, and incorporating new wave material in his politicized Galician-language urban folk/rock repertoire, such as in the song "El é o as dos flippers" [He is the pinball wizard] by Taxi, a neighboring Portuguese band well known in Vigo. Trenvigo was a professional rock group with highly competent, trained musicians and good-quality sound equipment, quite an anomaly in the early days of the *Movida* in Vigo, as in Madrid. Several of his musicians had parallel musical adventures and would go on to be fundamental participants in the emerging *Movida de Vigo*. Thus keyboardist Teo Cardalda created the particularly influential band Golpes Bajos with Javier Novoa, also from Trenvigo, and the former Siniestro Total singer Germán Coppini (Cardalda later founded the pop duet Cómplices, also nationally successful). Trenvigo's drummer Javier Martínez would also play in the emerging new wave band Bar with Silvino Díaz (who would soon form the celebrated pop-rock band Aerolíneas Federales with Siniestro Total's Miguel Costas), and later he joined the notorious "porno pop" band Semen Up, led by Alberto Comesaña (who later founded the pop combo Amistades Peligrosas). This very brief summary of the ramification of Bibiano's Trenvigo gives us a glimpse of both the undercurrent of fluidity and mobility that characterized the bands from the *Movida viguesa* and its own internal creative cannibalization.

Bibiano himself would also follow a secondary process of reconversion, leaving his performing and recording career to become the most important concert promoter and impresario of the *Movida viguesa*, and thus an instrumental figure in its development. He co-founded one of its mythical temples, the *Kremlin* club and concert venue, which was itself reconverted from the old village cinema in the town of Coruxo, in the rapidly urbanizing rural outskirts of Vigo.[9] Bibiano was instrumental in securing the support of

9 Quite symbolically of this conversion, as a form of material and cultural cannibalization, the former sound equipment of Bibiano's live shows was recycled as the permanent sound equipment for the *Kremlin* club. A similar cannibalization of locations took place with another of the original venues of the *Movida viguesa*, *Satchmo*, which transformed itself from a laid-back jazz pub to a new wave club and center of the *Movida*, where new groups rehearsed and played live, and band members were exchanged between different group formations. As a testament of the importance of these locales for the development of the *Movida*, Santiago Romero (from Radio Oceáno) said: "O Sachtmo en Vigo [...] representa [...] o que the Cave para Liverpool" ("The Satchmo in Vigo [...] represents [...] the same as The Cave for Liverpool") (Casal 118).

local authorities for the burgeoning youth culture, and was also the creator and director of the "Aula de Música Moderna e Electrónica" (Modern and Electronic Music Workshop) in the newly established Universidade Popular by the Vigo municipality, where the music demos of many of the *Movida galega* groups were recorded. In another important initiative, Bibiano was the designer and master of ceremonies of the official Madrid-Vigo *movida* exchange in 1986 (Madrid se escribe con V de Vigo [Madrid is spelled with V of Vigo]), which for many signified both the climax and the beginning of the end of the *Movida viguesa* (and the *Movida madrileña* also, as Gallero points out). It can be said, then, that Bibiano was thus a catalyst in the rise and fall of the *Movida*.

During the transition years in Galicia, there was a big gap between the established Galician cultural nationalism, the groups of nationalist intellectuals, writers, and artists considered as the establishment of the anti-Franco cultural resistance, and a new generation that did not share the same language, ideals, experiences, and vital attitude. There was a discernible generational disconnect with, and rebellion against, the discourse of established Galician intelligentsia, who appeared to live in a distant ghetto disassociated from contemporary youth. According to Bibiano, the discourse of cultural nationalism in the late 1970s, in the hands of Galician writers, mostly poets, was depressing and uninviting, and formed "un ermo intelectualmente triste" ("an intellectually sad wasteland").[10] There was also a reciprocal disconnect between the nationalist political front and the emerging urban youth culture identified with the *Movida*, dismissed as either imperialist, "cosmopolita," or "españolista."[11] Thus, there was an initial opposition on the part of the Galician nationalist orthodoxy, who saw rock as cultural imperialism and were suspicious of the connections of the *Movida viguesa* with *la Movida madrileña*.[12] Siniestro Total's leader, Julián Hernández, summarizes this disconnect:

10 Bibiano seemed to be referring to a manifesto of Vigo intellectuals from 1976 which used that expression (Bibiano.org).

11 Most of the repertoire of rock groups from Vigo, with the exception of Bibiano's Trenvigo and Os Resentidos, was sung in Spanish, reflecting the existing local sociocultural conditions of diglossia.

12 It is interesting to see the alliance of peripheries, and the lateral connections between segments of the *Movida viguesa* and the *Rock Radikal Vasco* (Kortaku, Neru Gorriak, etc.), who also rebelled against the established Basque *cantautor* movement and had similar antiestablishment attitudes to Siniestro Total and Os Resentidos. Kaki Arkarazo (from Negu Gorriak) produced Os Resentidos' last album and, after they dissolved, he formed with Antón Reixa the Galician–Basque band Nación Reixa. Arkarazo also played a key role in Reixa's later solo project *Escarnio*.

Las relaciones entre el rock y el nacionalismo no eran buenas. El nacionalismo pensaba que el rock era imperialista. Claro, nosotros cantábamos en castellano [...] En el Instituto del Calvario, el gallego era una postura más política, no era el idioma de todos los días, aunque podíamos hablarlo y entenderlo, claro.

'The relations between rock and nationalists were not good. Nationalists thought that rock was imperialist. The thing is we sang in Spanish [...] In the Instituto del Calvario high school, the use of Galician implied a more political position, it was not the everyday language, although we could speak it and understand it, of course'. (Turrón and Babas 55)

A significant figure of change in this debate, and another key figure and catalyst in the early developments of the *Movida viguesa*, is Antón Reixa, who formed the avant-garde poetic collective Rompente in Vigo in the late 1970s with Manolo Romón and Alberto Avendaño.[13] Rompente was an experimental and revolutionary cultural group on the alternative margins of Galician nationalism that aimed to bring modern Galician poetic discourse to the streets, with a new urban language and new channels of performance. They defined their work not as poetry but as "poetic communication" or "poetic 'agit prop'" (Avendaño 27), following the example of historical avant-garde movements, particularly Dadaism and Surrealism, and the association of aesthetic innovation with ideological agitation. Rompente presented a radical aesthetic practice of multidisciplinary happenings in local bars, cafes, and concert venues, where different media were juxtaposed and parallel creative processes converged. This typically included poetic performances on stage and contemporary musical collages while slides were shown and murals were painted. Rompente thus represented an exploration of a new Galician urban modernity. Several aspects of their innovative performances, such as the theatrical staging, the integration of distinct artistic practices, the intertextuality and inclusion of pop references to advertising and mass media, the provocative rupture with the past, and

13 Antón Reixa is undoubtedly one of the most iconic figures of contemporary Galician culture, being very well known across the Spanish cultural landscape as the former leader, singer, and composer of the Galician alternative agit-rock bands Os Resentidos and Nación Reixa in the 1980s and 1990s, and one of the key audiovisual performers and cultural promoters in Galicia today. Reixa's different multidisciplinary endeavors defy categorization. As the quintessential Galician multi-artist, he is, or has been, a visual poet, performance artist, alternative rock musician, avant-garde video artist, popular Galician TV series creator, film director, and audiovisual producer. Reixa's varied works amply demonstrate the dominant power of mass media in contemporary Galician culture.

the new and direct urban channels, were key recognizable elements of the *Movida de Vigo*. Rompente was thus a significant point of departure for the productive dialogue of intellectual discourse and popular culture that characterized the *Movida*.

The group also published their work, collectively and individually, through the self-made guerrilla press Rompente, combining contemporary poetic discourse and art design in a modern fanzine format, as well as political pamphlets and cultural manifestoes named "Follas de resistencia poética" (Leaflets of poetic resistance) under the influence of the Situationist movement (with an ironic nod to Rosalía de Castro's foundational poetry book *Follas novas*). They also had a weekly radio show known as "Rompente Radio Esquimal" on Radio Popular, one of the new media channels of the *Movida*. This experience was an important confirmation of Rompente's political and aesthetic conceptual project, as Avendaño remembers: "demostramos que a comunicación poética, para nós, non tiña límites, que o noso ser poético era político e cabareteiro e rockeiro e sentimental. E que todo, absolutamente todo, era factible e comunicable en lingua galega" ("We demonstrated that poetic communication, for us, didn't have any limits; that our poetic concept was political, with elements of cabaret and rock, and also sentimental. And that everything, absolutely everything, was feasible and could be communicated in Galician language") (Mejía 92). It was also possible to connect with a new public: not the minority Galician intellectuals of yore, but a new urban middle-class youth who accepted the use of Galician, even if their main linguistic code was Spanish: "O noso público dos pubs estaba composto maiormente por punkis tardíos, postmodernos adiantados, galeguistas reciclados e profesores recén chegados á profesión [...] Ollei para Reixa e sentinme coma un músico negro en Alabama tocando para unha audiencia de brancos. Nunca fun máis feliz na miña vida" ("Our audience in the bars was composed of latter day punks, postmodern types *avant la lettre*, recycled galleguistas, and educators just starting their careers [...] I looked at Reixa and I felt like a black musician in Alabama playing for an all-white audience. I never felt so happy in my life") (92). The confluence in time and space of Galician language, punk, and postmodern urban youth thus seemed like a real possibility for the first time, rather than a contradiction in terms.

During their years of active existence (1976–82) Rompente established contacts with many other young people with artistic interests, such as Julián Hernández, who often collaborated as a musician in their performances. This proved to be the beginning of a long and fruitful collaboration in years to come between Reixa, Romón, and Hernández, who would himself become the leader of the quintessential *Movida viguesa* band Siniestro Total. The contact with the local music scene opened new doors for Reixa, who was a high-school teacher of Galician language and literature by day and a Galician poet/intellectual by night. Following the early success of his friends with Siniestro Total, Reixa formed the band Os Resentidos (OR), one of the seminal bands of the *Movida viguesa*. This change of roles represents a significant transformation, and yet another highly symbolic epochal reconversion, from his former public role as avant-garde poet and radical minority intellectual to leader in a popular agit-prop rock band. The new channels that the rock group format opened, with recordings, bigger venues, concert tours, radio plays, and television appearances, far exceeded the necessarily limited reach of Rompente, but the conceptual vision was very much the same: the creation of a Galician modern and radical poetic discourse communicated through an urban medium. In that sense, OR represents a form of self-cannibalization, and successful commercialization, of Rompente.

OR made some lasting contributions to the *Movida* and to Galician culture in general, with the pioneering use of Galician in rock that would be the model for other groups, such as Os Diplomáticos de Monte-Alto and those of the *rock bravú* explosion of the 1990s, and the national projection of their music beyond Galicia (see Chapter 9). They were the first Galician rock band singing exclusively in Galician, and the only band of the 1980s *Movida viguesa* who did it consistently, as a political and aesthetic commitment to create a modern urban pop culture in Galician. Their success changed the perception of Galician nationalist purists who mistrusted the rock language as a submission to foreign dictates, and even Galician bands singing in Spanish came to be accepted as part of Galician culture. Rompente and Bibiano had tried to break the ice, but OR actually changed these perceptions and were able to bridge the gap between Galician nationalism and *Movida* youth culture. As Julián Hernández states:

Os Resentidos supuso una burrada de cambio en la opinión del nacionalismo, ellos hicieron un rock de vanguardia cantado en gallego, eso significó mucho y a mí me pareció genial [...] El nacionalismo cambió de pronto, gente de lo que ahora es el Bloque y que decía que éramos una panda de españolistas admitió que poca gente había hecho cosas así aquí aunque cantáramos en castellano, así que mejor decir que tampoco estábamos tan mal.

'Os Resentidos represented a huge change of opinion for [Galician] nationalism, they sang avant-garde rock in Galician, which was very important, and I thought it was wonderful [...] Nationalism suddenly changed, people in what today is the Bloque Nacionalista Galego and who used to say that we were a bunch of españolistas admitted that few people around here had done something like this before even if we sung in Spanish, so it was better to say that we were not that bad'. (Turrón and Babas 55)

Although OR claimed the use of the Galician language as the fundamental tool of creation and communication, they frequently changed linguistic codes (mixing Galician with phrases in Spanish, French, Italian, and English) or recorded different versions of their songs in other languages, such as the ironic post-punk anthem "Galicia caníbal (Fai un sol de carallo)," which was recorded in Basque, English, and Turkish. Their musical project was both profoundly Galician and yet completely immersed in internationalism. Ideologically their work was part of a militant project of cultural resistance in which the project of Galician nationalism aligned itself in solidarity with other postcolonial emancipating projects, mirrors of Galician peripheral subaltern status. This is the case of their recurrent crossing of geopolitical borders and creation of new imagined geographies, such as their celebrated rap litanies of the type "Lalín–Namibia–Mondoñedo–Angola ... ," juxtaposing Galician towns and African countries. This practice of deterritorialization was also a constant reminder of Galicia's subaltern status as a "colonized" nation, as were the continued allegorical references to first nations in their lyrics, which were also present in Rompente's texts, as Reixa himself has admitted: "Yo utilizo esa suma de periferias, la negritud, los sijs, los indios americanos, los esquimales, como metáforas de mi propio país, y la gente entiende ese guiño cómplice. [...] La miseria unifica la imagen. La visión periférica es lo más universal" ("I use that sum of peripheries, the Blacks, the Sikhs, the Native Americans, the Eskimos, as metaphors of my own country, and people understand that and feel the complicity. [...] Misery unifies the image. Peripheral vision is the most universal") (Rivas, "Antón Reixa").

Conceptually, musically, lyrically, as well as visually, in their concerts and videos OR produced an ironic recycling and mixing of old and new elements that resulted in something totally unique and immediately identifiable. Their albums offered an eclectic and fragmentary postmodern mix of heterogeneous elements, of tradition and modernity, deconstructing the traditional distinction between high intellectual culture (poetry, literature, avant-garde) and low popular culture (mass media, rock, video). Likewise, they integrated the rural and the urban (participating in the creation of a "rurban" cultural lexicon), Galician cultural roots and foreign influences, as can be seen in the integration of the autochthonous traditions and popular culture with an international pop language and the textual chaos of the modernity. Different discourses, such as political speech, literature, advertising, folk culture, and mass culture, are typically mixed in a hybridized new agit-prop idiom. This integration of old and new forms, as well as of different technologies, is a recurrent characteristic of their production, as has been analyzed by Xelís de Toro. Their musical experiments mix electric guitars with Galician bagpipes, tambourines, and traditional Galician dance rhythms, such as the *muiñeira*, with dance beats and electronic loops. Thus, the modern language of rap, R&B, ska, funk, and dance are seamlessly integrated with a Galician *cumbia* or a traditional *pandeirada*.

Irony, parody, pastiche, surrealism, and caricature are trademarks of Reixa and OR. Their signature song, "Galicia caníbal (Fai un sol de carallo)," with a mix of disco beats, classic hard rock guitar licks, and Galician bagpipes, was a smash national hit in 1986 and made Reixa a household reference in the Spanish media. "Galicia caníbal" is one of the few songs in Galician that made it into the lists of best Spanish songs of all time, and is considered one of the anthems of the *Movida galega*. Yet, the song is nothing but a self-parody of the modern urban *Movida* and its own self-cannibalization. The lyrics are sung with a pronounced *gheada* accent (a distinctive linguistic marker of social identity associated with parts of rural Galicia) and are full of *retranca* (characteristically Galician ironic hidden meanings). The first part of the song deals with the absurd modern parade of sunglasses at night in a club scene: "Con isto da movida/¡Qué movida!/ haiche moito yeyé/ ¡Qué movida!/ que de noite e de día/ ¡Qué movida!/ usa ghafas de sol./ Fai un sol de carallo." The lyrics alternate a playful pun on "a movida" (as in the night club scene) and the polysemic urban expression "qué movida," which can signify "what a party," but also "what a mess" or "what a sham." The *Movida* is seen from a distanced angle and identified with a superficial plastic modernity, as a sort of collective masquerade, and ironically rendered as a re-enactment of a 1960s fad ("moito yeyé"). The observer sarcastically uses a Galician expression, "Fai un sol de carallo" ("It's a hell of a sunny day"), to mock the trendy youth wearing sunglasses at night as a fashion statement. Against these modern images of urban leisure the song offers a collage of images of ancestral rural Galicia with a surreal and gory element (pig slaughtering, blood crepes), which are deterritorialized in a global geography that is both Galician and African, as in other lyrics of Reixa: "de Monforte ó Nepal" ("from Monforte to Nepal"), "safaris do porco" ("pig safaris"), "un parado occidental—Etiopía ten fame" ("an unemployed westerner—Ethiopia is hungry"). The postcolonial critical perspective re-emerges in the third part of the song, which offers a satirical critique of the West's inability to remedy the legacy of colonialism in the Third World through a corrosive cannibalization of the language of advertising and ineffective media campaigns, promoting a literal act of cannibalism.[14] With the bizarre juxtaposition of these images an ironically macabre solution is presented: "Doa os teus riles—Etiopía ten fame!" ("Donate your kidneys—Ethiopia is hungry!").

The surreal politicized imagery of the lyrics is further emphasized by the collage of visual images contained in the video clip for the song, directed by Xavier Villaverde, which has become a classic of Galician video production of the era. The video clip is a clever montage of images that includes vintage newsreel images of Franco's summer visits to Galicia in his yacht or as a pilgrim in Santiago de Compostela along with Warholized images of flying *botafumeiros* (giant incense burners), missiles, military airplanes, religious images of bishops, nuns, and pilgrims, next to censured television announcers, pig slaughtering, nightclubbing, and traditional Galician folk dancers overlaid on *Xacobeo* fireworks celebrations, punctuated by recurring lightning strikes and ending with a final explosion of Santiago's cathedral, with the addition in the audio track of church bells, people's clamoring voices, and thunder noises. This cacophony of recycled sounds and images, old and modern, forming a narrative collage of destruction, echoes the flow of television programming and seems to suggest an endless process of political and cultural cannibalization.

In Reixa and Villaverde's video of "Galicia caníbal" several distinct but complementary readings of cannibalization emerge. On the one hand, we can identify a critical view of Galicia as self-destroying (through parodic and negative images of Franco, social repression, religious superstition, media censorship, and forest burning). On the other, we perceive a more positive, but also ironic, view of the remaking of modern Galicia through the metabolization of the past with its old traditions (folklore, anthropological rituals, bagpipes) and its cultural reconversion into a modern society that integrates the rural and the urban in the new language of the *Movida*, performance, television, fashion, and rock.

To the primary readings of Galician cannibalization as a result of self-destroying and recycling mechanisms we should add a third one, more elusive and self-reflexive, which has already been hinted at earlier: Galicia as a peripheral factory of exoticism for consumption by the center. The year of the release of "Galicia caníbal," 1986, saw the organization of the official *movida* exchange entitled Madrid se escribe con V de Vigo (Madrid is spelled with a V for Vigo), arranged between the City Council of Vigo presided over by Manuel Soto and the Comunidad de Madrid presided

14 Reixa seems to be alluding sarcastically to feel-good campaigns organized by Western rock stars, such as Live Aid, orchestrated by rock superstar Bob Geldof in 1985.

over by the socialist Joaquín Leguina. This highly mediatic event included art exhibits, gastronomy, fashion, photography, music concerts, and video, and was indicative of the rapid institutionalization and co-option of the *Movidas* by the political elites. A trainload of the most representative *Movida madrileña* artists, designers, musicians, and photographers, along with some politicians (including Leguina himself), made the trip to Vigo for an intercultural exchange described as "encuentro de vanguardias" ("encounter of avant-gardes"). In reality, the event resembled more a tourist safari to an exotic distant location that ended up badly, and is considered by many as the beginning of the end of the *Movidas* (See Gallero; Alonso). In fact, the second part of the *Movida* exchange planned for the following year (Vigo se escribe con M de Madrid [Vigo is spelled with a M for Madrid]) never took place.[15] It is paradoxical that a movement that had originated as a peripheral underground countercultural expression, with punk, avant-garde, and anti-mainstream attitudes, ends up cannibalized by the official political machine eager to capitalize on its modern hip image. In the end, the *Movida* succumbed as a product of its own excess and consumption, in another act of cultural cannibalism.

For Reixa, there was an undeniable element of exoticism in the *Movida galega*, as seen from the center, which could also backfire: "La atención por algunos artistas gallegos vino inspirada por un cierto exotismo. Era muy simpático eso de *fai un sol de carallo*. Pero llega un momento en que quedamos poco exóticos y la gente te insiste en por qué seguir cantando en gallego" ("The attention towards some Galician artists was inspired by a form of exoticism. It was kind of cool that phrase, *fai un sol de carallo*. But there comes a time when we are no longer so exotic and people insist in asking you why you still sing in Galician") (Rivas, "Antón Reixa"). The exoticization of Galician *Movida*, and its cannibalization by *la Movida madrileña*, echoes the Spanish cannibalization of Galicia in a wider sense. For Reixa, the relationship between center and periphery is an unequal one in terms of the balance of power. "Si el centro existe es fundamentalmente como el polo poderoso de un intercambio desigual, allí donde se concentra, en lo que a mí me afecta, la industria de la música y la imagen" ("If the center exists it is fundamentally like the powerful pole of an unequal exchange, in the area that concerns me, the place that clusters the music and audiovisual industry"). Furthermore, the center dominates the relations

15 Antón Reixa and Os Resentidos parodied these official slogans in their song "Cumbia china," ("Chinese/Red-Light district Cumbia"), with the phrase "Ay, ay ay, Vigo, que se escribe con CH de chino" ("Ay-ay-ay Vigo, which is spelled with a CH for Chinese").

Figure 27  Postcolonial remappings from the periphery. Deterritorializing Galician culture in "Galicia Sitio Distinto" videoclip (1989), Videoesquimal S.A.

of power and cannibalizes its peripheries, as Manuel Rivas states, glossing Reixa's views: "El centro funciona también como un devorador de exotismos. 'Se acaba convenciendo a los músicos senegaleses para que hagan música disco'" ("The center also functions as a devourer of exoticisms. 'It ends up convincing Senegalese musicians to make disco music'"). Galicia is certainly not Senegal, although it is a metaphor that Reixa could easily use in his work, and many Galicians would just as easily understand.

The last project from OR I will examine is *Galicia Sitio Distinto* (Galicia Different Place/Galicia Place of Difference), conceived as a series of audio/visual cultural interventions (1989–90). *Galicia Sitio Distinto* (GSD) is among OS's most ambitious and enduring works, a continuation of "Galicia caníbal" and also in a certain way their farewell to the *Movida*. As much of Antón Reixa's other audio/visual work, GSD is highly conceptual and intermedial, with continual interplay between the song, the video clip, and the TVG program of the same name directed by Reixa, as well as the OS album *Delikatessen*, with songs taken from the TV program, and the poetry/song anthology by Reixa *Viva Galicia Beibe*. GSD imagines an alternate Galicia, a different Galicia, which is paradoxically a reflection as well as a negation of Galicia. As described by Reixa, "Galicia é un imperio e Sitio

Distinto é a súa colonia subconsciente" ("Galicia is an empire and Sitio Distinto is its subconscious colony"). As with Reixa's other projects, GSD is provocative, irreverent, and inventive, using humor, surrealism, hybridity, and postcolonial imagery as weapons of cultural resistance.

The video clip GSD, directed by Reixa, is a six-minute, thirty-second opus with an exuberant collage of images and sounds that aims to redefine Galicia and its peripheral condition against preconceived cannibalized notions of Galicianess created by both Galicians and non-Galicians alike. The video offers a parodic subversion of the picturesque notion of Galicia and the traditional motifs associated with a depoliticized folkloric vision of Galicia (*muiñeira* dances, folkloric costumes and traditions, and the pleasures sought by tourists and consumers: gastronomy, beaches, fashion, and so on). From the beginning, the video appears as a self-reflexive parodic performance, with Reixa in female Galician clothes holding a road sign indicating a viewing point, while the subtitle "Vista Pintoresca" ("Picturesque view") is superimposed on the video screen (see Figure 27). The video takes a deconstructionist approach, including suggestive images of urban destruction and forest fires, while musical hammers are used as instruments to break and destroy a display of kitsch Galician souvenirs: wine clay jars, dolls, and *hórreos* (raised granaries).

Visually and musically, the video clip exudes hybridity, mixing Galicia traditions and folklore with mass media images, pop and folk rhythms, Galician and global sounds. Side by side are country fair dodgems and global TV footage, images of nationalist heroes Arafat and Castelao, Galician dances and bagpipes, agit-prop rap and hip hop beats. The popular and the cultured mix, as do the traditional and the modern, the local and the global, the past and the imagined future, where the political is entertainment and vice versa.

GSD performs cultural identity as a series of role-playing representations in a new deterritorialized global map. Galicianess is performed as a series of transnational repressed identities characterized by border crossing and gender bending in the deterritorialized space of the TV studio, constituted as a site of cultural and political struggle. In a series of contradictory hybrid metamorphoses, Reixa appears cross-dressed in traditional Galician female costumes used for folkloric dances; then wearing a Galician red scarf as head gear associated with the Palestinian resistance, under a fedora hat (commonly wore by orthodox Jews), while performing a klezmer dance; and later metamorphosed into a Jewish prisoner from a concentration camp wearing a star sewn on his clothes with the initials OLP ('PLO').[16] Likewise,

16 As Reixa has written elsewhere about the deterritorialized and marginalized Galician identity: "Un galego é un refuxiado en terra de ninguén cunha estrela de David nos collóns e no centro da estrela as siglas da Organización para a Liberación

the other members of OR appear either in Galician bagpiper costumes or with Arabic tunics and hats.

The video's exuberant and dizzy display of fast images suggests the mobility associated with a globalized Galicia and the endless reproduction of images in our modern world, as symbolized by the recurrent appearances of the photo booth, the photocopy machine, the video camera, the road sign for photographs, and the large studio mirrors. The video thus reproduces the incessant flow of television, and the nature of the mass-media constructed world, with the impossibility of accessing an unmediated reality. This overload of images suggests the effect of a touristic photo album: paradisiacal pictures of A Toxa island with its shell-covered church, Rías Baixas maps, stone *cruceiros*, and fashion shows. In a visual remapping Galicia appears as an island in the middle of the ocean, a blue background texturized as a Braille text with the overtitle "Océano de Braille." In contrast with the overabundance of topical images, the video strongly suggests Galicia's real invisibility, trying to come out of the darkness, or even a blind Galicia, blinded by the oblivion of its historical reality (reinforced by the recurrent use of Galician sign language translators, blind readers, and telescopes in the video).

Against the postcard image of Galicia, the video inserts iconic pictures that have become symbols of Galician historic marginalization and identification with other subaltern identities, such as the images coming out of the photo booth and the photocopy machine, Castelao's dark and gloomy sketch of a black boy in NYC, or Manuel Ferrol's moving family photograph of the drama of migration, which was also featured on OR's *Fracaso Tropical* album cover. Reinforcing the mobility and postcolonial realignment of Galicia, the studio setting is continually changing, including textile banners in a patchwork pattern made out of Galician women's scarves and Palestinian *keffiyeh* headgear; a background of postcolonial flags of the world; and a set of big mirrors, which reflect and deform the reality around them. Likewise, maps, flags, banners, and road signs abound in the video, suggesting an alternative geopolitical and cultural cartography. Images of a globalized Galicia are offered with the audio/visual pun that juxtaposes the Italian pop song "Il Mondo" with the ancient Galician town of Mondoñedo and an inflatable plastic globe blown up by a black man; or a street banner remaps Galician postcolonial solidarity: "Em Galicia ninguen e forasteiro. Aupa Camerun" [*sic*] ("No one is a foreigner in Galicia. Up with Cameroon").

de Palestina" ("A Galician is a refugee in a no man's land with a Star of David in the bollocks and in the centre of the star the initials of the Palestine Liberation Organization") (*Viva Galicia Beibe*, 71). As Xelís de Toro has commented, "It would be hard to find a quotation that better describes the sense of deterritorialization" (251).

Figure 28　Postcolonial remappings from the periphery. Demarginalizing sounds and visions from "Galicia Sitio Distinto" videoclip (1989), Videoesquimal S.A.

The video presents an amalgam of cannibalized and recontextualized ready-made images and sound bites. Thus it mixes video and audio excepts from interviews with Galician women reminiscing about Galician migration and the discrimination suffered, such as the infamous conductor call in some Spanish train stations "Viajeros al tren, gallegos también" ("All aboard, Galicians as well," which was also used in their song "Galicia Express"), and the shocking sense of altered identity, suggesting "un poco alma [...] de travesti" ("feeling a bit [...] like a transgender person"), a recurrent image of non-conformity in Reixa's work (such as *As Ladillas do travesti* from Rompente). The video also inserts the famous monologue by O rubio de Camelle, the illegal fisherman who became a popular hero after his appearance on TV denouncing the conditions of fishermen in the Costa da Morte with a syllogism that begins "Quen come-los percebes? Os ricos! Quén son os ricos? Os políticos!" ("Who eats the barnacles? The rich! Who are the rich? The politicians!"). The insertion of O Rubio's monologue in the video is a form of cultural remapping and deperipheralization of marginal identities, as he becomes the voice and sound of a new Galicia, where the popular and subaltern struggle for space. The video images of O Rubio are framed within the shape of Galicia, which emerges from a static world map and moves to the center until it becomes its own continent–island, separated from the rest of the world, resituated in the center of the screen (see Figure 28).

As with some of the best tracks by Os Resentidos, GSD is a musical collage, hybridizing local and global sounds: a Galician traditional *muiñeira* dance overlaid with elements of hip hop and heavy rock guitar riffs, punctuated with electronic instruments against the rich wall of sound of bagpipes, and featuring musical intertexts of Andrés do Barro ("Vai e ven e baila do dereito e do revés," from "Pandeirada"). As in "Abdul" and other songs, a postcolonial remapping of Galicia occurs, juxtaposing the four Galician provinces "A Coruña, Lugo, Ourense e Pontevedra" next to "Namibia, Palestina, Nicaragua, Guatemala" as sites of collective struggle and resistance.

## Siniestro Total: A Permanent Reconversion

In their more than 30-year uninterrupted career, Siniestro Total (ST) have become one of the most solid bands in Spanish rock, with a long repertoire of classic songs, a history of collaborations with many other musicians, and a reputation as powerful live performers hard-earned across the national territory. Several books have been written about the band's trajectory and their story will not be retold here (Ordovás; Turrón and Babas). What I would like to explore is their role of "grupo visagra," or border band, between *la Movida madrileña* and *Movida viguesa*, and their participation in the process of cannibalizing Galicia.

Unquestionably, ST have been quite influential, both in Galicia and in the rest of Spain, as one of the seminal punk rock *Movida* bands, which is rather surprising coming from the fringes of the periphery. They constitute, however, an indispensable part of *la Movida* story, in Madrid or Vigo. Shortly after the group's formation, they were immediately adopted by the media promoters of *la Movida* in Madrid. Jesús Ordovás, himself a Galician from Ferrrol and one of the most influential musical journalists of *la Movida madrileña*, discovered ST in 1982 for the rest of the nation by playing and endorsing their home demos on state-run Radio 3's *Diario Pop*. Ordovás was instrumental in the promotion of ST as the front end of the "Galician invasion," and Paloma Chamorro was responsible for their even wider exposure on national television through her program *La edad de oro*.[17]

ST represent a particularly important force in the origins and development of the *Movida viguesa* as they were directly responsibility for the formation of some of its main bands, often with some members doubling in other

---

17 Likewise, the new group Golpes Bajos, born a year later from the split of German Coppini from ST (joining Teo Cardalda), would be fully embraced by *la Movida madrileña* and constitute one of its emblematic bands, with poignant and gloomy songs such as "No mires a los ojos de la gente" ("Don't look at people's eyes") or "Malos tiempos para la lírica" ("Bad times for poetry").

bands (such as Miguel Costas in Aerolíneas Federales and Julián Hernández in Def con Dos), and they experienced an organic relationship and a fluid interexchange of members with other bands (Os Resentidos, Golpes Bajos). Throughout the years they have gone through a continuing process of internal renovation. Since its beginnings in late 1981 Julián Hernández has been the conceptual engineer and driving force of the band, and 35 years later he remains the only original member still with the band. The creative impetus and restlessness of Hernández has made him one of the major catalysts of the *Movida viguesa*, as well as one of its popular-intellectual middle-class heroes. As Hernández has ironically acknowledged, in another parallel of the group's history with the history of the city, "Somos como los astilleros, en reconversión permanente" ("We are like the shipbuilding industry, in a permanent state of reconversion") (Ordovás 231). The story of ST, at the very core of the *Movida viguesa*, is thus one of a highly active and productive internal cannibalization.

Initially associated narrowly with the punk movement, ST typically showed an anti-system attitude, against common sense, good taste, and any political correctness. If in their beginnings they were often identified with gratuitous provocation, infantile jokes, and musical ineptness, they were also recognized for their eclecticism and vitality and the occasional glimpses of witty brilliance. Their main distinctive feature from British punk rock was the use of irony, the acidity of their lyrics, and black humor, and the references to local realities. As Hernández states: "Nosotros tirábamos por el lado de los Dead Kennedys: 'kill the poor', mata al pobre, que tenía mucho más sentido del humor para nosotros, algo más negro, más de humor y mala baba. Pero sí, se nos consideraba punk, todo el mundo así lo veía. Y nosotros también, para qué negarlo" ("We were leaning more towards the Dead Kennedys: 'kill the poor', which had much more sense of humor for us, something darker, with more humor and bad attitude. But yes, we were considered punk, everybody saw it that way. And we did too, there's no point in denying it") (Turrón and Babas 55).

Ideologically, ST's position does not fit squarely with the Spanish and Galician political system. Although relatively close to the positions of the left and Galician nationalism, they would be more in line with anarchist attitudes, on the margins of traditionally organized political groups. As Julián Hernández states, they belong to the generation of *desencanto*, when political commitment in established political organizations already seemed a thing of the past:

Nosotros, por el lado de vanguardia de Rompente, estábamos en el rollo nacionalista, pero al ser un poco más jóvenes, ya no éramos rojos al uso, ya era más el rollo ácrata punk. Al llegar a la edad en que podías empezar a militar en algún partido político ya éramos unos descreídos, había una parte nacionalista que miraba el rock como una cuestión imperialista.

On the one hand, with the avant-garde front of Rompente, we were in touch with the nationalist agenda, but being a bit younger, we were no longer traditional lefties, it was more the anarchist punk scene. Upon reaching the age when you could join a political party we were already nonbelievers, there was a nationalist fraction that considered rock as an imperialist issue. (Turrón and Babas 27)

With regard to the expression of political views, their message is characteristically not straightforward, but usually ironically twisted. They do not follow party lines from any side, and they see everything through the filter of humor. "Teníamos amigos en grupos radicales que decían en sus canciones 'la mili es una mierda', y eso es demasiado obvio. Nosotros preferíamos decir 'sin novedad en el potaje' que es lo mismo pero no es la misma cosa" ("We had friends in radical groups who said in their songs 'mandatory military service is a load of shit,' and that is too obvious. We prefered to say 'all quiet in the army chow front' which means the same but is not the same thing") (Turrón and Babas 99). Thus, their marginal position was a result of their disbelief in organized political parties and their rejection of the agenda of either Spanish nationalism or the traditional orthodoxy of Galician cultural nationalism.

En el fondo nosotros éramos unos descreídos, veníamos del punk, no creíamos en la nación española pero tampoco en una cultura gallega rancia y aburrida. El nacionalismo se demuestra andando, y en ese sentido, más profundo y telúrico, más nacionalista que nosotros no había nadie. Reixa le hizo un favor a la cultura gallega con lo de Os Resentidos, mostrándoles que eran posibles otros caminos.

Basically we were nonbelievers, we came from punk, we didn't believe in the Spanish nation, but neither in an obsolete and boring concept of Galician culture. Nationalism is shown by your actions, and in that sense, there was nobody more profoundly telluric, more nationalist than us. Reixa did Galician culture a favor with Os Resentidos, showing that other paths were possible. (Turrón and Babas 55)

As in the case of Rompente, and later Os Resentidos, ST's punk attitude had a certain affiliation with the rebellious spirit and provocative playfulness of the avant-garde, such as the dadaist and surrealist movements, which

Hernández has recognized as a personal fixation: "Desde adolescente he sentido fascinación por la vanguardia histórica: dadá, el surrealismo y todo eso, ahí todo eran mensajes" ("Since I was teenager I have been fascinated by the historical avant-garde: Dada, Surrealism and the rest, they were all full with messages") (Turrón and Babas 99). This connection appears explicitly and ironically in some of their lyrics, such as "Somos ultraístas" ("We're ultraists") and "Oye nena, yo soy un artista" ("Listen girl, I'm an artist"). The programmatic irreverence, the aggressive message of cultural demolition, the rejection of traditional aesthetic and hegemonic ideological values, the devaluation of high art, the recycling of the ready-made, and the incorporation of the collage are avant-garde trademarks that are recurrent in ST's opus.

Musically as well as lyrically, ST put into practice an extreme form of cultural cannibalism. They made musical plagiarism, intertextual quotation, and recontextualization into an art form. In Hernández's 1999 book *Hay vida inteligente en el rock and roll?* he reflects on his personal theory of artistic creativity, provocatively claiming that all new artistic movements are the result of bad imitation of originals, a credo that has guided ST's long career. Thus, their covers of songs by other groups are typically reconstructed into something else altogether, and often transformed so unrecognizably that they could pass for originals. They demonstrate a great ability to appropriate songs and completely resignify and reterritorialize their meanings. Thus international arena rock standards such as Lynyrd Skynyrd's "Sweet Home Alabama" or AC/DC's "Highway to Hell" become the ironically self-reflexive "Miña Terra Galega" and "Somos Siniestro Total" respectively, two of their signature anthems, the product of their distinct form of musical cannibalization. This practice of borrowing, recycling, and restructuring in its widest sense is related both to the avant-garde technique of collage and to new technological innovations, which Julián Hernández symbolizes in the post-modern notion of "sampling":

> Hay refranero, frases hechas y toda clase de ideas pilladas al vuelo. El collage es el único invento genuino del siglo xx y en el caso de textos produce una sensación extraña de familiaridad y desazón a partes iguales cuando se manipula bien.

> There are sayings, idiomatic expressions, and all types of ideas caught on the brink. The collage is the only genuine invention of the 20th century, and in the case of texts, it produces a strange sensation of familiarity and discomfort in equal measure when it is manipulated well. (Turrón and Babas 87)

Figures 29–30   Glocal iconicity. Record covers from Siniestro Total, cannibalizing Galician bagpipes and iconic English rock albums: *Sexo chungo* (1983) from The Clash, *London Calling*, and *Ojalá estuvieras aquí* (1993) from Pink Floyd, *Wish You Were Here*.

La frase sacada del contexto, la descontextualización. A eso se llama samplear, es la única invención real del siglo xx insisto, el sampler, el collage, entendiendo un sentido muy poliédrico en el robo, no sólo verlo en un sentido, sino todo lo multidimensional que se pueda; no sólo en la corrección política sino en la incorrección también; no solo en la música latina sino en Stockhausen.

The phrase taken out of its context, the decontextualization. That is called sampling, is the only real invention of the 20th century I insist, the sampling, the collage, with a polyhedral understanding of the theft; not seen in just one sense, but as multidimensional as possible; not just in the sense of political correctness, but of incorrectness as well; not just Latin music but also Stockhausen. (Turrón and Babas 99–100)

In their lyrics, as in their music, the process of cannibalization operates in a similar manner, twisting idiomatic expressions, political slogans, literary works, popular sayings and catchphrases, fossilized metaphors, or nursery rhymes. One can find in their songs learned references to Tristan Tzara, Eduardo Pondal, Quevedo, Apollinaire, Joyce, Shakespeare, Fray Luis de León, or Nietzsche, side-by-side with references of comics, films, television, advertising, and popular music. As Hernández says, "somos un grupo esponja" ("we are a sponge band") (Turrón and Babas 126). This programmatic cannibalization of recycled sources and subversive upheaval of traditional cultural values may be one of the most defining elements of their creative approach.

The song "La sierra es la familia," from the ironically titled album *Made in Japan* (a nod to the classic hard rock live album by Deep Purple, albeit recorded in Memphis, as a tribute to the blues tradition they embraced), is a good example of their deterritorializing cannibalist practices. It was written for the horror film *La matanza caníbal de los garrulos lisérgicos* (1993), a low budget production shot in video and directed by Antonio Blanco and Ricardo Llovo, which included the participation of several *Movida* musicians, including Julián Hernández himself, César Strawberry (Def Con Dos), and Silvia Superstar (Aerolíneas Federales, Killer Barbys), as well as Vigo actor Manuel Manquiña (from *Airbag* and *El lápiz del carpintero*).[18] The film is a black comedy that follows a traditional plotline in the horror gore genre: a group of four urban youngsters has a road accident and seeks refuge in an isolated house where a strange family lives. The bizarre twist is that this

18 *La matanza* has cult film status in Galicia. It was featured as an example of "cine perralleiro" (alternative, marginal, low cost) by director Jorge Coira in his manifesto "Por un cine perralleiro" in 1997, as part of the *bravú* movement.

Galician rural family had converted to cannibalism in the postwar "hunger years." The film is full of hilarious double entendres recontextualizing the discourse of global economic politics and sustainability ("En el mundo sobran personas y falta comida" ["In the world there is an overabundance of people and lack of food"]) or commercial advertising (the ad jingle for the "Isabel" canned fish brand, "Qué bien, hoy comemos con Isabel" ["How nice, today we eat with Isabel"]), while proposing an ironic endorsement of cannibalism. This discursive twist serves as a corrosive critique of plastic modernity and the new conspicuous consumption of the 1980s and 1990s. *La matanza caníbal* offers a kind of gore metaphor of retribution, by which the modern *Movida galega* is being engulfed by the rural backward Galicia that it had displaced. The film was a parody of the *Texas Chainsaw Massacre* film series, itself a parody of the original 1974 film, with the cannibalistic Sawyer family serving as a parody of traditional and repressive family values and capitalist profiteering. The song title "La sierra es la familia" was borrowed from a line used in several of the films in the series, the catchphrase "The saw is family." The song is thus a parody of a parody of a parody, in a process of endless cannibalization.

A number of different discourses are cannibalized in the song, with multiple references to television, advertising, cinema, and historical and religious discourses. Nothing is sacred, and even irreverent allusions to the Bible are not free from the gore treatment: "No hay devoción sin digestion / carne de mi carne / sangre de mi sangre / ábrete las venas que ya tengo hambre" ("There is no devotion without digestion / flesh of my flesh / blood of my blood / open up your veins because I'm getting hungry"). Similarly, the lines "Dame tu secreto ricoricorico / carne de primera botella de tinto / Santiago y sierra España / que salga sangre con serrín" ("Give me your delicious secret recipe / a top choice meat and a red blood bottle of wine / Santiago and charge the chainsaw Spain, and let the blood spill with sawdust") are a parody of Spanish television star chef Karlos Arguiñano's catchphrase "rico, rico" and rewrite the nationalist war cry of Spanish Christians, "Santiago y cierra, España" as "Santiago y sierra España." The song thus reconverts the rallying cry of unity into a gore admonition of fragmentation and cannibalization, with a desecrated image of Spain that has been sawed, dismembered, and prepared for consumption. From the margins of the cultural periphery ST offers a provocative and ironic subversion of the centralized concept of the nation. Santiago–España, Galicia–Spain, and Vigo–Madrid appear as the conflicting terms of a polarity of center and periphery that is replayed in the political and cultural arenas.

It is ironic that the peripheral counter-culture of the *Movida viguesa* would end up being cannibalized by the commercial and political interests of the center. For some it was a result of media inflation, as well as political intervention: "Fundamentalmente foi cousa de periodistas madrileños e cataláns, todo inflado de máis" ("Basically it was something created by journalists from Madrid and Catalonia, all overblown") (Casal 37). In the end the *Movida galega* also cannibalized itself, as a victim of its own success. Reixa's earlier mentioned efforts to resist cannibalization need to be put in a wider context, considering his own trajectory in recent years (first becoming a Spanish media personality and habitual commentator in the Spanish press and TV, and later a film director/producer of films primarily shot in Spanish, or international productions, and eventually the elected president of the discredited SGAE, the most powerful music copyright clearance agency in Spain). To mark the 25th anniversary of the song's release, Reixa created the idea for the musical spectacle *Galicia Caníbal: El Musical*, which was staged in Galicia and other cities around Spain in 2012–13. Sponsored by the beer company Estrella de Galicia, it included many of the best-known songs of the *Movida galega*, which attests to the enduring power of nostalgia and the continuing cannibalization of the *Movida galega*'s own past.

It is also ironic and symptomatic that the *Kremlin*, once the temple of the *Movida viguesa*, has been reconverted again, this time to a warehouse for leisure maritime and fishing equipment. Bibiano, once the promoter of the Kremlin, recognizes the element of cultural change that the *Kremlin* represented as a metaphor for the *Movida viguesa* with a pungent image that resists facile nostalgia: "... *esta sala e todos os que estivemos nela, como todos os que estiveron na movida, contribuimos a quitarlle a esta cidade o cheiro a sardiñas asadas*" ("... this club and all of us who were there, like all of those who were in the movida, contributed to remove the smell of grilled sardines from this city") (Bibiano.org, original emphasis). The reference to the smell of sardines is quite appropriate as we come full circle to the beginning, as with the classic image of the "ourobouros," or "a pescada que se morde a cola" ("the fish that bites its own tail"). In this case we could say, extending the metaphor, that the sardine has bitten its own tail and cannibalized itself, leaving behind only a memory of its former smell. The *Movida* is remembered as a breath of fresh air, as a cultural phenomenon that changed the face of the city and brought a fuller experience of modernity. From the remnants of the old factories, canneries, and shipbuilding docks, a new factory of ideas, sounds, and images was developed. As we have seen, this transformation has entailed a continued process of cannibalization that has constructed and reconstructed the modern sense of an urban identity that defies its cultural peripherality.

# CHAPTER NINE

# Smells Like Wild Spirit: Galician *Rock Bravú*, Between the Rurban and the Glocal

Nos anos 70 chegou á aldea a televisión. Nos 80 os electrodomésticos. Nos anos 90 as guitarras eléctricas. Bravura ancestral enchufada nun amplificador. En cada rueiro unha tropa da tralla, en cada aldea un conxunto arroutado. 'In the 1970s televisions arrived in the villages. In the 1980s it was domestic appliances. In the 1990s electric guitars. Ancestral wildness plugged to an amplifier. In each block a rowdy gang, in each village a furious band.'
Xurxo Souto

Dos pinchos e das flores do toxo máis agreste,
do monte máis salvaxe.
Da calor e dos aromas da augardente e da queimada,
que teiman do orballo e das xeadas nos ósos.
Dos aquelarres en covas, en noites perdidas,
con bruxas e trasnos danzando por riba do lume.
Das pedras nos valados, nas cabezas e nas gadañas,
cravuñando o asubío dalgún cantar popular.
Das guitarras compradas coa primeira paga do paro
ou da economía somerxida.
Do tabaco de batea adulterado con aromas tropicais.
Do amor, do odio, da frustración ou dunha borracheira
de vatios nun alambique clandestino.
De todos eses sitios e de moitos máis,
naceu, cun aturuxo na boca, este rock tan noso ... SEN CAPAR
'From the thorns and flowers of the roughest gorse,
from the wildest mountain.
From the heat and the smells of moonshine and *queimada*,
that protect from the persisting rain and frost in the bones.
From the covens in caves, in lost nights,
with witches and goblins dancing over the fire.
From the stones in the hedges, in the heads and the scythe,
whispering the whistling sound of a popular song.
From the guitars bought with the first unemployment check
or the underground economy.

From the contraband tobacco tampered with tropical aromas.
From love, hate, frustration or an intoxication
of watts in a clandestine distillery.
From all those sites and many more, was born,
with a Galician yell in the mouth, this rock of ours ... NON-NEUTERED'
*Manifesto Bravú* (quoted in Valiño)

I f the *movida galega* of the 1980s was fundamentally an urban phenomenon of modern cultural reconversion, centered mostly in Vigo, in a permanent tension with Madrid, the *rock bravú* explosion of the 1990s was a multicentered movement disseminated throughout the Galician geography, and with strong rural roots, which tried to reconcile Galician tradition and global modernity. Although with some obvious links to the *movida viguesa,* such as the afterpunk ironic style of Siniestro Total and the political commitment to Galician culture and language of Os Resentidos, who both acted as godparents to the new movement, *rock bravú* was on the fringes of the national music industry and its popular success was the result of a great degree of self-management and intermediality with other channels, particularly television, and different fields, such as video, comics, graphic design, multimedia, literature, and journalism.[1]

The *rock bravú* movement was first conceptualized in 1993 at the "Castañazo Rock" festival in the remote Galician village of Chantada and officially launched in the same place the following year. The location, in the periphery of the periphery, but also in the heartland of Galicia, was already a significant statement of the remapping of Galician culture. Less than 15 years later, commemorative celebrations were already taking place in what we could consider an example of what Pierre Nora referred to as the "acceleration of history," understood as one of the cultural signs of our times. A new "Castañazo Rock" festival was held in November 2007 with contemporary Galician bands playing homage to the leading band of the *bravú* movement, Os Diplomáticos de Monte-Alto, led by Xurxo Souto. A studio tribute album was also simultaneously released as a double CD (*120 capadores*) with covers of their songs by some 20 new and regrouped Galician bands. These facts suggest the lasting legacy of the band and their songs, reflecting their symbolic capital as founders of the tradition of Galician "rock with roots." They also point to the rurbanized "normalization" of rock sung in Galician and the development of a cultural industry able to turn collective

---

1 Cifuentes considers *rock bravú* as the true origins of Galician rock (156), and Fernández Rego names *bravú* as the only rock movement uniquely Galician.

Figure 31   Banners from the retrospective *Bravú XX* exhibit (2014). Design by David Lages.

nostalgia into a cultural commodity, even when the *bravú* movement is considered a closed chapter in Galician popular music history.

More elaborate commemorations were held throughout Galicia in 2014, on the occasion of the 20th anniversary of the launch of the *bravú* movement. A number of concerts and cultural activities took place, which included a series of Castañazo rock concerts from Galician bands, roundtables with writers, musicians, journalists, and cineastes related to the movement, the release of new documentaries, a special presentation at the Festival de Cans, the celebration of the *Semana Bravú* in A Coruña, and the large-scale *Bravú XX* retrospective exhibit at the Auditorio do Pazo da Cultura in Pontevedra, curated by Xurxo Souto, which traveled through different Galician towns.[2] Although undoubtedly these celebrations were tinted with some degree of

2  Visual documentation of the *Bravú XX* exhibit is available from http://bretemas. gal/onte-1155-bravu-xx-no-culturgal/ and http://www.davidlages.com/portfolio/ bravu-xx/ (accessed 1 March 2017). Some of the documentary films related to the *bravú* include: *Nor-noroeste, a viaxe bravú* (1997), by Sonia Barros and Marta Piñeiro; *Kompostela, Capital bravú* (1997), by Basilio Martín Patino; and *Galiza Bravú* (2010), by Xaime Miranda, Elena Albán Lombao, and Sabela Sampedro. A biography of Os diplomáticos by Rodri Suárez, *Non temos medo*, was also published to coincide with the *bravú* twentieth anniversary.

nostalgia and suggest a degree of retroactive institutionalization, they also reflect the growing awareness of the importance of the popular cultural movement that redefined traditional rural/urban relations and thus remapped modern Galician culture in the 1990s.

With hindsight, some critics might suggest that it was almost inevitable that a convergence between the great indie rock explosion of the Galician *movida* in the early 1980s and the strong Galician folk music revival movement developing in the late 1980s and early 1990s was likely to occur at some point. Both movements enjoyed mass popularity and success inside and outside of Galicia, and constituted two of the most important developments in popular Galician music since the restoration of democracy. A large number of Galician pop/rock bands surged and were able to cross the invisible *telón de grelos* ("the Galician greens curtain," the political, economic, and cultural glass ceiling holding up the dissemination of Galician cultural production in the rest of the state). These new bands became well-known and influential in the nation state in the years of the *movida* (Siniestro Total, Antón Reixa and Os Resentidos, Golpes Bajos, Aerolíneas Federales, and Semen Up, among others). In those days, the *movida galega* was only second in importance to the *movida madrileña* in terms of creativity and influence in the rest of the Spanish state. Likewise, the Galician neofolk revival that began with bands such as Milladoiro and Emilio Cao developed into a diversified movement with a strong following in all segments of Galician society. This revival boomed internationally in the 1990s, with performers such as Luar na Lubre and Carlos Núñez, attracting many international musicians towards Galician traditional music, including The Chieftains, Mike Oldfield, and Ry Cooder, among other well-known performers. Significantly, Galician folk music—hybridizing with Celtic and world music—has become one of the major forms of roots music successfully exported from Spain to the rest of the world (the other one, of course, is flamenco music).[3]

It was to be expected that these two very popular musical movements—one with urban origins, the other with roots in the village—would merge, and that this merging would produce a wide range of intersections in terms of their audiences. Indeed, the 1990s saw the emergence in Galicia of a new cultural phenomenon, as rock culture started to take root beyond its main cities throughout the region (and more specifically in the rural and coastal areas) and as Galician folk music became urbanized and commercially successful beyond its own borders. Accordingly, a new generation of bands was born that incorporated traditional Galician folk roots with rock, developing what was soon to be known as *rock bravú*. This phenomenon,

---

3  This will be the subject of analysis in Chapter 10.

festive and rebellious in spirit and culturally rooted in the local and the national, asserted a modern Galician cultural identity developing at the intersections of the old and the new, the rural and the urban, and the local and the global (where the new hybrid realities of the *rurban* and *glocal* occur). As we shall see, the explosion of *rock bravú* soon expanded to encompass other expressions of Galician popular culture, especially in mass media, literature, and the visual arts, thus creating a larger *movemento bravú* that aimed to have an impact on contemporary Galician popular culture and identity.

## A Whole Lot of Shaking: A Movement is Born

The new *rock bravú* movement was launched with the conscious intention of giving a name and a strong sense of identity to an emerging and diverse new reality that was already taking shape.[4] In the wake of other modern cultural movements, the *bravú* movement had its own official public presentation and its own programmatic manifesto. These basic aspects of the movement were primarily conceived and orchestrated by Xurxo Souto, the multifaceted writer, journalist, cultural promoter, and leader of the A Coruña-based band Os Diplomáticos de Monte-Alto—the most veteran and prominent group among those associated with the *bravú*.[5] As a symbolic gesture of vindicating and celebrating popular culture and ancestral roots,

4 The launch of the movement reflected the realization that there was something new in the air that needed a focus, a theoretical foundation, and a practical articulation. The first conceptualization of *rock bravú* took place at the 1993 "Castañazo Rock" festival organized in Chantada, where urban and rural culture converged at the hands of two pioneering bands, Os Diplomáticos (from A Coruña) and the local band Os Rastreros (organizers of the festival). The idea was to celebrate a larger festival the following year to gather all the new emerging bands performing in Galician as a united front to create momentum, with the ambitious-sounding, ironic name of "Primeiro Simposio Mundial Sobor do Rock Bravo, Bravú ou Arroutado," ("First World Symposium on Wild, Bravú or Furious Rock"). The 1994 festival, the official launching of the movement, also included the bands O Caimán do Río Tea, Skornabois, Os Papaqueixos, Os Bochechiñas, Yellow Pixoliñas, and Desfeita, coming literally from all corners of Galicia.

5 Os Diplomáticos formed in 1989 and released their first album, *Arroutada pangalaica*, in 1991, which was produced by the three members of Os Resentidos. Their third CD, *Avante toda* (1995), was produced by Kaki Arkarazo from Neru Gorriak. Their frequent collaboration with these artists reflects the links of the movement with both the *movida viguesa* and the Basque *Rock Radikal*. Their albums offered a new sound, a result of the successful blend of the festive dance rhythms of the Galician popular *charangas* with the accelerated syncopation of ska rock, marked by the sound of the accordion as the main solo instrument.

the movement made its first public appearance as such in 1994 in the small inner Galician town of Chantada, where they proclaimed their "Manifesto de Viana" in a local *parrillada* (grill) that was, of course, serving Galician wild meat. Aside from musicians, the event also included the support of key Galician writers and journalists (such as Manuel Rivas and Alberto Casal, author of *Rock and Grelos*, the first book on the history of Galician rock), who would participate in the development and dissemination of the *bravú* movement, as discussed below.

Because the notion of *rock bravú* was the result of the convergence of many different trends and denominations, a close examination of their diversity exposes the complexities, internal contradictions, and ludic and confrontational spirit inherent in the movement. Manuel Rivas defined the movement as *punkismo máxico* ("O bravú. Notas"), a pun on *realismo máxico galego*—a term he and other Galician writers have been often associated with—thus underlining its connection with a distinctive Galician literary culture and tradition. Others have used different descriptors for their work, sometimes interchangeably. Some examples include: *Tralla* (rowdy noise) and *Arroutada* (rapture, fit of fury) from Xurxo Souto, with solid urban roots; *Rock agreste* or *Agro-rap* from Pinto D'Herbón, a village farmer and practitioner of Galician *regueifa* (popular improvisational poetry); *Son da ferralla* (scrap tin can sound) from Os Skornabois, who originally used paint buckets and oildrums as percussion; *Agropunk* from Os Rastreros, who vindicate their rural roots in their punk anthems; *Rock irmandiño* (in reference to the medieval Galician popular uprising of Os Irmandiños) from the highly politized radical band Xenreira; *Música castrapa* (in reference to the Galicianized linguistic hybrid of *castrapo*) from Os Papaqueixos, the most folk-oriented of the *rock bravú* groups; and *Poésica bravá* (a double neologism, which privileges cultural hybridity and gender identity) from Marisol Manfurada, a sampler-driven poetic performer and one of the few women in a male-dominated rock movement.[6]

---

6 It should be noted that the majority of *rock bravú* performers were almost exclusively male, with a few notable exceptions, including Marisol Manfurada, a Galician raised in London, and Mercedes Peón, who started under the wing of Manu Chao. A female duo also related to *bravú*, As Garotas da Ribeira, was later formed among the Galician diaspora in Barcelona, and have also collaborated with Barcelona resident Manu Chao. Mixing the Galician tradition of *regueifa* and modern hip hop, their feminist, outspoken, and humorously biting lyrics are heard in songs such as "Nacín alerta" ("I was born alert"), "Non é Perfecta" ("She's no perfect"), and "Historia dunha muller" ("Story of a woman"), based on a poem by Celso Emilio Ferreiro. Galician pop-rock bands from the 1980s and 1990s singing in Spanish (Aerolíneas federales, Bar) and English (Killer Barbies) included some

The common thread in all of these works was a radical subversiveness and a strong sense of place, an affirmation of Galician identity, culture, and language, and a desire to connect with one's "roots." The unifying term *bravú*, with its etymological closeness to "bravío" and "bravura," connotes notions of an untamed, wild, and fearless nature, and a confrontational spirit of resistance. In some parts of Galicia *bravú* refers to free wild animals that have not been tamed. It was famously defined by Xurxo Souto as a reference "ó sabor e ó cheiro da carne de caza e, en xeral, de toda a carne sen capar" ("to the taste and smell of wild game meat and, in general, all meat from unneutered wild animals") ("O bravú").[7] The references to the metaphorical unneutered/uncastrated nature of the movement are common, as seen in the "Manifesto Bravú" in the epigraph of this chapter.[8] The term applied to Galician culture—with its references to wild game and its untamed, uncastrated nature—alludes directly to the vindication of rural roots and wild nature, and figuratively to the politically subversive aspects of cultural resistance, but, perhaps less consciously, to a certain fear of symbolic castration, reflected in the testosterone-filled music and lyrics.[9]

female performers, but they were also a minority. The situation is markedly different in the Galician folk scene, where female singers and performers are abundant and have much greater visibility.

7 Allegedly this term was coined in part because it rhymed with Siniestro Total's first song in Galician, "Corta o pelo, landrú" ("Cut your hair, you punk"), released in 1987 (Valiño 10; Souto, *A tralla*, 130); indeed, both words *landrú* and *bravú* are connected by the use of rhyme in the song by Os diplomáticos de Monte-Alto "Xa ven o Xabarín" ("Here comes Xabarín"), recorded for the popular television program *Xabarín Club*. The iconic logo of the *bravú* movement was a wild wolf, designed by Galician painter Xaime Cabanas and associated with the 1980s *Atlántica* art movement (see figure 31).

8 One of the songs in Os diplomáticos' first album was "120 capadores," ("120 castrators"), which is also the name of the double homage album published in 2007. Furthermore, in reference to the hybrid high–low mixing of poetry and popular song in Galicia, in the oral tradition as well as in modern commodities such as books, CDs, bookstores, and taverns, Manuel Rivas explained in an interview with Xosé M. Pereiro: "La cultura está viva en las librerías y en las tabernas. Lo que funciona en Galicia es lo indómito, lo bravú (sin castrar)" ("Culture is alive in the bookstores and taverns. What works in Galicia is the untamed, the bravú (non-neutered)") (Pereiro "Un saxofonista contra la literatura de karaoke").

9 The suggestion of Galicia as a castrated nation is strong. Cultural and political castration anxiety was also evident in one of the most important ideologues of modern Galician nationalism, Alfonso Castelao, and his reference to the "doma e castración de Galicia" (mentioned in Chapter 1), which reveals a masculine definition of the nation in spite of the traditional feminine association of the motherland and the symbolic central importance of female figures such as María Pita and Rosalía de Castro. From a queer studies perspective, occasional representations of alternative

The main architect and ideologue of the *bravú* movement was Xurxo Souto, who played the role of cultural catalyst and creator of watchwords and slogans. Souto exercised his public voice as journalist, writer, and Galician radio host. Moreover, as the leader, singer, main composer, and accordionist of his band, he was responsible for the recognizable sound and image of Os Diplomáticos de Monte-Alto.[10] In his theoretical opus *A tralla e a arroutada* (1995) he called for a cultural rebellion against the homogenizing trends of globalization, mobilizing Galician popular culture and affirming Galician cultural identity: "Vivimos no cume da repunancia. [...] As películas fanas en Hollywood, a música en Inglaterra, a política en Bruxelas, os maquinillos no Xapón. E nós a velas vir" ("We are living in the height of disgust. [...] Films are made in Hollywood, music in England, politics in Brussels, technical gadgets in Japan. And we are just helpless spectators") (9). His great ability to create audacious proclamations and bold language manifestoes has been instrumental on many levels: in the very definition of the movement, in the contagious energizing effect on the community, and in the echo effect created by the media. His vindication of the periphery as a location of cultural (and political) resistance and his affirmation of emotion over rationalism— articulated in a hyperbolic expressive language—are considered tenets of the *bravú* movement. The following proclamation is typical: "Vivimos no cu do mundo, sí, pero temos bravura para tronzar o Universo" ("We live at the far end of the world, yes, but we have enough bravery/fierceness to smash the Universe") ("Arroutada en Guitiriz" 17).

Cultural hybridity is a constant presence in the *bravú* movement, affirming Galicianess while rejecting essentialist notions of identity. Musically *rock bravú* was a hybrid form created mainly out of the combination of traditional Galician roots music and popular culture with various forms of modern rock (punk, ska, indie rock), often integrating other foreign alternative musical forms in the mix, resulting in something new and unique. *Rock bravú* has been described as a fundamental hybrid of the "fusión entre

sexualities and non-conformist gender attitudes were expressed in ironic/rebellious rock bravú songs such as "Marujo Pita" by Os diplomáticos (written originally when they were known as Opus Gay, a pun on the ultra-Catholic group Opus Dei), "Xuntos e revoltos" ("Together and Disorderly") by Korosi Dansas (one of the all-inclusive theme songs of *Xabarín Club*), and the festive "Son Maricón" ("I am a fag") by Heredeiros da Crus, which became one of their signature songs.

10   Souto was the leader of the band between 1988 and 2001, producing a total of five albums with them. He is also the author of several books associated with the *bravú*: *A tralla e a arroutada* (1995), *Fumareu* (1999), *O retorno dos homes mariños* (1999); *Tres trebóns* (2005), and *Contos da Coruña* (2007). After he left the band he became the director of programming for the public Radio de Galicia.

o rock e a muiñeira, a guitarra eléctrica e a gaita, o rap e as regueifas, a batería e as pandeiradas e como non o rural e o urbano" ("fusion between rock and *muiñeira*, electric guitar and bagpipes, rap and *regueifas*, drumkits and *pandeiradas*, and of course, the rural and the urban") ("O bravú"). But the musical hybridity of *rock bravú* also encompassed a more inclusive perspective of Galician popular culture, beyond a conservative notion of folk, as Xelís de Toro has noted: "enlarging the concept of traditional music by incorporating popular music played by *orquestas* at *verbenas*, which had never before been seen as part of Galician traditional music" (246). Some of the most significant musical influences on the Galician roots side include traditional Galician folk songs, such as sailor and peasant songs; Galician dance music (with the rhythms of *muiñeiras* and *pandeiradas*); traditional Galician bagpipers tunes; popular *orquestas* and rural bands known as *charangas*; the tradition of *regueifas* or popular improvisational poetry challenges; and the inclusion of Galician folk instruments (particularly bagpipes, accordions, *pandeiros*, and *pandeiretas*). On the modern side, some of the most prominent influences include punk rock (such as The Clash or the Dead Kennedys), the transnational agit-rock of Mano Negra (with Manu Chao, of Galician origin), and, within the state, the Basque *rock radikal* (such as Kortaku, Negu Gorriak, and Fermín Muguruza) and, of course, the earlier *movida galega* (particularly the mix of punk witticism and ludic spirit of Siniestro Total, and the politically combative Galician rap of Antón Reixa and Os Resentidos).[11] Other alternative musical sources include ska music (a close relative of punk and new wave), hard rock, rap, hip hop, indie rock, and Mexican *rancheras*, among many others.

It is curiously significant that the convergence of rock and folk—which had generated many successful folk-rock hybrid formations in Anglo countries in earlier decades, such as Fairport Convention, Dexys Midnight Runners, and The Pogues—had not taken place before in Galicia. Manu Chao, one of the early collaborators of *rock bravú*, made an interesting parallel between the cultural contexts of rock in Galicia and in Latin American countries. In all these peripheral locations, rock originated mostly as an urban, middle-class phenomenon, in which musicians and audiences tended to identify rock with urban Anglo culture, and to negatively perceive traditional folk and rural culture as being at odds with rock. At some point in the early 1990s the

11 While Siniestro Total and Antón Reixa/Os resentidos are catalysts of the *bravú* movement, and amply recognized as influential pioneers and collaborators, the rest of the bands from the *movida galega*, singing their songs in Spanish, do not seem to have had such great impact on *rock bravú*, having disappeared or relocated, literally and/or metaphorically, to Madrid (Germán Coppini, Cómplices, Amistades Peligrosas).

situation changed, due in part to the following factors: the newly established access, both for the lower classes and rural areas, to consumer goods such as electric guitars and amplifiers; the discovery and appreciation of roots music and a revived interest in world music; and the perceived decay of mainstream US and British rock ("David Byrne conversa con Manu Chao"). These factors were a response to a new world paradigm of radical changes, transnational movements, and cultural transformations involving new interactions between the local and the global, as well as new intersections between the urban and the rural, through urban migrations and suburban exodus. It appears that some of the most exciting musical and cultural events of the last two decades have been taking place precisely at these junctions in the peripheries of the old centers (the explosion of ethnic music and world music would be a clear reflection).

In that sense, the *rock bravú* movement is a *glocal* phenomenon as well as a *rurban* phenomenon. It was the result of the progressive process of modernization (and partial urbanization) of long-neglected Galician rural areas, which provided previously isolated local areas with growing access to global cultural and material goods, and vice versa.[12] The establishment of local television (particularly TVG and its *Xabarín Club*, extraordinarily successful among Galician youth) and the improvement of communication infrastructures and transportation brought not only the country closer to the city but Galicia as a whole closer to the rest of the world, thus remapping the periphery/center structure along a *glocal* axis. At the same time, the creation of large metropolitan areas, particularly along the densely populated Galician coast, also affected the clear separation of urban and rural areas. As a result of this relentless *rurban* growth, former rural areas became incorporated into the economic and cultural life of cities, and cities also received large numbers of migrants from rural areas, creating new neighborhoods. This meant that large factories could now be seen next to farmland, and rows of suburban townhouses were built in fishing villages, thus creating a new mixed reality that could be best described as *rurban*.

Although it is always difficult and dangerous to generalize about a cultural phenomenon as complex and diverse as the emergence of *bravú*, several recurrent characteristics of *rock bravú* seem particularly defining. First and foremost comes the affirmation of Galician national culture. As

---

12  This cultural transformation in the music scene should be seen in parallel to the audiovisual, with the contemporary landmark of the TVG series *Mareas vivas*, in its vindication of Galician small village life set in a fictional small fishing town in Costa da Morte. The series was directed by Antón Reixa and featured a new young actor by the name of Luís Tosar, who would become one of the leading actors in Galician and Spanish cinema in the following years.

part of this collective act of cultural resistance, the preferred and almost exclusive mode of linguistic expression of *bravú* bands is, on principle, Galician, with the occasional introduction of English or Spanish words, often in Galicianized hybrid form. Depending on the geographical origin of the bands, non-normative Galician dialectal varieties (exemplified, for example, by the frequent use of *gheada* and *seseo* by bands from the coastal areas) are often consciously employed for political effect as distinctive markers of origin and class identity.[13] Also common is the Galicianized written spelling of foreign words—such as *Capetón* (Cape Town) and Antuerpe (Antwerp) by Os Diplomáticos, following the manner of Galician sailors—and combative *radikal* spellings in group and song names—Korosi Dansas (a pun on the Francoist folkloric "Coros y Danzas de la Sección Femenina"), Skornabois, Skupe Skapa, Kaos, *Komunikando*, or "Kazikes" by Os Diplomáticos, "Tecknotrafikante" and "Skaramoucho" by Os Papaqueixos, "Kristo jipi" by Os Rastreros—signifying an oppositional and culturally specific alternative positioning.

In typical Galician fashion, cultural nationalism comes very often mixed with social and political criticism as well as cultural self-parody. Although Galician leftist and nationalist positions are prevalent, the *bravú* movement is not necessarily affiliated to a particular nationalist political agenda such as the BNG (Bloque Nacionalista Galego); this does not preclude frequent overlapping, as many *bravú* groups have performed in nationalist rallies and/or otherwise supported the BNG nationalist party. Politically there is a common spirit of resistance and defiance of the mainstream. *Bravú*'s radical political positioning is often times overt in the condemnation of the social and political *status quo* and official culture during the years of the PP's rule in Galicia with Manuel Fraga as president (1990–2005). Likewise, the criticisms of state oppression ("O porco" ["The Pig"] by Os Rastreros, "Os galisáns" ["The Galisáns"] by Korosi Dansas), multinationals ("O sacristán de Basán" ["The Sacristan from Basán"] by Os Rastreros), *caciques* ("O alcalde morreu" ["The Mayor Has Died"] or "Kazikes" by Os Diplomáticos), and EU-imposed milk quotas ("A brosa do verdugo" ["The executioner's axe"] by Skornabois), are also culturally specific and rooted in the local. The songs sometimes carry explicit political slogans encouraging resistance, such as: "Que contra os caciques temos que loitar" ("Against the local bosses we must fight") or "Primeiro o orghullo, e despois o bandullo" ("First our pride, and then our bellies") ("Ardentia" by Os Diplomáticos); "Galicia Ceibe—Poder Popular!" ("Free Galicia, Power to the People!") ("Gaiteiro" ["Bagpiper"] by

13 For a detailed study of these sociolinguistic phenomena in Galicia, see Fernández Rei.

Os Diplomáticos); or "Non pasarán. Cuotas non, cuotas non" ("They shall not pass. No to milk quotas, No to milk quotas") ("Tratorada" ["Tractor Rally"] by Os Rastreros). References to historical memory and the repression of Galicia also occur, such as "Mil nove 36" ("1936") and "Onde a loita se chama Encrobas" ("Where the Fight is Called Encrobas"), by Xenreira, or "Ai vos quedades" ("So long I'm leaving you") , by Os Diplomáticos, a *bravú* ode to Galician working men, migrants, and exiles during Franco's dictatorship, with the recurrent use of a phrase meaning goodbye employed by Galician sailors leaving for Capetón (as they call Cape Town): "Ai vos quedades, entre curas, frades e militares" ("So long I'm leaving you, among priests, friars and military men"). In a move designed to show international solidarity, the common historical fight of Galician and Irish nationalism is celebrated in "Mesmo berce, mesma loita" ("Same cradle, same fight") by Xenreira.

More generally, there is a common vindication and celebration of Galician local roots (either the rural milieu of origin, or the new locations in urban neighborhoods, or the *rurban* mixture). This is accompanied by the assertion of Galician working-class identities (Os Rastreros's "Cerebro proletario" ["Proletarian brains"] and Heredeiros da Crús's "Íscalle lura"), particularly identities marked by the mix of urban and agrarian roots ("Vimos do monte" ["We come from the hills"] by Apanda Rapaz; "Nitramón 15, 15, 15" ["15/15/15 Fertilizer"] by Pinto D'Herbón; and "Tratorada"), or seaport culture origins (predominantly from coastal bands such as Os Diplomáticos or Heredeiros da Crus). Galician mobility and migration is also a theme in "De Jalisia ó extranxeiro" ("From Galicia to a foreign land") by Heredeiros da Crus. Ecological messages are also common, with critical references to industrial pollution and toxic waste, such as "Urkiola" or "Estrume" by Os Diplomáticos and "Ozono" by Xenreira; likewise, "Os galisáns" by Korosi Dansas, which mixes ecological concerns about natural resources and mismanagement of waste with a mythical reconstruction of the Galisáns, an indigenous tribe whose lifestyle is endangered by white men. The song is ironically sung in "Indian" Galician (with verbs in infinitive, lack of articles, and so on), as in old Western movies. Similarly, the new realities of drug trafficking and drug consumption, with Galician ports becoming the entry point of cocaine in Europe after the reconversion of the old contraband routes, receives ironic treatment in "Teknotrafikante (Farloppo ma non troppo)" by Os Papaqueixos and "Manolo pescadilla" by O Caimán do Río Tea.

In general terms, there is a certain proud and strident vindication of Galicianess in both festive and rebellious ways, mixing the spirit of popular festive *pachanga* and punk/ska, as Manu Chao had done with his *patchanka*. Naturally, there are constant allusions in their songs to Galician popular culture (food, soccer, fiestas, myths, and places of collective memory) and recognizable Galician icons (bagpipes, scenery and landscape, such as cows and tractors, the symbolic wildness of the thorny *toxos* (gorse), and untamed animals such as the wild boar or *xabarín*). These signs of Galicianess are further reinforced visually through videos, logos, album covers, and publicity shots.

Particular noteworthy in the *bravú* is the defense of the rural environment, with the legitimation of its popular culture and lifestyle (not in the sense of an essentialist or idyllic return to the past, but as an acceptable way of living in the present with pride in one's roots) and the appreciation of the natural milieu. Privileging Galician rural culture has been a mainstay of Galician nationalism since the mid-nineteenth century, and of Galician literature in particular until the latter part of the twentieth century. This new interest, however, does not necessarily represent an essentialist vision of Galicia, a return to any idealized bucolic past or a nostalgic anti-modern gesture. Tractors and electric guitars look not back to the past but to the present. In that sense, it is more a reflection of a radical transformation of Galician society in the last decades, especially evident since the restoration of democracy and entry into the European Union, a period marked by the major changes that I have characterized as *glocal* and *rurban*, including the urbanization of its small towns and villages, resembling more and more urban and suburban neighborhoods; the progressive industrialization of the rural and coastal areas with the introduction of agricultural machinery and industrial cooperatives; and the transformation of the landscape and habitat. While there are obvious signs of increased standard of living, and migration is not as acute as it used to be, these changes have not all been for the better. With economic development also came deforestation, land speculation, and the chaotic excesses of unregulated *minifundio* culture allowed by the political parties in government, all of which had very serious social consequences and a huge environmental impact. Some of the most serious corollaries include the abandonment of farmland, the shrinking of the rural population, and massive migration to the coastal urbanized areas, which in fact represents the desertification of inner Galicia, with the shocking statistic than less than 10% of the Galician population currently dedicate themselves to agriculture. Environmental impacts have included the deterioration of the natural habitat and the progressive degradation or "uglification" of the landscape and living environment with substandard construction. Not surprisingly, consciousness-raising songs about issues of environmental economics are pervasive in *bravú* groups, and include the criticism of land exploitation, the environmental impact of chaotic development, and lack of planning (commonly known aesthetically as *feísmo*, and structurally as *a desfeita*). Also common are criticisms of the mismanagement of natural resources and foreign-mandated regulations that negatively impact Galicians, particularly the milk quotas imposed by the European Union that severely reduced milk production, took with them thousands of jobs, and contributed to the abandonment of farms.

As these aspects imply, the tensions between the local and the global are sometimes quite visible in the *bravú*. As a movement, it occupies a shifting border position between the local and the global, taking music from Galicia to the world and vice versa. A good example of this ambiguous position is O Caimán do río Tea, a border band from the village of Ponteareas in the south of Galicia, which takes border-crossing hybridity as a guiding principle. As the band's name suggests, making reference to the town's river and the amphibious nature of alligator, culturally they are locally situated while open to the world. Their border music mixes old traditions and modern realities, cutting acrosss geopolitical, cultural, and musical boundaries. As expressed in their programmatic manifesto, which appeared in the newspaper *Faro de Vigo* in 1992, they conceived the group as a border band, exploring hybridity and cultural connections along the Galician/Portuguese border, mixing Galician migrants and exiles, contraband and smuggling of goods, and cultures and music styles, and telling real and contemporary Galician-focused stories between the local and the global:

> O caimán do río Tea es un anfibio, un animal inquieto, un petardo con un hormigueo en el culo, es una arteria que hierve, un rapaz envenenadamente rapaz. *Es la música de estraperlo*, el salto al vacío. Es romper la frontera galaico–portuguesa con un alijo de café y unos calzoncillos rotos y no mirar atrás. O caimán do río Tea nace en Ponteareas para hacer música universal, música hecha en casa. Son historias de curas, de marujas de mandil, de pseudoamericanos que se fueron sin dinero de Galicia al exilio, de labradores de tasca adorando el vino como si fuera maná del desierto, de pescadores trasmutados en narcotraficantes, de lameculos de los políticos. Es un anfibio, por eso no se está quieto en un solo estilo musical, quiere hacer de todo, aunque sea poco. Es la música hecha aquí, hecha en casa, de frontera, buscando el contacto y no la marginación. Música universalmente hecha en casa. *Faro de Vigo* 4 Marzo 1992, 46. (quoted in Cifuentes)

> O caimán do río Tea [The alligator of the Tea River] is an amphibian, a restless animal, a firecracker with a tingle in the ass, it is an artery that boils, a venomously voracious youngster. It's the music of the black market, a jump into the unknown. It is crossing the Galician–Portuguese border with a stash of coffee and frayed underpants and

not looking back. O caimán do río Tea was born in Ponteareas to make universal music, music made at home. They are stories of priests, of housewives with aprons, of semi-Americans who left Galicia moneyless into exile, of farmers in the tavern worshiping wine like manna in the desert, of fishermen turned into drug-traffickers, of brownnosers of politicians. It is an amphibian, and that is why it does not stand still in one musical style, it wants to try everything, even if it is just a little. It is music made here, homemade, at the border, seeking connections and not marginalization. Homemade music universally made.

In terms of their form of operation, the *bravú* bands were mostly composed of non-professional young musicians, alternating their work in the bands with their studies or other jobs. Their anti-establishment attitudes were met with a lack of interest and support from major labels, mainstream channels, and public institutions (with some exceptionsm such as the TVG programs *Xabarín Club* or Antón Reixa's *Galicia sitio distinto*). As a result, they tended to follow the model of self-management employed by Basque *rock radikal* bands, organizing the concerts and music festivals themselves, recording and producing their own songs locally, commercializing their recordings through independent labels or self-releasing them, creating low-budget videos, and multi-tasking in the ventures of self-promotion. Importantly, even though these bands moved around alternative channels—rehearsing and recording in garages and granaries, playing in small villages, and producing low-budget self-made posters and fanzines—they were able to connect with a young and receptive Galician audience, eager to embrace something they could directly relate to, that spoke about their lives and realities, their aspirations and frustrations, in a modern idiom, and in their own language, for the first time.

## A Movement of the Land: *Galicia Terremota*

*Rock bravú* was an important musical phenomenon in its own right, but it was something more than just a musical trend or style. It was not only rock and roll, or simply Galician *rock and roots*. As Xelís de Toro has explained: "At first *rock bravú* was perceived as a cross between rock and folk; it later proved to be a more complex intersection of rock and folk, literature and music, politics and culture" (246). Indeed, from its inception the *bravú* had aspirations to be a part of something larger, a multifaceted cultural grassroots movement with diverse manifestations in different media and with significant social and political ramifications. Although the *bravú* was rooted in the popular— both traditional folk culture and mass media culture—it was also open to other high cultural forms (avant-garde manifestoes, contemporary poetry, and literary experimentation, in the vein of Os Resentidos or Marisol Manfurada). It was also prone to finding parallel expression through other channels, particularly in the areas of narrative—Santiago Jaureguízar, Xurxo Souto, Fran Alonso, Manuel Rivas—and the visual arts—video, comics, graphic design, multimedia (see articles by Salgado).[14] This variety of channels was frequently integrated in festivals, live performances, television and radio shows (*Galicia sitio distinto*, directed by Antón Reixa, *Xabarín Club* by Suso Iglesias, and *A tropa da tralla* by Xurxo Souto), fanzines and magazines, and multicultural events such as the "Semana Bravú," coordinated by Xurxo Souto, and "A feira das mentiras," organized by Manu Chao.

Many cultural figures participated directly and indirectly in the development of the movement, expanding its horizons and giving it intellectual credentials, cultural legitimation, and great visibility and exposure in the media. Well-known writers (such as Manuel Rivas) and musicians (such as Manu Chao) who had the ability to reach large sectors of the public inside and outside of Galicia were active participants in several projects directly related to the *bravú* movement.[15] Rivas frequently acted as

14  In the *Bravú XX* exhibit Xurxo Souto commented: "O Bravú comenzou sendo guitarra e distorsión, mais axiña estendeu o seu berro de vida por outros camiños. Nesta exposición queremos recoller ese proxecto de axitación xeral, alierce duha tradición, e tamén impulso creativo para os novos tempos" ("The Bravú started as guitar and distorsion, but it soon spread its living scream through other areas. In this exhibit we aim to recapture that project of general agitation, foundation of a tradition, and also creative impulse for a new age") ("Exposición Bravú XX").

15  Manu Chao's relation with Galicia is not limited to his Galician family roots, as son of exiled Galician writer Ramon Chao. With his first band in France, Los carayos, he wrote several songs with Galician airs, such as "Ai vai," a Galician topic song with the sound of bagpipes and a rockabilly rhythm that could easily fit in any *bravú* group's repertoire. Its refrain later reappeared in "La vacaloca" (from *Próxima estación, Esperanza*). Manu Chao spent long periods of time in Galicia in the mid-1990s, rediscovering Galicia during the years of the formation of the movement, and he collaborated with many of the people associated with the *bravú*, recording with, for instance, Mercedes Peón, Os Diplomáticos, and Pinto D'Herbón, and playing in the band Los tres de Monforte. He recorded part of his solo album *Clandestino* in the town of Herbón, and several motifs of the album are related to his *bravú* multi-spectacle "A feira das mentiras," which took place in Santiago in 1997. His album *Próxima estación* also has explicit references to *bravú* culture. Additional material from the album on the official web page (Manuchao.net) further develops the *bravú* connection: "Algunos montes resisten [...]/ Los montes Bravú./ Alli sobrevive la sabiduria./La sabiduria de la fiesta,/ la verdadera,/la irreverente,/ la popular,/la sabiduria del desbordamiento"; "Por eso me gusta la regeifa [sic]/ Por eso me gusta el vino/L'aguardiente/Tonino Carotone/Y Pinto D'Herbon" ("Some

an unofficial cultural liaison for the movement outside of Galicia.[16] In an article originally published in *El País*—coinciding with the release of the *Unión Bravú* collective compilation CD, and then reprinted in the record liner notes—Rivas addressed the question "¿E que é o bravú?" ("And what is the bravú?") in one of the first articles published about the movement in the general Spanish press:

> O que cheira a bravío, a salitre mariño e toxo montañés, a esterco e argazo, a terra incrustada nas unllas, a intemperie, ó contacto entre o balume, a choiva e a suor da pel. Para os xoves galegos máis inquedos, o *rock bravú* é o son bravo e a expresión musical sen andrómenas. Nas aldeas, nos pobos, nos arrabaldes simbióticos e nos sotos urbanos xurden, como plantas bravas, ducias de bandas de inspiración *bravú*. Nunha iniciativa sen divos, a primeira antoloxía colectiva, o disco *Unión Bravú*, está xa na rúa. (*Unión Bravú*)

> What smells like wild spirit, sea salt and mountain gorse, fertilizing manure and seaweeds, dirt in the nails, inclement weather; like the contact between mowed grass, rain, and skin sweat. For the restless Galician youth, *rock bravú* is the wild sound and the musical expression without nonsense. In the villages, in the towns, in the symbiotic outskirts and the urban basements spring up, like wild plants, dozens of *bravú*-inspired bands. In an initiative without divos, the first collective anthology, the record *Union Bravú*, is already on the street.

Rivas also wrote an extended commentary in the accompanying original booklet of the *Unión Bravú* CD from 1996, the first recording released with the name *bravú* in its title, with Xurxo Souto and Os Diplomáticos as executive producers. Rivas highlights there the collective act of resistance, the sense of unity in defense of a national popular culture, and the solidary and combative spirit of the movement, while establishing a reconnection

---

mountains resist [...]/ the Bravú mountains./There survives wisdom./ The wisdom of fiestas,/the authentic,/irreverent,/popular, uncontrolled wisdom'; That's why I like the *regueifa*,/that's why I like wine/moonshine/Tonino Carotone/And Pinto D'Herbon"). Chao wrote the song "Galicia tropical," also the name of a spectacle he presented in Lyon, which was released in the *Próxima estación B Side*, where he mixes samples of "Galicia caníbal" from Os Resentidos.

16 Not a surprising development, as many *rock bravú* songs reflect the same rurban and glocal atmosphere that Rivas masterfully described originally in his acclaimed *Un millón de vacas* (1989) and has continued to develop in his narrative, with its poetic construction of a Galicia that is a mix of old and new, urban and rural, local and universal.

with Galician historical memory in his reference to the democratically horizontal *Irmandiños* uprising against the power of the nobility (also employed by Xenreira in their own categorization as *rock irmandiño*): "Os bravús son unha Confederacion Irmandiña. Non hai programa, nin ideas preconcebidas, nin uniformes. Unidos pola terra, a lingua e a música, peiteados polo vento, os guerreiros desbrozan as corredoiras cegas" ("The *bravú* youth is a Confederation of Irmandiños. There is no program, nor pre-conceived ideas, nor uniforms. United by the land, the language, and the music, with their hair styled by the wind, these warriors are clearing the old blind country roads") (*Unión Bravú* 5, quoted in Mariño Davila and Noya Beiroa 119).[17]

Another important development in the *bravú* movement was the launching of *Revista Bravú* in Vigo in 1997. Its first issue was introduced with the "Manifesto do tractor bravú," also written by Manuel Rivas, which delineates the modern character of hybrid Galicia in a surreal parody of political manifestos and in the spirit of cultural resistance embodied in the *bravú* movement, here poetically symbolized in the strength and resistance of the tractor:

O tractor é unha baca do Gran Sol que sulca en
estribor a Nosa Terra,
O tractor non emigra, protesta.
O pantasma do tractorista percorre Europa cun doble
air-bag de nubes e collóns.
Un tractor bravú funga na Vía Láctea.
O tractor é un carro do país ao que lle arde o peito,
pon en rock de pistons a balada folk do eixo. ("Manifesto" 7)

The tractor is a boat from Gran Sol ploughing Our Land to starboard. The tractor does not migrate, it complains. The specter of the tractor-driver is haunting Europe with a dual airbag of clouds and guts. A *bravú* tractor is grumbling in the Milky Way. The tractor is an ox cart with its chest on fire, rocking with its pistons the folk ballad of the axis.

---

17 Xurxo Souto and Manuel Rivas, who share origins in the same working-class neighbourhood in A Coruña (Montealto), were frequent collaborators in other projects related to the *bravú* culture. Rivas recorded live with Os diplomáticos the "Pregón de Monte Alto," which was released on CD accompanying the second edition of his book *Toxos e frores* (1998), sung by Rivas, who also recites and sings part of the "Pregón" in the fisherman *ranchera* song "Taberna Monte Alto" on the album *Capetón* by Os Diplomáticos (1999). They also collaborated in the public presentations of Manuel Rivas's novel *Ela, maldita alma* in 1999.

*Revista Bravú* was short-lived, with only four issues printed (it continued online at bravú.net), but it provided a highly visible outlet for all the different areas covered by the *bravú* movement.[18] In an era of self-made low-budget fanzines, *Revista bravú* was an ambitious enterprise, published by the prestigious Galician publisher Edicións Xerais and bringing together some of the most talented and dynamic young Galician creators. Directed by Xosé Manuel Pereiro, journalist and former leader of the A Coruña band Radio Oceáno (as Johnny Rotring), the editorial board included a new wave of writers, musicians, and cultural figures associated with the movement, such as Santiago Jaureguízar, Manu Chao, Manuel Rivas, Fran Alonso, and Xurxo Souto. Regular collaborators also included a long list of young Galician writers, journalists, filmmakers, actors, graphic designers, painters, photographers, and artists, such as Suso de Toro, Ramón Chao, Antón Reixa, Alberto Casal, Alfonso Pato, Jorge Coira, Miguelanxo Prado, Din Matamoro, and Manuel Manquiña, among many others. The magazine was voluminous (each issue averaged more than a hundred pages) and incorporated a mosaic of *bravú* elements, short fiction, comics, reports, and cultural manifestos.

An important feature of the magazine was its covering of *Rock bravú*, with interviews, concert reports, and record reviews. Each issue of the magazine was accompanied by an original CD of collected *bravú* music especially constructed around a single unifying theme of Galician popular culture. As in the case of the magazine contents, the records were eclectic, innovative, and featured exciting collaborations. The first CD (*Selección Xa!*) was centered on the demand for a Galician soccer national team and included tracks by Os Diplomáticos, Mercedes Peón, Manu Chao, and Pinto D'Herbón with the voices of Galician soccer players. Some of the tracks experimented with dance, techno, and electronic music, hybridizing with traditional Galician folk songs with rock beats and accordion-driven polkas from popular *charangas*. The second CD (*Hai alguen ai fora?*, 1998) was presented as a message in a bottle sent from Galicia to the world. In the tradition of Galician ironic *retranca*, the message was formulated as a question ("Is there anybody out there?"). The title track by O Coro dos Rozadores (an open band formed with members from other *bravú* bands) covered Bob Dylan's "Knocking on Heaven's Door" and individual parts were sung by Manuel Rivas, Suso de Toro, Antón Reixa, and other magazine collaborators. The third CD (*Terra*

18 Other cultural Galician magazines created in the heyday of *movida galega* in the 1980s included *La naval* in A Coruña and *Tintimán* in Vigo, which in some ways preceded and prepared the way for *Revista Bravú*. The magazine *Animal+* ("Revista cultural para todas as especies") was another publishing outlet for the *bravú* movement.

*terremota*, 1998) used the earthquake as a metaphor for the seismic social and cultural movements taking place in the *rurban* and *glocal* Galicia, and went further in technological experiments with electronica, acid jazz, and samplers. Antón Reixa's own "Terra terremota" mixes funk with Galician drums and bagpipes, creating a surreal atmosphere of movement that gives a central focus to the project, while Marisol Manfurada mixes Miles Davis samplings with her Galician rap in "O Big Bang," a futuristic explosion of fury and biting emotions. O Coro dos Rozadores again performs another Galician cannibalization of a classic song, this time deconstructing the *movida madrileña* (Nacha Pop's anthem "Chica de ayer" becomes a Dylan-infected protest song about environmental pollution entitled "A resposta está no vento" ["The answer is blowing in the wind"]). Also included are some well-known anthems of the *rock agreste* variety such as "Tratorada" by Os Rastreros and "A motoserra" ("The power saw") by Pinto D'Herbón, and a videogame featuring Pinto D'Herbón. The fourth and last CD of the series (*7 portas, 7 mares*) focused on Galician sea culture, city ports, ships, and seafarers, highlighting the global outlook of Galician maritime culture. It included tracks by Os Diplomáticos and the popular metal band Astarot from the Morrazo peninsula (an area well known for its seafaring culture and leftist nationalist politics), next to sailors' songs, a choir of traditional Galician women *cantareiras*, a duet of accordion and *zanfoña*, and, in another effort to expand horizons, an ode to Fisterra/Finisterre in Galician by José Ángel Valente. As was mentioned in Chapter 1, Xurxo Souto summarized Galicia's new position in a remapped postperipheral cartography where Galicia extends towards the seas:

> Galicia é unha rocha cativa chantada no Atlántico e tamén un inmenso país marino que abrangue todos os Océanos. [...] Outra xeografía. As distancias enrúganse e estrícanse no mar. [...] Reclamamos para o bravú o país invisible do mar.[...] Non hai límites nin fronteiras. Existimos entre a realidade e o misterio. O fuciño no Océano, a porta de todos os camiños. [...] Desde a hiper-periferia cara Capetón. ("Galicia-Capetón" 73)

> Galicia is a small rock stuck in the Atlantic and also an immense marine country encompassing all the Oceans. [...] Another geography. Distances shorten and stretch in the sea. [...] We claim for the *bravú* people the invisible country of the sea. [...]There are no limits or frontiers. We exist between reality and mystery. Our snouts in the Ocean, the gate of all roads.[...] From the hyper-periphery towards Cape Town.

Figure 32  Rock and bagpipes. The Xabarín mascot from TVG program *Xabarín Club* (1994). Design by Miguelanxo Prado.

Another even more important channel and catalyst of the *bravú* movement was Galician television, and particularly the program *Xabarín Club [XC]*, the star of TVG's youth programming with the highest ratings in its category, which used the logo of a Galician wild boar, designed by Miguelanxo Prado. The reach and impact of *XC* on Galician youth as an instrument of cultural and language normalization was considerable, and it played a very significant role in the dissemination of *rock bravú* among young audiences. On the air seven days a week since its launch in 1994, *XC* became a mass phenomenon in the late 1990s, with over 100,000 youth affiliated in the club, about a quarter of all Galician youth ("A televisión en Galicia" 16). *XC* also reached youth audiences beyond Galicia, in the borderland areas of León, Zamora, and Asturias, as well as in the rest of Europe and the Americas through two satellite channels and the TVG website.

*XC* was an open format program that included imported animation series (dubbed in Galician), as well as self-produced short features, news, games, and, significantly for *rock bravú*, concerts and music video clips especially made for the show by new rock and folk groups in Galician. *XC* also produced and released highly successful compilation CDs for its club members (four CDs of the series "A cantar con Xabarín"—three of them dedicated almost

Figure 33   A new rurban/glocal sound and vision. Album cover for *A Cantar con Xabarín*. Vols 1 and 2 (1995). Design by Miguelanxo Prado. TVG/BOA Music.

exclusively to *rock bravú*—plus another CD of the soundtrack of the Galician animation series "Os vixiantes do camiño" directed by Miguelanxo Prado. Aside from records, members of the club received magazines and other tie-in merchandise, and could also participate in *Xabaxiras*, Xabarín music tours, fairs, and events throughout the towns and villages of Galicia. Although the target audience of the club was older children and teenagers, it is clear that many young adults were also part of the television audience and many managed to maintain their membership even after reaching the age limit for club membership, set at eighteeen (according to Xavier Viana, screenwriter and co-host of *XC*). In addition to songs and videos in Galician, there were also frequent Portuguese-language groups from Brazil, Portugal, or Cape Verde, which opened Galicia towards the Lusophone world.

The connection of *XC* to *rock bravú* existed from the original concept and early graphics of the program, created by Suso Iglesias and designed by Miguelanxo Prado. Xabarín, the mascot of the show, also known as *o porco bravo* ("wild boar"), created a natural link to the *bravú* concept, sharing the same vindication of Galician symbolic wildness, which was frequently reinforced in videos, graphics, and songs. Not surprisingly, references to the *xabarín* or *porco bravo* abound in many songs, such as "A vida nun pin"

("Life in a Pin") by Nación Reixa—"Imita a conducta do xabarín, porco bravo coma tin e coma min" ("Copy the behavior of the *xabarín*, a wild boar just like you and me")—or "Xa ven o Xabarín" ("Here comes Xabarín") by Os Diplomáticos—"Xa ven o porco bravo, xa ven o Xabarín ... cheirando a bravío, cheirando a bravú, licor de landra, licor de landrú" ("Here comes the wild boar, here comes Xabarín ... smelling like wildness, smelling like *bravú*, liqueur of acorns, liqueur of punks").

Since *XC* was a public television youth program, the songs featured in the videos and CDs offered a somewhat softer and gentler side of *rock bravú* for the younger audience, but without renouncing its principles. Profanity and overtly sexual themes were avoided, and expressions of radical political positionings were excluded. This was an obvious consequence of the directives from the PP-controlled public TVG. However, while the most aggressive or provocative parts of *rock bravú* were toned down for the videos and CD compilations, and overtly politized messages were absent, the spirit was still ludic, energetic, irreverent, rebellious, and definitively with an edge, still carrying a strong sense of vindication of Galician cultural identity. The videos and songs produced by *XC* proved extraordinarily popular with the young public, unifying the interests of the urban and rural Galician youth audiences and creating a new community around a common sense of shared identity (popularly known as "Xeración Xabarín" ["Xabarín generation"]). It could be said, then, that *XC* was the first TVG program to successfully bridge the *rurban* and *glocal* youth cultures of modern Galicia. In 2013 Antón Losada reminisced about the importance of *XC* for the "normalization" of Galician language and culture for a new generation of young Galician viewers and listeners, and its opening to the world. It represented a response from the periphery in opposition to the hegemonic programming emanating from the center, while opening up new channels of communication towards the world outside:

Frente al modelo de hipermercado y producción y consumo masivo del Club Disney, nuestro Xabarín aguanta como su admirado Asterix resistía frente a la uniformidad y la disciplina militar del imperio romano. [...] mercadotecnia alternativa e imaginación llevando la marca Galicia por el mundo globalizado de la televisión. ("Xabarín Forever")

Against the warehouse superstore model of massive production and consumption of Disney Club, our Xabarín stands just like his admired Asterix resisted against the uniformity and military discipline of the Roman empire. [...] alternative marketing and imagination taking the Galician brand out in the globalized world of television.

## And the beat goes on ...

Although now extinct as a movement, the legacy of the *bravú* still survives. The recent *bravú* homages and commemorations could be seen not just as nostalgic reflections of its completion as a movement but as an overdue acknowledgement of its historic relevance for the modernization of Galician culture and as an opportunity for its discovery by younger generations. Several cultural figures associated with the development of the *bravú* movement offered their retrospective assessment, highlighting different aspects of its lasting impact, particularly crucial issues of cultural self-esteem, decolonization, mobility, and modernity. For Xosé Manuel Pereiro, "O bravú foi un chute nacional de autoestima emocional e de ansia musical" ("The bravú was a shot of emotional self-esteem and musical urgency") ("O bravú regresa") and it represented "autenticidad en una era de plástico" ("authenticity in a plastic age") (Salgado, "El sabor de la carne"). María Yáñez, a former director of the online *Revista Bravú* website and later director of the Galician portal Vieiros, agrees that the movement was able to mobilize "a cuestión da autoestima e un certo proceso de descolonización mental [...] Para min, o grunge, Tarantino e Os Diplomáticos estaban, en 1994 ou 1995, no mesmo barco" ("the issue of self-esteem and a certain process of mental decolonization [...] For me, grunge music, Tarantino and Os Diplomáticos were, in 1994 or 1995, on the same boat") ("Castañazo Rock"). For Xurxo Souto, "se consiguió identificar el gallego con la vanguardia, como en Os Resentidos, en un país antiguo que se acaba y que choca con una modernidad de ferragancho; de esa colisión se desprende una energía maravillosa" ("we all managed to identify Galician language with the avant-garde, like in the case of Os Resentidos, in an old country that is dying away and clashes with a metallic modernity; from this collision emanates a wonderful energy") (Salgado, "El sabor de la carne").

In contrast, however, there have been some critical voices that showed considerable less enthusiasm. Iago Martínez, for example, has criticized the regressive and totalizing essentialism of the movement in the construction of an idealized conception of rural Galicia, although he admits that the ludic spirit as well as the normalization of the language and the consumption of self-made music were positive legacies:

> O bravú [...] foi unha nova volta de rosca á idealización da cultura rural en Galicia, que excluía o urbano, e tivo pretensións totalizadoras de se estender tamén á literatura [...] O bravú fabricou unha imaxe do país esencialmente reaccionario [...] Talvez o único positivo do bravú resultou o seu sentido lúdico e a constatación de que se podía facer

música aquí para consumir aquí; iso é o que aproveita do bravú a nova escena musical galega. (Salgado, "Cando a periferia")

The *bravú* was another twist on the idealization of rural life in Galicia, which excluded the urban, and had totalizing pretensions of including also literature [...] The *bravú* fabricated an image of the nation essentially reactionary [...] Maybe the only positive element of the *bravú* was its ludic sense and the realization that we could make music here to be consumed here; that is what the new Galician music scene takes from the *bravú*.

One aspect on which all commentators agree is that one of the most important consequences of the *bravú* was the normalization of Galician as a suitable language for rock music and Galician modern youth culture in general, something that was still quite atypical in the early 1990s. A new generation of Galician youth, for the first time, grew up listening to rock music (and watching the videos and concerts of their favorite bands) sung in Galician about Galician realities. YouTube comments on those video clips and concerts overwhelmingly attest to the huge impact they had and their lasting legacy, as well as the nostalgia associated with the movement. An important corollary of this is that, today, it is accepted and seemingly unsurprising, if still not the norm, for new Galician rock bands to sing in Galician.

The hybridization that occurred with the *bravú* movement of folk and rock—old and new, local and global, rural and urban cultural idioms—has also generated a rich and varied field in Galician popular music today. A case in point is the appearance of female performers in Galician who creatively mix roots and international influences: rappers such as As Garotas da Ribeira, rock singers such as Ses, and the "revolution" of women *gaiteiras* (Mercedes Peón and Cristina Pato, among others) in a traditionally masculine field using the performative language of rock while playing the traditional bagpipe. This would seem unthinkable without the cultural seismic movement created by the *bravú*. In some cases, this connection with the *bravú* is real and direct. A great deal of musical innovation has been brought about by avant-garde performance artists such as Mercedes Peón (who started in the *bravú* movement with Os Diplomáticos and Manu Chao, mentor and producer of her first recordings, and is now in the forefront of Galician experimental roots music in the international arena). The bold musical hybridity and audacious experimentation of *rock bravú* also opened the gates for new ways of approaching folk and popular music, Galician roots and foreign music, as the recent wave of exciting hybrid projects by Nordestin@s, Espido, and Marful, or the new Jazz galego, attests.

Figure 34  Leaving the audio/visual periphery behind. Poster inspired by *El método sueco* web series from *Porco Bravú*. Design by Guillermo Peláez González.

On the social and political front, although the *bravú* was never a unified political movement, its grassroots popular structure, its nationalist leanings, and its radical political positionings prepared the way for the kind of massive popular mobilizations in towns and villages that took place throughout Galicia after the *Prestige* oil spill catastrophe, where popular creativity, political confrontation, and defense of the land and sea converged with the angry attitude and ludic spirit of the *bravú* movement, under the umbrella of the NGO platform *Nunca Máis*.[19]

The rebellious and wild spirit of the *bravú* persists in a new generation of creative Galician artists, such as the A Coruña-based audiovisual collective *Porco Bravú*, who specialized in the production of alternative web series, having received the Mestre Mateo award two years in a row for their acclaimed series *El método sueco* (2014–2016). Working from the periphery and the margins of the mainstream, *Porco Bravú* have found in the Internet a suitable niche for provocative, rebellious, off-beat, humorous, minimalist, low-cost do-it-yourself productions.

*Bravú*'s vindication of local roots—the Galician people and culture from the inner rural areas and the sea coast, including working-class peasants, farmers, sailors, and fishermen (traditionally dismissed as ignorant and

19  For an overview of the mix of ludic creativity and political contestation in relation to *Nunca Máis* see Lobato.

backward)—and of Galician language (including that spoken by the working classes, with the frequent use of *gheada* and *seseo*, considered vulgar and non-normative) created a positive image of self-esteem that counteracted a long tradition of derision and neglect.[20] As Xurxo Souto has noted, the *bravú* leveled the playing field between cities and villages and demarginalized the conditions of Galician cultural production: "O bravú demoleu apriorismos e deixou á vista que se pode facer algo con personalidade desde a periferia da periferia" ("The bravú demolished prejudices and revealed that you can do something with personality from the periphery of the periphery") (Salgado, "Cando a periferia"). All these cultural experiences, which have been part of the "normalizing" process of Galician cultural life in recent years, were made possible in large measure as a consequence of the seismic cultural movements initiated with *Rock bravú*, and the larger struggle of the movement to resituate Galician cultural production and overcome the challenges in the deterritorialization of its polyperipheral condition.

20 The acknowledgement and vindication of the Galician *rurban* reality and the ludic and confrontational spirit of the *bravú* can also be seen behind the creation of the Festival de Cine de Cans, the *rurban* counter-response to the Cannes Film Festival, with its "agroglamour" and actors and directors parading in tractors, and film shows, press conferences, and presentations taking place in farm stables and granaries. See Pérez Gil.

# CHAPTER TEN

# Bagpipes, Bouzoukis, and Bodhráns: The Reinvention of Galician Folk Music

Anda vaite polo mundo
Non esquezas de onde vés
O que esqueza a súa historia
Pouco poderá aprender.

Anda vaite polo mundo
E aproveita a viaxe
Deixa que o mundo te vista
Coa roupa da mestizaxe.

'Go travel around the world
Don't forget where you come from
Those who forget their history
Will not be able to learn much.

Go travel around the world
And take advantage of the journey
Let the world dress you
With the clothes of metissage.'
"Vaite polo mundo," Traditional song/Leilía

## Reinventing Traditions

This chapter examines the contemporary redefinition of Galician folk music that has occurred since the transition to democracy and the establishment of Galician autonomy, and the role contemporary Galician folk music has played in the construction of a modern Galician cultural identity in the global age. Since the mid-1970s the recovery of Galician musical and cultural heritage has gone hand-in-hand, somewhat paradoxically, with innovation, transformation, and hybridization. In parallel, contemporary Galician folk music has become one of the key cultural expressions of a modern Galician identity that is to a large extent based in the distinctness and richness of its traditional music, even if this genre has undergone a complex process of hybridization entailing the merging of old and new forms, rural and urban manifestations, and local and global trends.

This redefinition of Galician folk music has developed in parallel to the major political and social changes occurring in Galicia during this period, and the significant cultural developments in literature, audio-visual arts, rock music, and fashion, which have all played a key role in the process of collective self-discovery and self-construction. Two major historical events have governed these developments: the process of cultural "normalization" as a result of the establishment of Galician political autonomy; and the globalization of the cultural industries with Galicia's response to the new cultural climate and the economic currents of our global age. The result of these processes has allowed the redefinition of Galician folk music as an organic entity that maintains strong and direct links with its own past, but is clearly heading towards new horizons.

The revival of folk music in Galicia has not been an altogether exceptional phenomenon, but has rather occurred largely in the wake of the great folk revival taking place in the second part of the twentieth century throughout the western world. This revival—influenced on the ideological plane by political leftist–nationalist activism—has been characterized on the musical plane by the recovery of traditional musical styles and by the incorporation of new instruments, hybridization, and dialogue across cultures (for example, the introduction of electric guitar in American folk or the banjo and bouzouki in Irish music). In its initial stages, the Galician folk music revival was part of the general reawakening of Galician cultural and political nationalism in the late 1960s and 1970s, and of the general resistance against the dictatorship in the waning days of Franco's regime and during the transition to democracy. A subsequent revival took place at the turn of the century, with the new 'boom' of Galician traditional and folk music, in part a natural development of the early folk movement and the result of strong institutional sponsorship, not always from the nationalist front, as Javier Campos has noted. But this process was also motivated by the appearance of new trends, such as the globalization of cultural markets and the concept of world music, which brought the discovery and rebranding of Galician music as "ethnic music," often categorized as part of the pan-Celtic international music scene.

Arguably, it is in the field of Galician folk music that some of the best examples of successful hybridization of local/global cultural production taking place in Galicia in the last few decades can be found. A well-established musical landscape has been formed which reflects not only the richness of its cultural heritage but also its development and innovation according to new musical tendencies, with wide public and critical acceptance both in Galicia and abroad.

The musical hybridization and redefinition of Galician folk music has not been an anomaly, but the result of the convergence of several historical forces that cut across geopolitical borders. Galicia's rich ancestral musical tradition was influenced by the flux of cultures traversing the area throughout the centuries, as well as by its continual cultural contact with others, perhaps best epitomized by the centuries-old Christian pilgrimage route of the Camiño de Santiago (see Chapter 3). Since the nineteenth century, Galician traditional music has been deeply affected also by the great waves of migration of Galicians to other parts of the world, particularly to Latin America, and the cultural and musical exchanges ensuing from these historical connections. And, while the new trends of globalization present a number of challenges to local cultures, they have also expanded and redefined political and economic horizons, providing additional channels and opportunities for potential cultural exchange and hybridization. This chapter will examine the complex cultural contexts of this surge of Galician folk music and its merging with other folk movements, particularly with Celtic music (from Ireland, Great Britain, and Brittany) and music from other parts of the world with strong historical and cultural links to Galicia, such as Latin America and the Lusophone world. In doing so, I will also remain attentive to other forms of hybridization, where Galician folk music has entered into contact with different musical currents and genres, including classical, medieval music, and world music as well as contemporary forms of popular music such as jazz, rock, new age, or chillout.

Historically, the theory of Galicia's Celtic origins has been the subject of much debate in discussions of Galician cultural identity, often being seen as another form of "invented tradition" in Eric Hobsbawm's sense (1983). The legendary re-encounter with Celtic cultures has run deep in the conception of Galician cultural identity since the nineteenth-century *Rexurdimento*, when a Celtic past was 'invented' as a central part of Galician identity based on uncertain historical, anthropological, and archaeological connections. This was a typically romantic, mythologized conception of the nation subsequently institutionalized in the Galician national anthem, based on Eduardo Pondal's poem "Os pinos" (The Pine Trees), as the "nazón de Breogán" (nation of Breoghan—the mythical Celtic king of Galicia). The central role of the *gaita* (bagpipe) in Galician traditional music has been repeatedly used as evidence of that Celtic link. As Xelís de Toro has stated, since the nineteenth century "the bagpipe has been seen as the 'true expression' of the 'Galician soul'" (238). Unquestionably, bagpipe music, and its well-established tradition of representation in Galician literature and the visual arts (with a rich iconography in art, advertising, and periodicals), have been tenets of national identity both in Galicia and in the great Galician diaspora. Although the debate is still open as to the actual extent of Galicia's Celtic past, the connections between Galicia and the Celtic world have been abundant throughout the centuries. The cultivation of a Celtic past, real or imagined, is also part of twentieth-century Galician nationalist intellectual history (as in the works of Vicente Risco and Alfonso Castelao) and Galician literature (in the poems of Ramón Cabanillas and Álvaro Cunqueiro's fictional prose), with a firm grab on Galician popular culture (festivals, soccer, advertising, and especially music).[1] The contemporary rebranding of Galician folk music as part of a large transnational pan-Celtic cultural map could be seen as the last chapter in that development, which has also contributed to its deperipheralization, positioning itself successfully on the global map of world music.

## New Beginnings

Around the mid-1970s Galician traditional and folk music were at a critical crossroads, hovering between popular tradition and innovation. On the one hand, Galician music was experiencing the decline of the politically engaged *cantautor* (singer–songwriter) movement, which had emerged as a form of cultural resistance to the dictatorship and was best represented in the "protest song" of the group Voces Ceibes.[2] On the other, Francoist co-option of Galician folk imagery and traditions as a way of demobilizing political nationalism, coupled with the rapid urbanization of the population, had brought about a sense of general neglect of Galician traditional folklore.[3]

The transition to democracy and Galicia's cultural and national affirmation after Franco's death saw the appearance of new voices and directions in Galician popular music. A renewed interest in Galicia's cultural heritage initiated a recovery of the traditional musical heritage, generally neglected during the dictatorship but still quite alive in Galician popular

1 For a review of Galicia's controversial Celtic status within the pan-Celtic movement, see Ellis.

2 For a personal history of *Voces Ceibes*, see Araguas.

3 There were exceptions to this general neglect during the Franco era. Aside from the regional groups of *Coros y danzas de la Sección Femenina* (Choirs and Dances of the Women's Section), the official propagandistic version of traditional song and dance enforced by the regime, there were important developments such as the creation of the Cultural Association *Cántigas e Frores* in Lugo (1948), the *Ballet Gallego Rey de Viana* in A Coruña (1949), and the successful tours of the group *Cántigas da Terra* around the migrant communities overseas.

culture, and originated an early revival in Galician folk music, which would only increase in future years. This revival included the recovery by folk musicians of old instruments that had fallen into disuse and the retrieval of traditional Galician tunes, songs, and dances through research in archives and *cancioneiros*, as well as through active fieldwork in villages throughout Galicia. This early folk revival was accompanied by the establishment of schools of traditional music, traditional instrument workshops, and dance academies, which had a big impact on the growth of the folk movement in later years. A case in point would be the *Escola de Gaitas de Ortigueira* (Ortigueira Bagpipe School), founded by Xavier Garrote in 1975, which lead to the establishment of the important *Festival Internacional do Mundo Celta de Ortigueira* (Ortigueira's International Festival of the Celtic World) in 1978, an annual event gathering thousands of folk music performers and aficionados from around the world. Antón Corral, at one time director of the School, would later direct the "Obradoiro de música tradicional" ("traditional music workshop") at the Universidade Popular de Vigo, from which a new generation of Galician folk musicians was to emerge.

At the same time, some *cantautores* who had abandoned the old "protest song" style came together under the Movemento Popular da Canción Galega (MPCG) (Popular Movement for Galician Song), which aimed to bring new life to Galician folk music by exploring more adventurous musical avenues.[4] They were interested in rebuilding Galician cultural identity as well as recovering the repressed and forgotten voices of the past, often recurring to musicalizing Galician poetry, both traditional and contemporary. This should not be surprising since the Galician poetic tradition (both popular and literary, religious and profane, old and new) has been one of the fundamental backbones of Galician literature and culture since the Middle Ages. While these *cantautores* found inspiration in traditional Galician music they were also in tune with modern musical sensibilities, influenced by other Iberian and international folk movements, and open to experimenting with other musical genres, such as blues, new age, or classical music.

One of the pivotal starting points of the *cantautor* revival was Luis Emilio Batallán, a participating member of the MPCG, whose first album *Ahí ven o maio* (Here Comes the Spring) (1975) is considered one of the most successful examples of Galician urban folk. The album is an outstanding collection

---

4 Although short-lived, the MPCG movement would be a breeding ground for the revitalization of Galician popular music. Participants included veterans Bibiano, Benedicto, and Jei Noguerol, and newcomers Luis Emilio Batallán, Emilio Cao, Antón Seoane, and Rodrigo Romaní, all of whom would play a key part in the redefinition of Galician folk in the years ahead. For more information, see Estévez and Losada.

of acoustic songs based on well-known poems from the Galician lyrical tradition, including poets from the nineteenth-century revival as well as twentieth-century poets such as Ramón Cabanillas, Álvaro Cunqueiro, and Celso Emilio Ferreiro. From a musical point of view, the album signaled a thoroughly innovative approach in the Galician context, featuring a rich and lush if delicate sound and meticulous production, with original musical arrangements that recovered traditional instruments and styles, while incorporating modern sounds (with musicians from progressive/symphonic rock band Granada). Batallán's style was influenced by international neo-folk singer–songwriters (such as Simon & Garfunkel and Cat Stevens), as well as modern Galician pop/folk (Andrés do Barro). The album incorporates for the first time traditional Galician instruments such as the *zanfona* (hurdy gurdy), the *gaita*, the violin, and church bells, but also makes use of the pop/rock sounds of electric guitars, drums, pianos, and synthesizers. The album was met with universal acclaim in Galicia, marking a new beginning for Galician popular music and setting an example for other *cantautores* and musicians working on the integration of Galician tradition (instruments, lyrical poetry, and melodies) with modernity (authors, musical arrangements, and instrumentation). Surprisingly, *Ahí ven o maio* became a bestselling album in Spain as well, at a time when the market for Galician music records, let alone Galician folk records, was practically non-existent. It is now widely considered a contemporary classic of Galician folk music.

As a testament of the permanence of the album in Galician popular culture, one of its songs, "Quen poidera enamorala" ("Who Could Make her Fall in Love"), has become a staple in Galician folk music. Based on a poem by Álvaro Cunqueiro written in the medieval Galaico-Portuguese *cantigas de amigo* tradition, it has been covered by many other artists and choirs throughout Galicia, including Amancio Prada, Milladoiro, and the heavy metal band Astarot, in addition to being used on the soundtrack of the widely acclaimed Galician film *Pradolongo* (2008). The album, in its successful marriage of lyrics and music, traditional and modern forms, reflects a strong sentiment of collective Galician cultural identity. The lead song, "Ahí ven o maio," based on Curros Enríquez's compelling anti-clerical and anti-*cacique* poem in defense of the Galician peasant class, sets the tone of the album. It incorporates Galician traditional elements of *saudade* and melancholy—"Camiño Longo" ("Long Way"), "Chove" ("It's Raining")— with a profound sense of irony and resistance against oppression—"Notas necrolóxicas" ("Death Notices"), "Nosa Señora" ("Our Lady"), and "Nocturno" ("Nocturnal")—or the joy of cultural celebration at the dawn of a new political era—"Ahí ven o maio" and "Agardarei" ("I will wait"). Unfortunately, Batallán disappeared from the musical scene for a long time, and his second album did not arrive for another two decades.[5] However, the seeds of creative dialogue between past and present planted by his first album were there for others to follow.

Another important singer–songwriter in the reawakening of Galician folk music after the dictatorship was Amancio Prada. Originally from El Bierzo, the Galician-speaking part of the region of León, he devoted several albums in the 1970s to Galician poetry, including his first album *Vida e Morte* (1974), which included poems by Rosalía de Castro, Celso Emilio Ferreiro, and Darío Xohán Cabana. This album was followed by *Rosalía de Castro* (1975), devoted completely to the Galician poet; *Caravel de caraveles* (1976), with traditional Galician songs; and *Leliadoura* (1977), devoted to medieval Galician–Portuguese lyrical poetry. Like most *cantautores*, he accompanied his music with an acoustic guitar, while also introducing traditional instruments such as the *zanfona* and the *cromorno* (crumhorn), and often a cello, thus mixing the popular tradition with medieval and classical music influences. Prada was an excellent connoisseur of the troubadour tradition, as well as a gifted singer and composer, and many of his covers of Galician poems have swiftly become contemporary standards of Galician popular music, with deep social resonance as songs of resistance against political and economic oppression—such as Rosalía de Castro's "Adios ríos, adios fontes" ("Farewell Rivers, Farewell Fountains") and "Pra Habana" ("Leaving for Havana"), about the Galician diaspora. Other important figures in the early revival of Galician folk song were María Manuela and Pilocha (Pilar Martínez Conde). María Manuela released her first album in 1975, *Cántigas ao meu xeito* (Singing My Way), followed by *Idioma meu* (My Language) in 1977, and Pilocha released her first, self-titled, album in 1978. Both singers anticipated the later emergence of a variety of strong female performers in Galician folk music, and can be considered early examples of the modern Galician–Portuguese folk music reconnection. Maria Manuela's cover of the *fado* "Habemos de ir a Viana" ("We Shall Go to Viana") and Pilocha's popular rendition of the Portuguese song "O sancristán de Coimbra" ("Coimbra's Beadle")—originally known as "Fado Serenata do Hylário" ("Hylário's fado serenade")—have in time become part of the repertoire of Galician popular music.

---

5 Significantly, Batallán's pioneering trajectory in music is parallel and remarkably similar to Chaño Piñeiro's in cinema, as both alternated their intermittent artistic careers with their full-time professional dedication (as rural doctor and pharmacist respectively), which reflects the limitations of cultural atomization and lack of an appropriate cultural infrastructure.

## The Celtic Reawakening

An instrumental figure in linking the Galician *cantautor* folk movement with the emergent Celtic music revival is Emilio Cao, a singer–songwriter and multi-instrumentalist who had been part of the folk group collective Voces Ceibes and subsequently joined the emergent MPCG. Cao's first solo album, *Fonte do Araño* (1977), marked another milestone in Galician folk music by starting the fusion—or perhaps reintegration—of Galician music with Celtic influences, and by becoming a bestselling record, still a rarity in those days. Mixing his own traditionally inspired compositions with Galician traditional pieces and traditional instruments such as the *gaita*, the *zanfona*, and the *cítola* (zither) with occasional electric guitar (in the New Age style of Mike Oldfield), Cao famously introduced the use of the Celtic harp into a Galician folk album. It was the first recording in which a Galician bagpipe could be heard side-by-side the harp on most of its tracks, thus singlehandedly reinstituting the harp—a traditional instrument in Galicia in the Middle Ages that later fell into disuse—into the musical scene.

For his musical undertaking, Cao followed the example of Alan Stivell, the master of the Celtic harp and one of the pioneers of the 1960s Celtic folk revival in Brittany, who in turn soon became an admirer and frequent collaborator of Cao. For his part, Stivell wrote a very strong and passionate endorsement of Cao's achievement in bridging Galician with Breton and Irish music, which can be found in a statement included in the album's inner sleeve. I reproduce here a part of Stivell's statement for its historical significance as perhaps the first formal instance of international recognition of Galician music as part of the pan-Celtic frame:

> ... teño para min que este xesto é coma una ponte galgando por riba do Atlántico, expresión dos vencellos que xuntan a Galicia e Bretaña, dous países que se atopan, ainda que en distinto degrau, na encrucillada das culturas latina e céltiga. Non quero facer colonialismo cultural ao afirmar que os celtas de Bretaña, Irlanda, e outras terras, logo de ter sido afogados até a agonía polos grandes Estados opresores (Francia, Inglaterra...) sentímonos satisfeitos ao ver aos galegos revalorizar a súa parte da herdanza céltiga común para mellor defender súa personalidade nacional frente a España. Penso que o elemento céltigo é o factor esencial que lle dá tanto ao pobo como ao país galego o seu carácter distintivo.

> ... I believe that this gesture is like a bridge crossing over the Atlantic, an expression of the connections that unite Galicia and Brittany, two nations that are, even if in different degrees, at the crossroads of Celtic

and Latin cultures. It is not my intention to make cultural colonialism when affirming that we the Celts of Brittany, Ireland and other lands, after having being suffocated to death by the great oppressive States (France, England...) are pleased to see Galicians revalorize their part of common Celtic heritage in order to better defend their national character in front of Spain. I believe that the Celtic element is the essential factor giving both the Galician people and its nation their distinctive nature.

Stivell's words were to prove prophetic, as *Fonte do Araño* became a turning point in Galician folk music that has, since then, resisted the test of time. Its success was directly responsible for the readoption of the harp for Galician folk music, and, with it, the entrance of Galician folk music into the circuit of international concerts and inter-Celtic music festivals. *Fonte do Araño* is characterized by its acoustic serene style, musical experimentation, and rich suggestiveness, which was evocative of the Galician landscape, traditionally considered one of the most distinctive depositories of Galician identity. Its expressive style, at once joyful and reflective, still resonates as fresh and modern as it was at the time of its launch.

If there is a track from *Fonte de araño* that deserves special attention it is "Pandeirada de Nebra" (Nebra's Tambourine Dance), a traditional Galician piece adapted and rearranged by Bernardo Martínez, a member of Cao's accompanying band. This lively tune features a dialogue between the harp and the bagpipe over the pounding rhythm of a *pandeirada*, one of the most recognizable traditional Galician dances, accompanied by a *pandeiro* and tambourines. This piece became very well known to Galicians of all kinds, as it was adopted as the theme music for the pre-opening of Galicia's midday television programming before the connection to Spanish national television—at the time, the only television available to Galician viewers before the creation of Television de Galicia in the mid-1980s. For a long time Cao's "Pandeirada de Nebra," with its eclectic, but still unmistakably Galician mix of sounds, could be heard on every Galician television set on a daily basis. This new/traditional *pandeirada* became synonymous with the new Galicia that was beginning to take shape, mediated by the power of modern telecommunication technology, as a new expression of Galician identity that was proud and respectful of its rich cultural heritage, while boldly innovative and modern.

The circumstances and timing of the album production are also of particular relevance. *Fonte de araño* was recorded in April 1977, a historic time for the recovery of political freedoms, when the reconstruction and celebration of Galician identity was at the forefront of public discourse.

Music was to be a key element in the rapid formation of a new Galician identity that could reconcile the rural and the urban, as epitomized in the ancestral dance of yesterday and the modern television set.[6] *Fonte do Araño* was also something of a collective musical experiment, and it would have a significant impact in the future development of the participating musicians, who would have a long and important trajectory in Galician folk music. These figures included Xoan Piñón and Bernardo Martínez (both from the emerging group Doa, one of the earliest Galician prog folk groups) and Antón Seoane and Xosé Ferreirós, who subsequently formed Milladoiro, perhaps the most influential Galician folk music band to this day.[7]

In parallel, another historic figure starting his career as part of the old protest song movement was Bibiano, who, influenced by Portuguese *cantautores* such as José Afonso, developed a modern career as an urban folk *cantautor* during the transition. Although occasionally using traditional instrumentation, including the incidental use of the harp and *gaita*, his recordings during the late 1970s experimented freely with jazz and rock. His experimental albums *Estamos chegando ao mar* (We Are Getting Close to the Sea) (1976), *Alcabre* (1977), and *Aluminio* (1979) did not bring him the wide popular success of the other above-mentioned figures, but his music certainly played a very important transitional role in linking the old *cantautor* movement with the new generation. In so doing, Bibiano became an instrumental catalyst and promoter of the great musical explosion of the *Movida galega* in the 1980s (as we saw in Chapter 8).

## Bringing Urban and Rural Galicia Together

An important vocal group playing a highly significant role in the modernization of Galician folk music was Fuxan Os Ventos (Let the Winds Flee). Originally emerging as part of the movement of cultural resistance in late Francoism, the band actively participated in the process of the assertion of Galician language and culture as well as the critique of Galicia's

---

6  In this sense, from the beginning television played a key role in the acceptance and dissemination of traditional/modern Galician folk music, as TVG would do later with folk and *rock bravú*.

7  Another pioneer in the recovery of traditional Galician instruments was Xosé Quintas Canella, with his album *Porque no mundo menguou a verdade* (1978), an early project in the renovation of the medieval Galician–Portuguese *cantigas* tradition, recorded with members of the group Malvís (Xoán Piñón, Bernardo Martínez, Enrique Fernández, and Miro Casabella), all of whom would eventually form part of Doa.

specific social problems, such as political repression, the traumatic legacy of migration, and the rapid abandonment of rural life.

The voice is clearly the protagonist of the musical project of Fuxan Os Ventos, with rich and powerful vocal arrangements, the use of recitatives, and a generally minimalist approach to musical accompaniment; eventually, however, more musical instrumentation, arrangements, and collaborations were incorporated. Their repertoire was a combination of Galician traditional songs, original compositions in traditional popular style, and covers of Galician poems (by Marica Campo, Darío Xohán Cabana, Manuel María, Celso E. Ferreiro, and Ramón Cabanillas, among others). Rejecting the use of electronic instruments in their recordings and concerts, and less prone to musical experimentation than other contemporary folk musicians, Fuxan Os Ventos represented a more traditional approach to folk music, which nevertheless proved very successful with Galician audiences. Their traditional-sounding, socially engaged songs had great appeal to a wide public, particularly in rural Galicia, which the previous *cantautores* rarely reached. Part of their success was due to their able transfer of old and familiar Galician popular forms into new, modern settings. Thus, they could effectively use the traditional format of a *canto de cego* (blind man's song) for the purposes of contemporary political commentary on the shortcomings of Galician autonomy. The song "Canto de cego II," included in *Sementeira* (Sowing) (1978) is a case in point. While also enjoying an international presence—performing twice at the Inter-Celtic Festival of Lorient in 1978 and 1979—several of their songs have become popular Galician anthems: "Fuxan os ventos" (a poetic call for Galician unity and struggle for national affirmation), "Sementeira" (a lyrical defense of the traditions of Galician rural lifestyle), and "Muller" (an ode to the suffering of women caused by emigration, written by Marica Campo). The widespread popularity of Fuxan Os Ventos and their crucial importance in the collective construction of a new Galician identity can be measured by Suso de Toro's statement that the ever-present icons in Galicians' homes during the 1970s were a Sargadelos ceramic and a Fuxan Os Ventos cassette tape, both seen as symbols of Galician modernization.[8]

8  Personal interview with the author included in my book *Galeg@s sen fronteiras* (2013). Other popular vocal folk group formations following the success of Fuxan Os Ventos include A Quenlla, A Roda and Xocaluma.

## Celtic Crossroads:
## Bagpipes, Bouzoukis, and Bodhráns

Milladoiro was probably the most important band in the reinvention of Galician folk music, for their pioneering role during the 1970s, their sustained trajectory for more than three decades, the diversity of their musical output, and their international recognition. Milladoiro are fundamentally an instrumental revivalist band, although on occasion they are accompanied by vocalists, particularly in their live performances. For this reason they stand in contrast to the *cantautores* and traditional vocal formations such as Fuxan Os Ventos. Milladoiro was the end result of the merging of two groups: the original formation was spearheaded by medievalist musicians Rodrigo Romaní, Antón Seoane, and Xosé Ferreirós, who had released the album *Milladoiro* in 1978 to wide critical acclaim; they were joined later by the group Faíscas do Xiabre, formed by Xosé Ferreirós, Nando Casal, and Ramón García Rei; a jazz player and a classical musician were later added to this line-up. The resulting formation was named Milladoiro and their first album was entitled *A Galicia de Maeloc* (Maeloc's Galicia) (1979), the first Galician folk album ever to be released internationally. Milladoiro experimented with antique instruments, thus pioneering the recovery and reintroduction of traditional Galician instruments such as the *zanfona*, the *gaita*, the *citola*, and the *dulcimer*, together with the incorporation of non-traditional instruments such as keyboards, flutes, and a series of imported instruments from other Celtic traditions, such as the Irish bodhrán, the uilleann pipes, the tin whistle, the Celtic harp, and even bouzoukis, all of which would become staples of the new Galician folk music in the years ahead. Rather than being a regular folk group, they progressively developed into a musical "ensemble," involving themselves in longer orchestral works, in a manner similar to The Chieftains in the Irish context. Milladoiro's ensemble make-up and merging of popular folk music and medieval art music have been described as "chamber-folk" (Winick), a style characterized by the rich yet intimate climate of their sound, their erudite approach, technical accomplishment, and careful arrangements.

While fundamentally inspired by Galician musical traditions, Milladoiro's music has also been open to modern and external cultural influences. Although a large part of their repertoire is based on newly arranged Galician traditional music, they also incorporate their own compositions, often inspired by traditional and medieval Galician music, while taking in influences from classical music and other Celtic cultures, particularly Irish, Scottish, and Breton. From their beginnings, Milladoiro had a clear understanding of their role as both absorbers and producers of a rich mix of musical traditions. A case in point is the symbolic reference in their own name to the medieval tradition along the Camiño de Santiago of creating *milladoiros*, stacks of stones or cairns piled up to indicate the way. According to this tradition, each passing pilgrim would add to the pile a stone brought with them from their original homes. This ritualized practice created useful milestones but, symbolically, it could also be understood as a silent witness of a collective creation—a result of the myriad cultural influences exchanged—that has withstood the test of time. Milladoiro aimed to follow the tradition represented by these Galician musical crossroads in the diversity of the instrumentation used and their open acceptance of multiple musical influences.

The back cover of the first album by Romaní and Seoane, precisely entitled *Milladoiro*, included a quote from the *Codex Calixtinus*, the medieval manuscript detailing the Way to Santiago, which contains a treasure for Galician musical historiography, as we saw in Chapter 3: "Some sing with zithers, others with lyres, others with kettledrums, others accompanied by flutes, others by flageolets, others by trumpets, harps, violins, others by Gallic and British wheel fiddles, others by psalteries, others by diverse musical instruments." The quotation from the *Codex* about the diversity of musical instruments played by the pilgrims along the Camiño was seen as a way to validate *Milladoiro*'s hybrid approach. This recognition also follows the modern tradition of universalist discourse by twentieth-century Galician nationalist intellectuals (from the Irmandades da Fala to the Xeración Nós), as reflected in the *Partido Galeguista*'s motto "Galicia, célula de universalidade" ("Galicia, cell of universality") in 1931 and Castelao's reference to Galicia as a "centro de universalidade" ("center of universality" 47), as a result of the influence of the Camiño de Santiago. More recently, in a collective statement posted on the band's official website (milladoiro. com), they have reaffirmed their original conceptual position, with their understanding of the Camiño as a historical and symbolic crossroads, as well as an example of cultural exchange and enrichment for our global age. Fully conscious of their own role as participants in that exchange, Milladoiro have commented on the ongoing process of Galician identity formation in a global framework:

> Compartíamos e compartimos a paixón pola música e polo noso país, pero sendo conscientes de que o camiño, o emblemático camiño de Santiago, é vía de dúas direccións e de aí o noso nome. Os milladoiros que guiaban os pasos dos peregrinos que se achegaban a Galicia, permitíronnos abrirnos ás moitas influencias que enriqueceron esta esquina de Europa. A nosa ilusión sería devolver o moito recibido en

forma de música fermosa e viva que nos axude como país a manter un lugar de identificación colectivo que nos permita seguir existindo baixo o irremediable manto da aldea global.

We shared and still share a passion for the music and for our country, but remain fully aware that the road, the emblematic Road to Santiago, is a two-way road, and that is where our name comes from. The *milladoiros* that guided the pilgrims coming to Galicia allowed us to receive many influences which have enriched this corner of Europe. Our wish would be to give back all that we have received in the shape of beautiful, live music, in the hope that it will help us as a country to maintain a sense of collective identity that will allow us to exist under the unavoidable cover of the global village.[9]

Throughout their long career Milladoiro have shown a great capacity for diversification. Thus they have channelled their creativity through a number of different productions, including film soundtracks (*La mitad del cielo* 'Half of the Sky', *Divinas palabras* 'Divine Words', *Tierra del fuego* 'Land of Fire'), TV series (*Martes de Carnaval* 'Mardi Gras'), major art exhibitions (*Galicia no tempo* 'Galicia through Time') and the exhibition of Galician surrealist artist Maruja Mallo, and especially commissioned institutional projects for the Xacobeo, the University of Santiago, and several Galician cities. Milladoiro are also responsible for some of the most ambitious efforts in Galician folk music, including orchestral pieces based on Galician folk music with classical and new age overtones, such as the albums *Gallaecia Fulget* and *Iacobus Magnus*, in conjunction with the London Symphonic Orchestra. Although sometimes criticized for marginalizing the voice in their performances, they were the first Galician folk group to use in their recordings a choir of female *cantareiras* and *pandereteiras*, traditional ensembles of women singers and tambourine players. The album *Galicia no país das maravillas* (Galicia in

9 This explanation is still used 30 years later in their international advertising, as is shown in this concert promotional material from Latvia and Lithuania (2010): "The name 'Milladoiro' is taken from the piles of stones that were installed by the pilgrims in order to mark the way of the Camino, and symbolizes this way of cultural exchange by which Galicia obtained and exported the elements that make up its identity. The objectives of Milladoiro are to adapt the Galician musical folklore to the modern urban world. Their compositions are remake of the traditional music preserved in songbooks or collected directly from oral sources, interpreting them with a wide variety of more than 20 instruments in total—modern as well as the traditional ones. The final result is the music of Celtic origin and inspiration, original in its fusion of other cultural influences, and that makes a synthesis between tradition and modernity" (www.sapnufabrika.lv).

Wonderland) (1987) included several collaborations with the group Cantigas e Agarimos (Felisa Segade, Montse Rivera, and Mercedes Rodríguez), who would also collaborate with the folk groups Berrogüetto and Xochilmica, and would later form the group Leilía. Milladoiro thus anticipated the boom of *cantareiras* in the Galician folk music scene that took place in the 1990s.

In relation to the sometimes heavily disputed use of the "Celtic" music label applied to Galician folk music, Milladoiro member Antón Seoane has expressed a clear positioning, accepting that Celtic is *one* aspect of Galician traditional and folk music out of other equally important influences, including medieval, classical, and other musical traditions from southern Europe and northern Africa, forming a rich and plural mosaic. This reconceptualization effectively subverts the frequent perception of the peripheral status of Galician folk music in relation to the "centers" of Celtic music in Ireland and Scotland. In consequence, it resituates Galician cultural production in an alternative imaginary geography at the crossroads and not at the periphery, suggesting a much richer musical tapestry:

> Nosotros decimos que la música gallega es un mosaico y una parte de ese mosaico es la música celta, la música de influencia atlántica. Pero partes grandísimas de ese mosaico tienen que ver con la música medieval, con la música de Occitania, del Norte de Italia, de todo el Camino de Santiago, otra parte tiene que ver con la música de influencia árabe y mediterránea ... Mientras que otras propuestas dicen que la música gallega forma parte de un mosaico superior que es la música celta. [...]
>
> Sin la influencia medieval la música gallega no se entendería. Sería quererla meter como un apéndice de la música celta, cuando yo creo que la música gallega es mucho más rica. Le pasa un poco como a la música bretona, que también se mete bajo el apelativo celta y sin embargo es infinitamente más rica que la música escocesa.
>
> Entonces las periferias respecto al poder central, que en música celta representa Irlanda, como Bretaña y Galicia tienen otra enjundia porque hay toda una influencia romana, una influencia latina, y eso hace que nuestra música yo creo que es más rica que la de ellos. (Marco)

> We believe that Galician music is a mosaic and a part of that mosaic is Celtic music, the music of Atlantic influence. But very large parts of that mosaic come from medieval music, whether these be Occitan, from northern Italy, from the Road to Santiago or from Arabic and Mediterranean influences ... While other opinions say that Galician music is a part of a bigger mosaic that is Celtic music. [...]

Galician music cannot possibly be understood without taking account its medieval influences. In other words, Galicia cannot be considered an appendix to Celtic traditions, when in reality it is much richer than that. This is also the case of Breton music, for example, which is also categorised under the Celtic label and yet is infinitely richer than Scottish music. Thus, when it comes to assessing the peripheries of the central powers of Celtic music—Ireland, in this case—I believe that Brittany and Galicia have a lot more to offer, because of the plethora of historical influences they have integrated, like Roman or Latin influences.

Milladoiro's positioning is thus not based in some mystical Celtic prehistorical communion, as the romantic invention of nineteenth-century *Rexurdimento*, but in the history of old and modern cultural exchanges. And this movement works in both ways, as has been repeatedly confirmed by their active collaborations with singers and musicians from Galicia and other musical cultures, and by how their repertoire has also been keenly adopted by other folk musicians around the world.

## New Sounds in the Air

Other Galician folk bands followed Milladoiro in the 1980s, such as Na Lúa and Luar na Lubre. Na Lúa were originally a strictly instrumental folk band in the tradition of Milladoiro, although more modern and experimental in vein, often fusing folk music with rock and jazz. The band was the brainchild of the multi-instrumentalist and composer Xosé Paz Antón, who was joined by two bagpipers and frequently by electric guitars and rock drums, as well as clarinets and saxophones. Following their first instrumental self-titled album, *Na Lúa* (1985), the singer Uxía Senlle joined the group as the lead singer and recorded two albums with the band, *A estrela de Maio* (May's Star) (1987) and *Ondas do mar de Vigo* (Vigo's Sea Waves) (1989), a modern reinterpretation of Martín Códax' famous medieval *cantigas* by contemporary Galician writers. One of the band's characteristic products has been in fact the musical covers of Galician poems by writers such as Manuel Rivas, Antón Reixa, and Xosé María Álvarez Cáccamo. The members of Na Lúa were from the industrial *rurban* periphery of Vigo, which explains their hybrid mix of urban folk, merging traditional and modern elements. Their proximity to the Portuguese border also explains their keen interest in exploring musical influences and exchanges from the Lusophone world. A frequent collaborator of Na Lúa was the well-known Portuguese folk multi-instrumentalist musician Júlio Pereira, who covered one of their songs, "Espabilator," in his album *O meu Bandolim* (My Mandolin) (1992), retitled as "Na Lua." After starting a successful solo career in the 1990s with Pereira as producer, Uxía would become one of the most prominent Galician female performers internationally and a strong promoter of Galician and Lusophone musical encounters.

Luar na Lubre (LNL) are among the most well-known Galician folk bands internationally. Since the mid-1980s the band have maintained a productive career that has left a profound mark in the modern development of Galician folk music, especially in its projection outside Galicia. The founder and leader of the group's vision is Bieito Romero, who started his training as a young bagpiper in the renowned Ballet Galego Rey de Viana—founded by José Rey de Viana in 1949—and in the traditional music and dance group Xacarandaina, one of the early schools of traditional Galician folklore established during the political transition. Trained in traditional Galician instruments (*gaita*, *zanfona*, and accordion), Romero is the composer of more than 200 musical pieces inspired by Galician traditional music and folklore, as well as a dynamic researcher of Galician folk sources, popular legends, and traditional Galician music.[10] He is also an advocate of Galicia's affinity with Celtic cultures, and has been the co-founder of important local folk music venues (such as *A cova folk*, *A casa da lubre*, and *A cova céltica* in A Coruña).

Throughout the years LNL have consolidated their position as the foremost Celtic folk band in Galicia. They also hold an unambiguous stance with regard to the pan-Celtic folk movement, embracing Celtic cultural traditions in perhaps more unequivocal ways than any other major folk group in Galicia.[11] This is reflected in the music and themes they tend to explore, their Celtic-styled graphic design in albums and concerts, and even in their own name: "Moonlight beam in the magic forest" is a reference to the sacred places of the Celtic druids. Their own official website (www.luarnalubre.com) endorses the band's Celtic character in a single phrase that voices their stance to the world: "Música celta desde Galicia" ("Celtic music from Galicia").

LNL's first album *O son do ar* (The Sound of the Air) (1988) firmly established their style and modus operandi. Their repertoire consists mainly of a combination of rearranged Galician traditional pieces and Romero's own compositions, occasionally incorporating some pieces from both Celtic cultures and other contexts. A case in point is their piece "AO-TEA-ROA" (the

10 Romero examines the presence of symbolic magical figures in Galician popular culture in his book *Xeometrías máxicas de Galicia*, 'Galicia's Magical Geometries' (2009), documenting abundant examples of Celtic crosses, knots, triskelions, and spirals with hundreds of photographs taken by him throughout years of study.

11 Romero discusses this issue at length in the personal interview with the author included in my book *Galeg@s sen fronteiras*.

native name for New Zealand in Maori: "The land of the long white cloud"), included in *Plenilunio* (Full Moon) (1997), an instrumental adaptation of the Scottish folk song "Leaving Nancy" by Eric Bogle, about a Scottish migrant leaving for Australia, which they learned from the Celtic fusion music band RUA from New Zealand. Another example is their song "No mundo" ("In the World"), included in *Hai un paraíso* (There is a Paradise) (2004), a universalist condemnation of the social injustices in the world, also based on a cover of another Irish song popularly known as "Master McGrath" or "The Old Orange Flute," about the Troubles in Northern Ireland. The absence of any acknowledgement of these songs' origins, which appear on the album booklet as of "traditional" authorship, may suggest a determined effort in the crossing of cultural and national borders and a belief in the common depository of folk music culture that transcends linguistic and geopolitical frontiers.

As in the case of other Galician folk revival bands, LNL incorporate both traditional Galician and "imported" instruments from the pan-Celtic folk movement (bodhrán, tin whistle, Irish flute, and bouzouki). Similarly to Na Lúa, they also regularly include the accompaniment of a female vocalist. After their second album, this role was taken by cellist Rosa Cedrón, whose expressive and melancholic voice added a distinctive sound to the band.[12] Their repertoire typically offers a varied mix of fast-paced joyful dance tunes and atmospheric lyrical tunes. Their sound often resembles pan-Celtic folk music, although with clear inflections from Latin music, particularly in the use of percussion. This undoubtedly is a reflection of both Galicia's and LNL's extensive cultural connections with Latin America, as two of the band members, the percussionist and violin player, came from Venezuela and Cuba respectively. Thus, their album *Saudade* (2005) was a fascinating musical journey devoted to Galicia's relationship with Latin America and the musical and cultural hybridity resulting from the history of Galician migration, and included stellar collaborations with Latin American singers Lila Downs, Adriana Varela, and Pablo Milanés.

LNL had a major international breakthrough in the 1990s as a result of a series of collaborations with the world-renowned multi-instrumentalist star Mike Oldfield, which catapulted them to international renown as one of the most important groups in the pan-Celtic music scene.[13] Although LNL

12  Also, as in the case of Na Lúa with Uxía Senlle, Rosa Cedrón would have an acclaimed solo career after her departure from the band in 2005.

13  The events were as follows. The Galician band and Mike Oldfield, a self-professed admirer of the group, first met in 1992 upon Oldfield's request. He then recorded a version of LNL's "O son do ar," the emblematic composition by Bieito Romero which was used as title of their first album. "O son do ar" (literally "The sound of the air," but later retitled as "The Song of the Sun" by Oldfield) served as the starting

already had some exposure outside Galicia, nationally and internationally, their collaborations with Mike Oldfield enabled them to reach a much bigger sector of the public and to play for large arena rock audiences. LNL thus became the most popular folk group in Spain, and their albums *Plenilunio* (Full Moon) and *Cabo do mundo* (Cape of the World) (1999) reached gold status, thus consolidating the Galician folk music boom of the late 1990s. In 2004 LNL were the subject of a documentary feature film, *Un bosque de música*, directed by Ignacio Vilar, one of the few documentaries ever made on a music group for the big screen in Spain.

## The Brotherhood of the Stars

There was something in the air indeed for the Galician musical scene. LNL's extensive international projection was one of the clear signs of a "boom" starting to form in Galician folk music in the mid-1990s. For once, serious attention was being paid to Galician folk music outside of Galicia. Galician folk musicians regularly played in international folk festivals, had frequent collaborations with some of the biggest names in Celtic music, and were signed and released internationally by multinational record companies. Thus, the prestigious international folk music magazine *Roots World* stated: "Galicia has become the focus of the latest 'Celts of the world' fad" (Furnald). New young stars started to emerge in the Galician folk music scene, selling records and receiving awards internationally.

A particular case in point is Carlos Núñez, who has become one of the most recognizable names in Galician folk music, indeed reaching the unusual status of an international folk superstar. His emergence in the world music scene was part of a new generation of Galician folk musicians that came of age in the 1990s as a result of the seeds cast in the 1970s and 1980s, with the proliferation of schools and workshops of Galician traditional music. At the age of 12 he played at the Inter-Celtic Festival of Lorient in Brittany, and only a few years later he was invited to accompany The Chieftains in their live concerts, which he has continued to do through the years in their worldwide

point for Oldfield to record a Celtic-themed album. This piece became the leading track for his new album *Voyager* (1996), which set the mood for Mike Oldfield's most Celtic album, with a mix of traditional and folk music (Irish, Scottish, and Galician). Oldfield later invited Rosa Cedrón to join his band as singer and cello player for his 'Tubular Bells III' concerts in 1998, and she recorded the lullaby "The Inner Child" on the *Tubular Bells III* album. LNL was also invited to tour with Oldfield as his support band in the "Live Then & Now" tour (1999). Bieito Romero's "The Song of the Sun" was later released again in the chart-topping compilation double album *Two Sides, The Very Best of Mike Oldfield* (2012), with selections chosen by Oldfield himself.

tours and recordings. Their collaboration solidified with The Chieftains' ground-breaking album *Santiago* (1996), which explored the connections between Irish and Galician music through a symbolic journey along the Camiño. The album had been long in the making and was the result of their close collaboration over the years. The overwhelming worldwide success of *Santiago* allowed large audiences around the world to "discover" Galician music and its connections with Celtic music, and generated an interest in Galician folk music internationally that would grow in future years (see Chapter 3).

The reinvention of Galician folk had many different protagonists, as it was a collective undertaking, but if there is one single record that had a definitive impact on its transformation at home and abroad it would be *A irmandade das estrelas* (The Brotherhood of the Stars) (1996), the first solo album by Núñez, which marks a before and after in the development and recognition of Galician folk. The album was produced by Paddy Moloney and Ry Cooder, promoter of the worldwide success of the Buena Vista Social Club, developed in parallel with The Chieftains's *Santiago* and released almost simultaneously. *A irmandade* was the result of years of work and research, as well as extensive collaborations with some 50 international musicians, in which The Chieftains also participated actively. The album was met with universal critical and popular acclaim and catapulted Núñez to a hugely successful international solo career. The unprecedented crossover success of this record also represented the definitive confirmation of the new Galician folk boom, both at home and abroad.

The album's title was a poetic reference to the Milky Way, traditionally pointing to Galicia in the sky and "The way of the stars," another popular name for the Camiño de Santiago, and indirectly to the long history of cultural connections between Galicia and the rest of the world, as well as Galicia's history of global migration. It thus touched conceptually on some of the legendary and defining aspects of Galician history and culture, its geographic mobility and cultural hybridity. But the title also evokes Núñez's personal experience of "brotherhood" with other musicians from lands far away and near, particularly his lasting collaboration with The Chieftains, who Núñez described as treating him "as a brother" (Llevellyn 91), thus reflecting the strong sense of closeness and cultural affinity underpinning this album. Núñez's multiple talents were obvious from the start. First and foremost was his evident virtuosity as multi-instrumentalist and musical arranger. Núñez also demonstrated a great ability as researcher, retrieving fundamental pieces of the Galician folk tradition and unearthing lost or half-forgotten treasures of Galician music and giving them a brilliant definitive form. Likewise, he displayed a great talent for successfully aligning and harmonizing different musical traditions, and gathered an impressive list of illustrious international collaborators (which, throughout his career, has included a veritable *who's who* of pan-Celtic folk music, combined with renowned musical figures such as Ry Cooder, Jackson Browne, Linda Rondstadt, Carlinhos Brown, and Compay Segundo).

In some sense, *A irmandade* created a new imaginary geography of affinities, cultural overlaps, and movements in different directions, from the past to the present, from Galicia to the world, and vice versa. It stands as a metaphor of Galicia as a crossroads of traditions. The album follows a conceptual circular movement, or perhaps more accurately a spiral movement, widening the circle from beginning to end and enlarging the point of view towards a peripheral vision that encompasses the plurality of cultural exchanges and musical traditions crossed. It begins appropriately with "Amanecer" ("Dawn"), an expressive tune in the tradition of the lyrical Galician *alborada* to welcome the rising sun of a new day, which introduces the progressive blending of different instruments and musical traditions, and thus establishes the character of the album; this is immediately followed by "A irmandade das estrelas," another instrumental tune which creates its own musical constellation with the musical stars pointing to the peripheries of the Basque Country, Andalusia, and Galicia. The album travels through Portugal, and moves back and forth between the different Atlantic shores, from Ireland to Cuba. The album ends, in circular motion, with a festive "return" to the motherland and a closing of the circle: "Para Vigo me voy" ("I'm Leaving for Vigo"), the celebrated conga written by Cuban pianist Ernesto Lecuona which celebrates the strong Cuban/Galician historical connection and the experience of the Galician migrant retuning home.[14]

*A irmandade* is a journey that deterritorializes and deperipheralizes Galician music and culture. The journey proposed crosses musical, cultural, geopolitical, and language boundaries, alternating the sacred and profane, the melancholy and the jovial, the popular and the erudite, *roots and routes*, in a movement back and forth across the Atlantic, from Galicia to Portugal, Ireland, or Cuba, including the music of the *fado*, jig, and *conga*. Two national Galician literary heroes are expressly invoked in this journey, which underlines the foundational aspect of the album. These are Rosalía de Castro and Alfonso Castelao, mother and father of Galician literature and fundamental figures of Galician nationalism, who were both personally familiar with the experience of migration and exile. Their respective poetic texts generated two very significant songs in Galician cultural history

14  It was premiered in Havana at the Gran Teatro in the Centro Gallego in 1935 in preparation for Lecuona's European tour, which would take him to Vigo.

which Núñez both give deep resonance and bring to new heights. One is the emblematic profound and dark "Negra sombra" ("Black Shadow"), based on one of the most well-known poems by Rosalía de Castro. The song has a double connection with Cuba, as the poem was originally published in *Follas Novas* in Havana by the Galician migrant community, and the music used is that of a traditional Galician *alalá*. The song was also premiered in Havana in 1892 and has since been considered a Galician classic. Carlos Núñez's musical arrangement and Luz Casal's vocal performance are masterful renditions of this piece and have received wide global acclaim (it was later included in the soundtrack of the Academy Award-winning film *Mar adentro*). The other song is "Lela," based on a text by Castelao and part of his play *Os vellos non deben de namorarse*, written during his exile in New York and premiered in Buenos Aires, which is the most popular piece of Galician theatre of all time. Originally it was a farse reflecting old Galician customs, the social repudiation of age differences in relationships that may alter family's inheritances. The song, originally following the musical tradition of the *tuna compostelana* (university student ensemble), was remusicalized by the director of the Galician choir Cantigas e Agarimos in 1961, and here it is performed by Portuguese singer Dulce Pontes with an undeniable *fado* cadence, elevating the song from satire to a powerful expression of unrequited love and longing across time and space boundaries.

The album received wide acclaim, generating a lot of interest for Galician folk music internationally. It gave a new sound and image to Galician folk and opened a way to the discovery of a modern and vibrant Galicia, connected to its past and connected to the world, just as open to finding affinities with other musical traditions, near and far. If the musical production and conceptualization were brilliant and innovative, Núñez's stage persona was also outstanding, and his live concerts proved to be equally popular. As a performer who grew up on stage from a very early age, he is at home when performing, and his concerts have repeatedly proven all-round crowd-pleasers. From the point of view of representations of the bagpiper, Núñez has certainly innovated traditional images, bringing to it a rock-star energy and charisma unknown before. For that reason he has been referred to as "the Jimi Hendrix of the bagpipe" in *Billboard* magazine (Llevellyn 10). For the first time in history, a Galician bagpiper was filling entire stadiums around the world.

Núñez was an important part of the great international Celtic music renaissance of the 1990s, exemplified also by *Riverdance* in the USA and *L'Héritage des Celtes* in France. His overwhelming success is unquestionable. His solo albums—produced by legendary Argentinian rock musician Alejo Stivel—have gone platinum in Spain and have reportedly sold several million worldwide. Aside from his regular solo albums and concerts, he has written scores for several films and received a Goya award for the soundtrack of Alejandro Amenábar's film *Mar adentro* in 2004. However, in spite of the universal consensus on Núñez's artistry and his crucial role in taking the Galician folk music revival to a new level worldwide, his huge commercial success and superstar status have exposed him to the scorn of purists. Rightly or wrongly, some see his collaborations with rock stars such as Supertramp's Roger Hodgson and his flirting with pop as selling out, and the mixing of Galician and flamenco or *andalusí* music as simply unnatural.[15]

## New Accents

Núñez may have set the tone, but there was much more below the tip of the iceberg. In addition to the continued success of historical groups such as Milladoiro, Luar na Lubre, and Na Lúa, and the successful careers of solo singers such as Uxía Senlle internationally, there was a whole new generation of young voices, bagpipers, and neo-folk groups taking the Galician folk music scene by storm and ready to be heard in the world. It is important to underline in this regard the key role played by the newly developed schools of Galician traditional music, some of them built upon the smaller schools of earlier decades, in the emergence of a new generation of well-trained players, innovative group formations, and musical projects. This new wave of musicians had a most auspicious start with Matto Congrio (*Matto Congrio* 1993), the formative instrumental band from which Carlos Núñez and his band musicians, as well as Berrogüetto, emerged. Other key albums were released in the mid-1990s to great acclaim, such as *Navicularia* (by Berrogüetto, 1996) and *Paralaia* (by Xosé Manuel Budiño, 1996), which pushed the boundaries of Galician traditional folk music into new territories and set the tone for fertile musical trajectories. The ETRAD (*Escola Municipal de Música Folk e Tradicional*, previously known as the *Universidade Popular*), sponsored by the Vigo municipality, and *aCentral Folque/Centro Galego de Música Popular* in Santiago (formerly the *Conservatorio de Música Tradicional e Folque* in Lalín) are two of the most dynamic schools to this day, constantly developing innovative projects and creations. Thus, ETRAD has created the *Orquestra Folque SondeSeu*, one of the first European orchestras of folk music and today the leader of the ENFO project (European Network of Folk Orchestras). Likewise, *aCentral Folque*, directed by folk singer Ugía Pedreira—one of the most recognized voices in Galician music with original projects such as Nordestin@s and Marful—has created a series of shows and an international network of

---

15  For Carlos Núñez's illuminating perspective, see his conversations in Rodríguez.

concerts, collaborations, and co-productions, with special emphasis on the Lusophone, Latin American, and European connections.

An important revolutionary development in this new wave of folk music was the incorporation and improved visibility of female musicians and singers. Although there had been previous examples of important female figures in Galician folk music, only in recent years has there been a profusion of successful female performers.[16] As mentioned earlier, María Manuela and Pilocha were pioneers, establishing their careers as Galician folk singers in the 1970s. In the international arena, Uxía's *Estou vivindo no ceo* (I am living in heaven) (1995), produced by the Portuguese multi-instrumentalist Júlio Pereira, received the applause of the world's folk scene as a fresh take on Galician *cantautor* folk song, opening connections with the Lusophone musical world. Uxía's popular and critical success also inaugurated the boom of Galician folk women soloists of the late 1990s. A revolutionary wave of female bagpipers followed, with the release of seminal albums such as Cristina Pato's *Tolemia* (1999), Susana Seivane's self-titled album (1999), and Mercedes Peón's *Isué* (2000), and have remained at the forefront of musical innovation in folk music internationally. Mercedes Peón is a good example of the new age of Galician folk music. Her eclectic mix of Galician traditional music in the style of ancestral *cantareiras*, world ethnic music influences, and new age electronica, with originally choreographed avant-garde performances such as her 2009 spectacle *Kiosko das almas perdidas* (Kiosk of the Lost Souls), choreographed by Roberto Oliván and the *Centro Coreográfico Galego*, is one of the most creative productions in modern Galician folk. Also revolutionary was the emergence of professional female groups of *cantareiras* and *pandereteiras*, such as Xiradela, Leilía, Ialma, and Donicelas, rediscovering a traditional musical form that had been generally outside of the mainstream music industry circuits until then.[17] These parallel developments headed by female musicians represent the rediscovery of the importance of female musicians in Galician traditional

16 The tradition of female bagpipers in Galicia goes back at least to the beginning of the twentieth century. The first documented female Galician bagpiper was Áurea Rodríguez, leader of the four-piece band Os Maravillas established in 1910 and popularly known as the "Raíña da Gaita Galega" ("queen of Galician bagpipe"). In the 1960s the band Saudade was the first Galician group of female bagpipers.

17 The development of Galician folk groups in the migrant communities spread around the world is another important dimension of the present global boom of Galician folk. Interestingly, one of the biggest names in *cantareiras*, Ialma, brings together a group of Belgium-born daughters of Galician migrants. Ialma's leader, Verónica Codesal, already had a successful singing career, including being Belgium's representative at the Eurovision Song Contest. As a group, they have reworked the traditional Galician style of *cantareiras* and introduced new modern musical arrangements with the accompaniment of Belgian musicians.

music, not only as accompanying vocalists and percussionists but as leading bagpipers and fiddlers, as well as of a "forgotten" and uniquely Galician form of female group singing.[18] Other imaginative musical experiments in the renovation of Galician folk music include the group Marful, fronted by Ugía Pedreira, which reinvented the music of the ballroom dance era, and Nordestin@s, a project by Guadi Galego, Ugía Pedreira, and Abe Rábade, which mixed traditional Galician song with new jazz arrangements and harmonies. These female soloists and groups provided the missing link in Galician folk music, in a tradition where female instrumentalists had rarely occupied the central stage and female vocals were heard only as part of male folk groups, not as the performers of their own music.[19]

The ground-breaking emergence and prominence of Galician female voices and musicians cannot be underestimated. It is important to note in this regard that Cristina Pato, perhaps more than any other Galician artist, can be said to represent a truly global musician in every sense of the word. Cristina Pato has traveled far and wide musically, from early collaborator of new folk band Mutenrohi to the first Galician female bagpiper releasing a solo album to establishing a solid international career as bagpiper, pianist, and singer. Her explorations of Galician music and mixing with other cultures, contemporary classical, jazz, and Middle Eastern music are the result of her own professional and vital trajectory. Pato has been based in New York since the mid-2000s, and has constantly been on the move around the world with different projects, particularly as a member of the Silk Road Ensemble accompanying Yo-Yo Ma, with whom she has recorded highly praised albums, winning two Grammys in 2010 and 2017, and played live on American TV for millions of viewers.

Critically acclaimed by *The New York Times* and *The Wall Street Journal*, Pato has developed a successful career recording and releasing Galician roots music albums on American labels with titles in English: *The Galician Connection* (2010), where she experiments freely with the Galician bagpipe, jazz, and world music, *Migrations* (2013), and *Latina* (2015), the first bagpipe albums ever published by an American jazz label. The work of Cristina Pato encapsulates the experience of border crossing, the mix of influences, and the multiple facets of her personality, as well as the possibilities of Galician music in the global age.

18 An example of this new generation of female performers is the fiddler Begoña Riobó, who, after accompanying Carlos Núñez on stage for several years, created her own band, *Riobó*, which released their first self-titled album in 2011.

19 A recent anthology of Galician folk music by female groups and soloists is the album compiled by Uxía, *Cantigas de Mulleres* (2013), which is meant as an introduction to a wide range of Galician female artists, with inside credits in Galician, Spanish, and English.

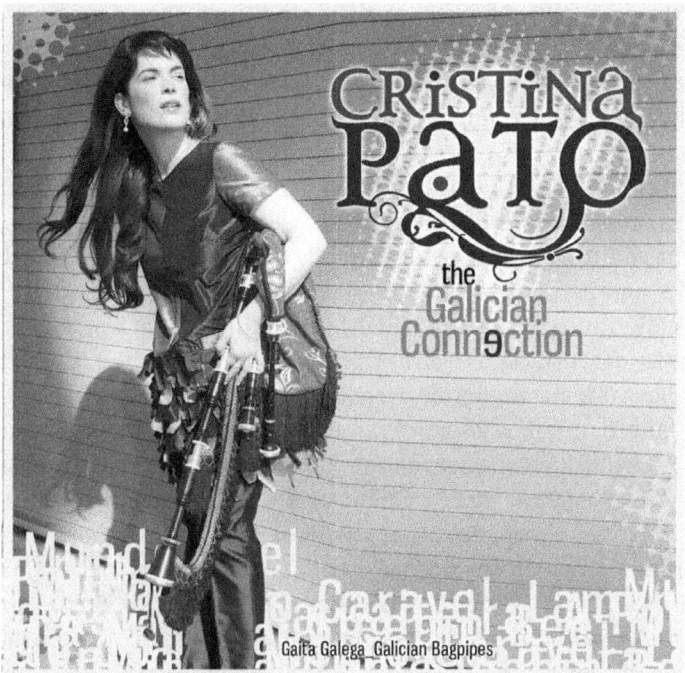

Figures 35–36   Galicia beyond Galicia. Album covers from Cristina Pato's local/global recordings in New York, *The Galician Connection* (Zouma Records, 2010) and *Migrations* (Sunnyside Records, 2013).

The hybridization with other musical traditions and practices across the world has also provided the context for Galician music's more sustained rapport with that which is historically, geographically, linguistically, and culturally closest—and yet often forgotten—that is, the Lusophone world. Uxía has been an avid promoter of Lusophone connections through her continued collaborations with musicians and singers from Portugal, Brazil, the Azores, and Cabo Verde, the artistic direction of the Lusophone festival "Cantos na Maré," and the mentoring of groups such as Batuko Tabanka, a group of singing and *batuko* drum-playing women from the Cape Verdean migrant community in Galicia. Their first album (*Djunta mô*, 2012) included collaborations from Uxía, as well as from Xosé Manuel Budiño, Mercedes Peón, Rodrigo Romaní, Berrogüetto, Treixadura, and Segundo Grandío, among others. The urban folk *cantautor* Fran Pérez (Narf), who lived in Lusophone Africa, has also helped strengthen the connection with Portuguese-speaking areas of Africa and the development of an Afro-Galician sound with his albums *Directo en Compostela* (2003), *Totem* (2007), and *Aló Irmao!* (Hello brother!) (2010), which includes the collaboration of Manecas Costa from Guinea-Bissau. Ugía Pedreira collaborated with Brazil's Fred Martins on the album *Acróbata* (2011), the symbolic title of which is a reference to the Brazilian name of a migratory bird who flies between Galicia and Brazil, the *carrán* (common tern). Carlos Núñez also deserves special mention in this regard for his album *Alborada de Brasil* (Brazil's *Alborada*) (2009), a tour de force work devoted to the often unexplored musical and cultural connections between Galicia and Brazil.

## Galician Folk Music and the Instruments of Cultural Identity

The Galician folk music revival of the last three decades, and the recent international boom, has undoubtedly had a big impact on Galicia's self-image and projection. Rather than emphasizing the undeniable commercial dimension of this phenomenon, however, it would be more appropriate to highlight how the redefinition and recognition of Galicia's folk music in the past decades has gone hand-in-hand with the process of cultural redefinition of Galician identity. Galician folk music has certainly played a key role in the process of Galician collective affirmation, showing that popular music can be an important instrument for constructing cultural identity.

As a form of cultural expression with an extraordinary capacity for collective identification, music transcends borders and boundaries and has the capacity to resist, confront, or conform to hegemonies. Galician folk music has also been an effective instrument to correct Galicia's peripheral condition, contesting its historically subordinate position within the

Spanish state and voicing issues that have been integral to Galician history and society, such as the effects of migration, the abandonment of the rural life, the subaltern marginal position of Galicia vis-à-vis the Spanish nation state, the recovery of its heritage and cultural roots, and the self-affirmation and construction of Galician identity in dialogue with a global audience.

*Music travels well.* The bagpipes, bouzoukis, and bodhráns that have taken root in the Galician folk scene are more than mere musical instruments. They are instruments of collective identity formation as well as vehicles of cultural hybridity, always looking in multiple directions that are centripetal and centrifugal at the same time, looking inside and outside, towards tradition and innovation.

# Coda:
## Leaving the Periphery Behind

The Galician audio/visual fields have been key areas of cultural deperipheralization and means of reimagining Galicianess on the global map in recent years. From a historical point of view, the contemporary developments in audio/visual production in Galicia need to be understood within the general context of two fundamental phenomena that have reshaped the traditional concepts of nation and culture in the last few decades: one at the level of the reconfiguration of the nation state—the consequences of the ongoing process of political devolution and autonomous decentralization initiated since the 1978 Spanish constitution; and the other at the transnational level—the effects of political, economic, technological, and cultural globalization in local environments. Together they have redrawn a new cultural map that we could call postnational. Against this complex and evolving backdrop, we can distinguish several stages in the development of modern Galician audio/visual culture.

The 1980s are a foundational period for Galician audio/visual production, part of a larger project of nation (re)building which occurred in the context of the general "reconversion" crisis, primarily an economic and industrial process, but profoundly intertwined with the political and sociocultural transition of the late 1970s and early 1980s. These changes should be seen in relation to the beginning of the deperipheralization of Galician culture in broader terms (and particularly in the areas of music, media, literature, fashion, and the visual arts) and its opening to the world at large. Some major collective undertakings represented the concerted launch of a new and modern culture in dialogue with national and international trends, including new cultural "brands" such as the *Movida galega*, *Cinegalicia*, Galician Celtic music, and the *Atlántica* visual arts movement, which acquired momentum and wide projection throughout the 1980s with diverse degrees of institutional support. These projects are characterized by a very high degree of intermediality, which could be synthesized in the pioneering avant-garde multidisciplinary work of Rompente, and cut across the conventional categories of high and low, local and global, tradition and modernity, and the areas of music, literature, and image. The work of Siniestro Total and Os Resentidos, which represent two opposing poles of the Galician *Movida* rock of the 1980s, are deeply intertwined. Likewise, the musical *Movida* movement is connected with the new wave of video production (Antón Reixa and Xabier Villaverde), as seen in such emblematic videos as *Galicia caníbal*, *Veneno Puro*, and *Galicia sitio distinto*, which redrew Galician culture on the global map. Likewise, Chano Piñeiro's short film *Mamasunción* is widely considered the foundation of the Galician film auteur model and of modern Galician cinema, preparing the way for the subsequent launch of *Cinegalicia*. These years also witnessed the formation of the new Galician folk movement, which often engaged in dialogue with pan-Celtic musical trends, from the late 1970s with pioneering groups and musicians such as Milladoiro, Emilio Cao, Na Lúa, and Luar na Lubre. These wider cultural and artistic movements, including folk, pop and rock music, and video and cinema production, set the foundation for the development of a post-Franco modern Galician audio/visual culture.

The 1990s epitomized the boom and institutionalization of Galician audio/visual production. The contemporary surge in popularity of the Camiño de Santiago, starting with the official Xacobeo 93 celebrations, directly and indirectly stimulated a sudden increase in related audio/visual productions: Chano Piñeiro's *O Camiño das Estrelas*, Milladoiro's *Via Lactea* and *Iacobus Magnus*, Carlos Núñez's *A irmandade das estrelas*, The Chieftains's *Santiago*, Alberto Comesaña's *Jacobsland*, and the television miniseries *Os vixiantes do camiño* by Miguelanxo Prado and *Camino de Santiago* by Robert Young are some of the prime examples. We should also note the important role of TVG as catalyst, generator of content, and channel of distribution for Galician music, videos, and films, even if sometimes they clashed with official institutional directions. This was notably the case of the program *Xabarín Club*, which was extremely popular among younger audiences and often the subject of political controversy, as the cultural programming did not always match the political directions of the Xunta. *Xabarín* became a key conduit for the wide expansion of the rebellious *rock bravú*, which turned out to be the most successful and widespread modern music movement in Galicia in the 1990s, partly owing to the ripple effect of television.

The 1990s also saw the consolidation and international boom of Galician folk, hybridizing and merging with world music and pan-Celtic music, epitomized by the spectacular success beyond Galicia of Carlos Núñez and Luar na Lubre and the emergence of a new generation of folk musicians, with many highly visible women, such as Uxía, Cristina Pato, Susana Seivane, and Mercedes Peón, who revolutionized and modernized the field of Galician folk and gave it an international projection. The new Galician folk movement found in TVG an ambivalent ally, giving exposure to Galician folk music but often trying to downplay its political charge. Clearly TVG had favorites, and black-listed Galician folk musicians according to the different political winds.[1] The safe populism of Ana Kiro was thus often preferred to the politically charged Fuxan os Ventos, and the institutionally backed *escolas de gaitas* (bagpipe schools) were typically given preference over more experimental or personal projects, which gave TVG the popular title of "telegaita" (bagpipe TV).

During the 1990s the "made in Galicia" cinema model also took off, frequently on a co-production basis partially financed through a system of subsidies from the Xunta. Opening the way was *La lengua de las mariposas*, directed by José Luis Cuerda, a long-term Galician filmmaker by adoption since *El bosque animado* (1987). *La lengua* was successful both nationally and on the international art cinema circuit, establishing a filmic style that is recognisably coded as Galician and travels well outside of Galicia, thus creating a model for other directors to follow, and leading to such productions as *Los lunes al sol* and *Mar adentro*.

In the twenty-first century Galician audio/visual production has been characterized by efforts towards "normalization" and diversification, with a variety of different genres and styles and the implementation of diverse strategies to overcome the effects of the economic crisis. This has meant the recourse to alternative forms of (co)production, and frequently of self-production and self-management, in the areas of both music and cinema. The access to affordable tools through new digital technologies has meant that emerging artists can circumvent the limitations of the mainstream audio/visual industry and the difficulties in access to traditional financing. Thus, except for the most commercially viable and well-established productions, most Galician local bands produce their music outside the channels of traditional record companies, and a new generation of audiovisual artists regularly works on the fringes of the mainstream.

The new Galician audiovisual panorama is thus diverse, atomized, and eclectic, striving to make of the periphery a position of strength. Two particularly strong areas in Galician cinema production in this era are the development of the animation industry and the *Novo Cinema Galego*, which have achieved a number of technical and artistic successes and important projection beyond Galicia, from *El bosque animado* to *De Profundis*, and from

---

1 See, for example, the comments by Bieito Romero and Uxía in my *Galeg@s sen fronteiras*. The "censorship" of musician activists critical of the government during the popular mobilizations after the Prestige oil spill would be perhaps the zenith of this practice.

*Todos vós sodes capitáns* to *Vikingland*. These are areas that show great promise for the years ahead.

One work that illustrates well the new audiovisual panorama in Galicia is the 2007 film *Hotel Tívoli* (Light my Fire), directed by Antón Reixa. This film epitomizes the conditions of possibility and the conceptual eclecticism and border crossing of contemporary Galician cinema, with all its shadows and lights. Significantly, it was made and released just before the onset of the crisis, as today it would probably have been much more difficult to produce such a logistically and structurally complex film. In some ways it could be said to represent the end of an era and the beginning of a new one.

*Hotel Tívoli* is a postmodern film looking for a home, a deterritorialized fiction in the global no-place of hotels, airplanes, *starquitect* museums, and virtual spectacles, seen through a peripheral Galician lens. It presents a multicultural mosaic of fragmented visions, made out of 11 intersecting stories, with ten different locations in five countries, and is spoken in seven languages (Spanish, Portuguese, Galician, English, Basque, Catalan, German, and Danish) with 34 main actors. This sort of polyperipheral hyper-Babel follows the "multiplex" model of intersecting stories and of literal and metaphorical border crossing.[2] The different stories are loosely united by a single flame (that of a hotel cigarette lighter passed around from hand to hand), with Mexican singer Julieta Venegas miraculously illuminating the narrative transitions as a sort of magical realist apparition. The film locations include Lisbon, London, Bilbao, Madrid, Vigo, Copenhagen, Greenland, and Argentina. The film is structured as a series of international "random" encounters in the neo-surrealist fashion of Luis Buñuel, as in *The Phantom of Liberty* (1974), where the camera follows a different character in every new sequence, with no intention of creating obvious narrative links other than their randomness, perhaps an appropriate metaphor for global nomadic uprootedness. These encounters include a very diverse typology of characters, young and old, black and white, European, African, American, and Asian, as well as indigenous people from the remote Intuuc Island in Greenland and the San Luis province in Argentina. Their paths cross for brief intervals—Japanese pilgrims on the road to Santiago de Compostela, African and Latin American migrants in Spain, European businessmen, families separating and reuniting. Cutting across the east/west, north/south dynamics, their stories intersect, creating new relationships, alliances, and spaces of cultural exchange, which is also an appropriate metaphor for the mode of transnational co-production scheme employed in the film.

2 I used the term "multiplex" after Walescka Pino-Ojeda to refer to the crisscrossing of stories within the story, as in Alejandro González Iñarritu's *Babel*.

Figure 37   Peripheral sounds and global visions. Image from *Hotel Tívoli* (2006), Filmanova. Paradoxical juxtaposition in the global map of anonymous homelessness and international stardom (Guggenheim, Frank Gehry, Mikel Erentxun). A crossroads of cultural anxieties questioning center/periphery power dichotomies, the spectacularization of culture and global nomadic uprootedness.

*Hotel Tívoli* is a postnational nomadic story, with a constant crossing of national languages and cultures. Migrants, tourists, businesspeople, street people, all identities in a constant state of flux. It is a plural story of a world made flat. These postnational visions are presented as a collection of tourist postcards, moving through a series of postmodern no-place locations: hotels, airplanes, taxis, franchise museums, and souvenir shops. The stories are ironically punctuated with the presence of a number of extravagant Galician characters, the quintessential migrant travelers, away from their homeland in the four corners of the world.

The transnational nature of the film is also reflected in the music soundtrack, which features several prominent Hispanic singer-songwriters— the Mexican Julieta Venegas, the Uruguayan (transplanted to Spain) Jorge Drexel, and the Basque singer Mikel Erentxun, formerly from Duncan Dhu—as well as in the complex transnational production by Filmanova, with four different financial partners (Galician, Portuguese, Argentinian, and Danish—Lars Von Trier's Zentrope) and the transnational co-operation programs of Ibermedia (with Latin America) and Euroimages (with the EU).

The multiplex, multisectional, and multilingual multiperspectivism of *Hotel Tívoli*, and its eclectic collage of narrative fiction and non-narrative performance, can be seen as a metaphor of the redefinition of traditional time and space conditions in the global age, and, self-reflectively, of the Galician glocal audiovisual field as a whole. Can we say that *Hotel Tívoli* is a movie simply "made in Galicia," any more than it is a "Galician film"? It might be more correct to speak of a global movie made out of Galicia.

Perhaps because of its structural complexity and loose narrative, *Hotel Tívoli* was not a critical or popular success, and Antón Reixa has acknowledged that it was a turning point for him to devote himself full-time to audio/visual production and management (Cid Cabido and Xestoso). Reixa, the well-known former leader of the legendary Galician post-punk rap band Os Resentidos, and also performance and video artist, TV series director and producer, filmmaker and president of the Filmanova Production Company, later became the President of the national Sociedad General de Autores y Editores (Spanish Society of Authors and Publishers) in 2012–13, a powerful entity which oversees the copyright management of audio/visual productions in Spain. Currently Reixa is president of the Filmanova group, which includes Filmanova SL (a film and TV production company), Filmanova Invest (a film investment company), and Filmanova Show (dedicated to advertising, TV, and musical productions). In 2014 Filmanova launched a new transnational company, Madmex Filmanova, with branches in Mexico and Brazil, to increase their presence and collaboration with Latin American film productions. In a way, his singular trajectory, from local punk performance artist and semi-amateur video artist to executive manager and international producer, correlates to the enormous leap taken by the audio/visual industry in Galicia in the last few decades in moving out of the periphery.

*Hotel Tívoli*, which effectively became Reixá's swansong as filmmaker before his reconversion into musical and film producer, can be seen as a metaphorical self-reflective film. The story of the random transmission of a lighter from hand to hand, a typical surrealist motif, appears as symbolic of the continuity and circularity of life and the power of the imagination, the passing-on of stories, the crossing of borders across traditions and languages, and the interconnectedness of a collective if fragmented project. The circular movement of the spiral suggests the widening of the circle, the departure from the periphery, and the link between the past and the future. In a way, passing the lighter around could be seen as passing on the torch to a new generation of filmmakers.[3] In this sense, it would be interesting to compare *Hotel Tívoli* with one of the most acclaimed new Galician films

3 Interestingly, Reixa himself seemed to acknowledge this transition in Galician cinema at the time, candidly admitting that perhaps his generation had not produced an "incontestable" film masterpiece, but, with characteristic intuition, prophesizing the arrival of a new generation of talent that would raise Galician cinema to new heights, reflecting something that was already in the air. See my interview in *Galeg@s sen fronteiras*.

of the last few years, *18 comidas* (Jorge Coira, 2010)—made in a similar "multiplex" format, with multiple stories crisscrossing, this time around the motif of sharing food, and also a multilingual production (Spanish, Galician, English, and Macedonian), with Luis Tosar acting as the narrative and performative thread as a nomadic street singer.

In that sense *Hotel Tívoli* marks the transition into a new paradigm of filmmaking in Galicia, a border-crossing cinema with multiple production schemes. This paradigm is characterized by the coexistence of different models: cinema made in Galicia, Galician cinema, and a third model, cinema made out of Galicia (such as that of Reixa, Peque Varela, or Oliver Laxe). It includes fiction and non-fiction, traditional and non-traditional, commercial and non-commercial or alternatively commercial, with new outlets and new forms of production—self-funded, crowdfunded, low cost, and transnational co-productions. Of course, these distinctions are necessarily reductive, since the boundaries are often blurry. The point is the coexistence of different styles and modes of production, sharing, distribution, and exhibition. There can be, side-by-side, the low-cost approach of the NCG or the crowdfunding of *O Apóstolo*, small-budget film productions of local interest (*Pradolongo*) and dogma-style movies (Juan Pinzás), mid-budget auteur art cinema (*De Profundis, Arrugas*) and transnational co-productions, all able to travel around the international circuits.

In regard to the Galician music scene of recent years, we could say that it has been following similar patterns of diversification and "normalization," and is also characterized by a great mobility, multiple border crossings, and outward projection beyond Galicia. The dominant note is the coexistence of a wide variety of well-established different musical trends, in dynamic dialogue with international currents, and in several languages: Galician and Spanish, as well as Portuguese, English, and even Arabic. Overall, this diversity has created a rich tapestry of musical styles: from traditional, folk, singer–songwriters, and "canción de autor" to indie rock, electronica, jazz, and pop-rock, in various degrees of cross-fertilization.

As in the case of the audiovisual sector, Galician music has received considerable institutional support from the Xunta to reach beyond Galicia, particularly during the bipartite government, which established its own Departamento de Internacionalización da Música (Department of Internationalization of Music) for the dissemination of Galician music overseas. Even with the onset of the economic crisis and the change of government, the support has continued, although in diminished form, as a testament to the importance of this area of Galician cultural production. Some of the main institutional strategies have been the activation of the network of Centros Galegos overseas (in the rest of Spain, Europe, and Latin

America), the participation of Galician musicians at international events, and the organization of promotional festivals and conferences, such as the WOMEX 2014 in Santiago, the most important roots music festival in the world. One particularly important channel for the diffusion of Galician music has been the Centros Galegos, through which workshops of traditional Galician music, instruments, and dances organized by the Xunta have been regularly offered, and this practice has built important connections and bridges between musicians from within and without Galicia. Mercedes Peón started her music career as an instructor of Galician *pandeireta*, and traveled for months giving workshops throughout Latin America. Likewise, institutional support has facilitated the organization of performances and tours of Galician musicians overseas and facilitated collaborations with other foreign artists.

One official program that illustrates well the contemporary diversity of Galician musical styles, their solidification, and their outward projection "from Galicia to the world" is Galician Tunes, an institutional project by the Xunta aiming for the deperipheralization of Galician music. Galician Tunes was one of the main institutional initiatives established by the former bipartite government in regard to the international promotion of Galician music, an initiative which has continued with subsequent administrations. Its main objective is to showcase new and upcoming Galician music through the creation and implementation of the brand "Galician Tunes" in the world music market. This objective has been carried out by way of the sponsorship of music festivals, participation in international music fora, and the dissemination of Galician music online through its own dedicated website and other platforms, such as Facebook and Twitter, and album releases such as *Galician Tunes, Music is in the oven* (2010). The Galician Tunes website is announced as "The web platform for music made in Galicia."[4] Not surprisingly, the "made in Galicia" marker echoes the same denomination widely used in the audiovisual sector. The website contains hundreds of musical videos, Spotify songs, and video playlists, along with information about Galician current music, groups and artists, music companies, and festivals. More than 50 different categories are covered in the platform, indicating both the great diversity of music being "made in Galicia" and the

---

4 The website was developed through AGADIC in collaboration with AGEM-Asociación Galega de Empresas Musicais (Galician association of musical producers), formed in 2007, and Músicos ao Vivo, the professional association of Galician live-performing musicians, formed in 2008. The website, in Galician, Spanish, and English, houses promotional videos of the brand, introduced by different foreigners with the catchphrase Galician tunes, "music in action" in different languages of the world.

dialogue with other musical traditions, including Latin, Lusobrazilian, and American folk music made in Galicia.[5]

The overall impression of Galician music today is that of a very lively and varied panorama, fully in sync with the world, which *Rootsworld* has recognized as a "dynamic music scene" in their review of Marful's first album release (rootsworld.com). The consolidation and coexistence of different trends and styles means that several types of Galician rock, pop, and jazz are found side-by-side next to different styles of folk, Celtic, and Latin music, and are frequently merged and hybridized in new forms. A bagpiper in a rock band or a tambourine player in an indie ensemble are not unusual sights in Galicia, as they would have been 30 years ago, but are an accepted part of the "normalization" and diversification of Galician music.

Similarly, the music scene is characterized by the establishment of fluid networks of collaborations and performance circuits, in Galicia, Spain, and other parts of the world, and of intersecting projects, reaching out to other musical traditions with different degrees of closeness to Galicia, be it Iberian, Celtic, Latin American, or Anglo-American. Hybridization with other "foreign" musical styles is an ongoing phenomenon. Having musicians and singers from other parts of the world collaborating with Galicians, and vice versa, is an everyday occurrence in Galician music today. Cristina Pato tours around the world and records with Yo-Yo Ma and the Silk Road Ensemble, and organizes the international Galician Connections concerts in A Coruña. Narf collaborates with Guinea Bissau's Manecas Costa, and Uxía with numerous Cabo Verde musicians and singers. Luar na Lubre has a Venezuelan flutist and a Cuban percussionist, and had a Portuguese lead singer as well as guest collaborations with Lila Downs from Mexico, Adriana Varela from Argentina, and Pablo Milanés from Cuba. Likewise, Basque accordionist Kepa Junkera dedicates a whole album, *Galiza* (2014), to collaborations with Galician musicians he has played with throughout his career.

Part of this diversity is the result of the continuing legacy of formerly established musical movements. Such is the case of the Galician *Movida*,

---

5  As an example of the variety and comprehensiveness of styles, the different tabs for musical categories on the Galician Tunes website include the following: acoustic, alternative, ambient, ancient, soundtrack, baroque, blues, cabaret, Celtic, classical, contemporary, country, dance, disco, electronic, experimental, folk, American folk, funk, fusion, garage, gothic, grunge, hard, heavy, hip-hop, humor, indie, industrial, children's music, instrumental, jazz, metal, minimal, Brazilian music, singer-songwriter, Portuguese music, new age, pop, pop-rock, post-rock, psychedelic, punk, rap, reggae, Latin, rock, progressive, rhythm and blues, ska, soul, surf, tango, techno, Galician traditional, vintage, world music.

most visibly through the ongoing career of foundational group Siniestro Total, still recording and touring widely, and the enduring work of Antón Reixa and Os Resentidos, particularly with the revival of *Galicia Caníbal, el musical*, directed and produced by Antón Reixa.[6] Similarly, the lasting legacy of *rock bravú* is notable in the glocal musical tradition of politically explicit rock in Galician, with active bands such as Heredeiros da crus and Ruxe Ruxe (Salgado, "A última banda bravú"), and the explicit homage to Os Diplomáticos de Monte-Alto by Galician indie rock bands in *120 capadores*. The legacy of those movements is clearly felt in the diverse musical panorama of today. Without the Galician *Movida* of the 1980s and the *bravú* of the 1990s it would be very difficult to explain the contemporary explosion of modern music in Galicia, where Vigo alone has some 200 rock bands.

Even more remarkable, perhaps, is the extraordinary folk diversity in contemporary Galician music, where folk is just an umbrella term that includes many different styles, from traditional female singing groups of *cantareiras* and *pandeireteiras*, bagpipe groups, and folk orchestras to new musical projects with modern instrumentation and arrangements, and experimentation and hybridity with different musical forms, such as jazz, new age, and other musical traditions (Lusophone, Latin American, Spanish, and Iberian). Also noteworthy is the coexistence of several generations and the continuing legacy of pioneering folk groups and musicians such as Milladoiro or Luar na Lubre, and those associated with the folk boom of the 1990s (such as Núñez, Budiño, Berrogüetto, Seivane, Pato, and Mutenrohi), and the emergence of new voices and musicians, with such innovative groups as Nordestin@s and Marful, who mix traditional Galician rhythms and melodies with jazz and dancehall music from the mid-twentieth century respectively, and add to this mix contemporary social themes.

In terms of the use of Galician as the language of popular music, there is no uniform pattern. Galician is the *de facto* language of traditional and folk music in all its variants, and often in jazz and "canción de autor," but less so in rock or pop, where English and Spanish are more common. In that sense, the "normalization" of popular music in Galician is still a work in progress. In parallel to the "cinema made in Galicia"/"Galician cinema" dichotomy, and the philological criteria employed in the demarcation of literary systems, the use of Galician language generally appears as a marker of authenticity and commitment to Galician cultural identity and the idea of the Galician

---

6 Diverse attempts to regroup by other *Movida*-era bands such as Golpes Bajos and Aerolíneas Federales have met with only limited success. This is not surprising, and is no different than other national and international music revival acts fuelled by nostalgia.

nation. Still, there is some fluidity in the language used in Galician music. Thus Xoel López started his successful career at the national level in English with his indie group Deluxe and then changed to Spanish, partly as a result of his years living in Latin America and being influenced by its music, from samba to milonga, and especially by *rock argentino*, with occasional songs sung in Galician ("Caetano Veloso," "A serea e o mariñeiro").

Although the choice of one language versus another is frequently explained as a matter of reaching a wider audience, as singing in English or Spanish would supposedly translate to larger numbers of followers than doing so in Galician, that is not necessarily so. In fact, curiously, the groups and singers who sing in Galician, predominantly those associated with folk, such as Carlos Núñez, Luar na Lubre, Cristina Pato, and Uxía, are the ones with a wider audience worldwide, through the different but overlapping networks of folk, world music, and Celtic music, and the circuit of international festivals. In this terrain the use of Galician is the norm. It would thus appear that the most successful artists beyond Galicia are those that are clearly identified with a connection to Galician roots and are able to bridge tradition and modernity, local and global idioms. While this trend certainly represents a deperipheralization of Galician folk music, other non-folk-based groups and singers often occupy more marginal positions, regardless of the language used.

Non-folk singing in Galician is "normalized" to the extent that it is now considered a viable channel to be employed, but it is not the norm. The trend to rehabilitate Galician pop singer Andrés do Barro is interesting in this regard, as he was the first singer to cross over to mass audiences in Spain and Latin America while singing in Galician in the 1960s–1970s (which would be soon emulated by others, such as Juan Pardo and Julio Iglesias). The tribute double album *Manifiesto Dobarrista* (2007) brings together some of the most recognized contempory Galician indie rock and power pop bands, such as Ataque Escampe, Homens, Narf, and Projecto Mourente, singing in Galician, as well as bands who normally sing in English (Niño y Pistola) or Spanish (Elodio y los seres queridos), which updates the sound and relevance of Andrés do Barro's ground-breaking Galician pop songs and aims for the deperipheralization of music in Galician at the same time.

Some of the most innovative and politically relevant voices in modern music in Galician, aside from folk, include pioneering *bravú* bands Heredeiros da Crus and Ruxe Ruxe, the eclectic work of Ataque Escampe, rap band Dios Ke Te Crew, and the newer voices of Gaudi Galego and Ses, among others. Ruxe Ruxe continues the *bravú* tradition of mixing punk attitude, rawness, and provocation with strongly Galician musical and social undertones and a critical political perspective. Thus the concern with the recovery of historical memory and the awareness of the reality of the Francoist repression in Galicia are highlighted in songs such as "Buratos" ("holes"), which refers both to holes in the ground (of the victims of the history of violence during the war and dictatorship), and the holes in the historical record as a result of the official "pact of forgetting." Emphasizing this recovery of the past, the video clip represents a literal trip to the past told in backwards motion. The commitment of Ruxe Ruxe to Galician history and cultural identity is also palpable in the anthem-like song "Rock do país" ("rock of the nation"), a post-punk energetic rock song played with the accompaniment of Galician tambourines and bagpipes, claiming "rock da terra, rock do país [...] rock da língua, rock da nosa xente [...] rock bravú, rock compromiso" ("rock of the land, rock of the nation [...], rock of our language, rock of our people [...] bravú rock, engaged rock").

The work of rap band Dios Ke Te Crew also represents a very explicit political position in defense of Galician culture, language, and identity. The internationally popular idiom of rap meets the literary and oral Galician tradition of *regueifa* in a form of hybrid agitprop Galician hip hop, as seen in their musicalization of "Deitado frente ao mar" ("Lying down by the sea"), one of the most combative poems of Celso Emilio Ferreiro, written in defense of the language of the working class and rural origins.[7] Their collaboration with folk band Quempallou, from the Morrazo area, in "Nenguén" ("Nobody"), offered a radical critique of the impact of global multinationals and neoliberal policies on local economies and cultures. The musical contrast of the hip hop beats and vinyl scratching with the lyricism of Galician tambourines, harps and melodies accentuates even more the ecological and political charge of the piece.

A similar mix of literature, activism, and modern music is noticeable in the alternative rock band Ataque Escampe, a group of former students of Galician philology at the Universidade de Santiago, whose lyrics use many literary and cultural references, from Rosalía de Castro to Celso Emilio Ferreiro. Ataque Escampe occupy a unique place in Galician music, being critically acclaimed for their powerful lyrics and unique mix of

---

7 Lingua proletaria do meu pobo/eu faloa porque si, porque me gusta/ [...] falar a fala nai/a fala dos abós que temos mortos,/e ser, co rostro erguido,/mariñeiros, labregos da linguaxe,/remo e arado, proa e rella sempre./ [...] e quero estar cos meus, coa xente que sufren longo/unha historia contada noutra lingua. (Proletarian language of my people/I speak it just because, because I like it/ [...] to speak in the mother tongue,/the tongue of our dead grandparents,/and to be, with the chin up,/ sailors and farmers of language,/oars and plow,/ prow and ploughshare/ [...] and I want to be with my people,/ with those who have long suffered/ a (hi)story told in another language.)

contemporary musical trends, creating an intertextual literary and musical postmodern collage that questions traditional boundaries. They are a self-produced band, ideologically positioned on the margins of the mainstream industry, releasing their records through the collective music company Discos da máquina under open license: all their albums can be listened to in their entirety and downloaded free from their website (discosdamaquina.com). Ataque Escampe represent a very distinct approach in their music, lyrics, and performance style, which are highly polished and sophisticated. Their sound is much less raw than that of *rock bravú* or Ruxe Ruxe and it does not have the immediacy of Dios Ke Te Crew. They have a more melodic and acoustic sound, mixing modern instruments with unusual kazoos and saws, ukeleles, and glockenspiel. Their songs are biting, with typical Galician "retranca" (ironic double meaning). Their videos are more conceptual and their lyrics less direct, more ironic and intellectual, but just as powerful as forms of cultural resistance. They often perform their songs using costumes, props, or even blackface, as in their video for "A cabana do tío Tom" ("Uncle Tom's Cabin"). In this song, played in a southern rock style, they recontextualize the famous analogy that Rosalía de Castro drew between Galicians with blacks as oppressed peoples, quoting her poem "Castellanos de Castilla." The lines of the song, "Respect yourself, galegos de Alabama, tratade ben aos galegos" "(respect yourself, Galicians from Alabama, treat Galicians well") offer a biting critique of the "auto odio" (self-hatred) complex as a product of internalized colonization.

Although the majority of Ataque Escampe's songs are in Galician, one of their most memorable ones is provocatively titled in Spanish "Galicia es una mierda" ("Galicia is a piece of shit")—also the title of their second album, which was chosen by popular vote on the group's website. "Galicia es una mierda" is a sarcastic comment about the pervasive disregard for Galician culture and language and the ideological "Spanishization" that occurs frequently as a result of the linguistic and cultural diglossia which privileges Castilian over Galician, the foreign over the local, and the urban over the rural.

New female voices and musicians providing powerful affirmations of Galician cultural identity have also been one of the dominant tones of the music scene of recent years. After the ground-breaking example of Uxía and the explosion of musical innovation and hybridization in the late 1990s with Cristina Pato and Mercedes Peón, the presence of these female voices in Galician music has grown and solidified. An exemplary trajectory which reflects the quality and diversity of women's musical projects is Guadi Galego, who has traveled musically from traditional to folk to *canción de autor* and jazz. The former singer of acclaimed folk band Berrogüetto, she has developed an eclectic career alternating her solo endeavours with her participation in some of the most innovative Galician musical projects of the last few years, including Espido, Nordestin@s (with Ugía Pedreira and Abe Rábade), aCadaCanto (with Xabier Díaz, Guillerme Fernández, and Xosé Luis Romero), Rosalía 21, and the Portuguese group Vozes da rádio with "Ponte do meu lado," advocating for cultural and linguistic unity with the Lusophone world. Her songs undoubtedly offer a strong female perspective, positioned at the intersection of gender and nation, often having females figures as central focal point, such as "Matriarcas," "Santa muller," "Dama," or "Madama." "Matriarcas" has had popular success, with around 200,000 viewings on YouTube. Shot in stark black-and-white, the video features a collective of women (and mothers with their children) each appearing to sing a line of the song, with words from the lyrics appearing on the screen in Galician, English, French, Catalan, Basque, and Greek as a form of transcultural/transnational solidarity. Although considered by some as an essentialized vision of women and motherhood, the song intends to be an ode to the often forgotten role of Galician women in the construction of the nation, an affirmation of an alternative version of the historically masculine definition of "Nós" ("Us"): "E nós pouquiño a pouco ímonos situando,/ construíndo barricadas no país dos alalás./ [...] Nós aleitadoras, nós conquistadoras,/brillantes activistas da vida cotiá./E nós que resistimos a séculos de forza,/e nós as matriarcas do país dun tal Breogán" ("And little by little we are getting in place,/ building barricades in the nation of alalás / [...] We nurturers, we conquerors, brilliant activists of daily life/And we, resisting centuries of force/and we, the matriarchs of the nation of someone named Breoghan").

Another provocative voice who has recently emerged with force is Ses (María Xosé Silvar). Ses is an alternative singer–songwriter/rock performer with a feminist perspective, a rebellious look, and a non-conformist attitude, who has gathered a large following in the last few years. In her songs and live performances she projects a contemporary Galician cultural identity totally at ease with international musical idioms, both modern and traditional. Her style is thus eclectic and hybrid, recurring to diverse musical forms, particularly American rock, rockabilly, and blues, and also Latin American traditional rhythms, from Argentinian *milonga* ("Milonga de aquí" ["Milonga from Here"]) to Cuban *son* ("Canto aquí canto na Habana" ["I sing here, I sing in Habana"], "Concordias de papel" ["Paper Concords"]), and "Labregha Berghantiñana," an ode to peasant women from Bergantiños with the rhythm of "Guantanamera." This constant crossing of musical borders creates a deterritorialized imaginary Galicia and a connection with the historical Galician diaspora in Latin America (particularly strong in Cuba and Argentina), while projecting a very strong sense of cultural identity.

All of Ses's songs are in Galician, using dialectal *gheada* and *seseo*, which are particular marks of local and popular non-normative Galician. Their use is intentionally provocative and rebellious, calling attention to alternative non-conforming identities. Ses represents a contemporary urban voice of struggle and a modern image, giving voice to the concerns and perspectives of a new generation. Her songs usually provide social commentary, sometimes ironic, always compelling, as in "Tempestades de sal" ("Tempests of Salt"), a politically charged song of collective resistance, which evokes the widespread popular mobilizations after the *Prestige* oil spill. Ses's performances are energetic and iconoclastic, like her popular and lively music videos shot in contemporary modern urban settings, some of which have reached several hundred thousand viewings on YouTube.

As in the case of other acts mentioned, intermediality is an important part of the music, often completely integrated as video clips, one of the most common channels of the dissemination of songs, adding new layers of significance, from the performative to the conceptual. As in the case of the new cinema, the new technological tools available—including Internet websites, video platforms, apps, and blogs, as well as digital recording—have been key avenues for creating, developing, distributing, and sharing new musical projects, sometimes on the margins of the industry. In that regard, technological development has been a key aspect of deperipheralization.

All these developments in the Galician audio/visual sector point to a lively and eclectic cultural scene. A new and diverse generation of Galician creators, musicians, and filmmakers who are in dialogue with international trends are coming out of the periphery. The affirmation of cultural identity and the building and expansion of a creative community through collaborations, both at home and abroad, are progressively deperipheralizing the periphery. Perhaps technically peripheral, geographically remote, territorially small, and economically disadvantaged cultures such as Galicia have some advantages after all in the global era, in both the musical and the audiovisual realms. Close networks are created, circuits of affinities, complicities, and collaborations generated, innovative and inventive strategies developed, and connections and bridges with other cultures established, both in Galicia as well as in the outside world. Paradoxically, new things appear from the fringes, but in the avant-garde. As we already know, waves are born in the periphery. In this case, musical and film waves are born in the periphery, from Galicia to the world.

# Works Cited

"A mellor película galega!" Listas. *20minutos*. 20minutos.es. Web.

"A televisión en Galicia." *Libro Branco do Audiovisual Galego*. Observatorioaudiovisual. org. Dirección Xeral de Comunicación Audiovisual, 2004. Web.

Aaron, Jane, and Chris Williams, eds. *Postcolonial Wales*. Cardiff: U of Wales P, 2005.

Acuña, Xoán. *Chano Piñeiro. Unha historia do cinema galego*. Vigo: Edicións do Cumio, 1999.

*Alalá*. Chapter 35. *Televisión de Galicia*, 16 January 2007. Web.

Alonso, Emilio. *Vigo a 80 revolucións por minuto. Unha crónica da movida*. Vigo: Xerais, 2011.

Alonso García, Luis, ed. *Once miradas sobre la crisis y el cine español*. Ocho y Medio. Madrid, 2003.

Amago, Sam. "Reflexivity in Iberian Documentary Film." *Routledge Companion to Iberian Studies*. Eds. Javier Munoz-Basols, Laura Lonsdale, and Manuel Delgado Morales. Forthcoming.

Araguas, Vicente. *Voces Ceibes*. Vigo: Xerais, 1991.

"As cifras da industria cultural galega." *Xunta de Galicia*. Xunta.es. 2011. Web.

"Audiovisual galego, as cifras." *Vieiros*. vieiros.com. 11 November 2002. Web.

Aula Castelao de Filosofía. *Globalización e cambio de milenio*. Vigo: Edicións Xerais de Galicia, 2001.

"Aula de cine. Novo cinema galego." *Universidade de Oviedo*. Uniovi.es. 14 September 2015. Web.

Avendaño, Alberto. "O meu Rompente." *Madrygal* 4 (2001): 25–32.

Axeitos, X.L. "A Real Academia Galega no discurso construtivo do Rexurdimento." *Grial* 171 (2006): 16–25.

Azalbert, Nicolas. "Loin de Madrid." *Cahiers du Cinéma* 693 (2013): 58.

Baamonde, Antón. "Voto emigrante." *El País* Galicia ed. 19 February 2008. Web.

Baltar, Ramón. "De Galicia para el mundo." *La Voz de Galicia*. 28 September 2005. Web.

Baltrusch, Burghard. "Tradución e nación. Galicia entre a lusofonía e o posnacionalismo." *Grial* 179 (2008): 60–67.

Beiras, Xosé Luis. *O atraso económico de Galicia*. Vigo: Galaxia, 1973.

Bergner, Verónica, Sebastián Rosal, and Geraldine Salles Kobilanski. "Entrevista a Xurxo Chirro." *Marienbad*. marienbad.com.ar. June 2013. Web.

Bermúdez, Silvia. "La Habana para un exiliado gallego: Manuel Curros Enríquez, La Terra Gallega y la modernidad nacional transatlántica." *Modern Language Notes* 117.2 (2002): 331–42.

—. "Poetry and Performance: The Renewal of the Public Sphere in Present-Day Galicia." *Contemporary Galician Cultural Studies: Between the Local and the Global.* Eds. Kirsty Hooper and Manuel Puga Moruxa. New York: Modern Language Association of America, 2011. 289–304.

Bermúdez, Silvia, et al. *From Stateless Nations to Postnational Spain/De naciones sin fronteras a la España postnacional.* Boulder: Society of Spanish and Spanish-American Studies, University of Colorado at Boulder, 2001.

Bhabha, Homi. *The Location of Culture.* London: Routledge, 2006.

—, ed. *Nation and Narration.* London: Routledge, 1990.

Bibiano.org. "Capítulo VI: A Movida viguesa, de Trenvigo ó Kremlim." Web.

Blanco, Uxía. "Galicia es el centro del mundo." *El País* Galicia ed. 13 June 2008. Web.

Bolaños, Alejandro. "Se buscan directivos listos para coger el avión." *El País* 3 December 2008. Web.

Bouzada Fernández, Xan Manuel, and Xesús Adolfo Lage Picos. "O retorno como culminación do ciclo da emigración galega." *Grial* 162 (2004): 26–35.

Bringas López, Ana, and Belén Martín Lucas, eds. *Identidades multiculturais: revisión dos discursos teóricos.* Vigo: Universidade de Vigo, 2000.

"Cadro de mando do sector audiovisual galego." Observatorioaudiovisual.org, *Observatorio Audiovisual Galego.* Web.

Calzada, Marta de la. "Cine gallego: viento del norte, a favor." *El País* 18 January 2015. Web.

Campos, Débora. "La memoria que llegó en barco." *Planeta gallego.* Degalicia.org. 4 July 2005. Web.

Campos Calvo-Sotelo, Javier. "We're on the Celtic Fringe! Celtic Music and Nationalism in Galicia." *Made in Spain. Studies in Popular Music.* Eds. Sílvia Martínez and Héctor Fouce. New York: Routledge, 2013. 53–63.

Cao, Emilio. *Fonte do araño.* LP. Madrid: Movieplay, 1977.

"Castañazo Rock—Homenaxe o 'rock bravú'." *Troula na banda.* Troulanabanda.info. 17 October 2007. Web.

Casal, Alberto. *¿Rock & Grelos?* Santiago de Compostela: Edicións Lea, 1994.

Cascudo, José Antonio. "*Vikingland* e a epopeia da emigración." *Madrygal* 18 (2015): 541–46.

Castelao, Alfonso R., *Sempre en Galiza.* 1944. Vigo: Galaxia, 1996.

Castells, Manuel. *The Information Age: Economy, Society and Culture.* Oxford: Blackwell, 1997. 3 vols.

Castro Vázquez, Olga. "Do local ao global. Achegas feministas e poscoloniais á relación entre antípodas (Galicia-Australia)." *Australia e Galicia.* Eds. Lorenzo Modia and Roy C. Boland, 153–79.

Castro de Paz, José Luis, ed. *Historia do cine en Galicia.* A Coruña: Vía Láctea, 1996.

Cebrián, Leonardo. "El bosque animado. España entra en el mundo del largometraje animado." *ANY fx* November (1999): 74–80. Web.

Cerdán, Josetxo. "Vindicación de la periferia. Revisión crítica de los márgenes del documental español contemporáneo." *Archivos de la filmoteca: Revista de estudios históricos sobre la imagen* 49 (2005): 146–69.

Chao, Manu. "A feira das mentiras." *Manu Chao.* Manuchao.net. N.d. Web.

Cid Cabido, Xosé, and Manuel Xestoso. *Antón Reixa. Ghicho distinto.* Vigo: Edicións Xerais de Galicia, 2012.

Cifuentes, Gonzalo. "La génesis del rock gallego: el rock bravú." *Rock Around Spain. Historia, industria, escenas y medios de comunicación.* Eds. Kiko Mora and Eduardo Viñuela. Lleida: Edicions de la Universitat de Lleida, 2013. 155–70.

Clifford, James. *Routes. Travel and Translation in the Late Twentieth Century.* Cambridge, MA: Harvard UP, 1997.

Cohen, Anthony P., ed. *Signifying Identities. Anthropological Perspectives on Boundaries and Contested Values.* London and New York: Routledge, 2000.

Coira, Jorge. "Por un cine perralleiro." *Bravú* 1 (1997): 62.

Colmeiro, José. "The Spanish Detective as Cultural Other." *The Post Colonial Detective.* Ed. Edward Christian. London: Palgrave-St. Martin's P, 2001. 176–92.

—. "Peripheral Visions, Global Positions: Remapping Galician Culture." *Bulletin of Hispanic Studies* 86.12 (2009): 213–30.

—. *Galeg@s sen fronteiras: Conversas sobre a cultura galega no século XXI.* Vigo: Edicións Xerais de Galicia, 2013.

—. "Quen somos, de onde vimos, a onde imos: Reflexións sobre os estudos galegos desde Estados Unidos." *Madrygal. Revista de Estudios Gallegos* 16 (2013): 131–38.

Correa, Anxa. "Preferimos as historias clásicas, ás que lle aportamos unha visión diferente." *Vigo Metropolitano.* Vigometropolitano.com. September (2006). Web.

Crofts, Stephen. "Reconceptualizing national cinema/s." *Film and Nationalism.* Ed. Alan Williams. New Brunswick, NJ: Rutgers UP, 2002. 25–51.

Cruz, Ángel de la. "El bosque animado. El éxito de la iniciativa gallega de animación." Issuu.com. *Código cero. Revista de novas tecnolóxicas de Galicia* 2 (2002): 23. Web.

Cunqueiro, Álvaro. "Las geografías imaginarias." *La Voz de Galicia* 4 May 1952. *100 artigos.* Ed. Dorinda Rivera Pedredo. A Coruña: La Voz de Galicia, 2001. 6–7.

"David Byrne conversa con Manu Chao." *DDOOSS.* ddooss.org. December 2001. Web.

Davies, Catherine. "Rosalía de Castro: Cultural Isolation in a Colonial Context." *Recovering Spain's Feminist Tradition.* Ed. Lisa Vollendorf. New York: The Modern Language Association of America, 2001. 176–97.

Deleuze, Gilles, and Félix Guattari. *Anti-Oedipus: Capitalism and Schizophrenia.* Minneapolis: U of Minnesota P, 1983.

—. *A Thousand Plateaus: Capitalism and Schizophrenia.* London/New York: Continuum International Publishing Group, 2004.

Donnan, Hastings, and Thomas Wilson. *Borders: Frontiers of Identity, Nation and State.* Oxford: Berg, 1999.

Dunne, Jonathan. *Anthology of Galician literature, 1196–1981/Antoloxía da literatura galega, 1196–1981.* Vigo: Xerais /Galaxia, 2010.

—. *Anthology of Galician Literature, 1981–2011 /Antoloxía da literatura galega, 1981–2011.* Santiago de Compostela: Xunta de Galicia; Vigo: Xerais/Galaxia, 2012.

Duque, Andrés. "Lo que me dijo un escocés." *Atlas Ilustrado da Periferia.* S8cinema. com. 1 April 2011. Web.

"Dygra Films Selects the Solaris 10 Operating System and Sun Systems to Advance Rendering Applications and Increase Production by 50 Percent For 3D Animated Films." *Sun Microsystems.* Sun.com. 23 August 2005. Web.

"El lápiz del carpintero. Denuncia dunha mentira." *Redes Escarlatas.* redesescarlata. org. N.d. Web.

"El audiovisual gallego, el primero en contar con su particular enciclopedia de todas las películas rodadas en Galicia." *Lukor.* Lukor.com. 1 June 2005. Web.

Elena, Alberto. *Los cines periféricos*. Barcelona: Paidós, 1999.

Ellis, Peter Berresford. *The Celtic Dawn: The Dream of Celtic Unity*. Talybont: Y Lolfa, 2002.

Enciso, Eloy. "Director's Statement." *Arraianos*. arraianos.wordpress.com. 2012. Web.

—, et al. "La celebración del viajero." Booklet, *Arrianos*, Zeitun Films. DVD 2013.

*Escolma do cine galego*. Vigo: Asociación Xuvenil Abertal, 1980.

Estévez, Xoán Manuel. *Milladoiro. Moito máis que un grupo de música folk*. Vigo: Ir Indo Edicións, 1999.

—, and Óscar Losada. *Crónica do folc galego. Vintecinco anos de historia*. Lugo: TrisTram. 2000.

Estrada, Javier. "No sólo se le puede ganar a los americanos, sino que se debe intentar permanentemente." *Metrópoli*. Elmundo.es. 29 June 2005. Web.

"¿Existe o cine galego?" *Vieiros*. Vieiros.com. 11 November 2002. Web.

Fernandez, James W. "Peripheral Wisdom". *Signifying identities. Anthropological Perspectives on Boundaries and Contested Values*. Ed. Anthony P. Cohen. London: Routledge, 2000. 117–44.

Fernández Labayen, Miguel, and María Mallol González. "Existimos, luego periféricas." *Atlas Ilustrado da Periferia*. S8cinema.com. 3 April 2011. Web.

Fernández, Miguel Anxo. "Distribución e exhibición." *Libro branco de cinematografía e artes visuais en Galicia*: 289–300.

—. *Rodado en Galicia*. Santiago de Compostela: Consorcio Audiovisual de Galicia, 2005.

Fernández Rego, Fernando. *50 anos de pop, rock e malditismo na música galega*. Noia: Soutollos, 2014.

Fernández Rei, Francisco. "Gheada e seseo no galego colloquial e no galego estándar dos anos 90. Notas sobre a súa presencia nos media e nos textos musicais." *A Lingua Galega, historia e actualidade: Actas do I Congreso Internacional, Santiago de Compostela, 16–20 de setembro 1996*. Vol 2. Eds. Rosario Alvarez Blanco et al. Santiago de Compostela: Consello da Cultura Galega, 2004. 307–36.

Fitzpatrick, Eileen. "Marketer Brings Music to U.S. Ethnic Groups." *Billboard* April 5 1997: 1–86. Web.

Frey, Nancy Louise. *Pilgrim Stories: On and Off the Road to Santiago*. Berkeley: U of California P, 1998.

Friedman, Thomas L. *The World is Flat. A Brief History of the Twenty-first Century*. New York: Picador, 2007.

Furnald, Cliff. "Na Lúa, Galician Musical Adventure." Review of *Os tempos son chegados* by Na Lúa, *Roots World*. RootsWorld.com. 2001. Web.

Gabilondo, Joseba. "The Hispanic Atlantic." *Arizona Journal of Hispanic Cultural Studies* 5 (2001): 91–113.

—. "Postnationalism, Fundamentalism and the Global Real: Historicizing Terror/ism and the New North American/Global Ideology." *Journal of Spanish Cultural Studies* 3.1 (2002): 57–86.

—. "The National Primal Scene: On the Global Emergence of Basque and Andalusian Cinemas." *Companion to Spanish Cinema*. Eds. Jo Labanyi and Tatjana Pavlović. Malden, MA: Blackwell, 2012. 85–98.

Galán, Eduardo. *O bosque inanimado. Cen anos de cine en Galicia*. A Coruña: Centro Galego de Artes da Imaxe, 1997.

Galiñanes, Juan. Blog. *Juan Galiñanes*. Juangalinhanes.wordpress.com. 13 October 2014. Web.

Gallero, José Luis. *Sólo se vive una vez: esplendor y ruina de la movida madrileña*. Madrid: Ardora, 1991.

García Canclini, Néstor. *Hybrid Cultures: Strategies for Entering and Leaving Modernity*. Minneapolis: U of Minnesota P, 1995.

—. *La globalización imaginada*. Buenos Aires: Paidós, 2005.

García Fernández, Emilio Carlos. *Historia del cine en Galicia (1896–1984)*. A Coruña: La Voz de Galicia, 1985.

García Mañá, Luís Manuel. *Couto Mixto. Unha república esquecida*. Vigo: Xerais, 2005.

Gemie, Sharif. *A Concise History of Galicia*. Cardiff: U of Wales P, 2006.

Gilroy, Paul. *The Black Atlantic. Modernity and Double Consciousness*. Cambridge, MA: Harvard UP, 1993.

Glissant, Édouard. *Poetics of Relation*. Ann Arbor: U of Michigan P, 1997.

Godón, Nuria. "Desde las antípodas. Conversación con José Colmeiro." *Transitions: Journal of Franco-Iberian Studies* 9 (2013): 9–27.

Gómez Viñas, Xan. "Cinema in Galicia: Beyond an Interrupted History." *A Companion to Galician Culture*. Ed. Helena Miguélez-Carballeira. 135–56.

Gómez-Montero, Javier. "Santiago de Compostela and the Obsession with Identity." *Iberian Cities*. Ed. Joan Ramon Resina. New York: Routledge, 2001. 18–32.

González, Alicia. "Japón quiere copiar el Camino de Santiago." *El País* 2 September 2015. Web.

González, Manuel. *Cine restaurado. Nuestras fiestas de allá (1928) Galicia y Buenos Aires (1931)*. A Coruña: CGAI—Consello da Cultura Galega, 2000.

González, Xurxo (Chirro). "Posicionamento periférico." *Atlas Ilustrado da Periferia*. S8cinema.com. 3 April 2011. Web.

—. "Novo Cinema Galego: Forza centrífuga." *Academia galega do audiovisual*. academiagalegadoaudiovisual.com. 20 January 2015. Web.

González-Millán, Xoán. "O criterio filolóxico e a configuración dunha literatura nacional: achegas a un novo marco de reflexión." *Cadernos da lingua* 17 (1998): 5–24.

González Fernández, Helena. *A tribo das baleas. Poetas de arestora = Antología de la poesía gallega última = An Anthology of the Latest Galician Poetry*. Vigo: Edicións Xerais de Galicia, 2001.

—. "La ausencia y la espera de la mujer sola como afirmación en Rosalía de Castro y Xohana Torres." *Del instante a la eternidad. Exégesis sobre "la espera" en la escritura de mujeres*. Eds. José Luís Arráez Llobregat and Amelia Peral Crespo. Alicante: Universidad, 2012. 93–111.

—. "Como prenden elas da nación? Sobre a poesía épica a comezos do século XXI." *452ºF. Revista de teoría de la literatura y literatura comparada* 8 (2013): 13–27.

Guasch, Anna Maria, and Joseba Zulaika. *Learning from the Bilbao Guggenheim*. Reno: Center for Basque Studies, U of Nevada, 2005.

Habermas, Jürgen. *The Postnational Constellation. Political Essays*. Cambridge, MA MIT, 2001.

Halter, Marilyn. *Shopping for identity.The Marketing of Ethnicity*. New York: Shocken Books, 2000.

Hernández, Julián. *¿Hay vida inteligente en el rock and roll?* Madrid: Temas de hoy, 1999.

Herrera Torres, Ramón. *Cine Jacobeo: el Camino de Santiago en la pantalla*. Bilbao: La Cineclopedia Edicion, 2009.

Higson, Andrew. "The Concept of National Cinema." *Film and Nationalism*. Ed. Alan Williams. New Brunswick, NJ: Rutgers UP, 2002. 52–67.

Hobsbawm, Eric. "Introduction: Inventing Tradition." *The Invention of Tradition*. Eds. Eric Hobsbawm and Terence Ranger. Cambridge: Cambridge UP, 1983. 1–14.

Holohan, Conn. *Cinema on the Periphery: Contemporary Irish and Spanish Film*. Dublin: Irish Academic P, 2010.

Hooper, Kirsty. "Novas cartografías nos estudos galegos: nacionalismo literario, literatura nacional, lecturas posnacionais." *Anuario de Estudos Literarios Galegos* (2005): 64–73.

—, ed. "New Spaces, New Voices: Notes on Contemporary Galician Studies." Special issue of *Journal of Spanish Cultural Studies* 7.2 (July 2006).

—. "Galicia desde Londres desde Galicia: New Voices in the 21st-century Diaspora." *Journal of Spanish Cultural Studies* 7.2 (2006): 171–88.

—. "New Cartographies in Galician Studies: From Literary Nationalism to Postnational Readings." *Reading Iberia: Theory, History, Identity*. Eds. Helena Buffery, Stuart Davis, and Kirsty Hooper. Oxford: Peter Lang, 2007. 123–39.

—. *Writing Galicia into the World: New Cartographies, New Poetics*. Liverpool: Liverpool UP, 2011.

Hooper, Kirsty, and Helena Miguélez-Carballeira. "Critical Approaches to the Nation in Galician Studies." Special Issue, *Bulletin of Hispanic Studies* 86.12 (2009).

Hooper, Kirsty, and Manuel Puga, eds. *Contemporary Galician Studies: Between the Local and the Global*. New York: Modern Language Association of America, 2011.

Hopewell, John. "Hit and Myth in the Deep North. Forward-looking Rural Area Transforming into TV and Film Heavyweight." *Variety* 19 September 2004. Web.

Hueso, Ángel Luis. "Anos de efervescencia política (desde as posturas ideolóxicas cara ó mundo industrial)." Castro de Paz, *Historia do cine en Galicia*. 180–93.

—. "Galicia." *Cine español: Una historia por Autonomías*. Ed. José María Caparrós Lera. Vol 1. Barcelona: Centro de Investigaciones Film-Historia/PPU, 1996. 265–86.

Iglesias, Óscar. "Os problemas dun poeta nacional." *El País* Galicia ed. 14 September 2007. Web.

Iordanova, Dina, David Martin-Jones, and Belén Vidal, eds. *Cinema at the Periphery*. Detroit: Wayne State UP, 2010.

Izquierdo Escribano, Antonio, and Montserrat Golías Pérez. "A poboación extranxeira en Galicia. Do dominio portugués á latinoamericanización." *Grial* 162 (2004): 44–53.

Kinder, Marsha. *Blood Cinema: The Reconstruction of National Identity in Spain*. Berkeley: U of California P, 1993.

King, Stewart, ed. "Mas allá de la periferia: narrativas de identidad en Cataluña, Galicia y el País Vasco." *Antípodas. Journal of Spanish and Galician Studies* (2007).

Koza, Roger. "Efectos Especiales." ojosabiertos.otroscines.com. *Con los ojos abiertos*. 15 April 2013. Web.

Labanyi, Jo. "Globalización, cosmopolitismo y traducción cultural." *Encrucijadas globales. Redefinir España en el siglo XXI*. Ed. José Colmeiro. Madrid: Editorial Iberoamericana/Vervuert, 2015. 35–60.

*Libro branco de cinematografía e artes visuais en Galicia*. Santiago de Compostela: Consello da Cultura Galega, 2004.

Liñeira, María. "Santiago de Compostela: Fact and Fetish." *A Companion to Galician Culture*. Ed. Helena Miguélez-Carballeira. *A Companion to Galician Culture*. 53–71.

Llevellyn, Howell. "Carlos Núñez Exports Gaita from Spain." *Billboard* 2 August 1997: 10, 91.

Lobato, Xurxo. *No país do Nunca Máis*. Vigo: Galaxia, 2003.

Lobo, C.L. "La magia de la animación gallega." *La razón* 1 July 2005: 38.

López-Claros, Augusto. *The Search for Efficiency in the Adjustment Process: Spain in the 1980s*. Washington, D.C.: International Monetary Fund, 1988.

Lorenzo Modia, María Jesús, and Roy C. Boland. *Australia and Galicia: Defeating the Tyranny of Distance/Australia e Galicia: vencendo a tiranía do afastamento*. Jannali, Australia: Antípodas monographs, 2008.

Losada, Antón. "Xavarín Forever." *El País* 4 March 2013. Web.

McGovern, Timothy. "Camping Up the Nation: Antón Lopo's Ganga and the Queering of Iberia." *Contemporary Galician Cultural Studies: Between the Local and the Global*. Eds. Kirsty Hooper and Manuel Puga Moruxa. New York: Modern Language Association of America, 2011. 166–81.

MacKenzie, John M. *Orientalism. History, Theory and the Arts*. Manchester: Manchester UP, 1995.

Marco, Mercedes. "Entrevista a Antón Seoane, integrante de Milladoiro." *Mujer actual*. Mujeractual.com. N.d. Web.

Mariño Davila, Esperanza, and Raquel Noya Beiroa. "A planificación lingüística en Galicia: Un balance do último lustro (1990–1995)." *A Lingua Galega, historia e actualidade: Actas do I Congreso Internacional, Santiago de Compostela, 16–20 de setembro 1996*. Vol 2. Ed. Rosario Alvarez Blanco et al. Santiago de Compostela: Consello da Cultura Galega, 2004. 103–34.

Martín Núñez, Marta. "Representación en el cine de animación: Reflexiones en torno al concepto de mimesis." *Fòrum de Recerca* 11. Uji.es. *Onzenes jornades de foment de la investigación*, Castellón: Publicacions de l'Universitat Jaume I, 2006. 1–16. Web.

Martínez, Guillem. *CT o la cultura de la transición: Crítica a 35 años de cultura española*. Barcelona: Debolsillo, 2012.

Martínez Martínez, Isabel, and María Gallego Reguera. "El Novo Cinema Galego, propuesta de definición y clasificación." *Revista Comunicación* 10.1 (2012): 264–75.

Mato, Mar. "Pili Carrera, de Galicia para el mundo." *La opinión A Coruña*. Laopinioncoruña.es. 3 May 2013. Web.

—. "La vanguardia del cine se filma en Galicia." *Faro de Vigo* 20 April 2014. Web.

Mejía, Carmen. "Estéticas da poesía galega e signos de ruptura. Unha nova ollada ó *Grupo de Comunicación Poética Rompente*." *Madrygal* 4 (2001): 89–94.

Mella, Carlos. *A Galicia posible*. Vigo: Edicións Xerais de Galicia, 1992.

Michelín, Gerardo. "Productor Ejecutivo de Dygra Films. Manuel Cristóbal: 'La animación española tiene todas las cartas y ahora tenemos que empezar a jugar'." *CINEinforme* February (2004): 30–31.

Miguélez-Carballeira, Helena. *Galicia, a Sentimental Nation. Gender, Culture and Politics*. Cardiff: U of Wales P, 2013.

Miguélez-Carballeira, Helena, ed. *A Companion to Galician Culture*. London: Tamesis, 2014.

Moreiras-Menor, Cristina. "El secreto revelado y los horizontes del nacionalismo gallego en Rosalía de Castro." *Revista Hispánica Moderna* 52 (1999): 322–40.

—. "Galicia Beyond Galicia: *A man dos paíños* and the Ends of Territoriality." *Border Interrogations: Questioning Spanish Frontiers*. Eds. Benita Sampedro and Simon Doubleday. New York/Oxford: Berghahn, 2008. 105–19.

Moreno Caballud, Luis. *Cultures of Anyone. Studies on Cultural Democratization in the Spanish Liberal Crisis.* Liverpool: Liverpool UP, 2015.

Moure, Erín. "The Public Relation: Redefining Citizenship by Poetic Means." *Global Neo-Imperialism and National Resistance. Approaches from Postcolonial Studies.* Eds. Belén Martín Lucas and Ana Bringas López. Vigo: Universidade de Vigo, 2004. 223–31.

Naharro Calderón, José María. "Mitos de la memoria: La obsesión del regreso (globos y sondas)." *Encrucijadas globales. Redefinir España en el siglo XXI.* Ed. José Colmeiro. Madrid: Editorial Iberoamericana/Vervuert, 2015. 141–70.

Naughten, Rebecca. "Voyage of Discovery. Xurxo Chirro on *Vikingland* and New Galician Cinema." *Eyeforfilm.co.uk*, Eyeforfilm.co.uk. 2015. Web.

Niall, Julia. "Speaking in Tongues? Language Policies of Minority Languages in Spain." MA thesis, University of Auckland. 2015.

Nogueira, Xosé. *O cine en Galicia.* Vigo: Edicións A Nosa Terra, 1997.

—. "As temáticas." *Libro branco de cinematografía e artes visuais en Galicia*: 71–164.

—. "O bosque animado (2001)." *Grial* 39.151 (2001): 503–08.

Nora, Pierre. "Between Memory and History: Les Lieux de Mémoire." *Representations* 26 (1989): 7–25.

—. *La Republique.* Vol. 1. *Les Lieux de mémoire.* 6 vols. Paris: Gallimard, 1984–92.

"Nueva York acogerá el Galician Cinema Festival." *La Región Internacional.* Laregioninternacional.com. 17 June, 2015. Web.

"O Audiovisual agora. Pintan Ouros." *Vieiros.* Vieiros.com. 11 November 2002. Web.

"O bravú regresa coa forza de '120 capadores'." *Vieiros.*Vieiros.com. 6 December 2007. Web.

"O bravú. Notas sobre o movemento." *Proxecto Estrume.* Proxectoestrume.fiestras.com. 8 September 2008. Web.

"O cine na Dictadura (1937–1970)." *Historia do cine galego (1896–1979).* Culturagalega.org. N.d. Web.

O'Donnell, Mary, and Manuela Palacios, eds. *To the Winds Our Sails. Irish Writers Translate Galician Poetry.* Cliffs of Moher, Ireland: Salmon Poetry, 2010.

Ordovás, Jesús. *Siniestro Total. Apocalipsis con grelos.* Madrid: Ediciones Guía de Música, 1993.

Oroz, Elena, "Las afinidades electivas." *Atlas Ilustrado da Periferia.* S8cinema.com. 1 April 2011. Web.

Ortega y Gasset, José. *España invertebrada. Bosquejo de algunos pensamientos históricos.* Madrid: Calpe, 1922.

Ortiz, Fernando. *Contrapunteo cubano del tabaco y del azúcar.* Caracas: Biblioteca Ayacucho, 1987.

*Os 80. Moda en Galicia. Singularidades.* Exhibition Catalog. 2009.

"Os europarlamentarios reciben a Nunca Máis." *Vieiros.* Vieiros.com. June 13 2003. Web.

"Paco Leiro, escultor de Galicia para el Mundo." *El Correo Gallego.* 21 July 2015. Web.

Pagán, Alberte. "A toupeira." *Atlas Ilustrado da Periferia.* S8cinema.com. 1 April 2011. Web.

—. "Vikingland, película perfecta." *Alberte Pagán.* Albertepagan.eu. 6 July 2011. Web.

—. "Algumhas consideraçons sobre a língua de Costa da Morte." *Acto de Primavera* Actodeprimavera. 2014. Blog.

Palacios, Manuela, and Laura Lojo. *Writing Bonds: Irish and Galician Contemporary Women Poets.* Bern: Peter Lang, 2009.

Patiño, Lois, "Director's Notes." *Zeitun films.* Zeitunfilms.com. 2013. Web.

Parker, Noel, ed. *The Geopolitics of Europe's Identity.* New York: Palgrave Macmillan, 2008.

Pato, Alfonso. "A muiñeira faise mestiza." *El País* Galicia ed. 3 March 2006. Web.

Pena, Jaime. "A produción", *Libro branco de cinematografía e artes visuais en Galicia*: 13–30.

Pereiro, Xosé M. "Un saxofonista contra la literatura de karaoke." *El País* 20 May 1996. Web.

Pérez de Eulate, Esther. "El bosque animado. Un bosque digital gallego al estilo de Hollywood." *Cinevideo 20* 186 (2001): 42–48.

Pérez Gil, Lila. "El festival de Cans celebra el 'agroglamour' gallego." *El País* 23 May 2005. Web.

Pérez Touriño, Emilio. "Presentación." *Rodado en Galicia.* rodadoengalicia.galiciafc. org. 2005. Web.

*Periféricos.* Directed by Tamara Blanco, Xosé Holgado, and Carlos Méndez. Pontevedra, Spain: Productora Periféricos, 2006.

Pino-Ojeda, Walescka. "Devolviendo la mirada: *Biutiful* y la globalización de *Los olvidados.*" *Encrucijadas globales: Redefinir España en el siglo XXI.* Ed. José Colmeiro. Madrid/Frankfurt: Editorial Iberoamericana/Vervuet, 2015. 257–81.

"'Pradolongo': o cinema normalízase." *Vieiros.* Vieiros.com. March 14 2008. Web.

Prout, Ryan. "Speaking Up /Coming Out: Regions of Authenticity in Juan Pinzás's Gay Galician Dogma Trilogy." *Galicia 21: Journal of Contemporary Galician Studies* B (2010): 68–91. Web.

Quintas Froufe, Natalia. "The 'Galicia Moda' Project: The First Attempt to Launch Galician Fashion." *Journal of Design History* 23.2 (2010): 181–94.

Rábade Villar, María do Cebreiro. "Spectres of the Nation: Forms of Resistance to Literary Nationalism." *Bulletin of Hispanic Studies* 86.2 (2009): 231–47.

—. "Centro e periferia." *Facebook.com.* June 23, 2015. Web.

Rabón, Xosé M. "A percura dun cine galego." *Grial* 40 (1973): 235–38.

Rasch, Nicole. *Cultural Representations of Galician Identity: Contemporary Narratives of Santiago de Compostela and the Camiño de Santiago.* Diss. Michigan State University, 2014.

Redondo Neira, Fernando. "Lo procesual como marca de modernidad en el Novo Cinema Galego." revistalatinacs.org. *Actas VI Congreso Internacional Latina de Comunicación Social.* Universidad de La Laguna, December 2014. Web.

Rei-Doval, Gabriel. "Los estudios gallegos en los Estados Unidos." *Informes del Observatorio/Observatorio Reports.* Instituto Cervantes at FAS—Harvard University. N.d. Web.

Reimóndez, María. *A alternativa está aquí.* Vigo: Edicións Xerais de Galicia, 2014.

Reixa, Antón. *Viva Galicia Beibe.* Santiago: Edicións Positivas, 1994.

Reizbaum, Marilyn. "Canonical Double Cross: Scottish and Irish Women's Writing." *Decolonizing Tradition. New Views of Twentieth Century 'British' Literary Canons.* Ed. Karen R. Lawrence. Urbana: U of Illinois P, 1992. 165–90.

"RESOLUCIÓN do 23 de marzo de 2010." Xunta.es. *Diario Oficial de Galicia* 86. 7 May 2010. Web.

Richardson, Nathan E. "Animals, Machines, and Postnational Identity in Julio Medem's *Vacas.*" *Journal of Iberian and Latin American Studies* 10.2 (2004): 191–204.

Ríos, Xulio, and Carlos Teijo, eds. *Galicia solidaria. O sistema galego de cooperación ao desenvolvemento.* Vigo: Edicións Xerais de Galicia, 2009.

Rivas, Manuel. "Antón Reixa: 'El centro siempre nos derrota'." *El País* 18 May 1989.

—. "Tres películas gallegas." *El País* 2 December 1989. Web.

—. "¿E que é o bravú?" *Unión Bravú.* CD. Pontevedra: Ediciíns do Cumio, 1996.

—. "Manifesto do tractor bravú." *Bravú* 1 (1997): 7.

—. "Galicia contada a un extraterrestre." *El País* 14 October 2001. Web.

—. "A Galicia transn@cional." *El País* Galicia ed. 22 December 2006. Web.

Rodríguez, Salvador. *Entre Fisterras. Conversas con Carlos Núñez.* Vigo: Xerais, 2003.

Rolfe, Pamela. "Spain Animators Drawing Attention." *The Hollywood Reporter.* 20 March 2007. Web.

Romaní, Rodrigo, and Anton Seoane. *Milladoiro.* LP. Madrid: Novola, 1977.

Romero, Bieito. *Xeometrías máxicas de Galicia.* Vigo: Ir Indo Edicións, 2009.

Romero, Eugenia. "Amusement Parks, Bagpipes and Cemeteries: Fantastic Spaces of Galician Identity through Migration." *Journal of Spanish Cultural Studies* 7.2 (2006): 155–69.

—. *Contemporary Galician Culture in a Global Context: Movable Identities.* Plymouth: Lexington Books, 2012.

Romero Suárez, Brais. "Low cost, crisis y cine en España." *A cuarta parede.* Acuartaparede.com. 21 June 2015. Blog.

—. "Idioma e identidad en el Novo Cinema Galego." *Fonseca. Journal of Communication* 11 (2015): 9–31.

Roseman, Sharon R. "Santiago de Compostela in the Year 2000: From Religious Center to European City Culture." *Intersecting Journeys. The Anthropology of Tourism and Pilgrimage.* Eds. Ellen Badone and Sharon R. Roseman. Urbana and Chicago: U of Illinois P, 2004. 68–88.

Rozados, Francisco. "Dúas décadas sen Chano Piñeiro." *La Voz de Galicia.* 21 March 2015. Web.

Rutherford, John. "Os estudos galegos nos contextos globais." *Novas achegas ao estudo da cultura galega.* Vol 2. *Enfoques socio-históricos e lingüístico-literarios.* Eds. Olivia Rodríguez González et al. A Coruña: Universidade da Coruña, 2012, 15–26.

Salgado, Daniel. "El sabor de la carne sin castrar." *El País* Galicia ed. 5 November 2007. Web.

—. "A existencia dunha literatura bravú." *El País* Galicia ed. 23 February 2007. Web.

—. "Cando a periferia da periferia tamén se move." *El País* Galicia ed. 5 May 2008. Web.

—. "La cultura cierra filas con la Xunta." *El País* Galicia ed. 28 February 2008. Web.

—. "A última banda bravú. Ruxe-Ruxe rematan a xira do seu sexto disco e entran de novo en estudio." *El País* 5 December 2008. Web.

Sampedro, Domingos. "El censo del voto emigrante aumenta cuatro veces más que el de Galicia." *La Voz de Galicia* 21 March 2007. Web.

Sánchez Albornoz, Claudio. *Santiago, hechura de España: Estudios Jacobeos.* Ávila, Fundación Sánchez Albornoz, 1993.

Sande, José Manuel. "Periferia eres." *Atlas Ilustrado da Periferia.* S8cinema.com. 3 April 2011. Web.

Santos, Ángel. "Periferia(s)." *Atlas Ilustrado da Periferia.* S8cinema.com. 1 April 2011. Web.

Sempere, Isabel. "O apoio da Administración á creación audiovisual." *Libro branco de cinematografía e artes visuais en Galicia*: 251–88.

Sequeiro, Mónica. "La emigración gallega tiene más peso en el censo electoral que los habitantes de Lugo y Ourense." *Galiciaé.* Galiciae.com. 27 January 2008. Web.

"'Serramoura', un thriller rural desde Galicia para el mundo." *Audiovisual451.com.* Audiovisual451.com. 7 April 2015. Web.

Sojo, Kepa. "El Camino de Santiago en el cine." *El Camino de Santiago y el cine en las aulas.* Eds. Isabel Cantón Mayo and Luis Miguel Alonso Guadalupe. León: Universidad de León/Festival de Cine de Astorga, 2010. 65–83.

Sommer, Doris. *Foundational Fictions: The National Romances of Latin America.* Berkeley: U of California P, 1991.

Souto, Xurxo. *A tralla e a arroutada.* Vigo: Ed. Xerais, 1995.

—. "Galicia-Capetón." *Bravú* 4 (1998): 73.

—. "Arroutada en Guitiriz." *Xermolos. Asociación Cultural de Guitiriz.* Xermolos.org. 24.49 (August 2005): 17–18. Web.

—. "Exposición Bravú XX. Tanta paixón quen poderá detela!" *Espacio FEE. Revista da Facultade de Economía e Empresa* 7 (2015): 5. Web.

Spivak, Gayatri Chakravorty. *The Post-Colonial Critic: Interviews, Strategies, Dialogues.* Ed. Sarah Harasym. London: Routledge, 1990.

Starkie, Walter. *Spanish Raggle-Taggle. Adventures with a Fiddle in North Spain.* New York: EP Dutton, 1935.

Stivell, Alan. "Prólogo." Emilio Cao, *Fonte de Araño.* Madrid: Novola, 1977.

Suárez, Pablo. "O 'Novo Cinema Galego'. Galiza na senda da vangarda." *Madrygal* 17 (2014): 123–30.

Suárez, Rodri. *Non temos medo. Historia oral de Os diplomáticos de Monte Alto.* A Coruña: Nicetrip, 2014.

Toro, Suso de. "Silencio se rueda." *Santiago de Compostela Film Commission.* Santiagoturismo.com. N.d. Web.

Toro, Xelís de. "Bagpipes and Digital Music: The Remixing of Galician Identity." *Constructing Identity in Contemporary Spain. Theoretical Debates and Cultural Practice.* Ed. Jo Labanyi. Oxford: Oxford UP, 2002. 237–54.

Turrón, Kike, and Kike Babas. *Tremendo Delirio. Conversaciones con Julián Hernández y biografía de Siniestro Total.* Zaragoza: Zona de obras, 2002.

"Un total de 324.388 emigrantes gallegos tienen derecho a voto en las generales, un 5,57 % más que en 2004." *La opinión A Coruña.* Laopinioncoruña.es. 23 February 2008. Web.

*Unión Bravú.* CD. Pontevedra: Edicións do Cumio, 1996.

Valiño, Xavier. *Rock bravú. A paixón que queima o peito.* Vigo: Xerais, 1999.

Varela, Lara. "Las hombreras del cambio." *El País* April 4, 2010. Web.

Veiga, Raúl. "A lingua do noso audiovisual." *Libro branco de cinematografía e artes visuais en Galicia*: 311–30.

Villarmea Álvarez, Iván. "Un canon para el cine gallego." *A Cuarta Parede.* Acuartaparede.com. 13 September 2013. Blog.

—. "Transnational Identities in Galician Documentary Film: Alberte Pagán's *Bs. As.* and Xurxo Chirro's *Vikingland.*" Eds. Elena Oliete-Aldea, Beatriz Oria, and

Juan A. Tarancón. *Global Genres, Local Films: The Transnational Dimension of Spanish Cinema*. New York and London: Bloomsbury, 2016. 231–45.

Villaverde, Xavier. "20 anos de Cinegalicia." Academiagalegadoaudiovisual.com, Academia Galega do Audiovisual 2009. Web.

"Votación películas gallegas." *A Cuarta Parede*. Acuartaparede.com. 2 September 2013. Blog.

Williams, Bruce. "Frysky Business: Micro-regionalism in the Era of Post-nationalism." *Film History* 14 (2002): 100–12.

Winick, Steve. "Between Fish & Chips. Milladoiro Talks to Steve Winick." *Dirty Linen* 45. Clip.dia.fi.upm.es (April/May 1993). Web.

# Index

www.ingramcontent.com/pod-product-compliance
Lightning Source LLC
Chambersburg PA
CBHW071753110726
47908CB00006B/1793